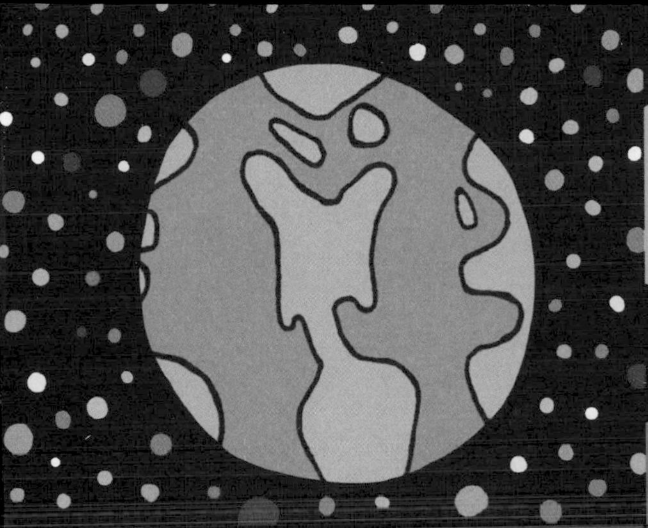

Earth is a planet located in the Universe.

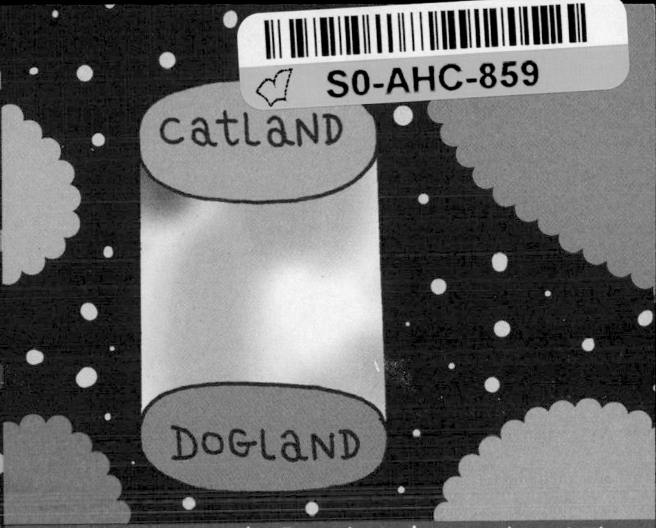
CATLAND
DOGLAND

Catland and Dogland are located in an otherwise unused area at one far end of the Universe.

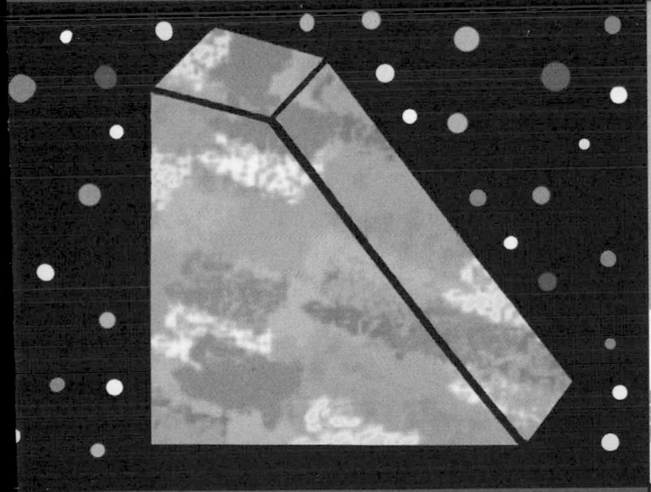

Universe City is where all life in the Universe resides after death and before birth.

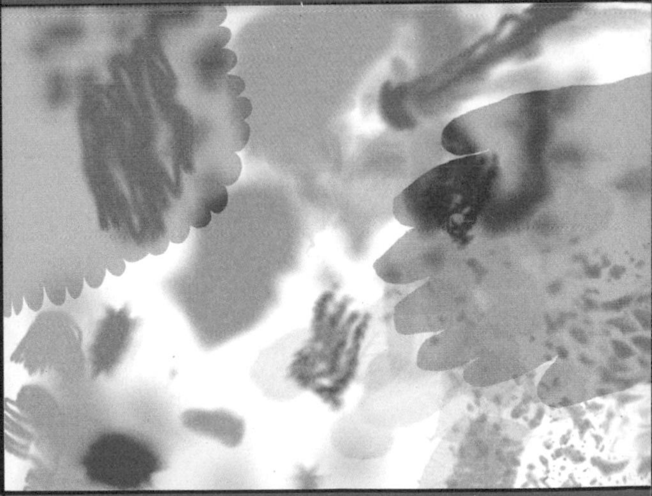

The Great Plain at the bottom of the Universe is an empty unused vastness located at the bottom of the Universe.

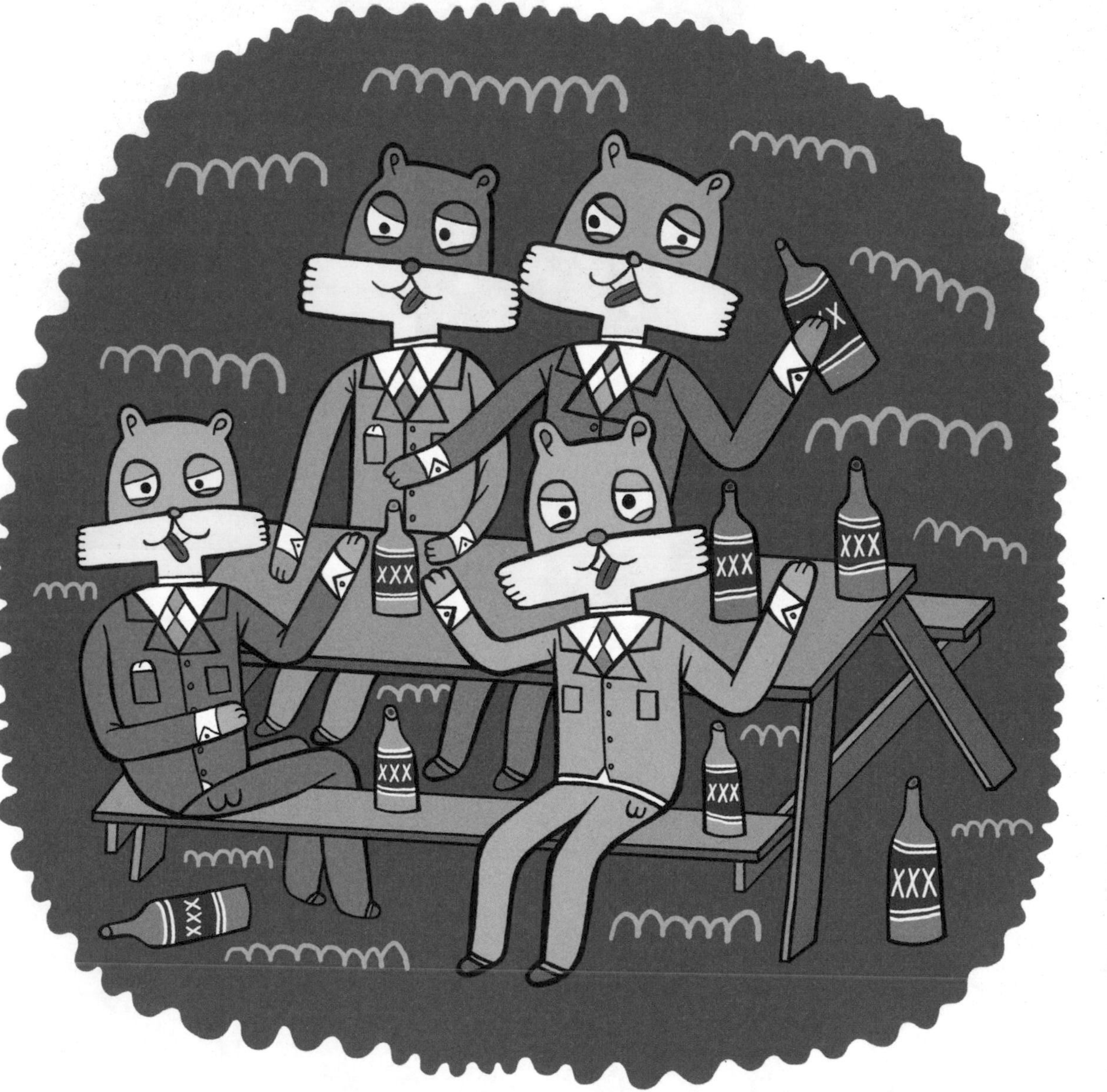
XXX
XXX
XXX
XXX
XXX
XXX
XXX

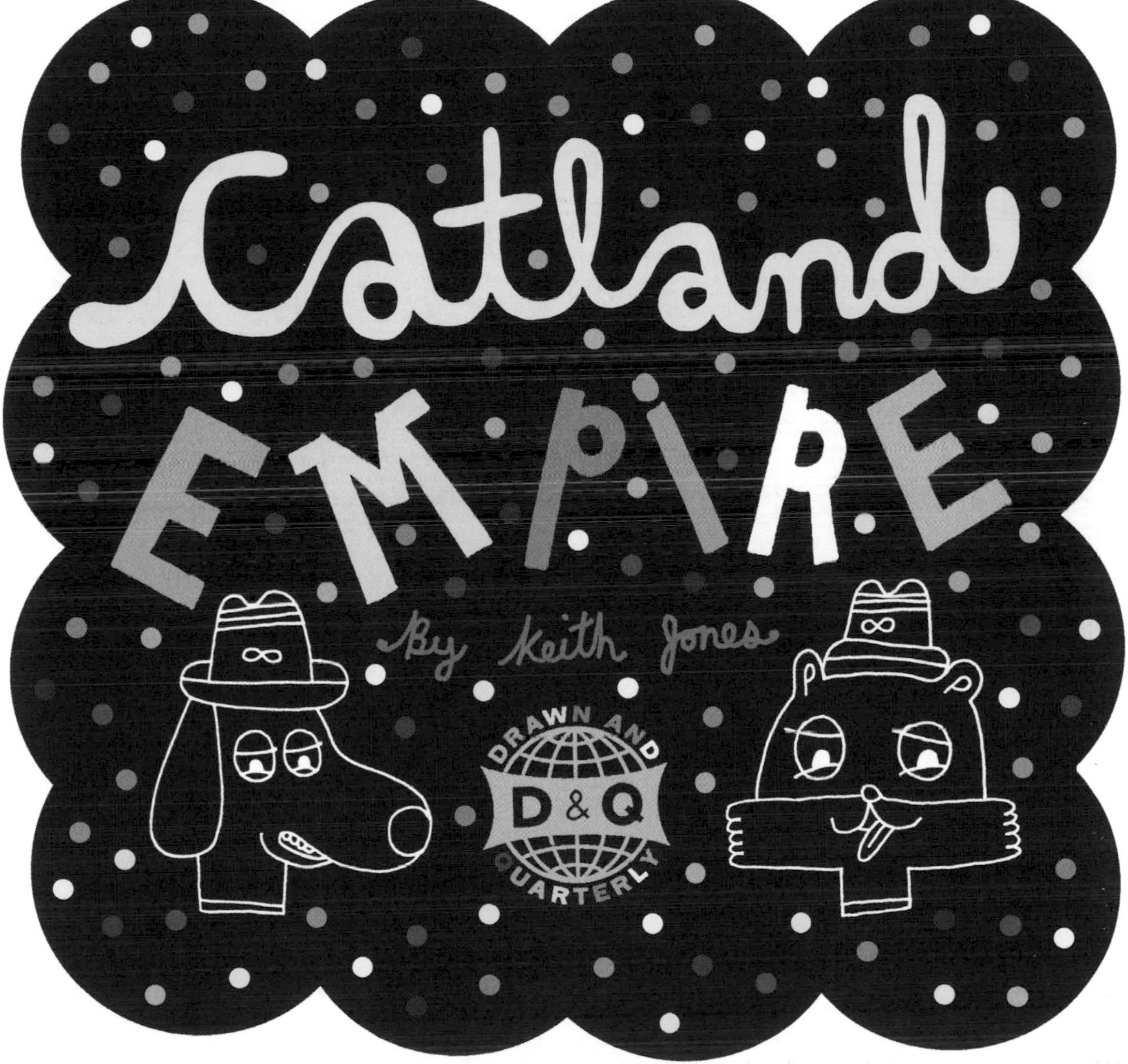
Catland
EMPIRE
By Keith Jones
DRAWN AND QUARTERLY
D & Q

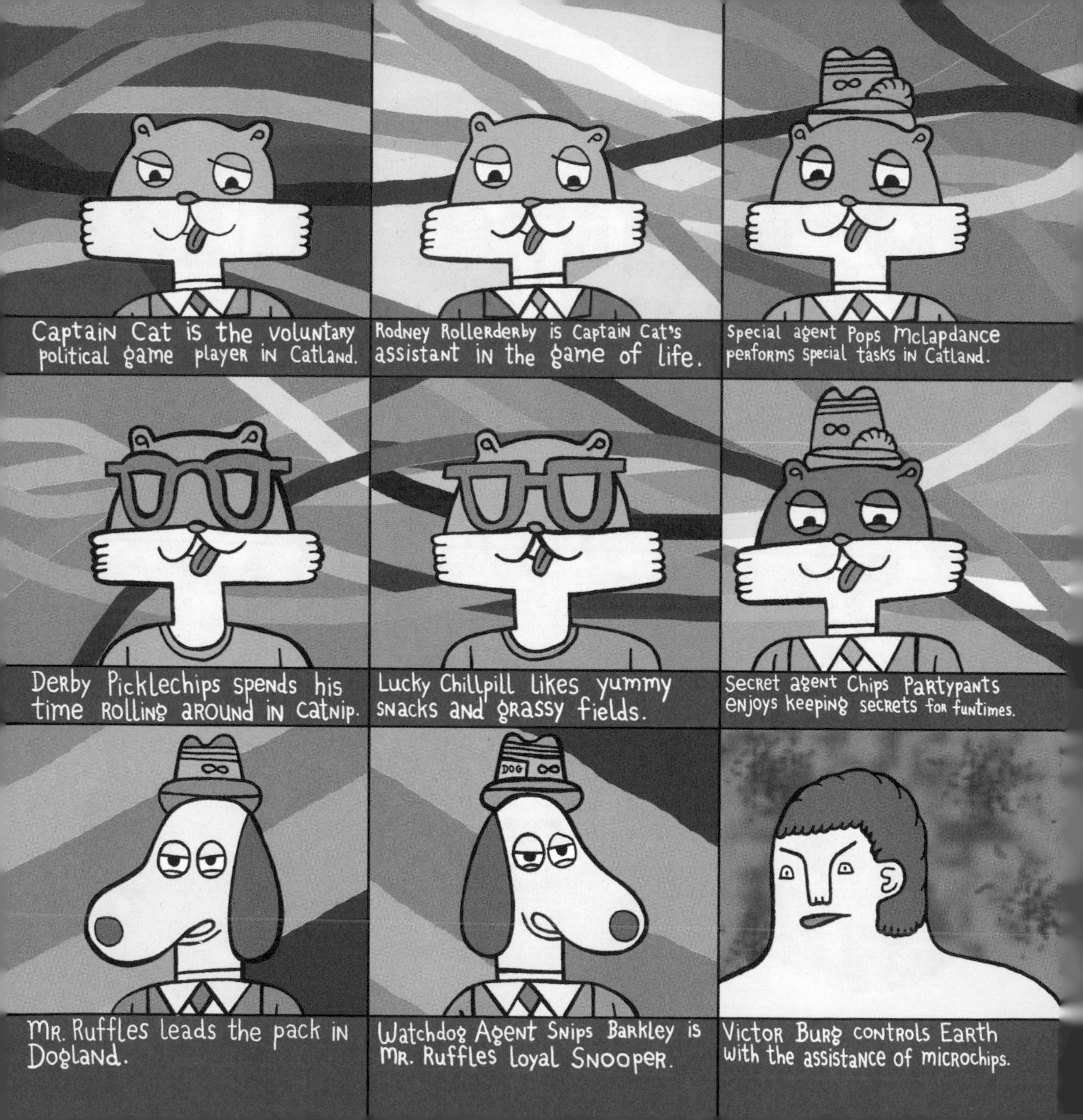
Captain Cat is the voluntary political game player in Catland.
Rodney Rollerderby is Captain Cat's assistant in the game of life.
Special agent Pops Mclapdance performs special tasks in Catland.
Derby Picklechips spends his time rolling around in catnip.
Lucky Chillpill likes yummy snacks and grassy fields.
Secret agent Chips Partypants enjoys keeping secrets for funtimes.
DOG
Mr. Ruffles leads the pack in Dogland.
Watchdog Agent Snips Barkley is Mr. Ruffles loyal Snooper.
Victor Burg controls Earth with the assistance of microchips.

Ricky Bowles is Victor Burg's assistant.

A human Responder Unit is controlled with a microchip implant.

Gyzop Narobi came to Earth via a Reverse Black Hole in order to Destroy the Universe for his Boss, Sir Cosmos.

Mysos Templar assists Gyzop Narobi in destroying the Universe.

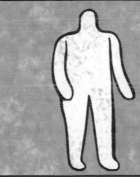

Zaxxier Beoulifolius is a Universal Life force that experiences human life as Victor Burg in this book.

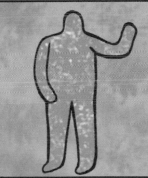

Blathesphierus Danub is a Universal life force that experiences life as an unknown cat in Catland during the time of this story.

Mr. Time manages Universal Order with Mr. Space.

Mr. Space manages Universal Order with Mr. Time.

Mr. Universe is the creator of the Universe and dean of operations at Universe City.

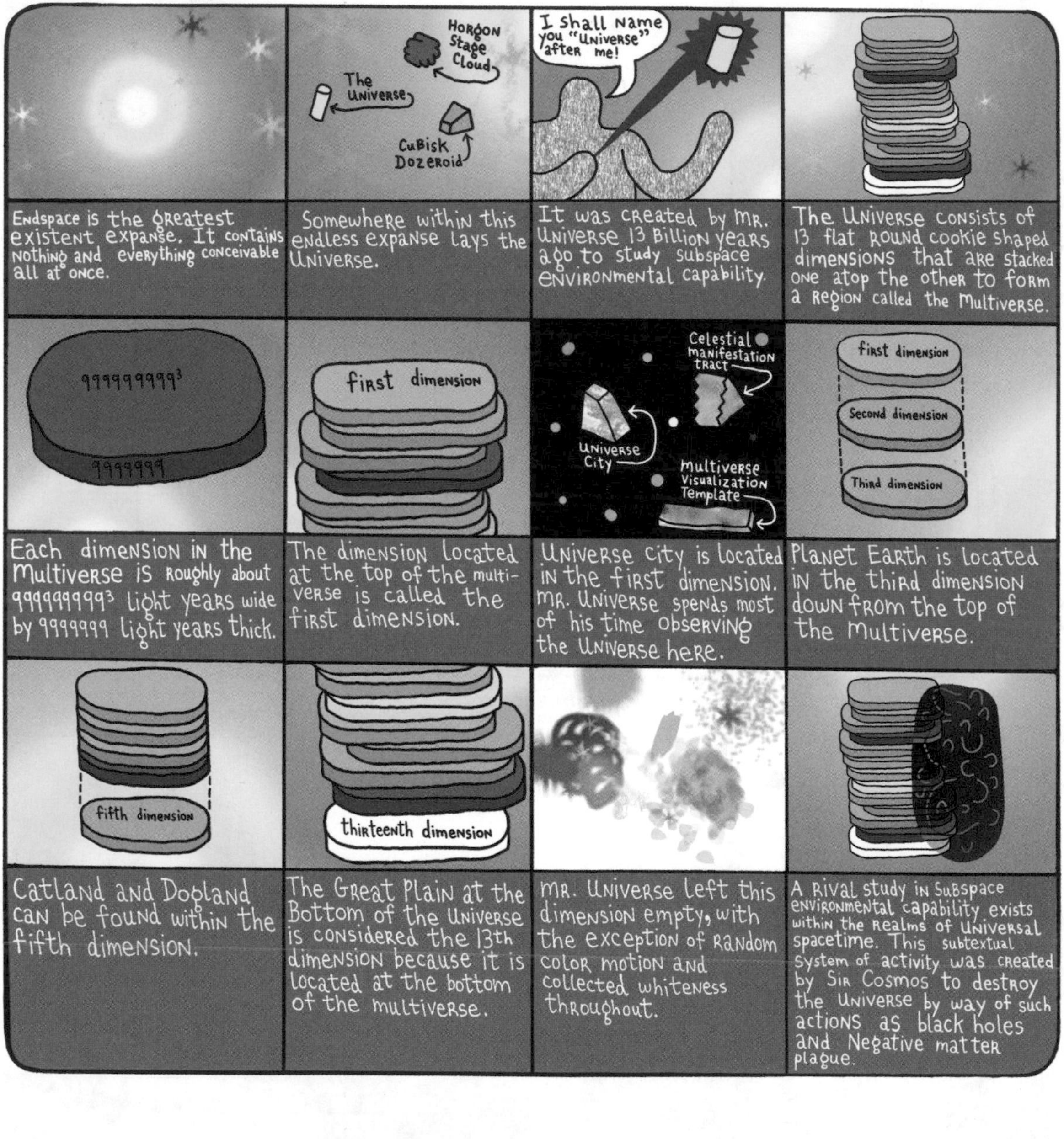
Endspace is the greatest existent expanse. It contains nothing and everything conceivable all at once.
Horgon Stage Cloud
The Universe
CuBisk Dozeroid
Somewhere within this endless expanse lays the Universe.
I shall name you "Universe" after me!
It was created by Mr. Universe 13 Billion years ago to study subspace environmental capability.
The Universe consists of 13 flat round cookie shaped dimensions that are stacked one atop the other to form a region called the Multiverse.
999999999³
9999999
Each dimension in the Multiverse is roughly about 999999999³ light years wide by 9999999 light years thick.
first dimension
The dimension located at the top of the multi-verse is called the first dimension.
Celestial manifestation tract
Universe City
multiverse Visualization Template
Universe City is located in the first dimension. Mr. Universe spends most of his time observing the Universe here.
first dimension
Second dimension
Third dimension
Planet Earth is located in the third dimension down from the top of the Multiverse.
fifth dimension
Catland and Dogland can be found within the fifth dimension.
thirteenth dimension
The Great Plain at the Bottom of the Universe is considered the 13th dimension because it is located at the bottom of the multiverse.
Mr. Universe left this dimension empty, with the exception of random color motion and collected whiteness throughout.
A rival study in subspace environmental capability exists within the realms of Universal spacetime. This subtextual system of activity was created by Sir Cosmos to destroy the Universe by way of such actions as black holes and Negative matter plague.

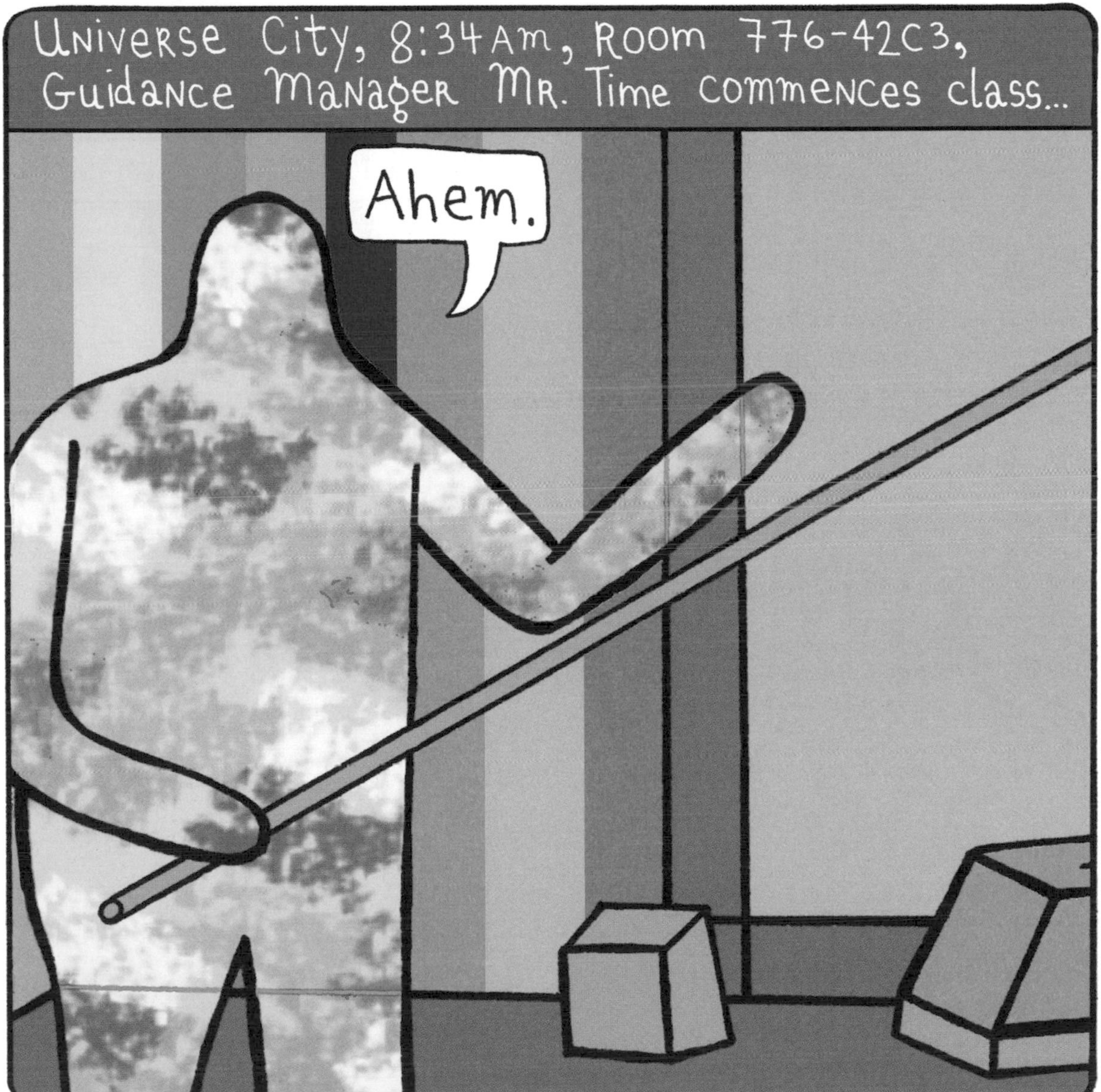
Universe City, 8:34Am, Room 776-42C3,
Guidance Manager Mr. Time commences class...
Ahem.

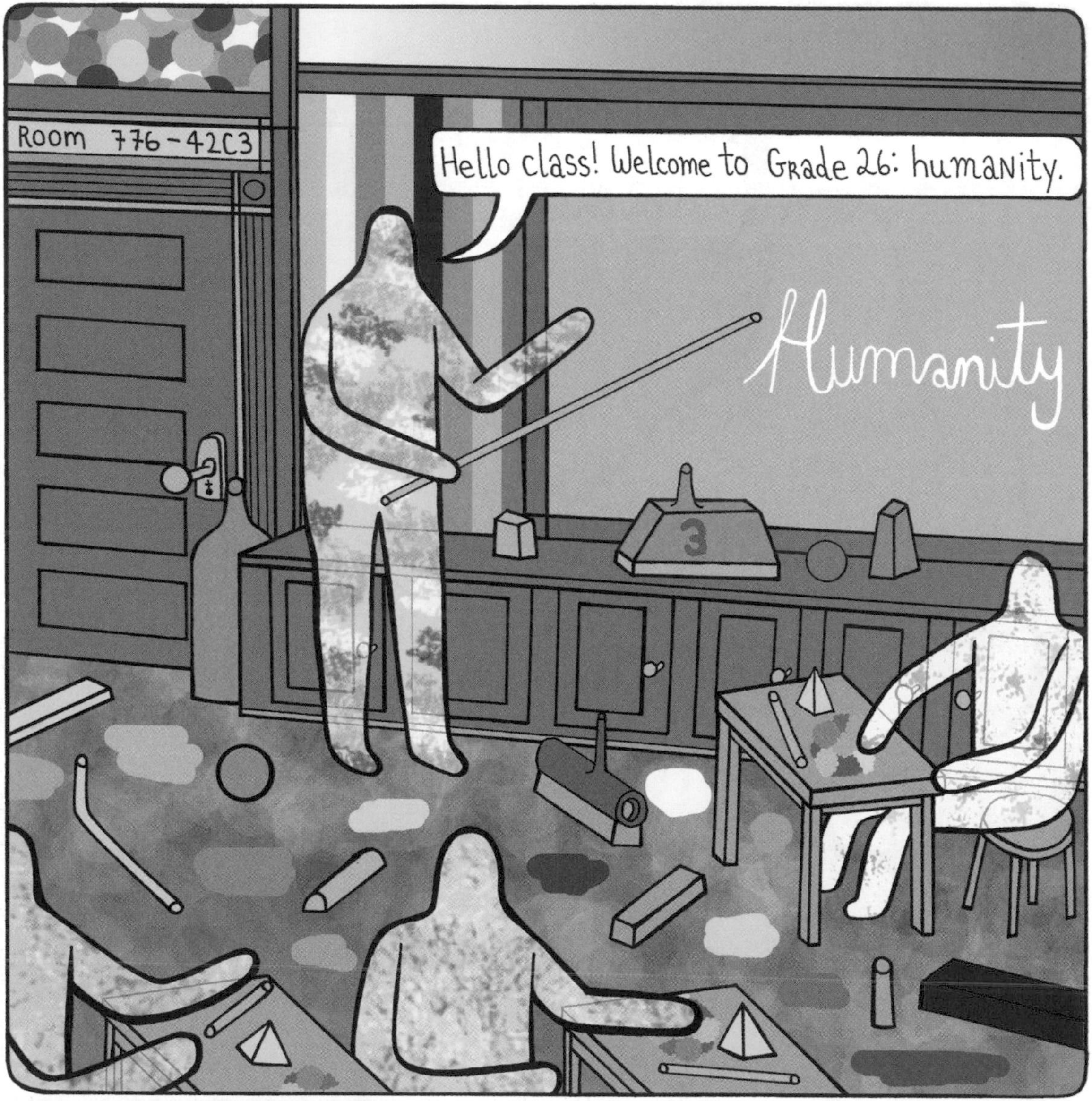
Room 776-42C3
Hello class! Welcome to Grade 26: humanity.
Humanity
3

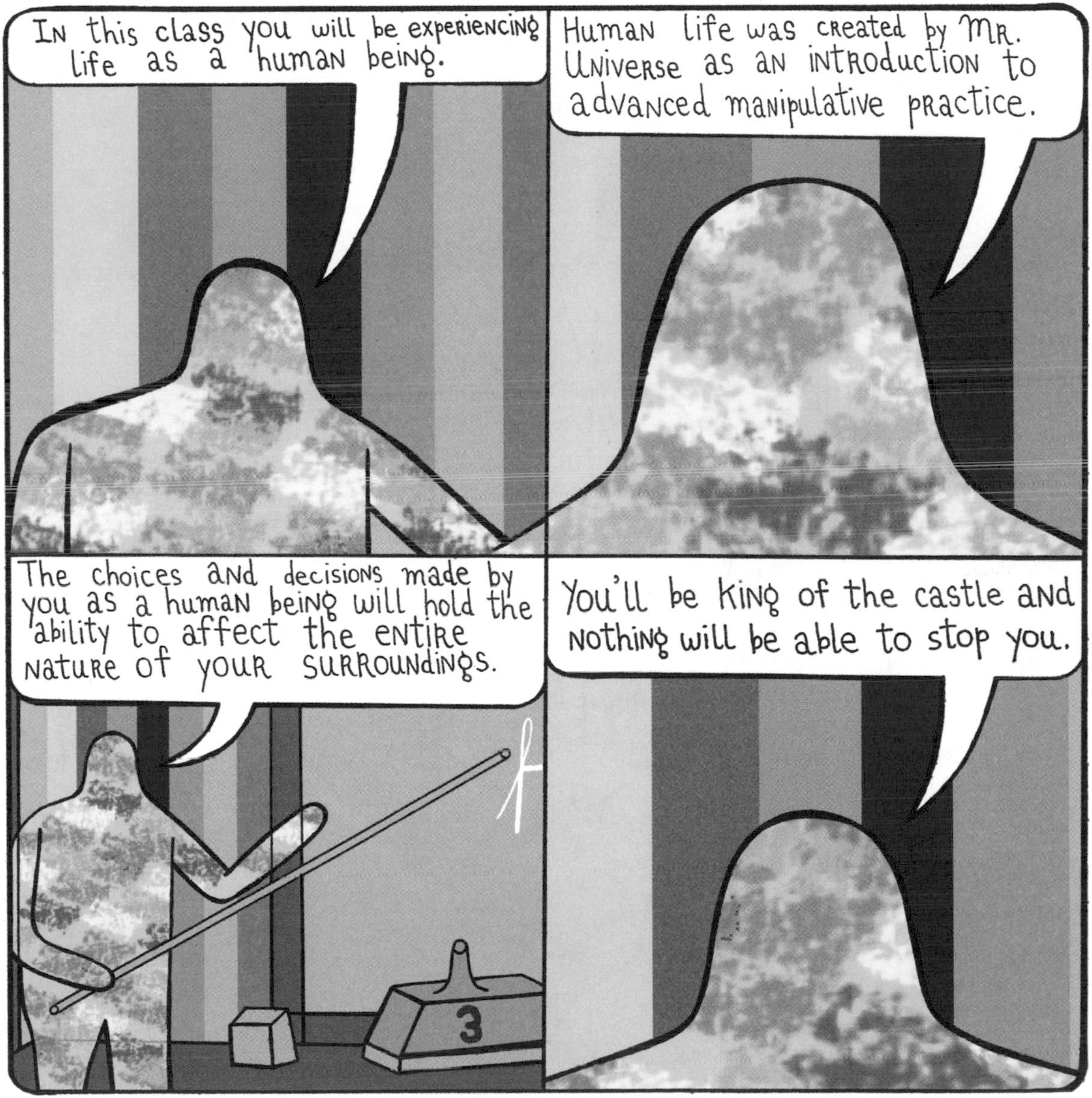
In this class you will be experiencing life as a human being.
Human life was created by Mr. Universe as an introduction to advanced manipulative practice.
The choices and decisions made by you as a human being will hold the ability to affect the entire nature of your surroundings.
You'll be king of the castle and nothing will be able to stop you.
3

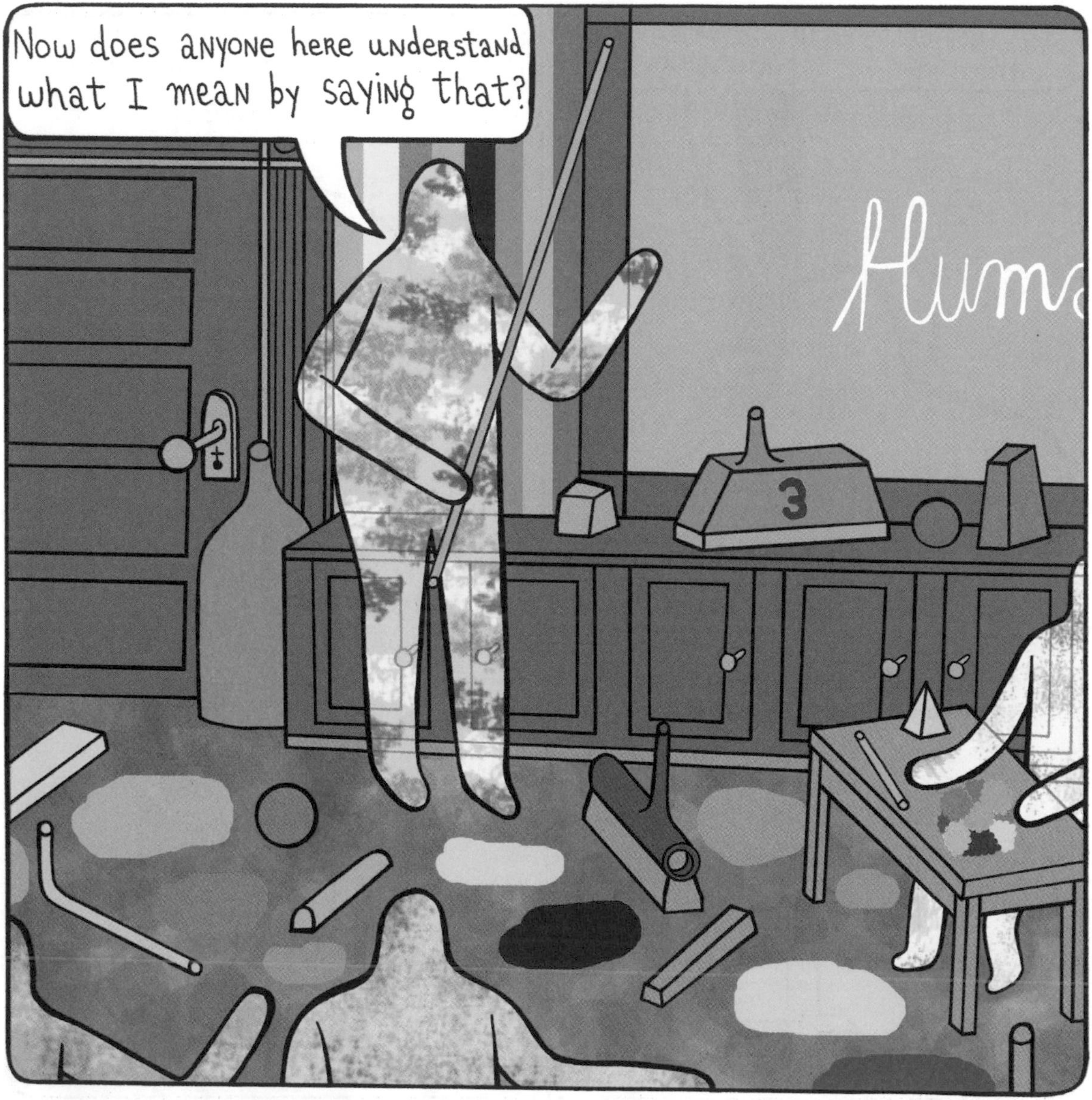
Now does anyone here understand what I mean by saying that?
3

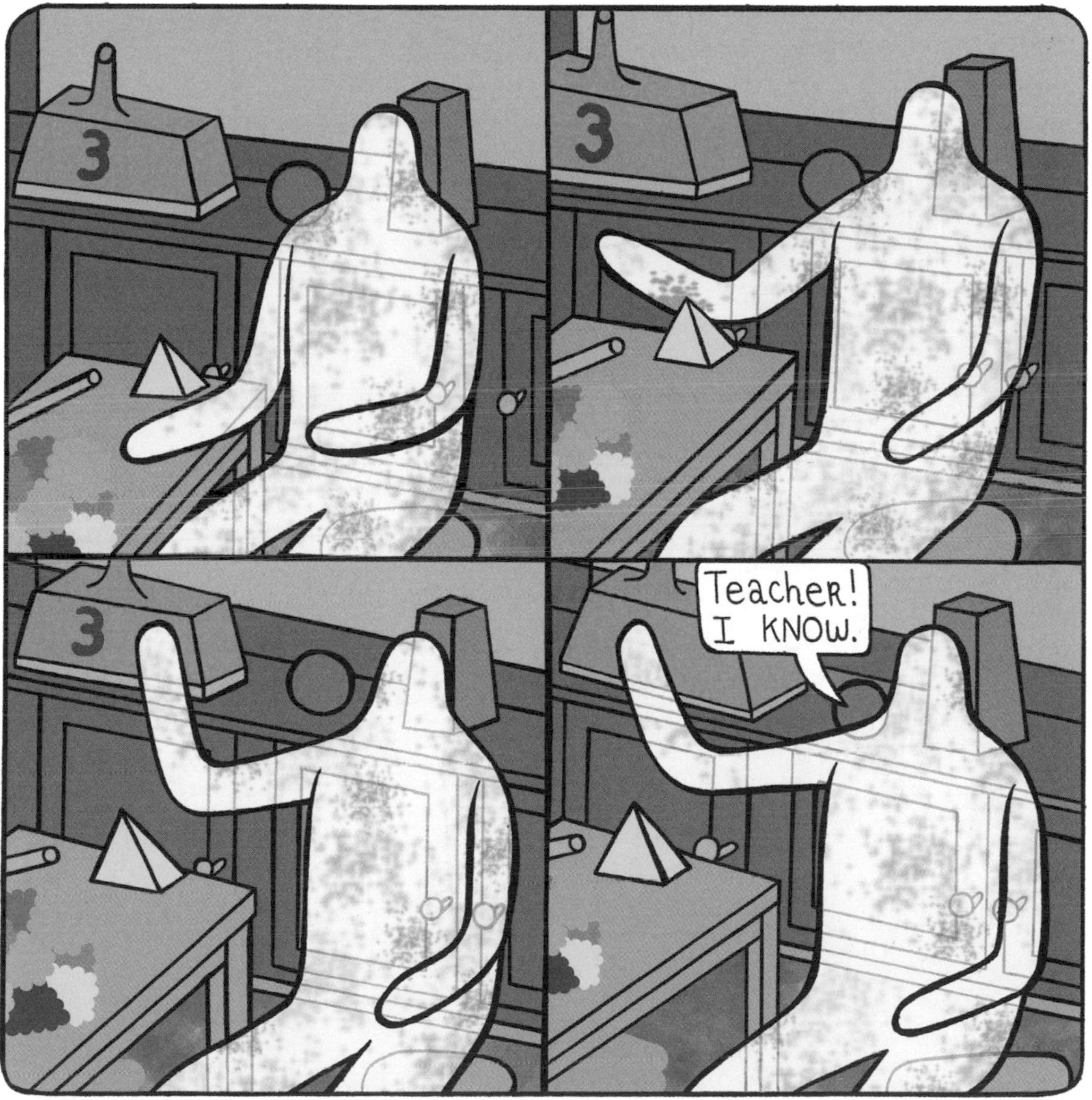
Teacher! I KNOW.

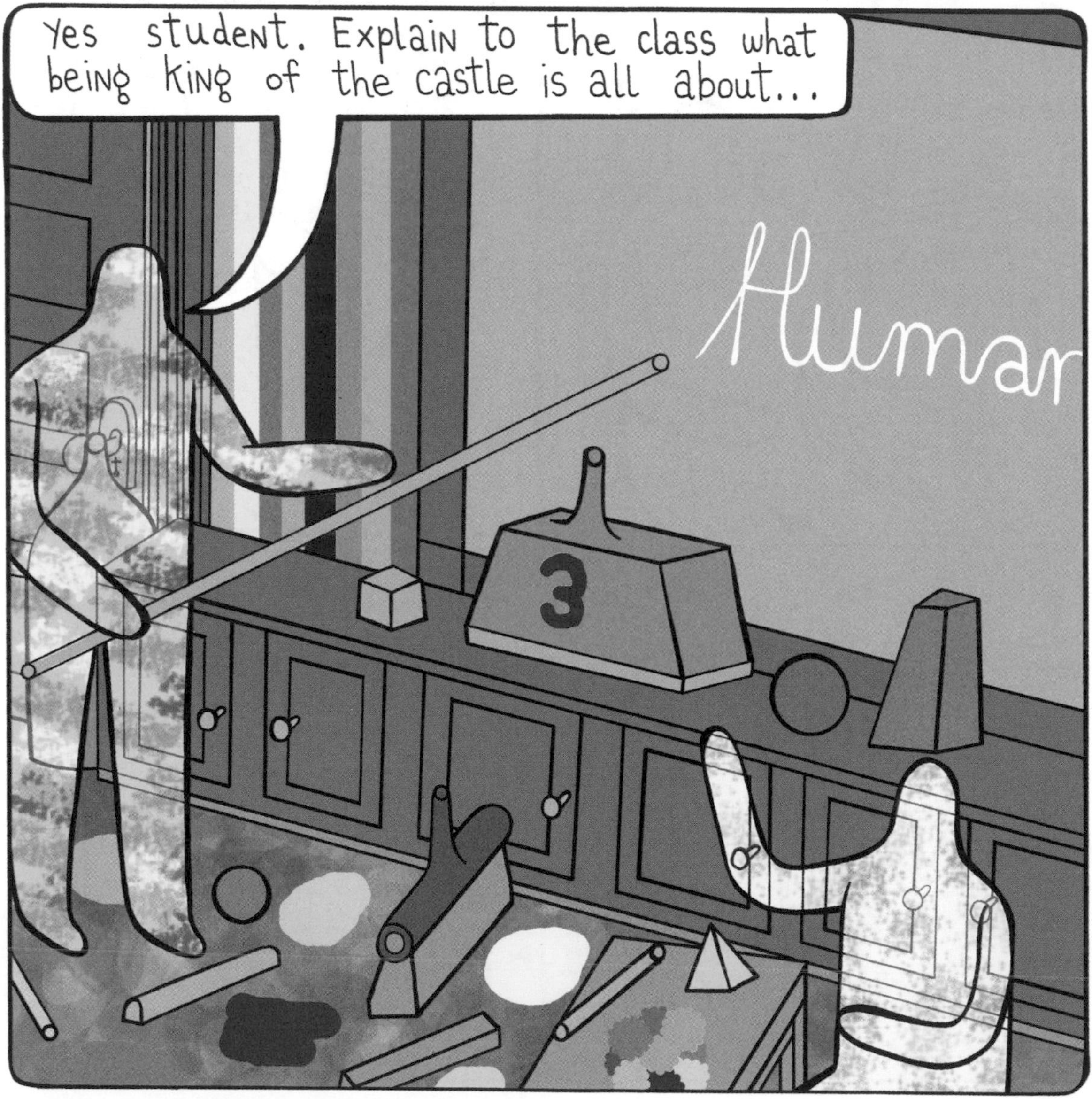
Yes student. Explain to the class what being King of the castle is all about...
Human

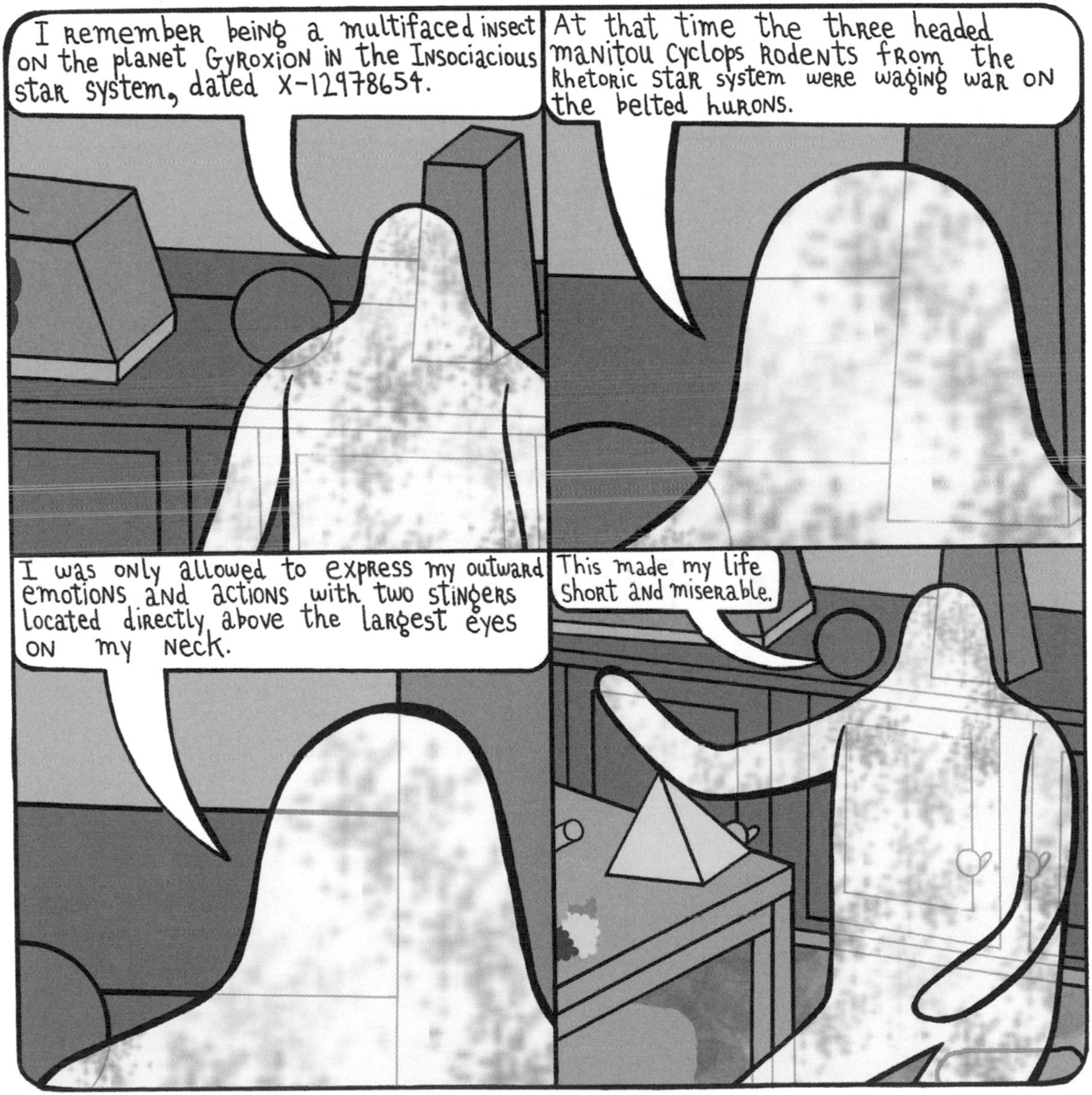
I remember being a multifaced insect on the planet Gyroxion in the Insociacious star system, dated X-12978654.
At that time the three headed manitou Cyclops Rodents from the Rhetoric star system were waging war on the belted hurons.
I was only allowed to express my outward emotions and actions with two stingers located directly above the largest eyes on my neck.
This made my life short and miserable.

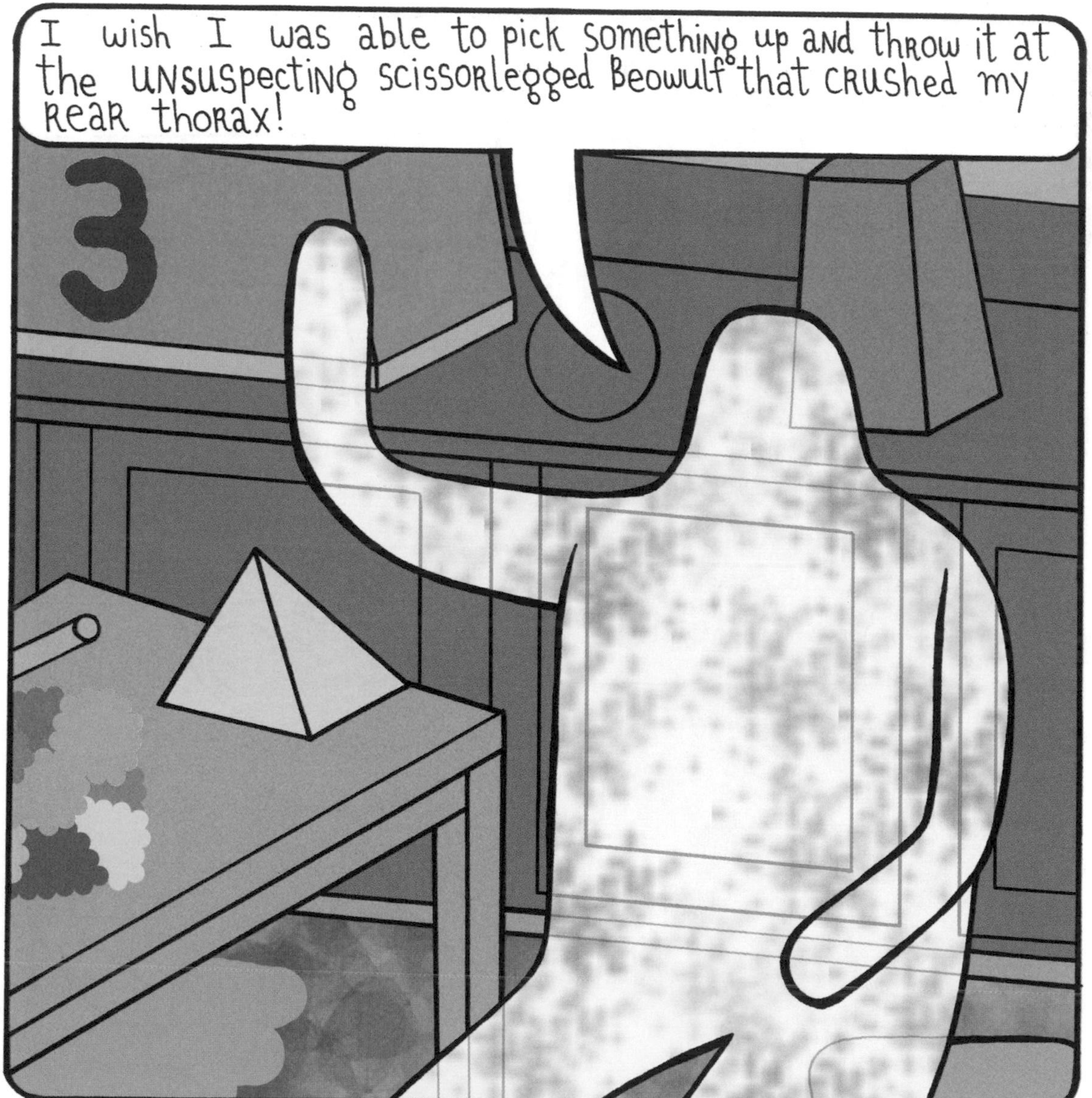

I wish I was able to pick something up and throw it at the unsuspecting scissorlegged Beowulf that crushed my rear thorax!
3

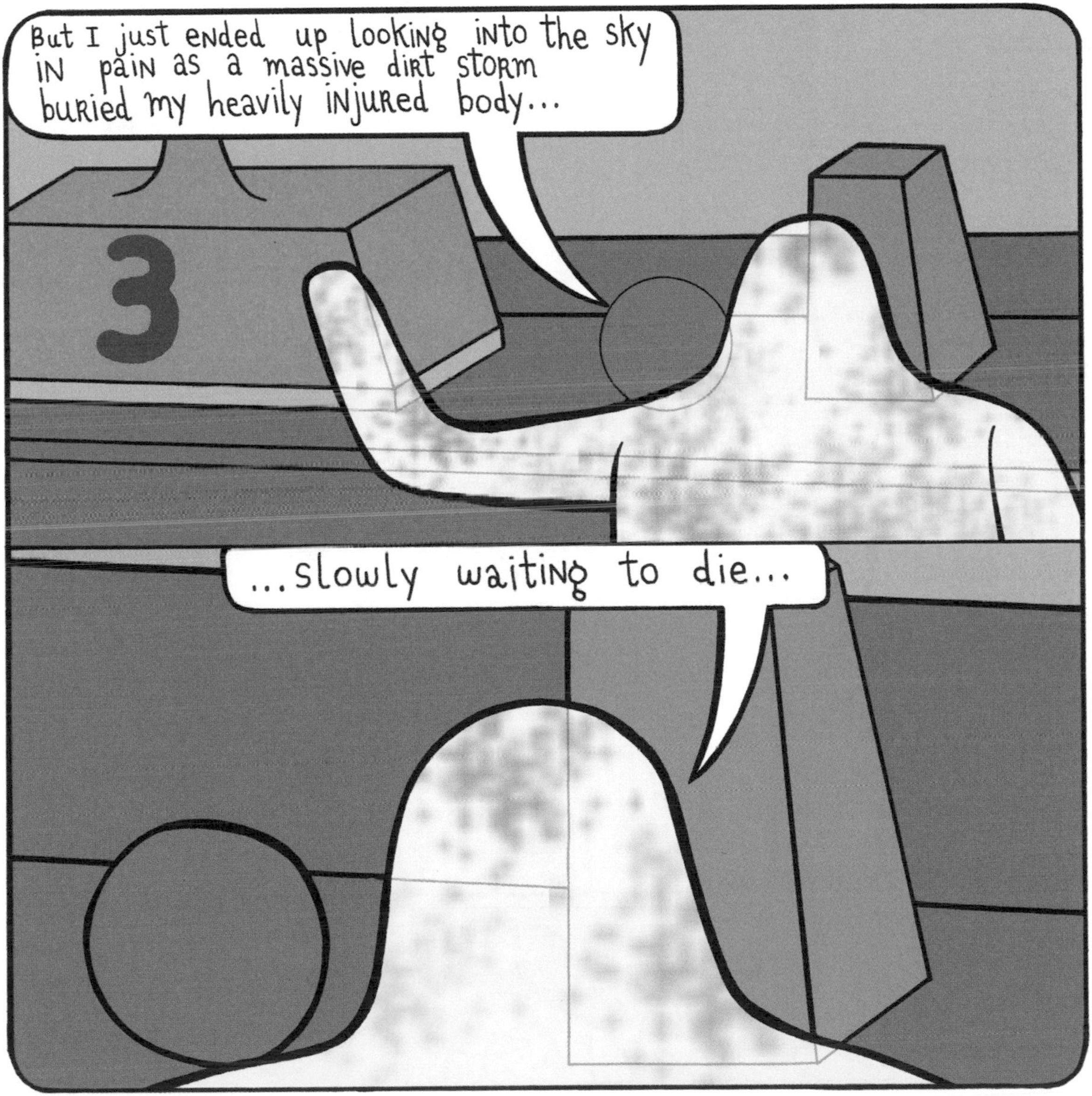
But I just ended up looking into the sky in pain as a massive dirt storm buried my heavily injured body...
...slowly waiting to die...

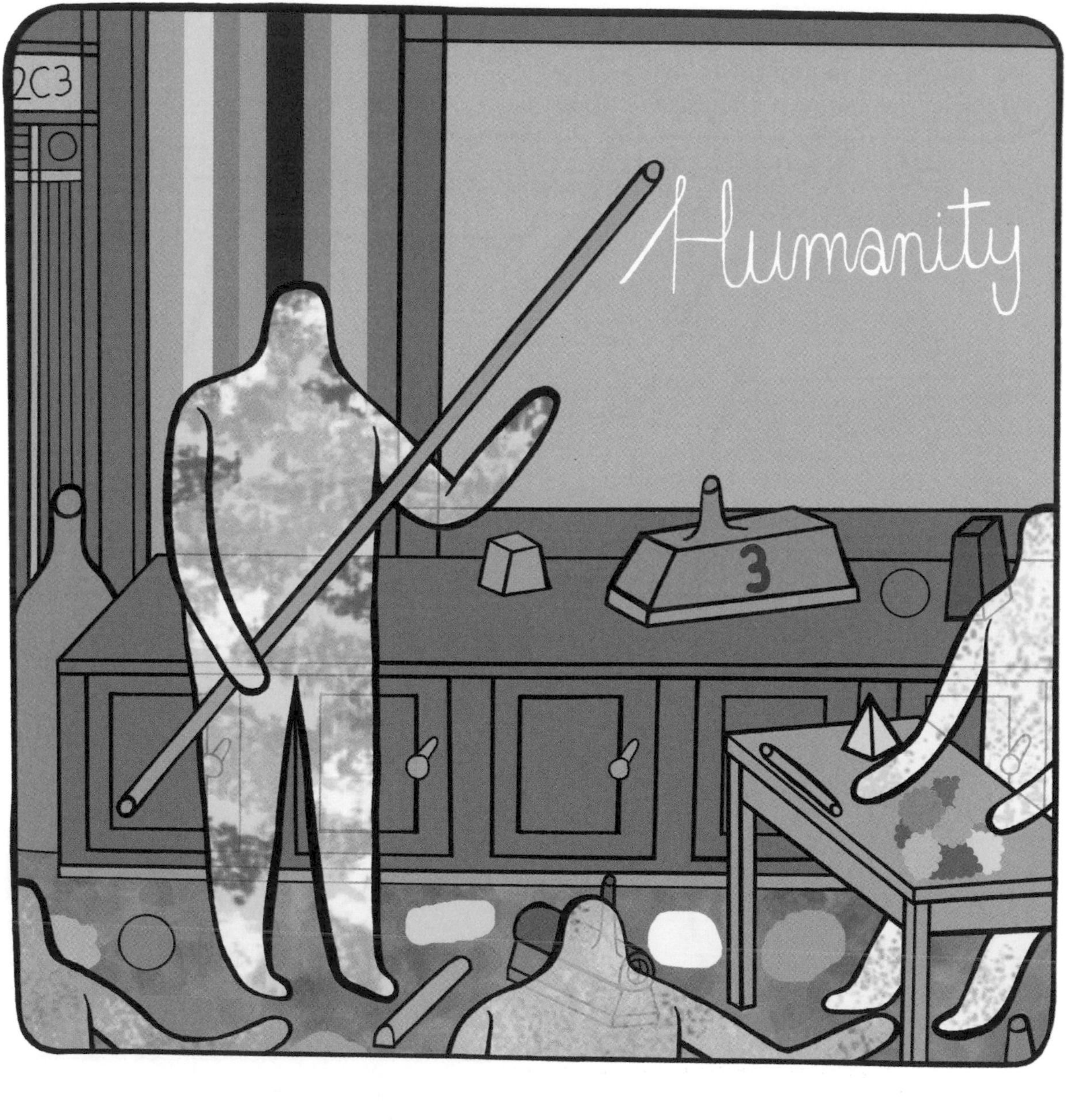
2C3
Humanity
3

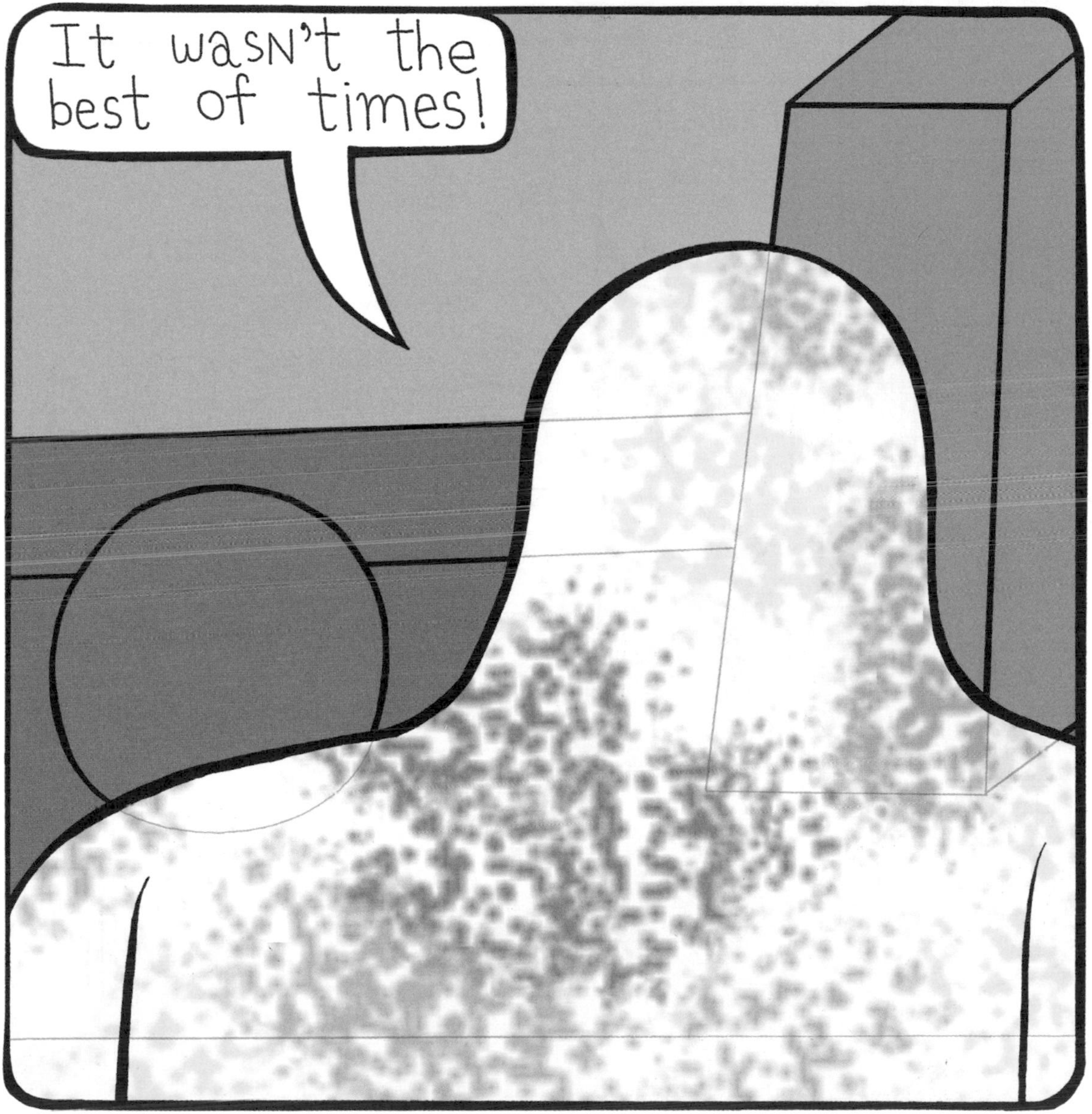
It wasn't the best of times!

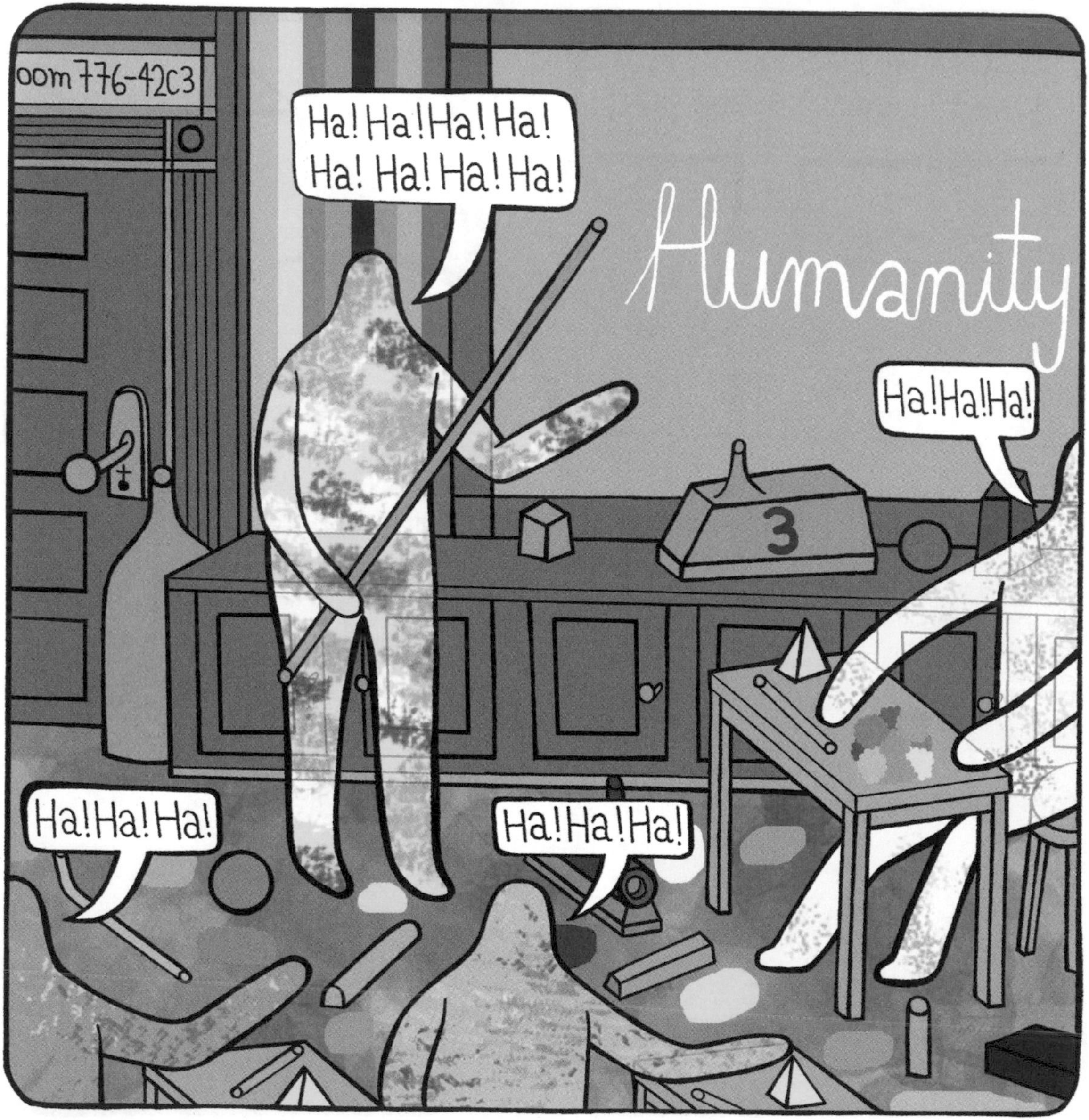
oom776-42C3
Ha! Ha! Ha! Ha!
Ha! Ha! Ha! Ha!
Humanity
Ha!Ha!Ha!
3
Ha!Ha!Ha!
Ha!Ha!Ha!

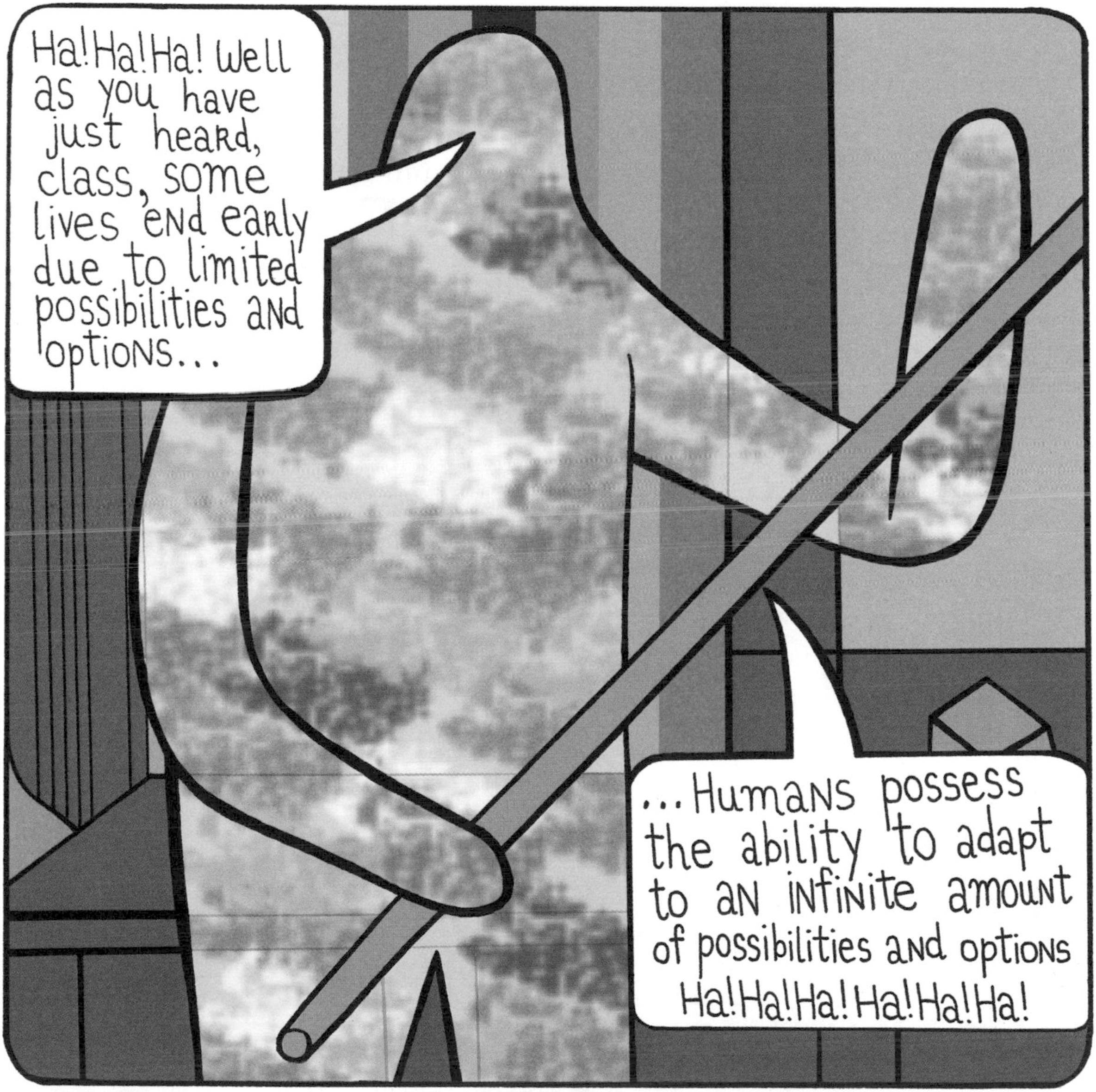
Ha!Ha!Ha! Well as you have just heard, class, some lives end early due to limited possibilities and options...
...Humans possess the ability to adapt to an infinite amount of possibilities and options Ha!Ha!Ha!Ha!Ha!Ha!

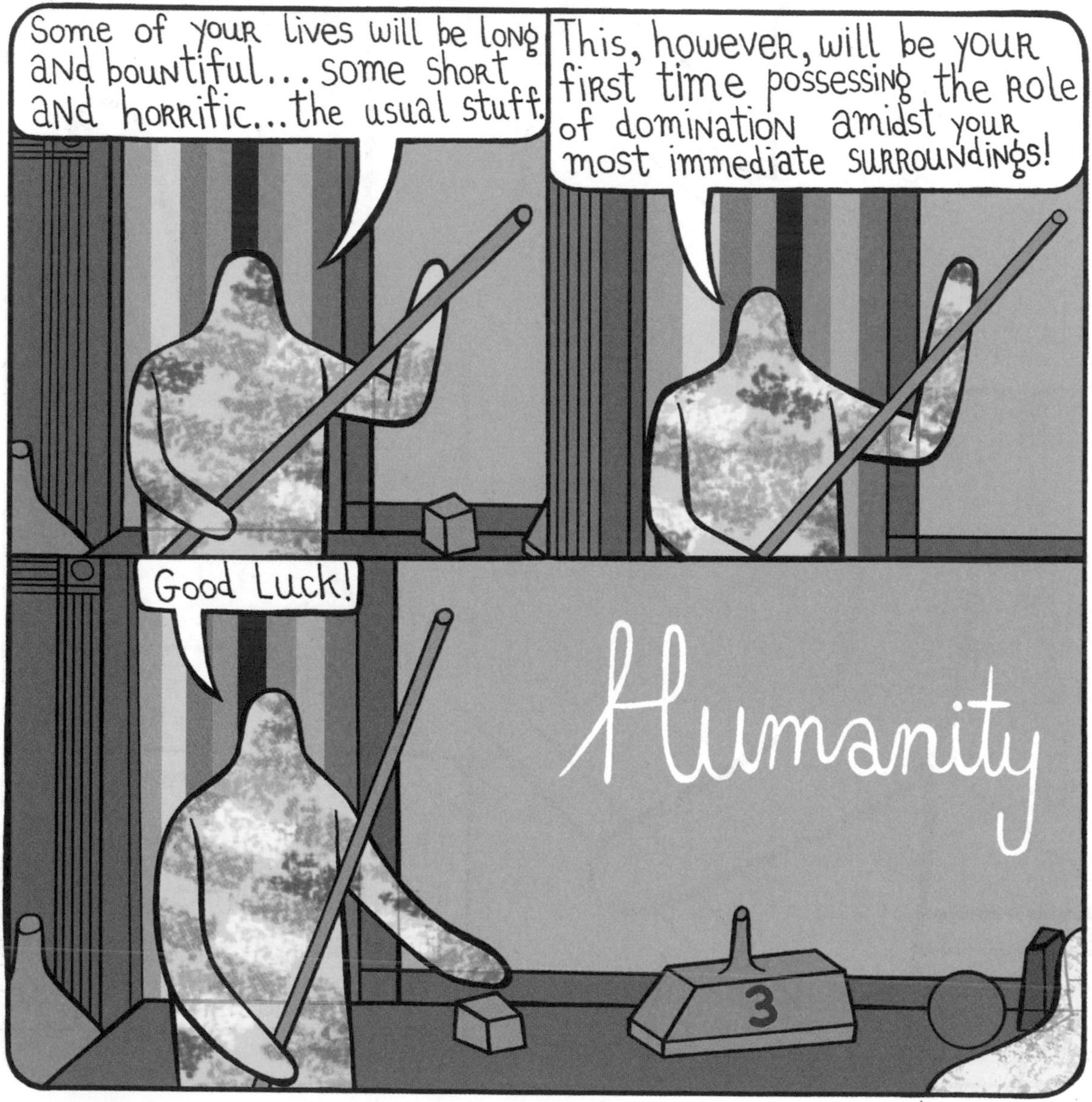
Some of your lives will be long and bountiful... some short and horrific... the usual stuff.
This, however, will be your first time possessing the role of domination amidst your most immediate surroundings!
Good Luck!
Humanity
3

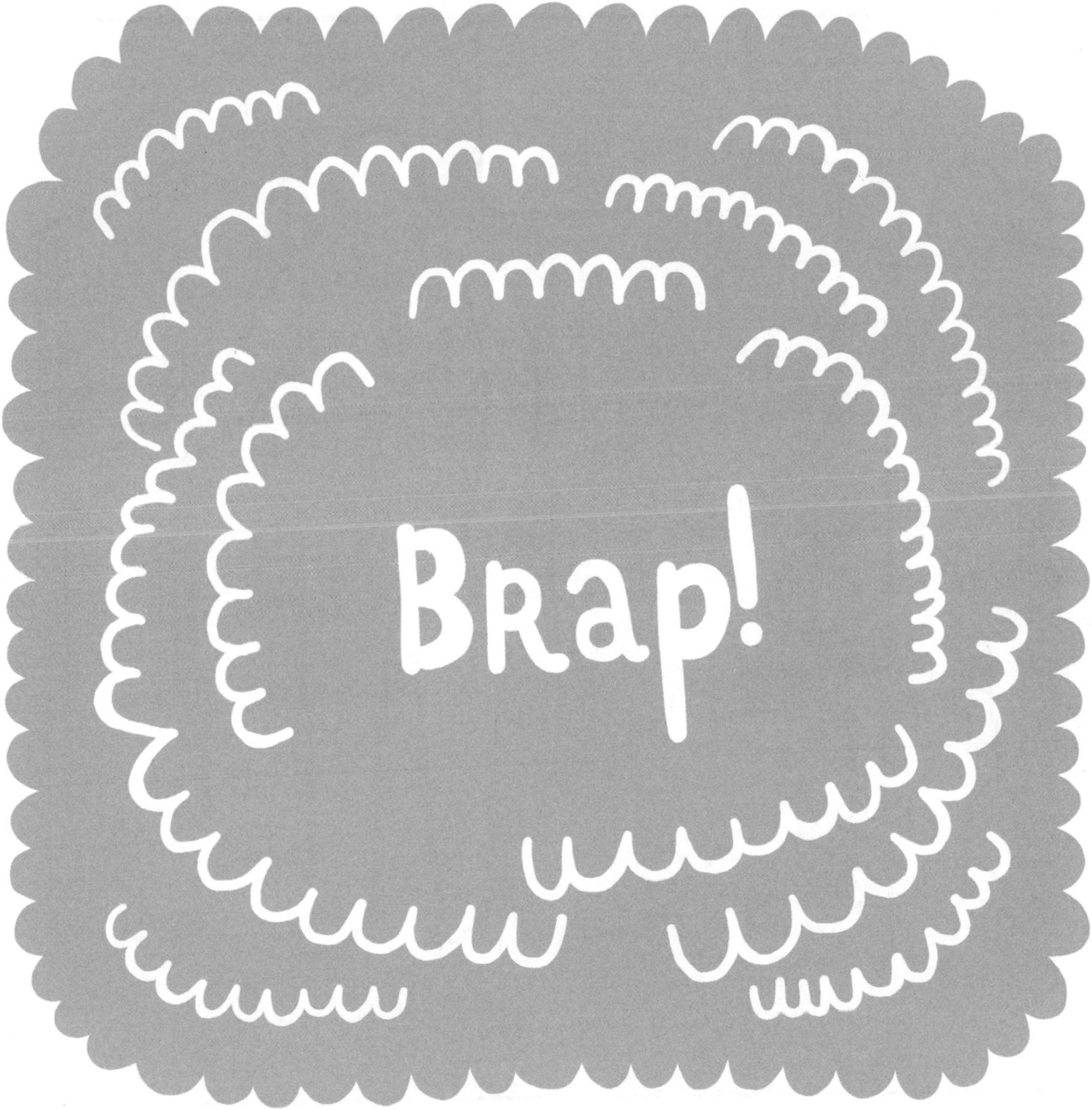
Brap!

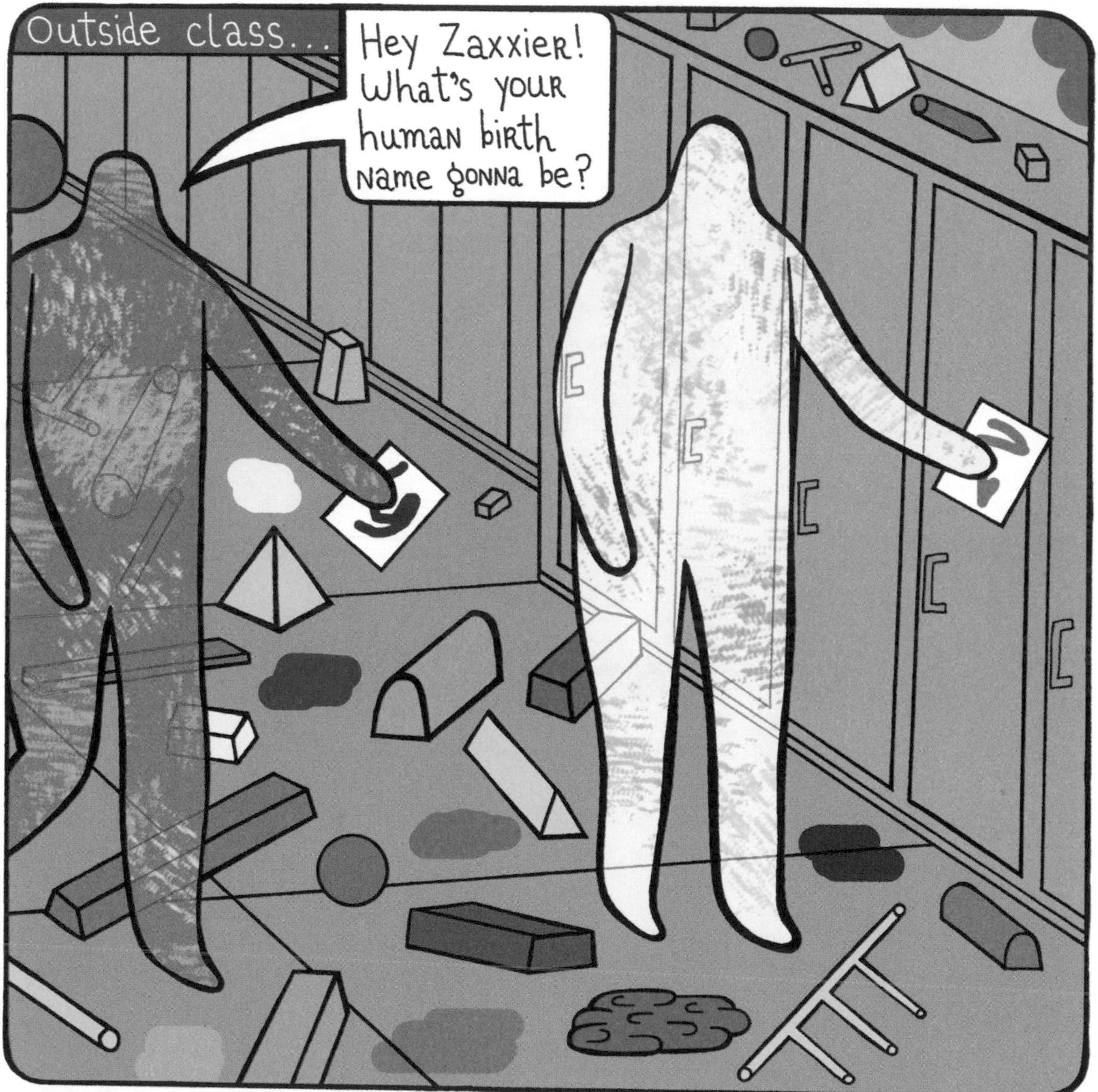
Outside class...
Hey Zaxxier! What's your human birth name gonna be?

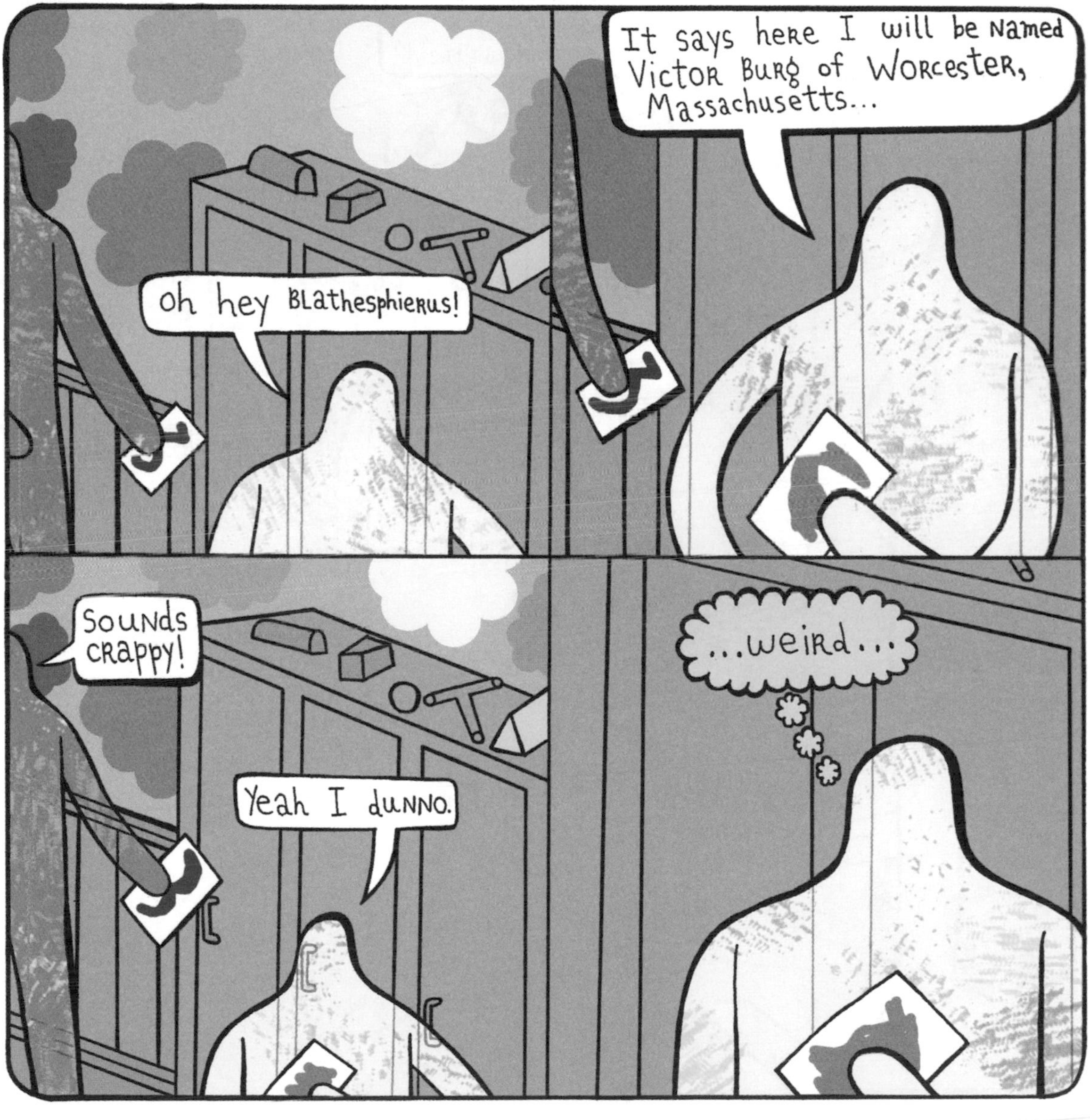
oh hey BLathesphierus!
It says here I will be Named Victor Burg of Worcester, Massachusetts...
Sounds crappy!
Yeah I dunno.
...weird...

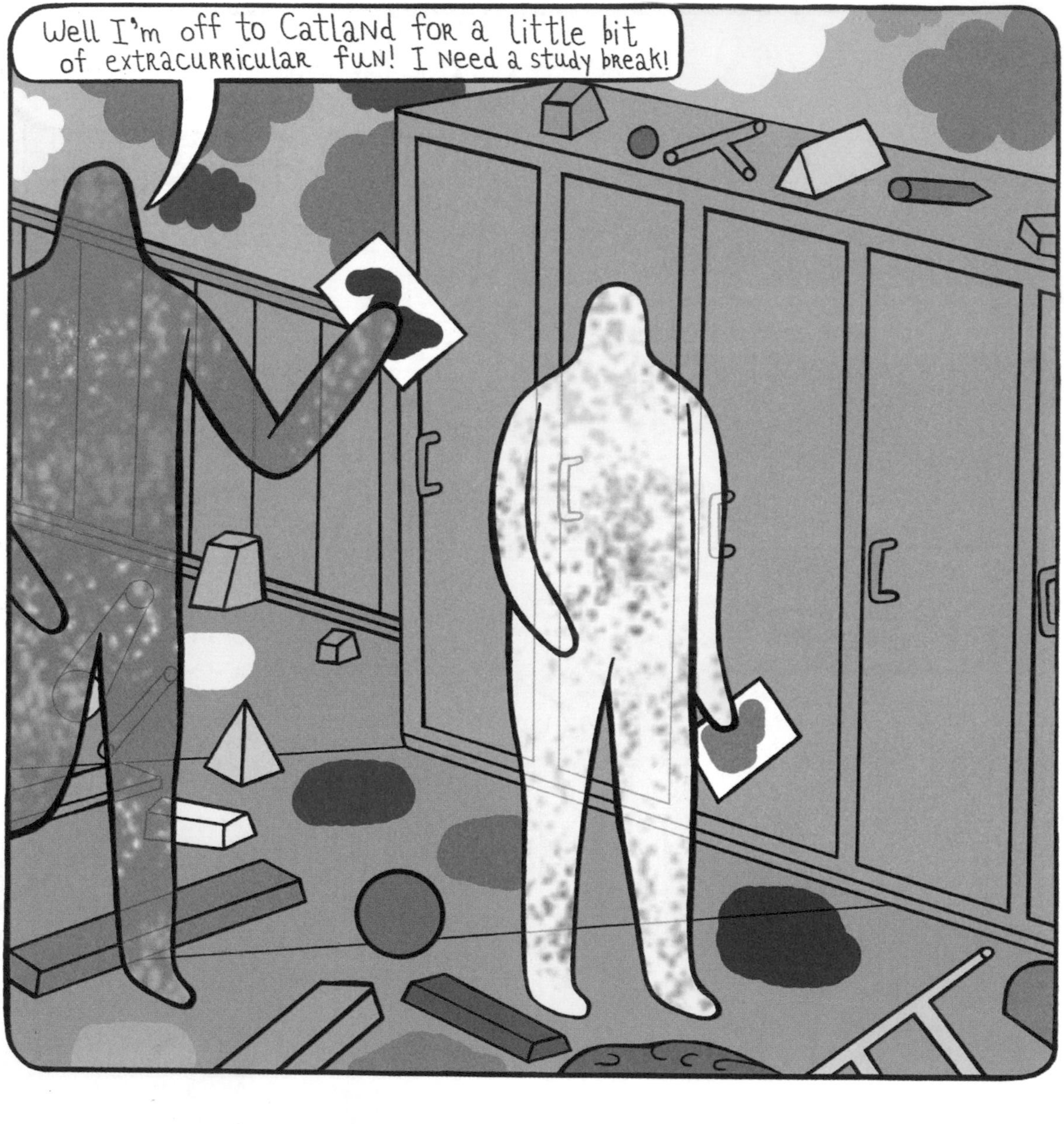
Well I'm off to Catland for a little bit of extracurricular fun! I need a study break!

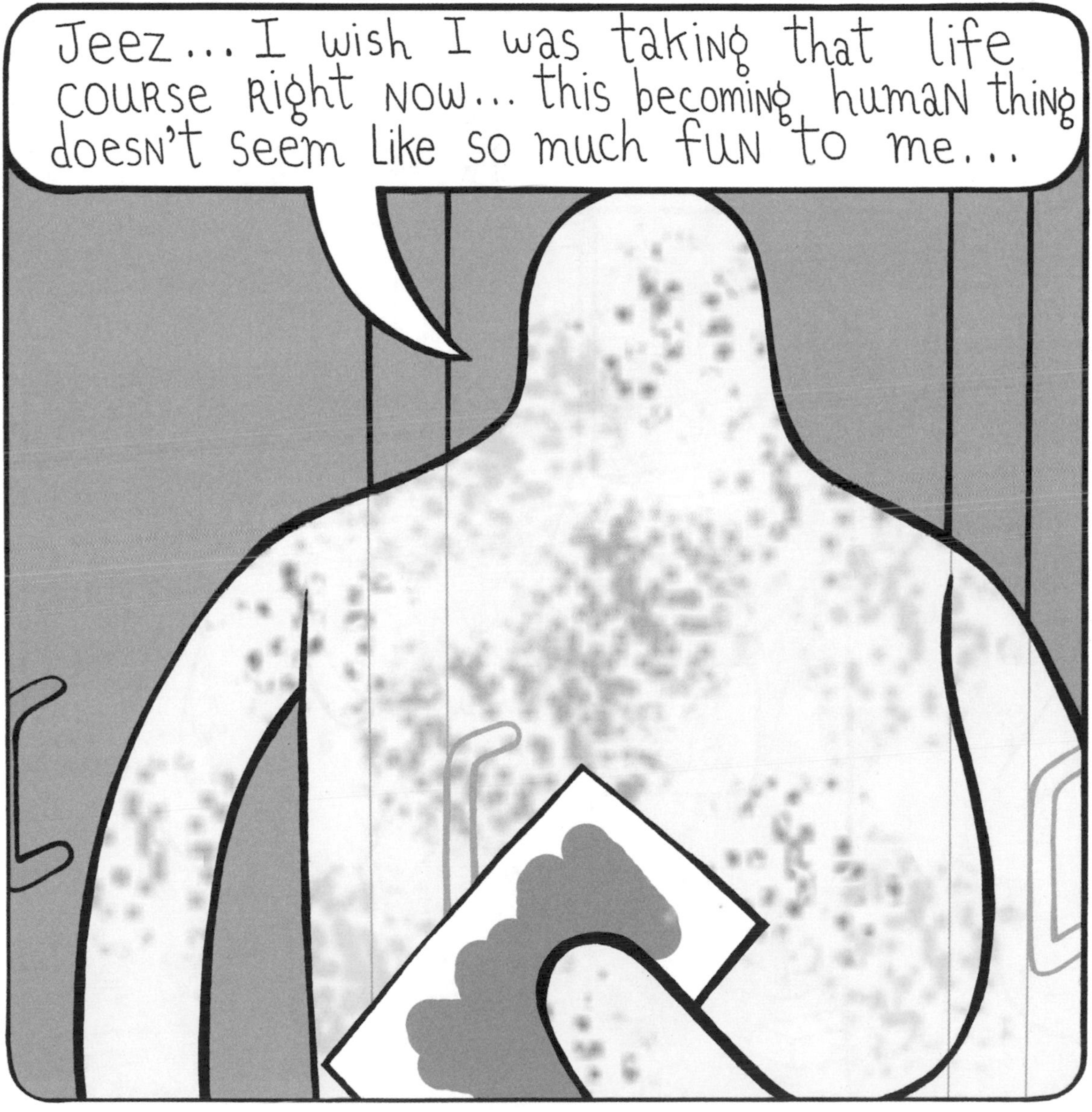
Jeez... I wish I was taking that life course right now... this becoming human thing doesn't seem like so much fun to me...

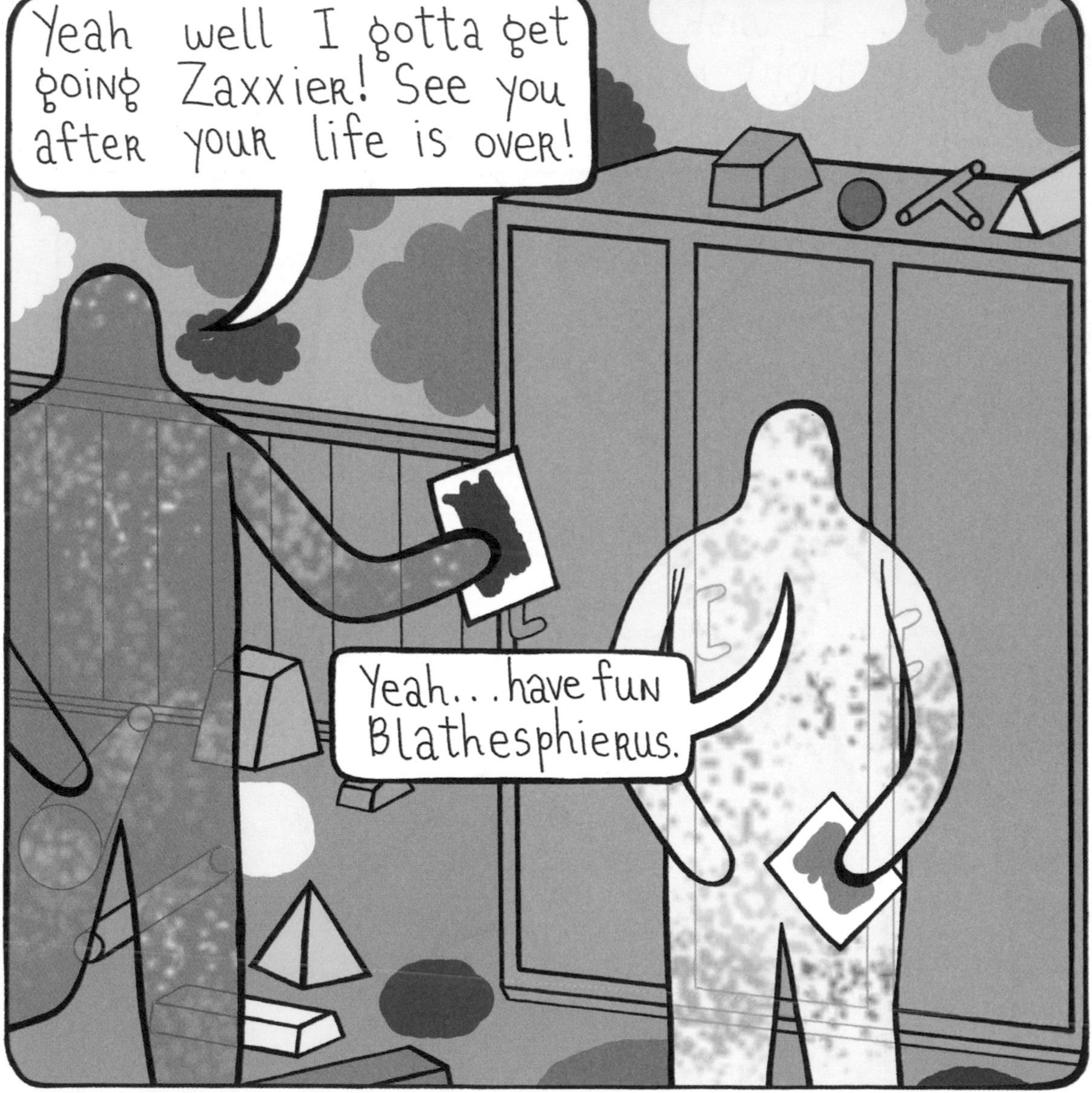
Yeah well I gotta get going Zaxxier! See you after your life is over!
Yeah... have fun Blathesphierus.

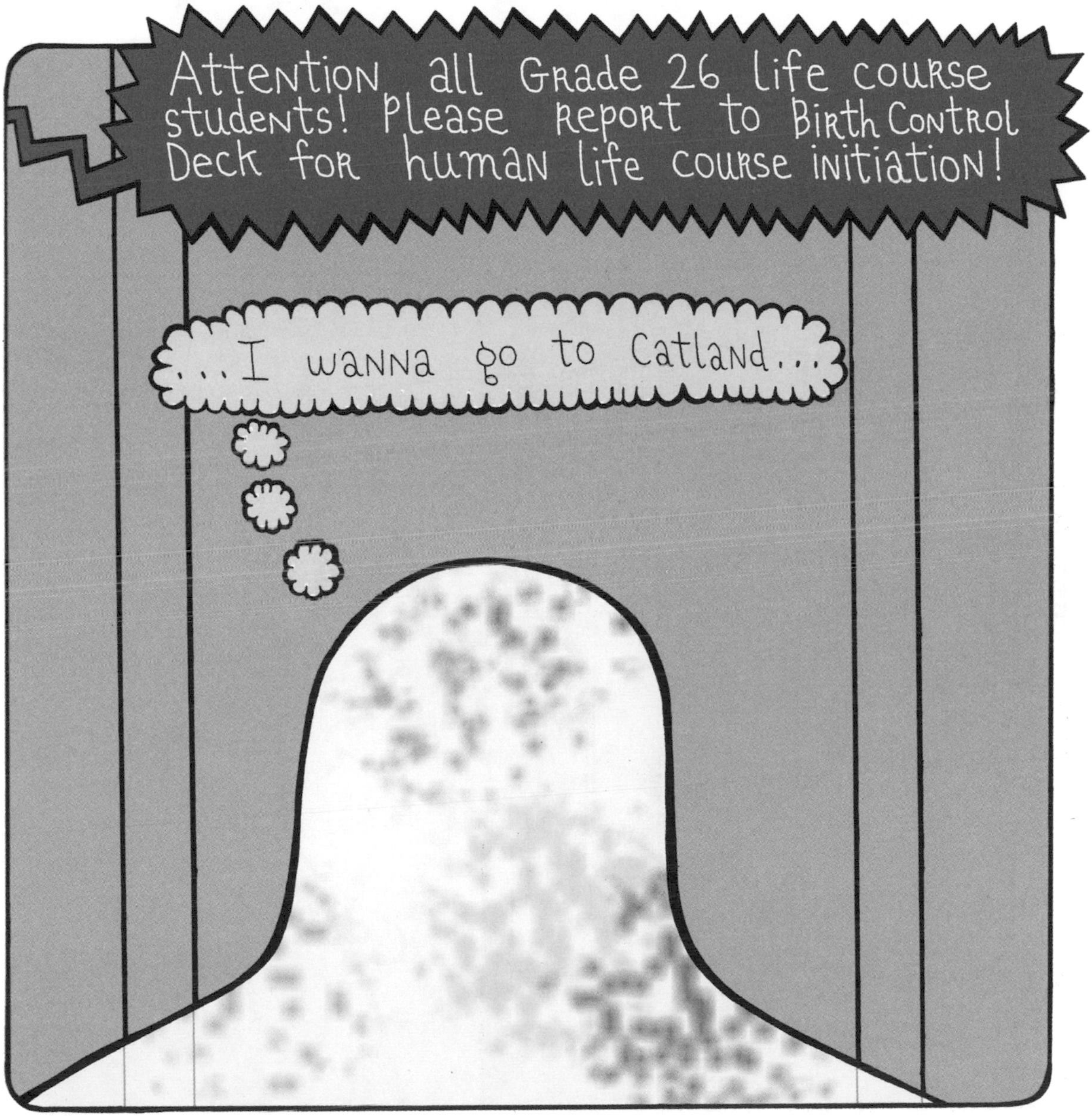
Attention all Grade 26 life course students! Please report to Birth Control Deck for human life course initiation!
...I wanna go to Catland...

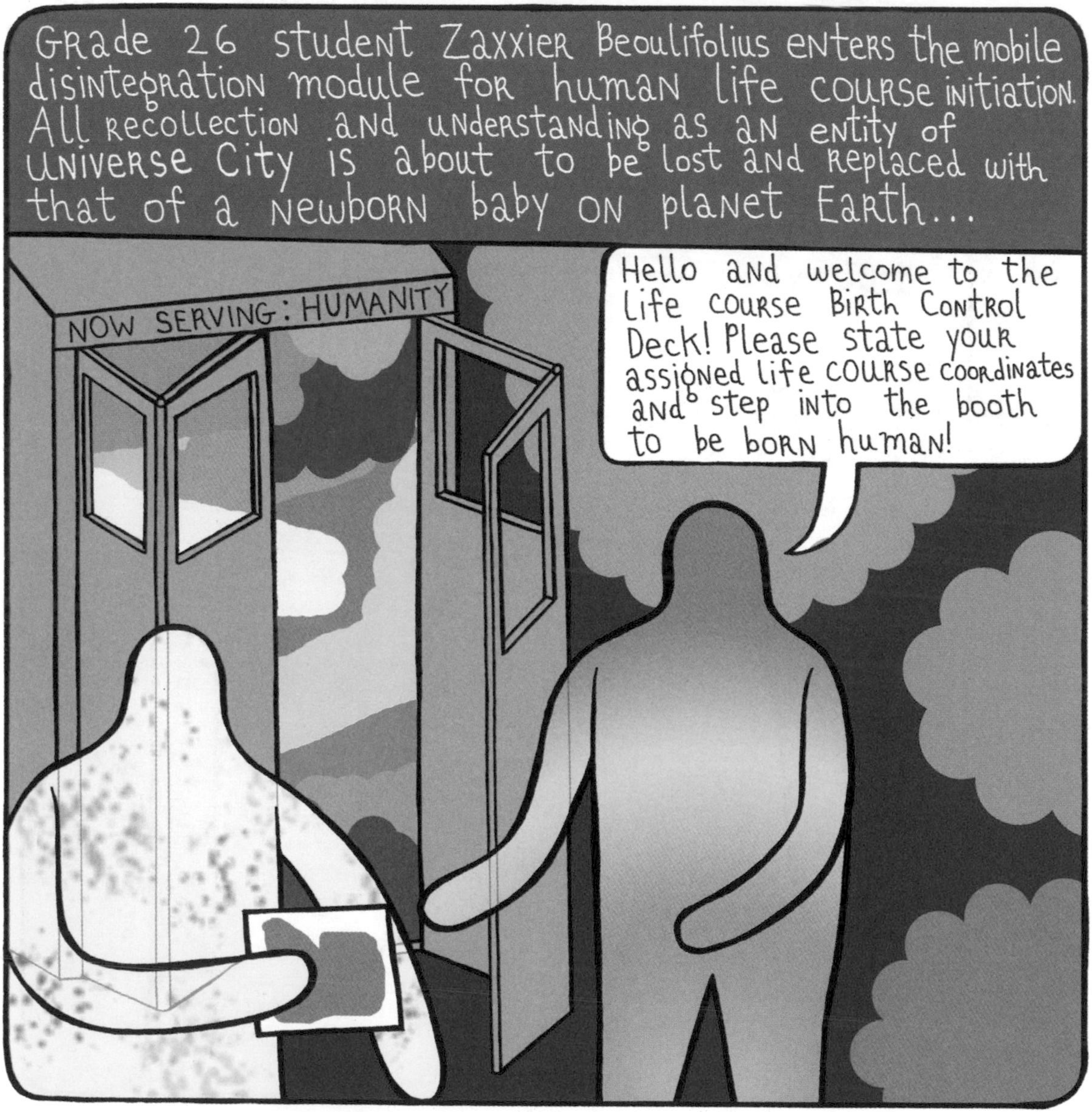
Grade 26 student Zaxxier Beoulifolius enters the mobile disintegration module for human life course initiation. All recollection and understanding as an entity of Universe City is about to be lost and replaced with that of a newborn baby on planet Earth...
NOW SERVING: HUMANITY
Hello and welcome to the Life Course Birth Control Deck! Please state your assigned life course coordinates and step into the booth to be born human!

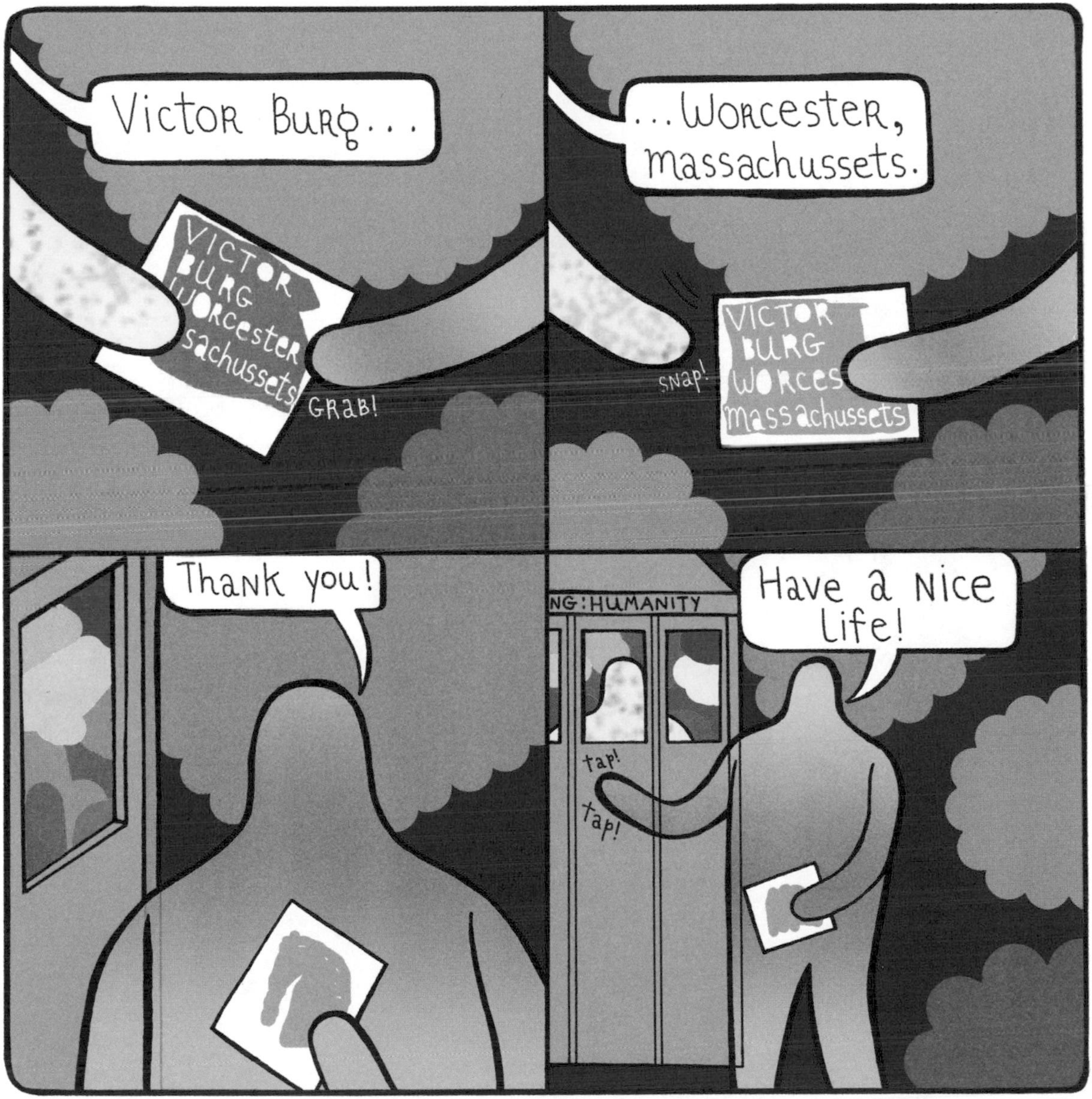
Victor Burg...
VICTOR
BURG
WORcester
sachussets
GRAB!
...WORCESTER,
massachussets.
VICTOR
BURG
WORCES
massachussets
SNAP!
Thank you!
NG:HUMANITY
Have a Nice
Life!
tap!
tap!

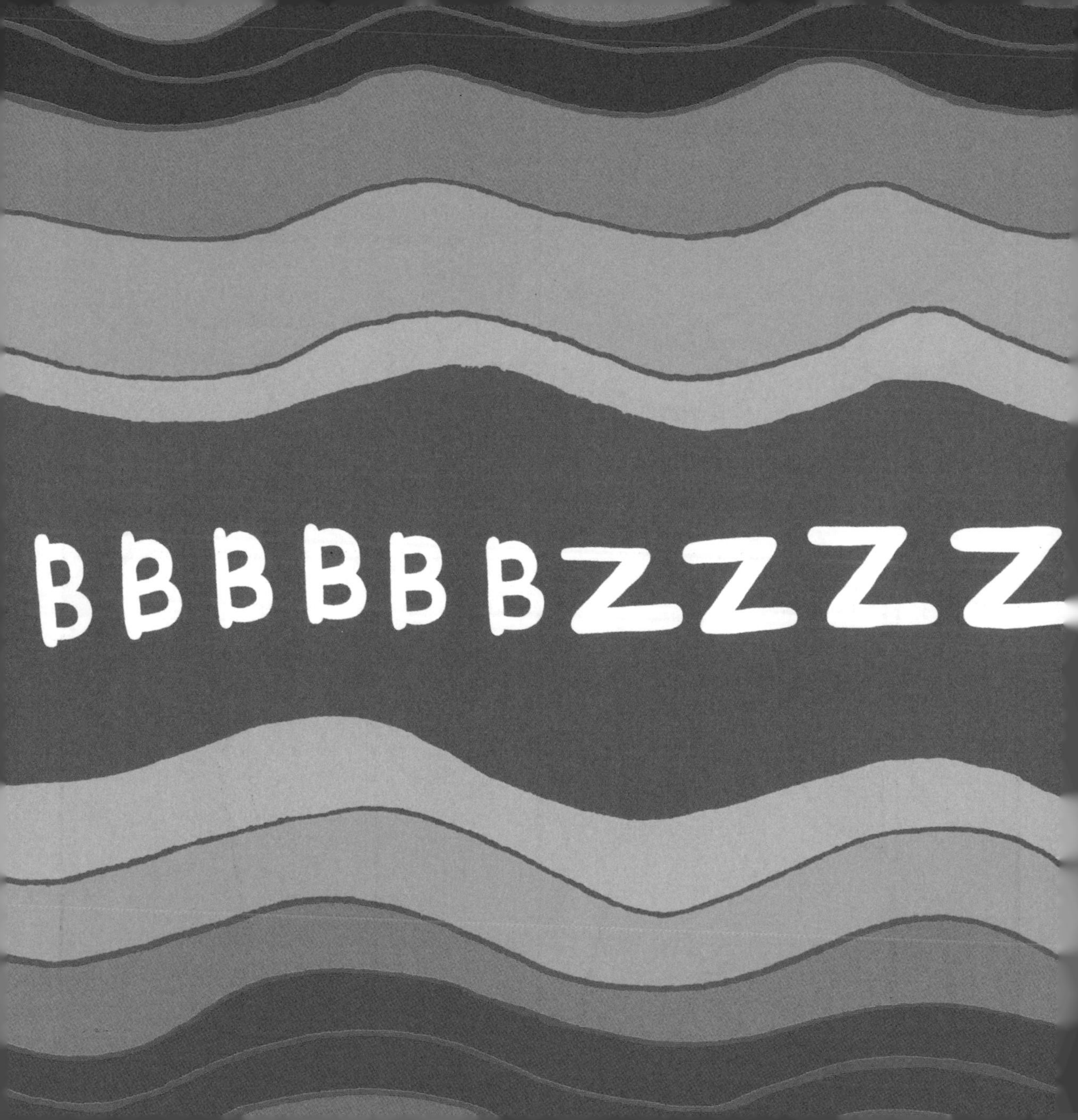
BBBBBBZZZZ

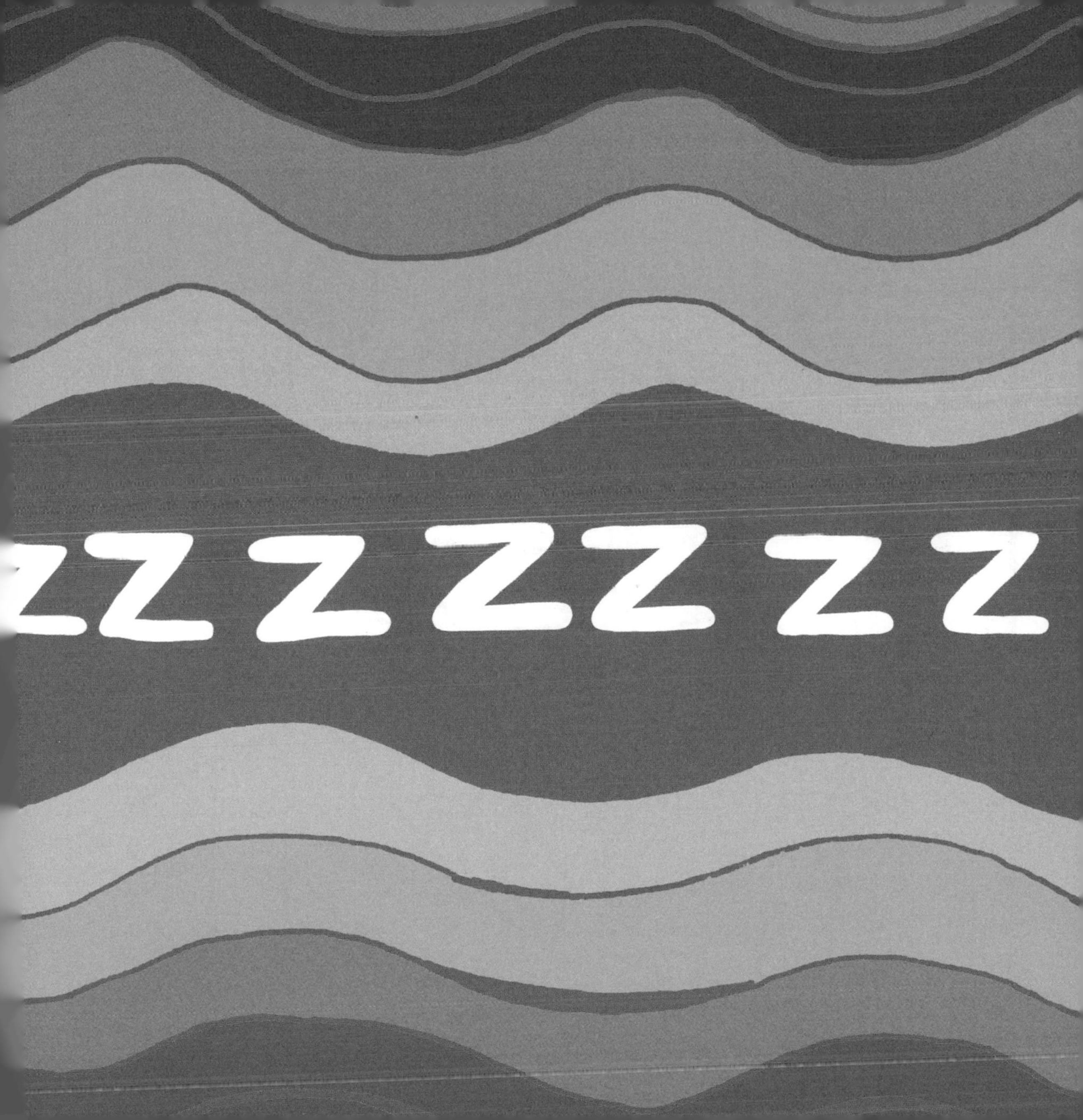
ZZZZZZ

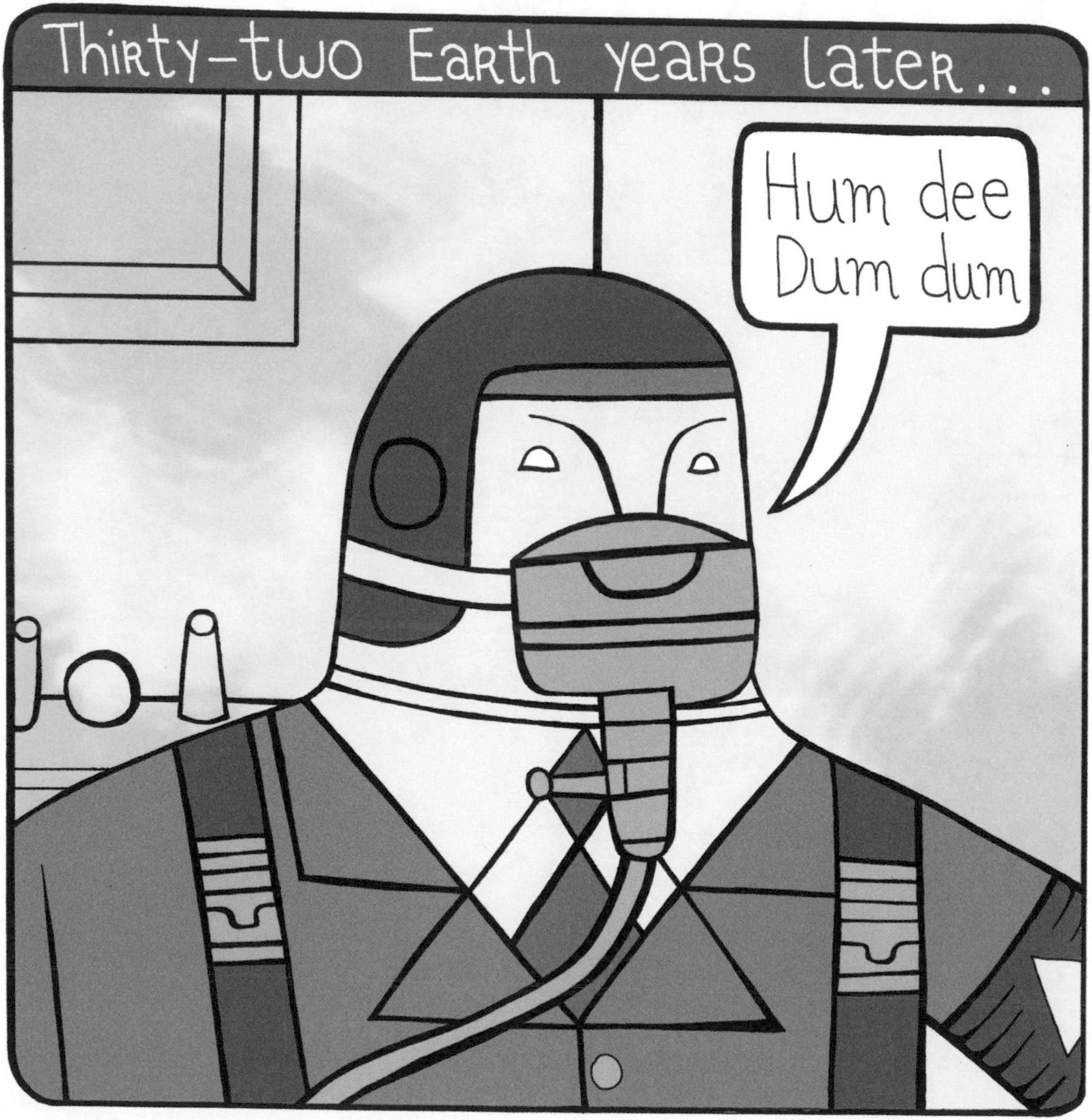
Thirty-two Earth years later...
Hum dee Dum dum

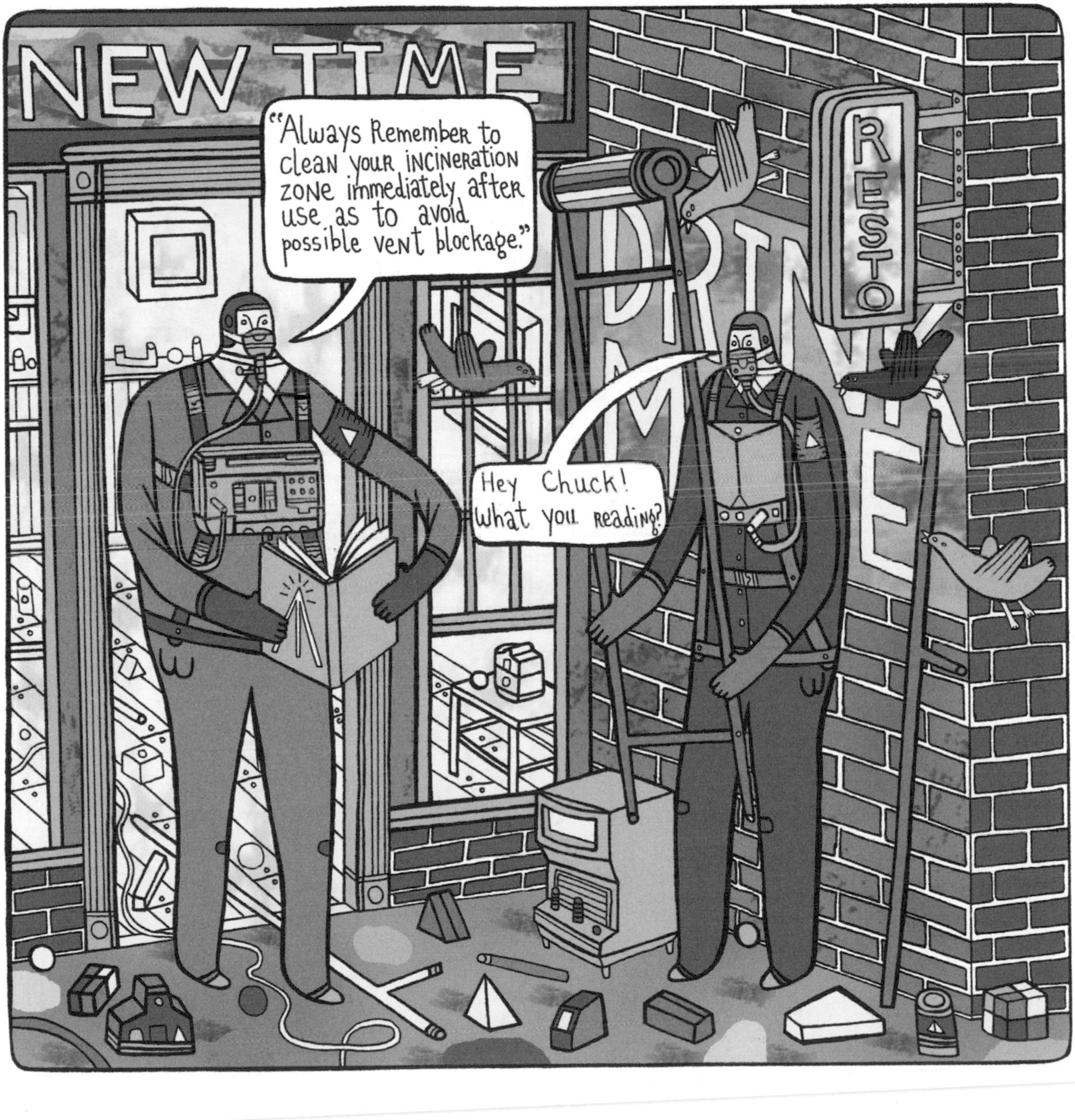
NEW TIME
"Always Remember to clean your incineration zone immediately after use as to avoid possible vent blockage."
RESTO
Hey Chuck! What you reading?

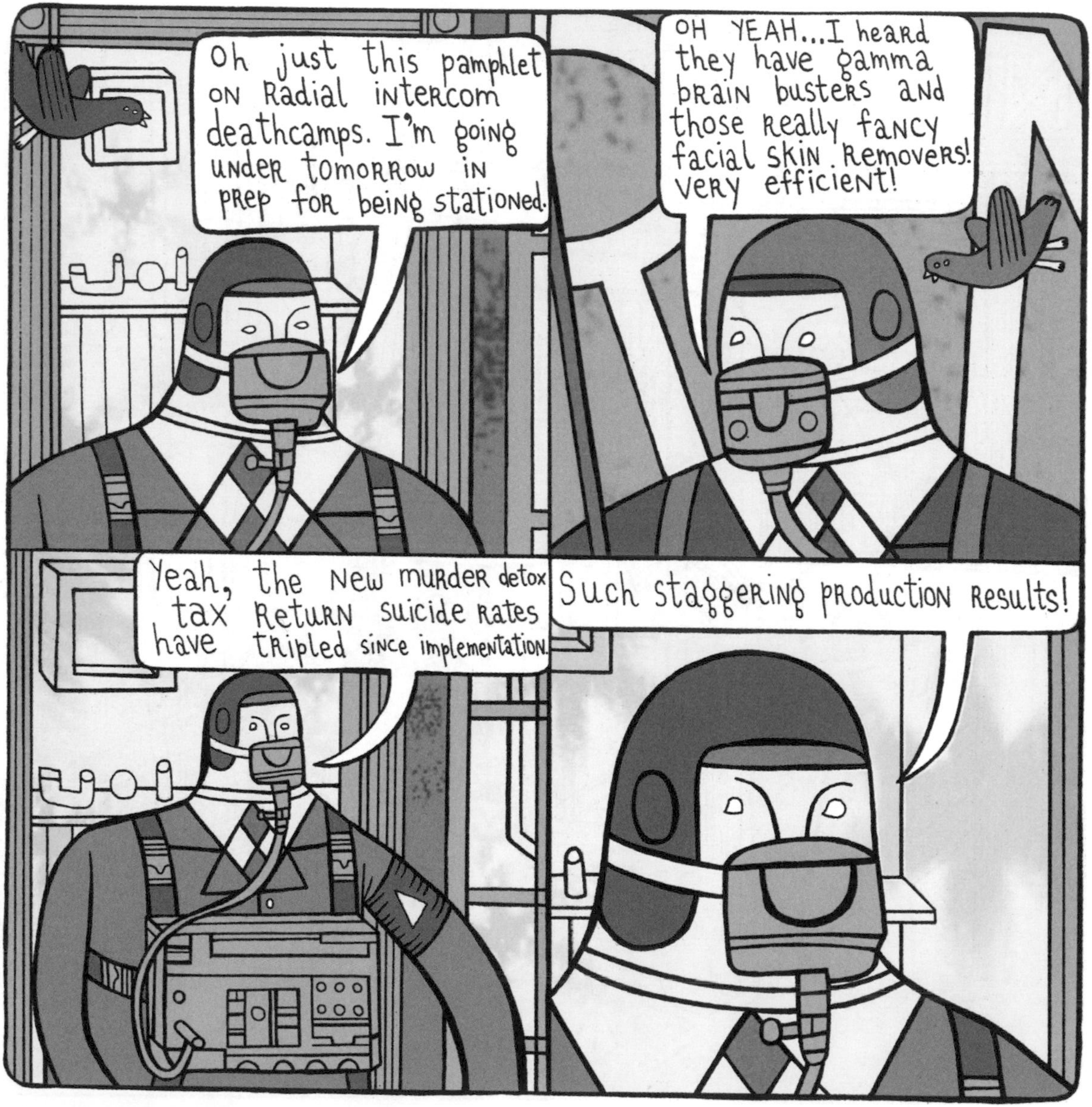
Oh just this pamphlet on Radial intercom deathcamps. I'm going under tomorrow in prep for being stationed.
OH YEAH...I heard they have gamma brain busters and those really fancy facial skin removers! Very efficient!
Yeah, the new murder detox tax return suicide rates have tripled since implementation.
Such staggering production results!

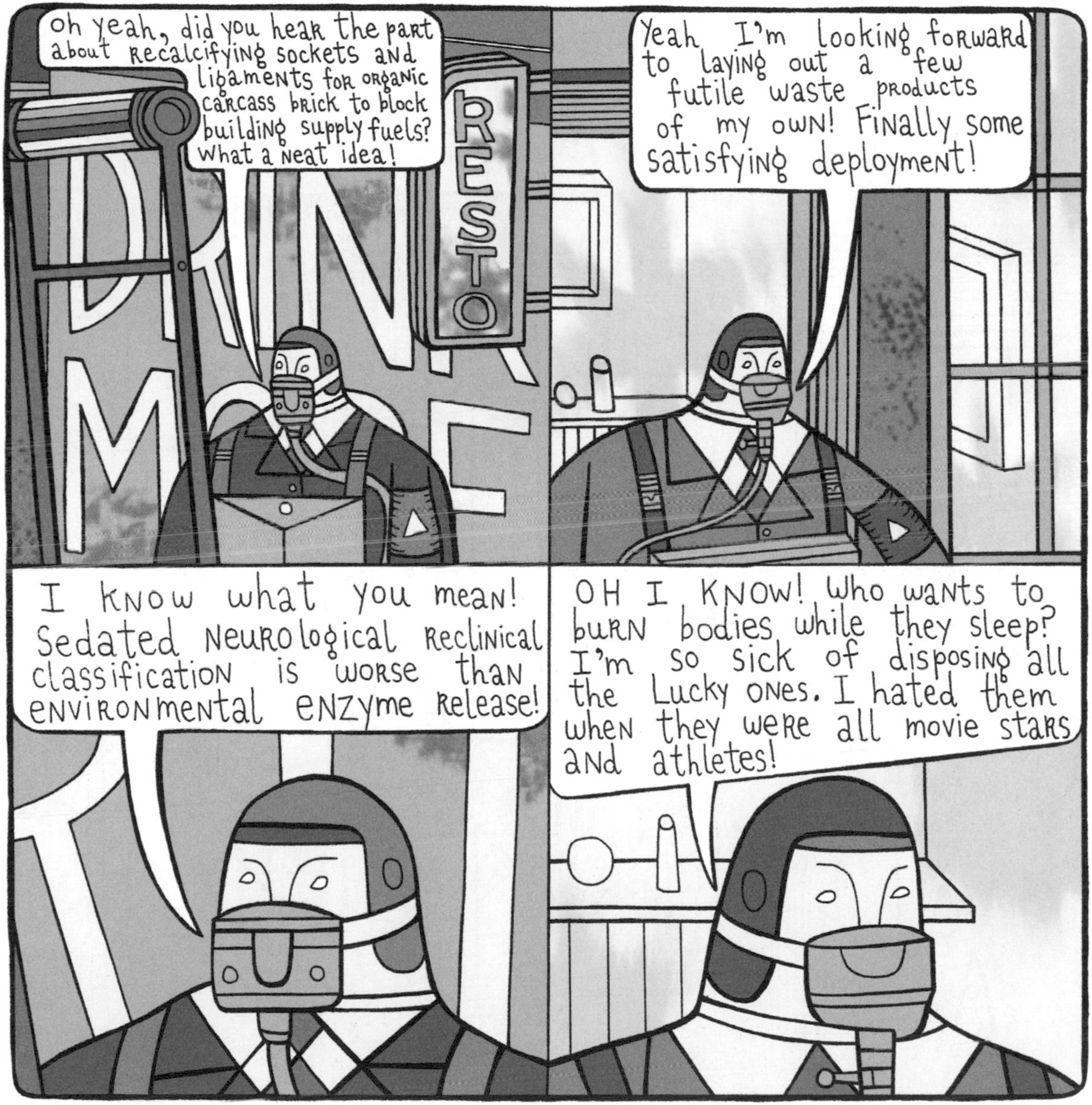
Oh yeah, did you hear the part about recalcifying sockets and ligaments for organic carcass brick to block building supply fuels? What a neat idea!
RESTO
Yeah I'm looking forward to laying out a few futile waste products of my own! Finally some satisfying deployment!
I know what you mean! Sedated neurological reclinical classification is worse than environmental enzyme release!
OH I KNOW! Who wants to burn bodies while they sleep? I'm so sick of disposing all the lucky ones. I hated them when they were all movie stars and athletes!

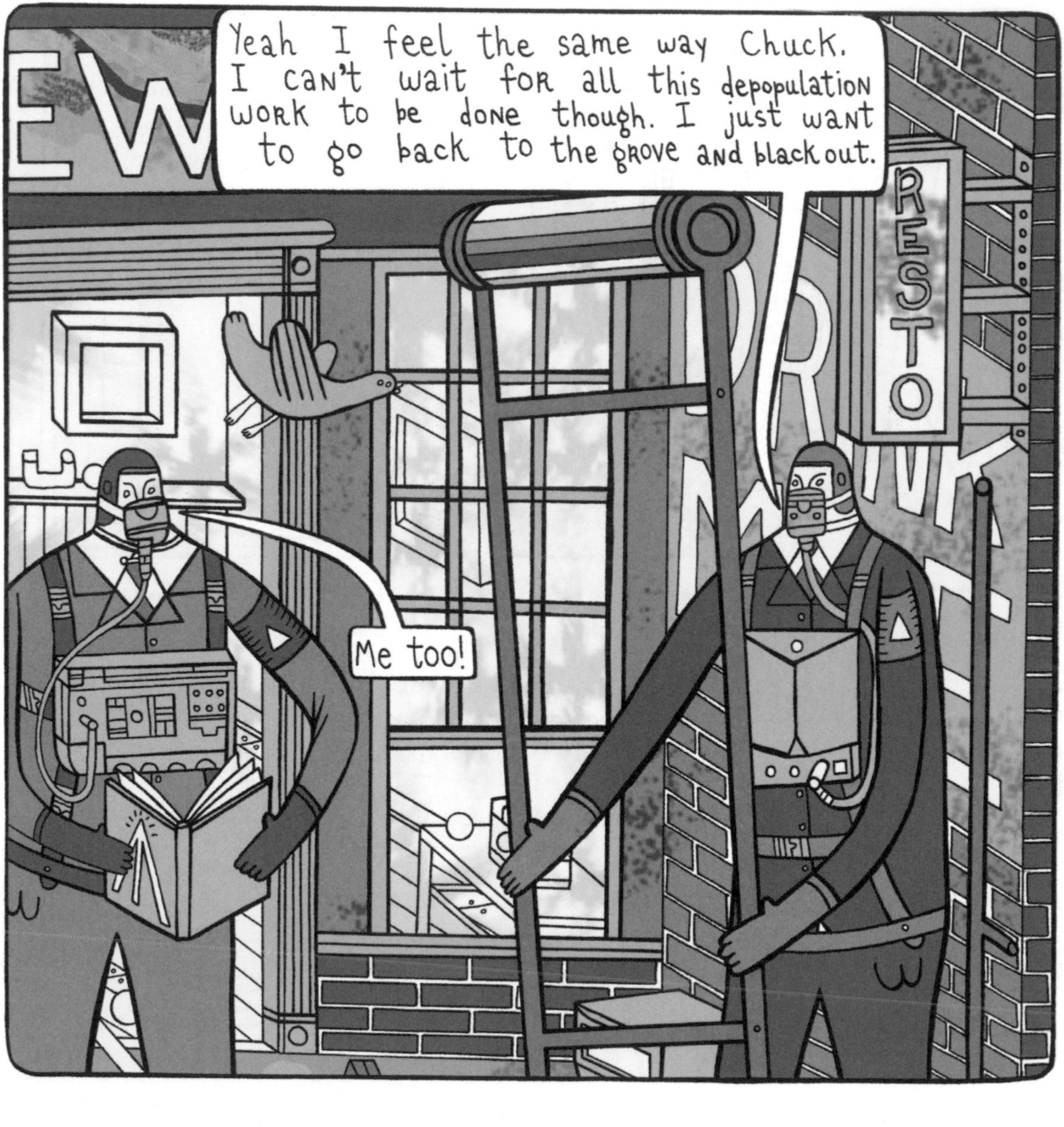
EW
Yeah I feel the same way Chuck. I can't wait for all this depopulation work to be done though. I just want to go back to the grove and black out.
RESTO
Me too!

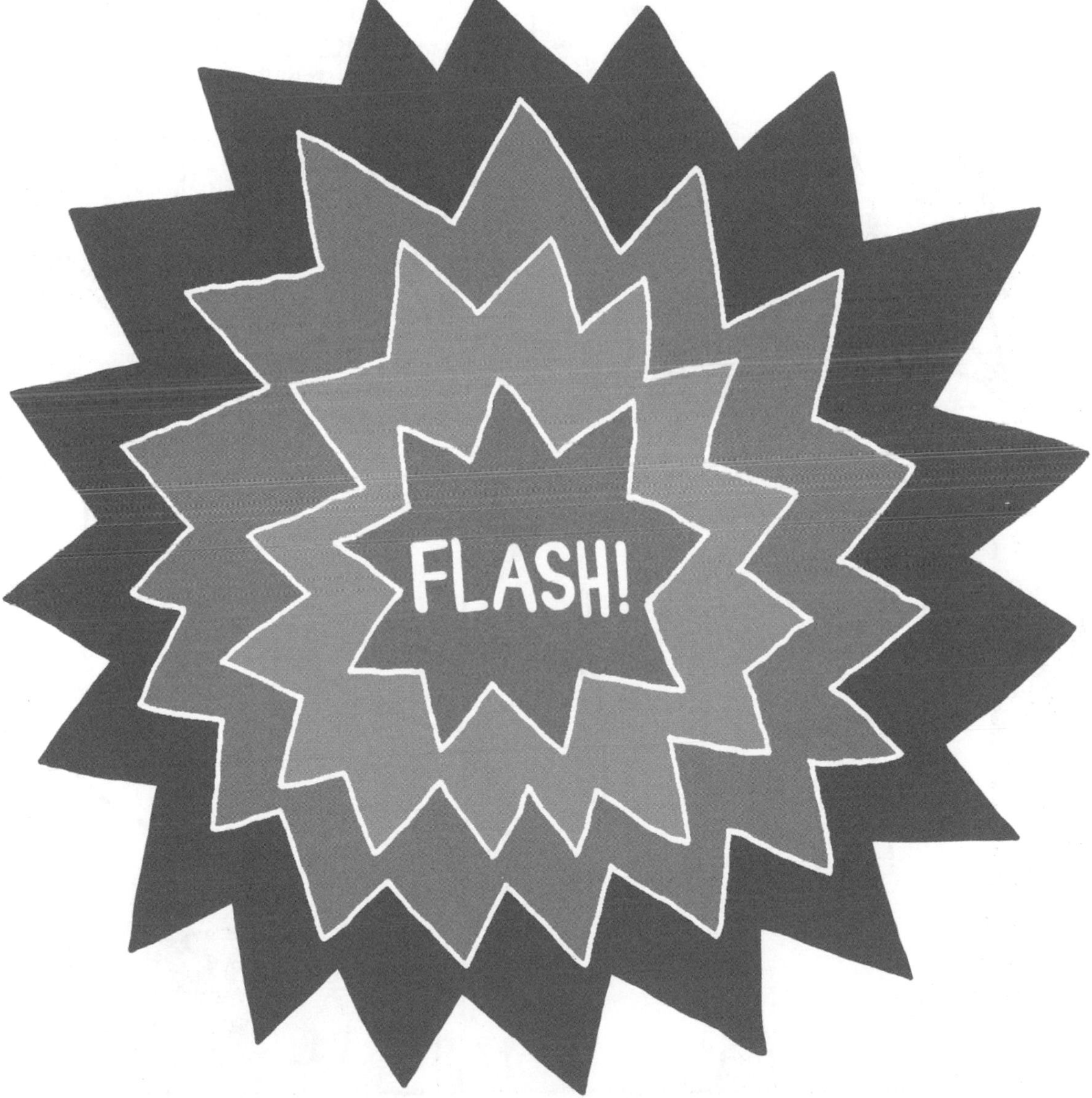
FLASH!

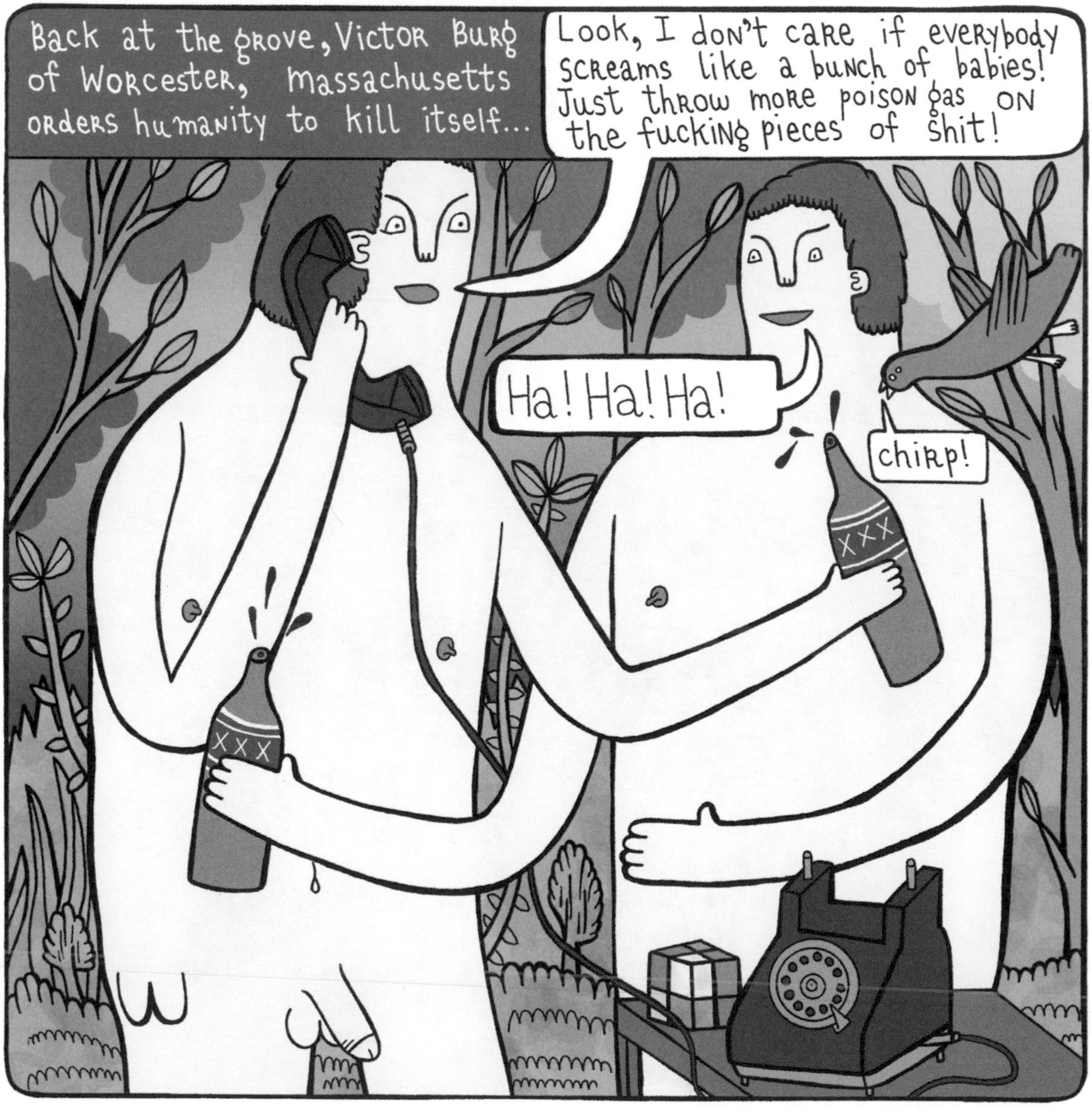
Back at the grove, Victor Burg of Worcester, Massachusetts orders humanity to kill itself...
Look, I don't care if everybody screams like a bunch of babies! Just throw more poison gas on the fucking pieces of shit!
Ha! Ha! Ha!
chirp!

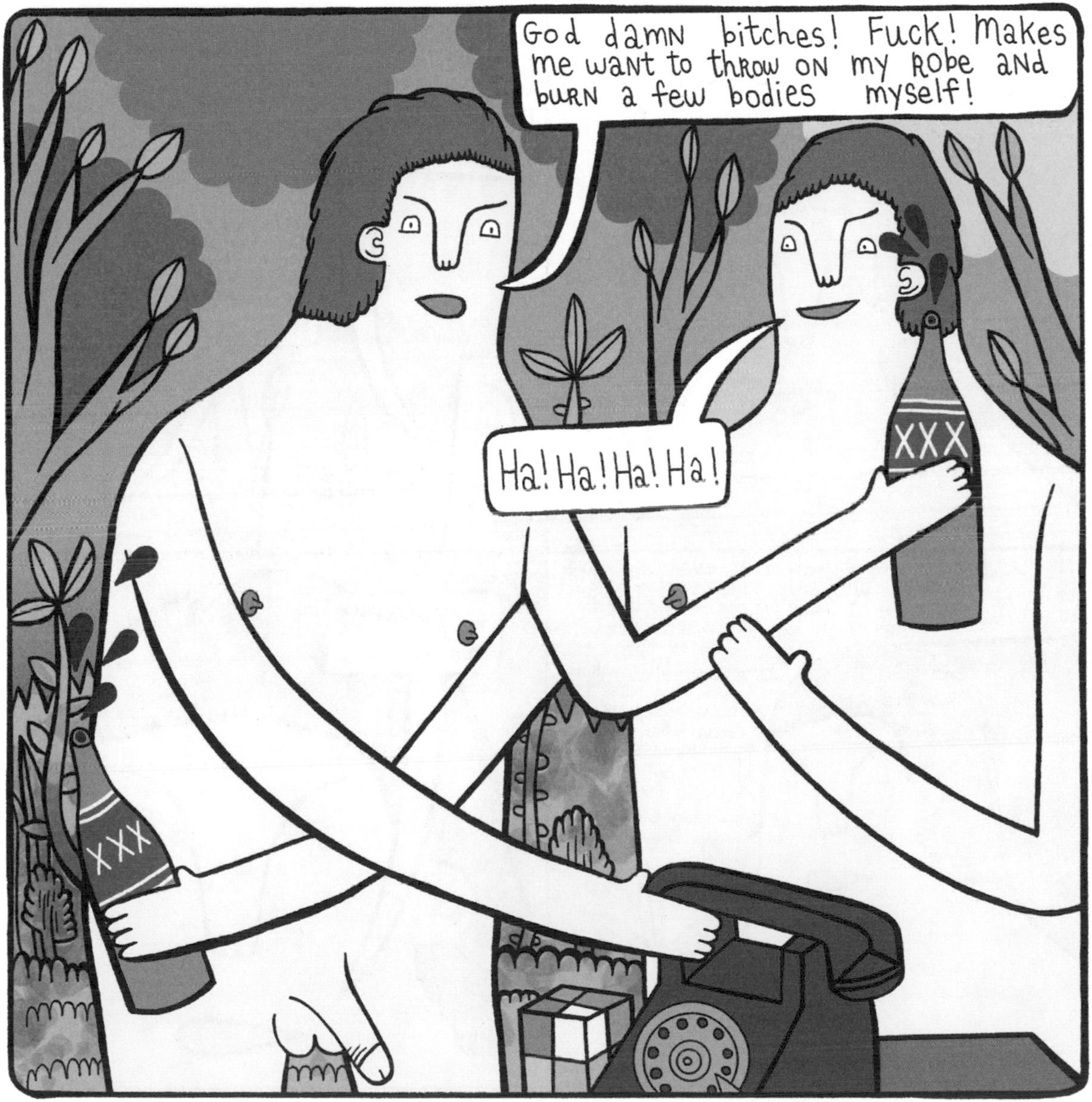
God damn bitches! Fuck! Makes me want to throw on my robe and burn a few bodies myself!
Ha! Ha! Ha! Ha!
XXX
XXX

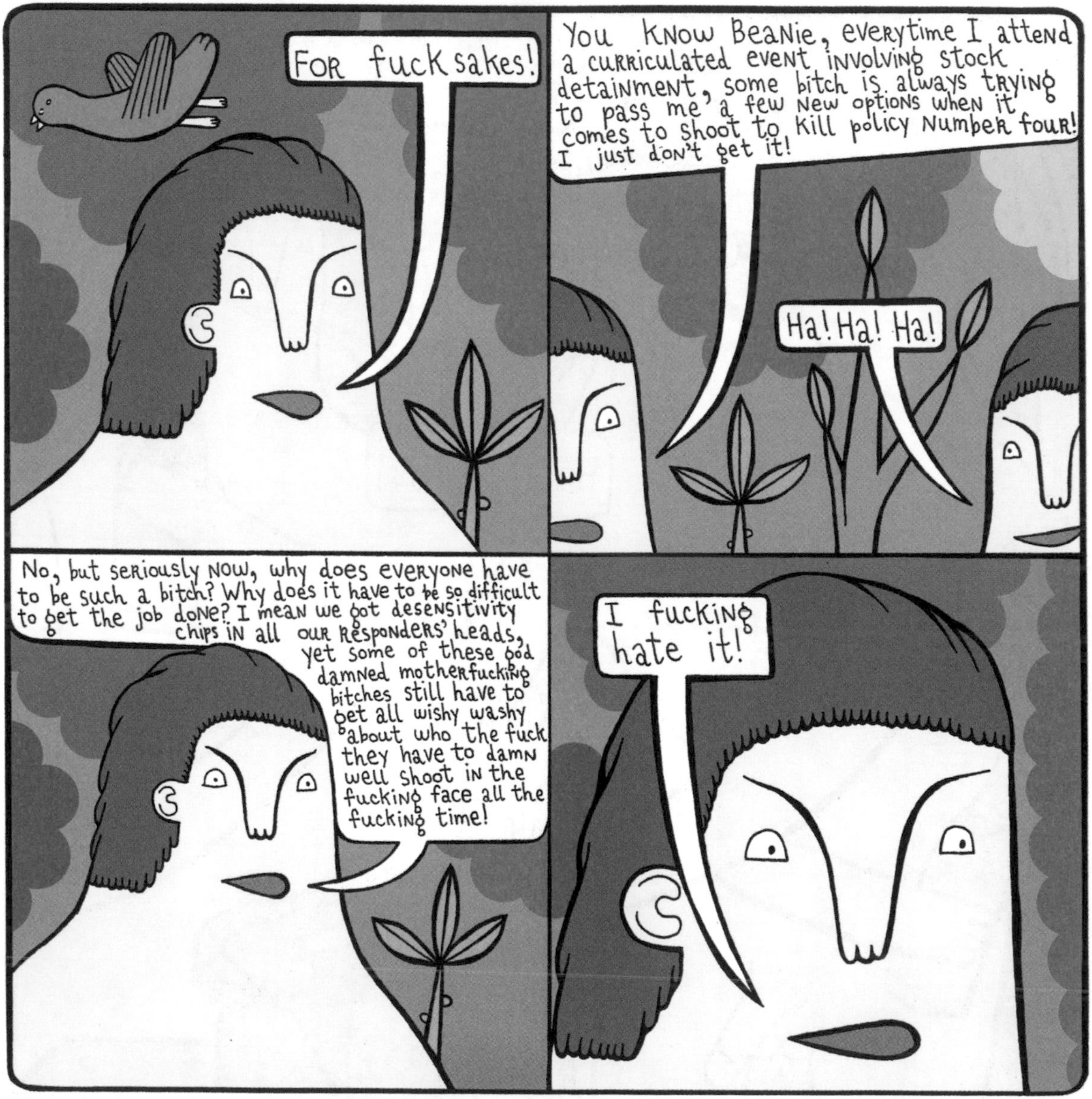
For fuck sakes!
You know Beanie, everytime I attend a curriculated event involving stock detainment, some bitch is always trying to pass me a few new options when it comes to shoot to kill policy number four! I just don't get it!
Ha! Ha! Ha!
No, but seriously now, why does everyone have to be such a bitch? Why does it have to be so difficult to get the job done? I mean we got desensitivity chips in all our responders' heads, yet some of these god damned motherfucking bitches still have to get all wishy washy about who the fuck they have to damn well shoot in the fucking face all the fucking time!
I fucking hate it!

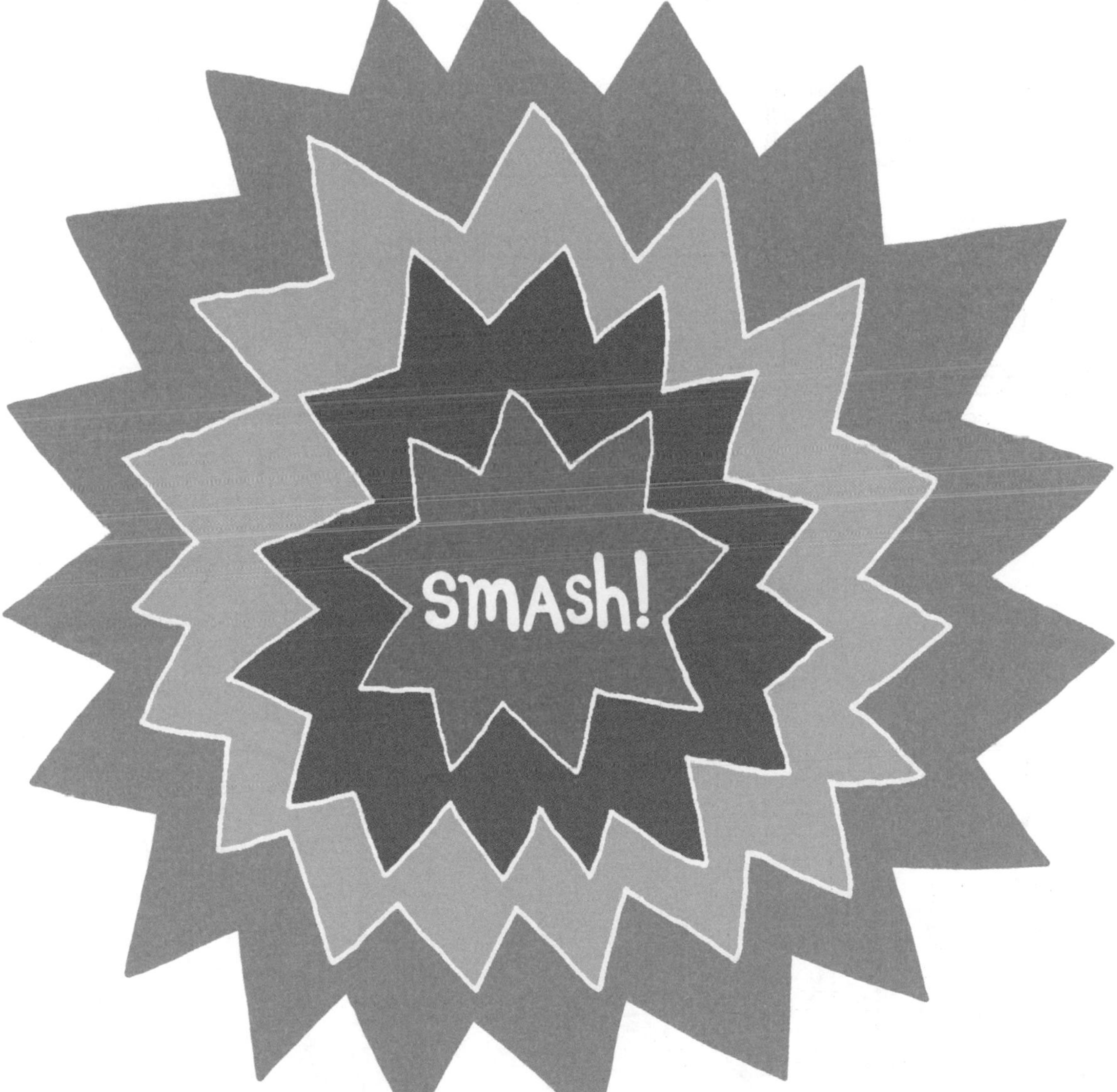
SMASH!

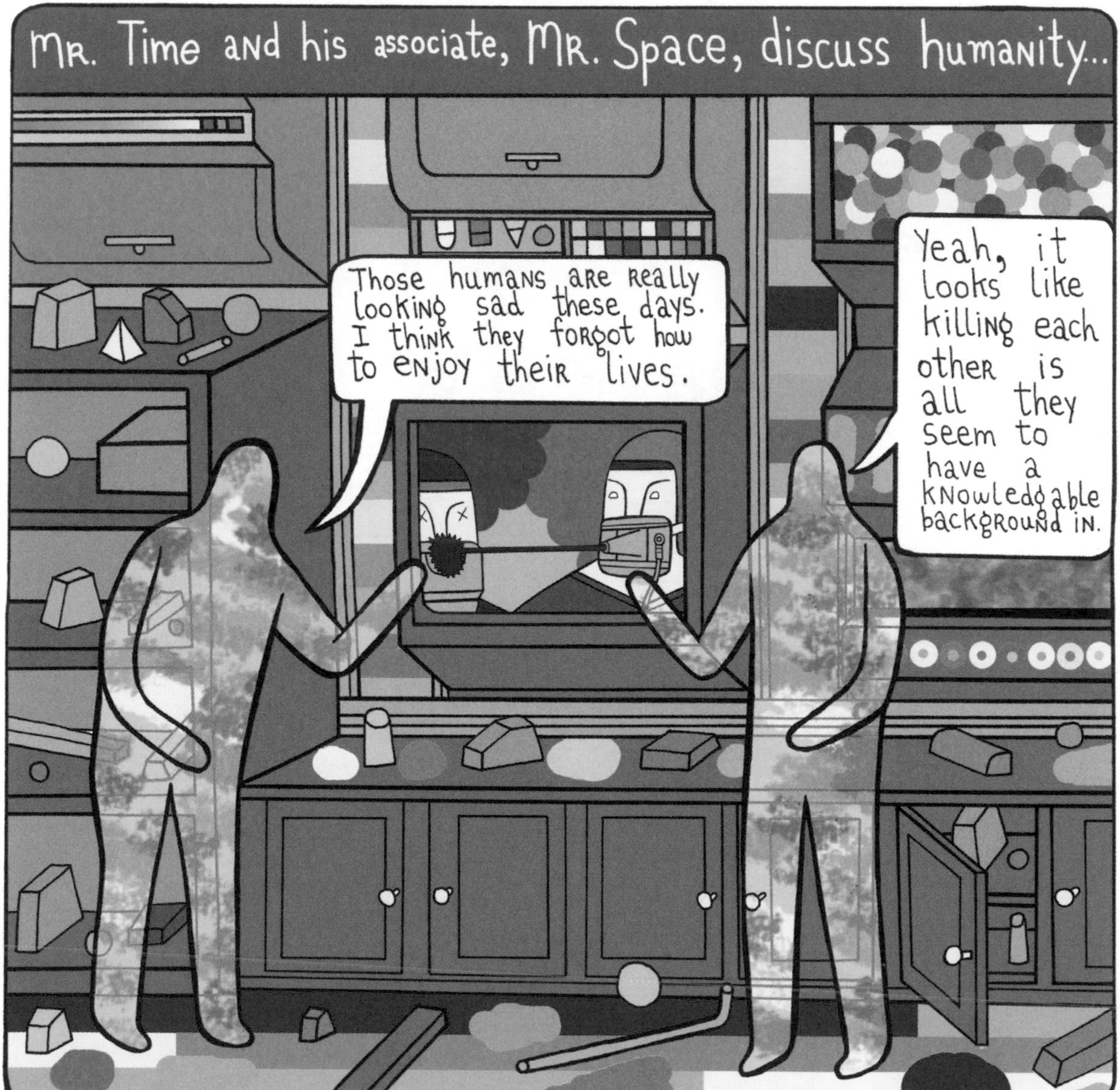
Mr. Time and his associate, Mr. Space, discuss humanity...
Those humans are really looking sad these days. I think they forgot how to enjoy their lives.
Yeah, it looks like killing each other is all they seem to have a knowledgable background in.

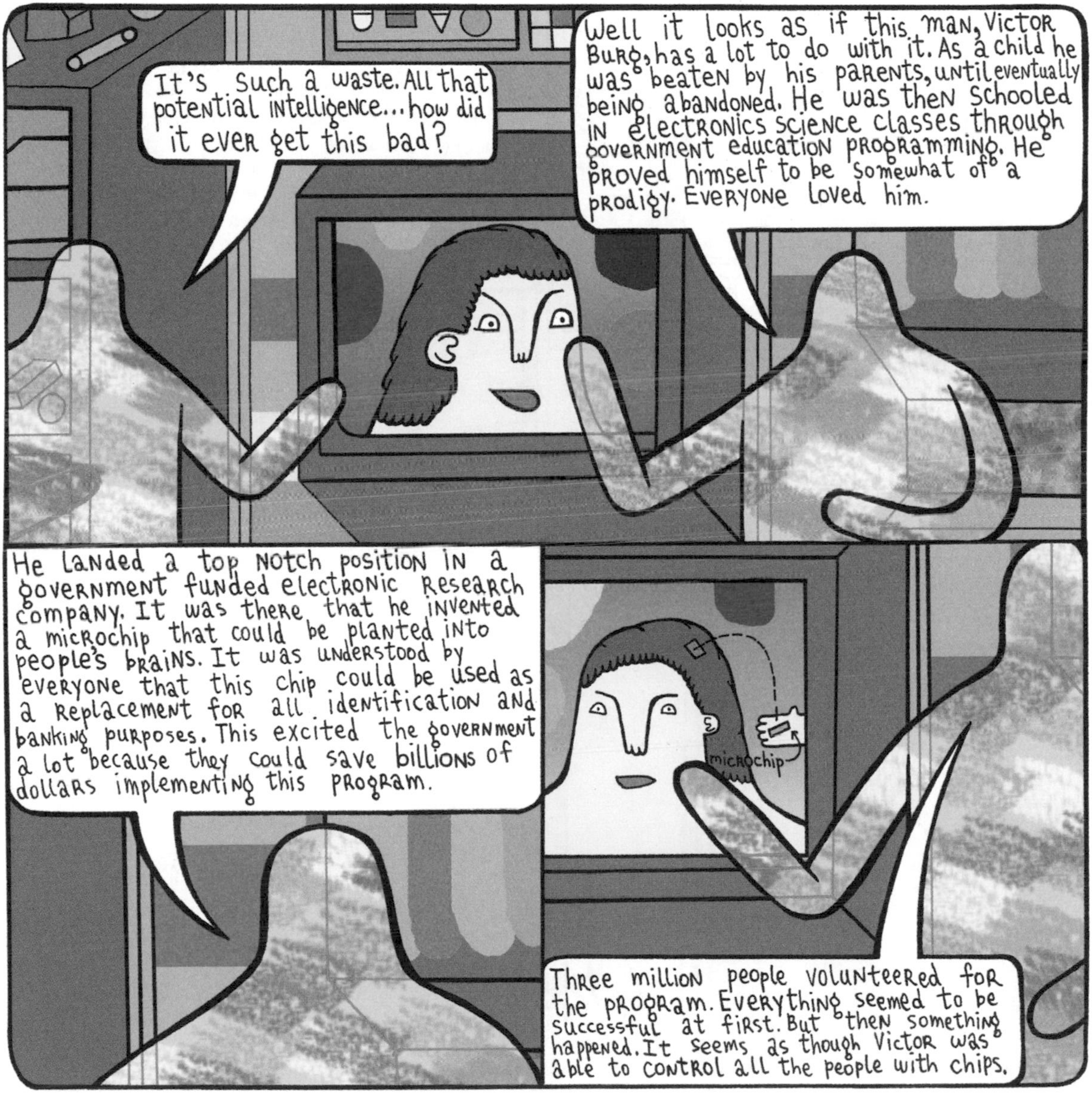
It's such a waste. All that potential intelligence... how did it ever get this bad?
Well it looks as if this man, Victor Burg, has a lot to do with it. As a child he was beaten by his parents, until eventually being abandoned. He was then schooled in electronics science classes through government education programming. He proved himself to be somewhat of a prodigy. Everyone loved him.
He landed a top notch position in a government funded electronic research company. It was there that he invented a microchip that could be planted into people's brains. It was understood by everyone that this chip could be used as a replacement for all identification and banking purposes. This excited the government a lot because they could save billions of dollars implementing this program.
microchip
Three million people volunteered for the program. Everything seemed to be successful at first. But then something happened. It seems as though Victor was able to control all the people with chips.

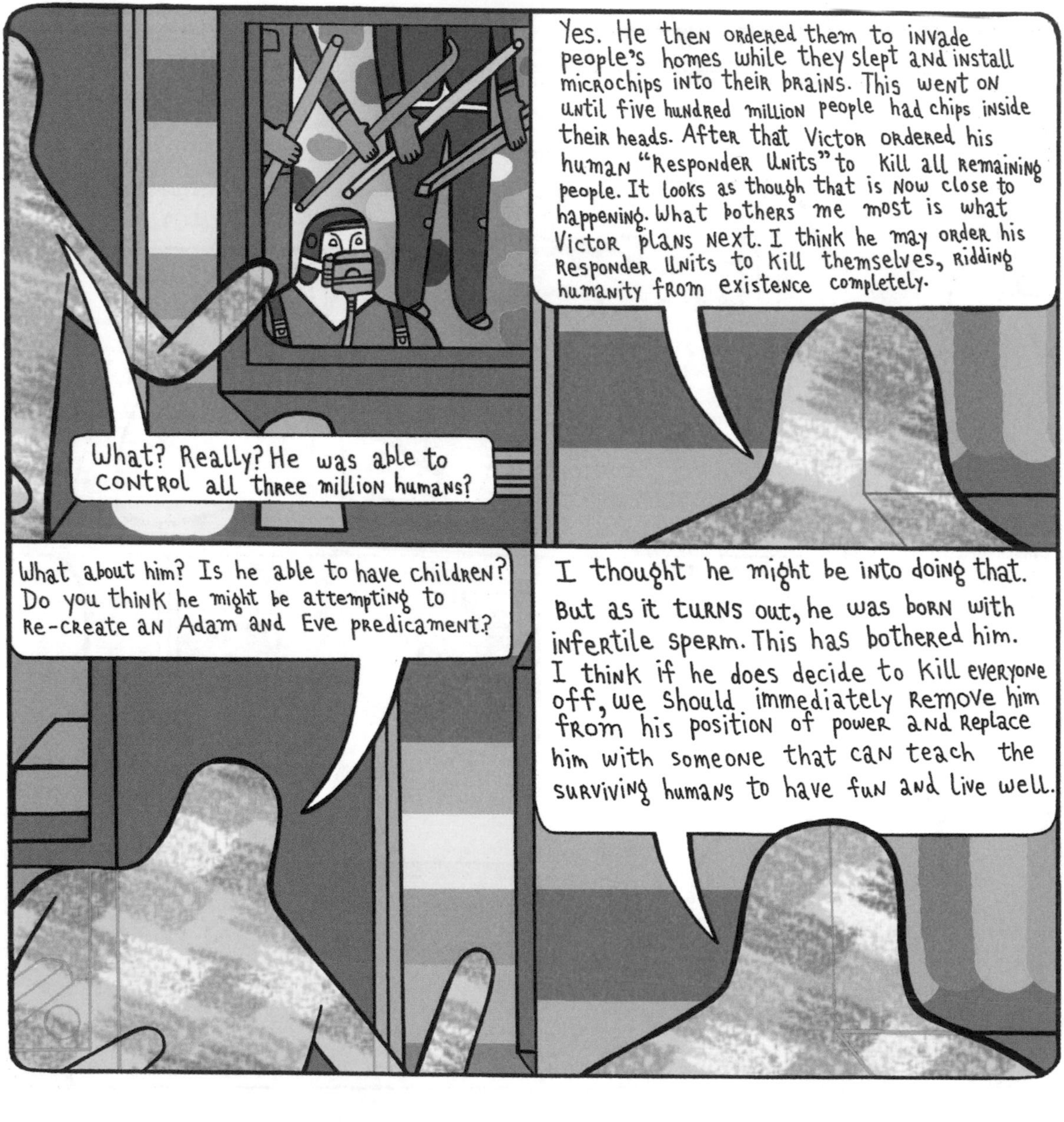
What? Really? He was able to control all three million humans?
Yes. He then ordered them to invade people's homes while they slept and install microchips into their brains. This went on until five hundred million people had chips inside their heads. After that Victor ordered his human "Responder Units" to kill all remaining people. It looks as though that is now close to happening. What bothers me most is what Victor plans next. I think he may order his Responder Units to kill themselves, ridding humanity from existence completely.
What about him? Is he able to have children? Do you think he might be attempting to re-create an Adam and Eve predicament?
I thought he might be into doing that. But as it turns out, he was born with infertile sperm. This has bothered him. I think if he does decide to kill everyone off, we should immediately remove him from his position of power and replace him with someone that can teach the surviving humans to have fun and live well.

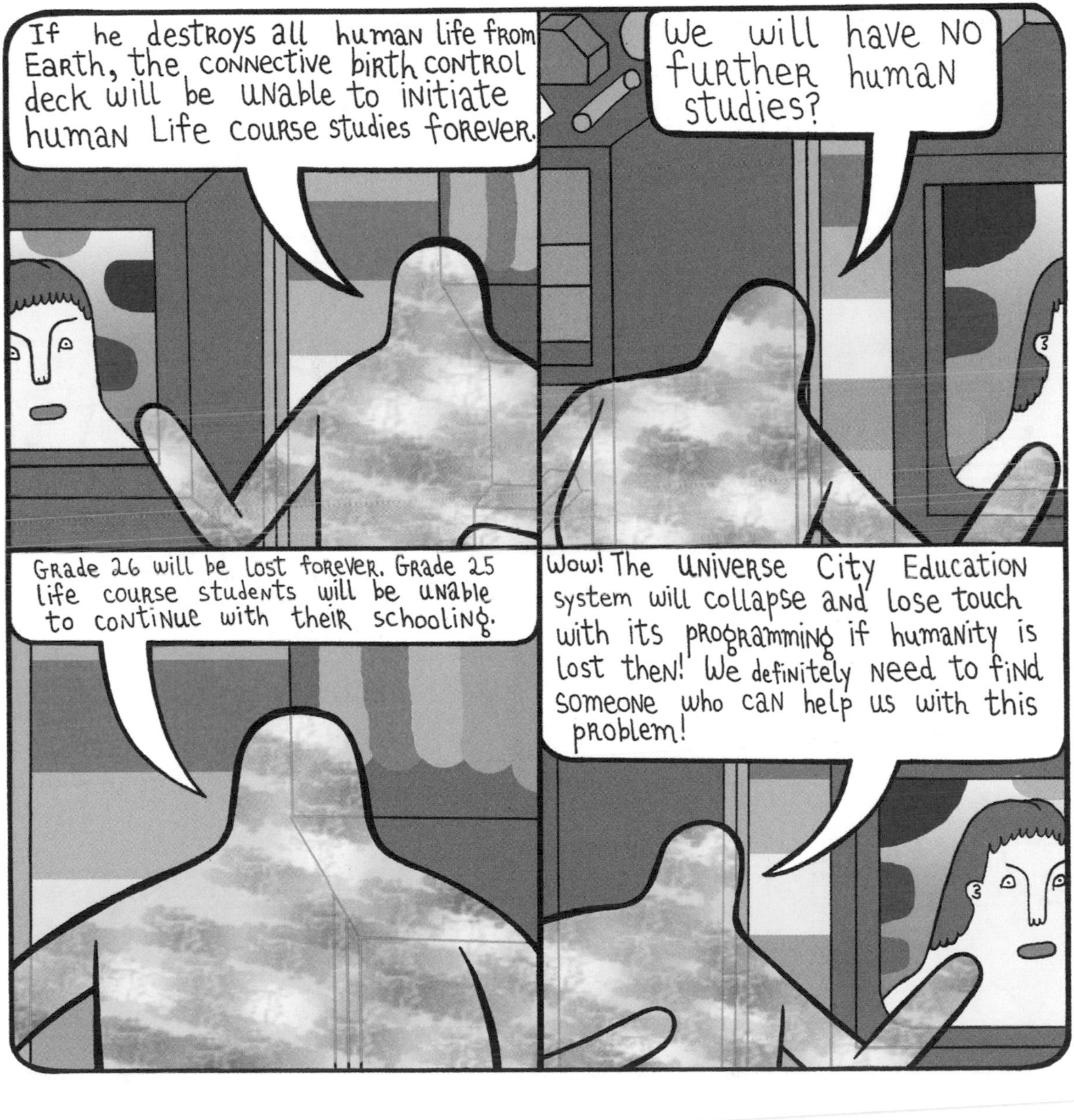
If he destroys all human life from Earth, the connective birth control deck will be unable to initiate human Life course studies forever.
We will have NO further human studies?
Grade 26 will be lost forever. Grade 25 life course students will be unable to continue with their schooling.
Wow! The Universe City Education system will collapse and lose touch with its programming if humanity is lost then! We definitely need to find someone who can help us with this problem!

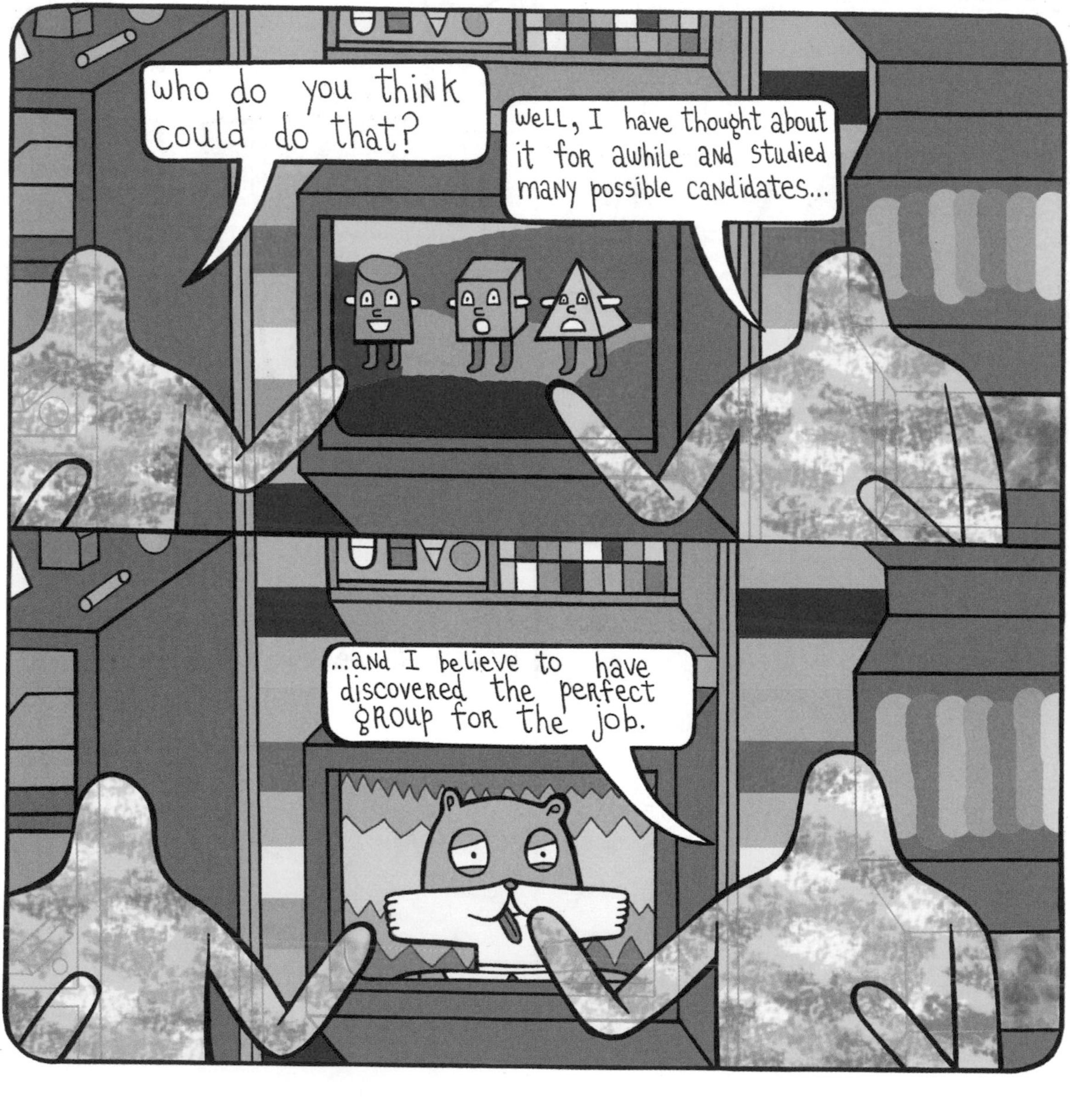
who do you think could do that?
WELL, I have thought about it for awhile and studied many possible candidates...
...aNd I believe to have discovered the perfect group for the job.

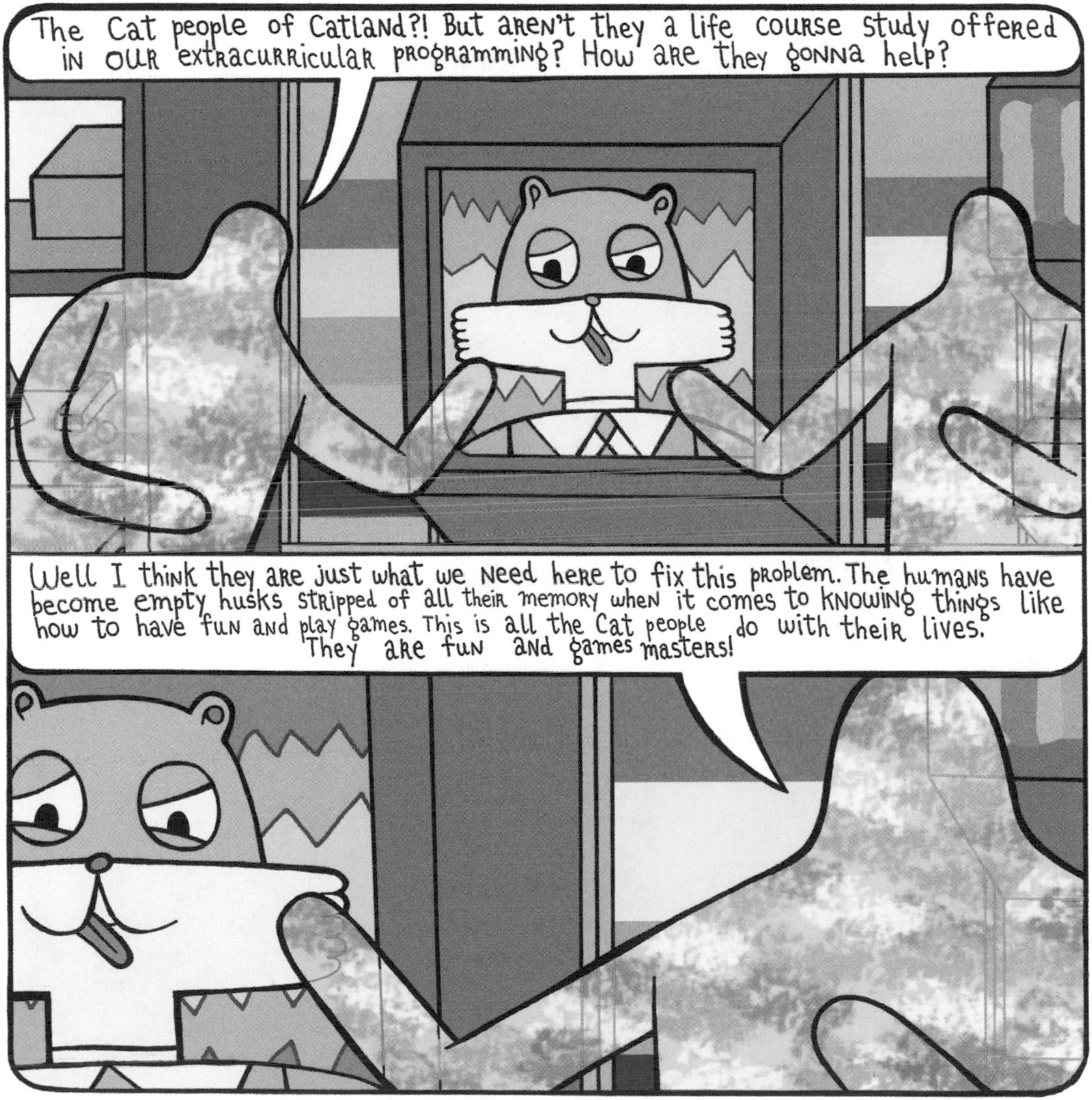
The Cat people of Catland?! But aren't they a life course study offered in our extracurricular programming? How are they gonna help?
Well I think they are just what we need here to fix this problem. The humans have become empty husks stripped of all their memory when it comes to knowing things like how to have fun and play games. This is all the Cat people do with their lives. They are fun and games masters!

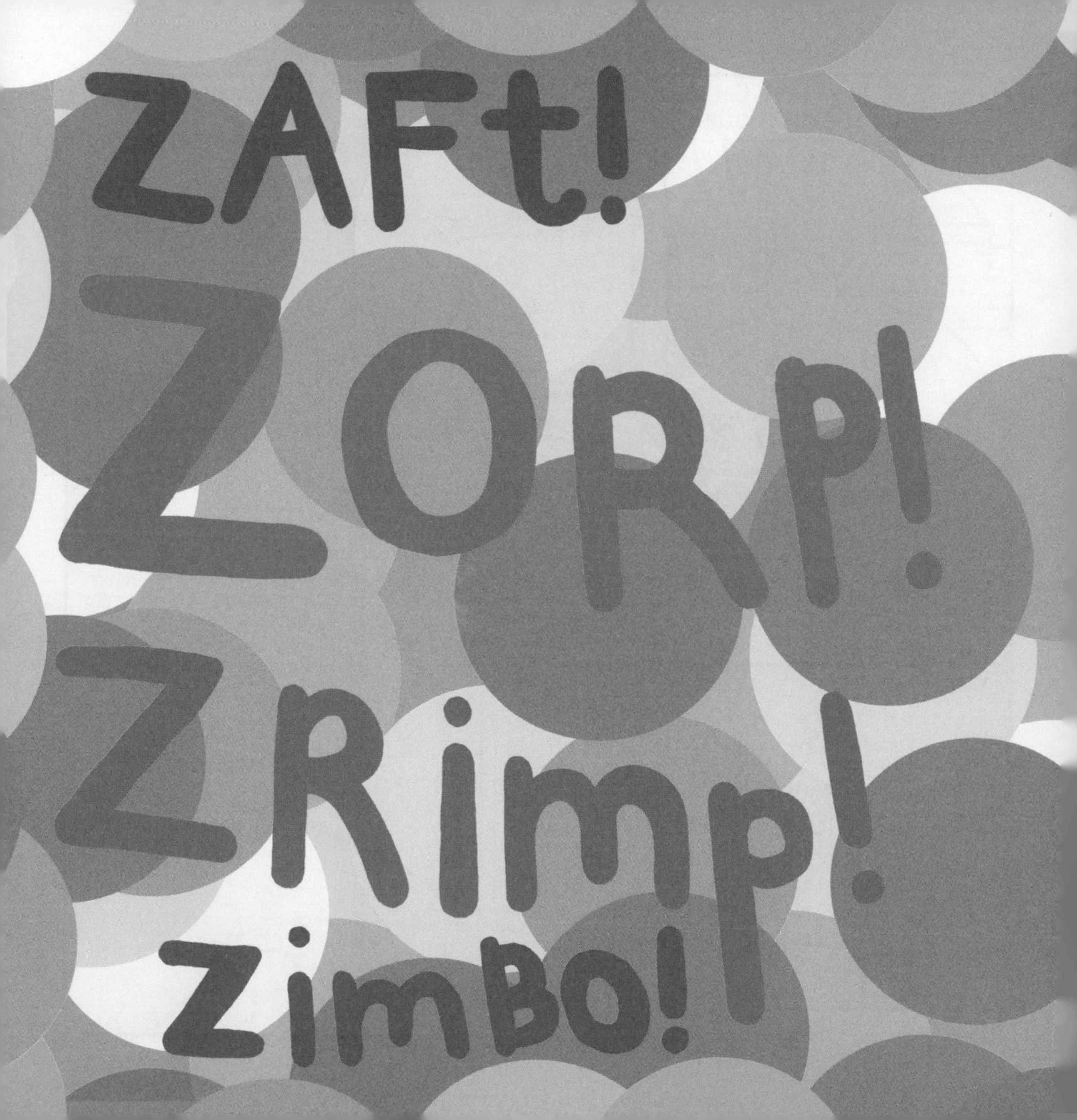
ZAFt!
ZORP!
ZRimp!
zimBO!

ZUVEN!

ZALLY!

ZERM!

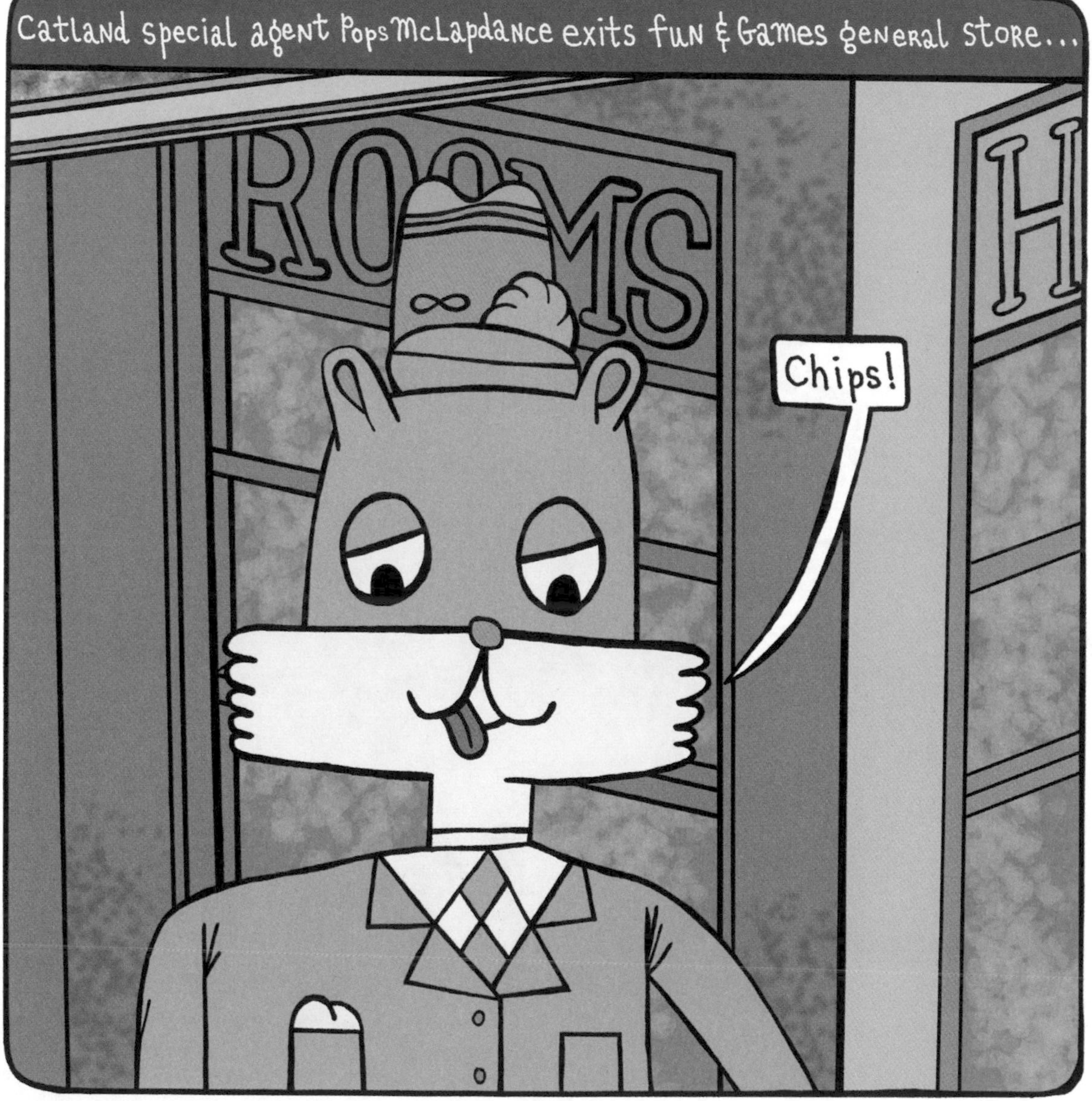
Catland special agent Pops McLapdance exits Fun & Games general store...
ROOMS
H
Chips!

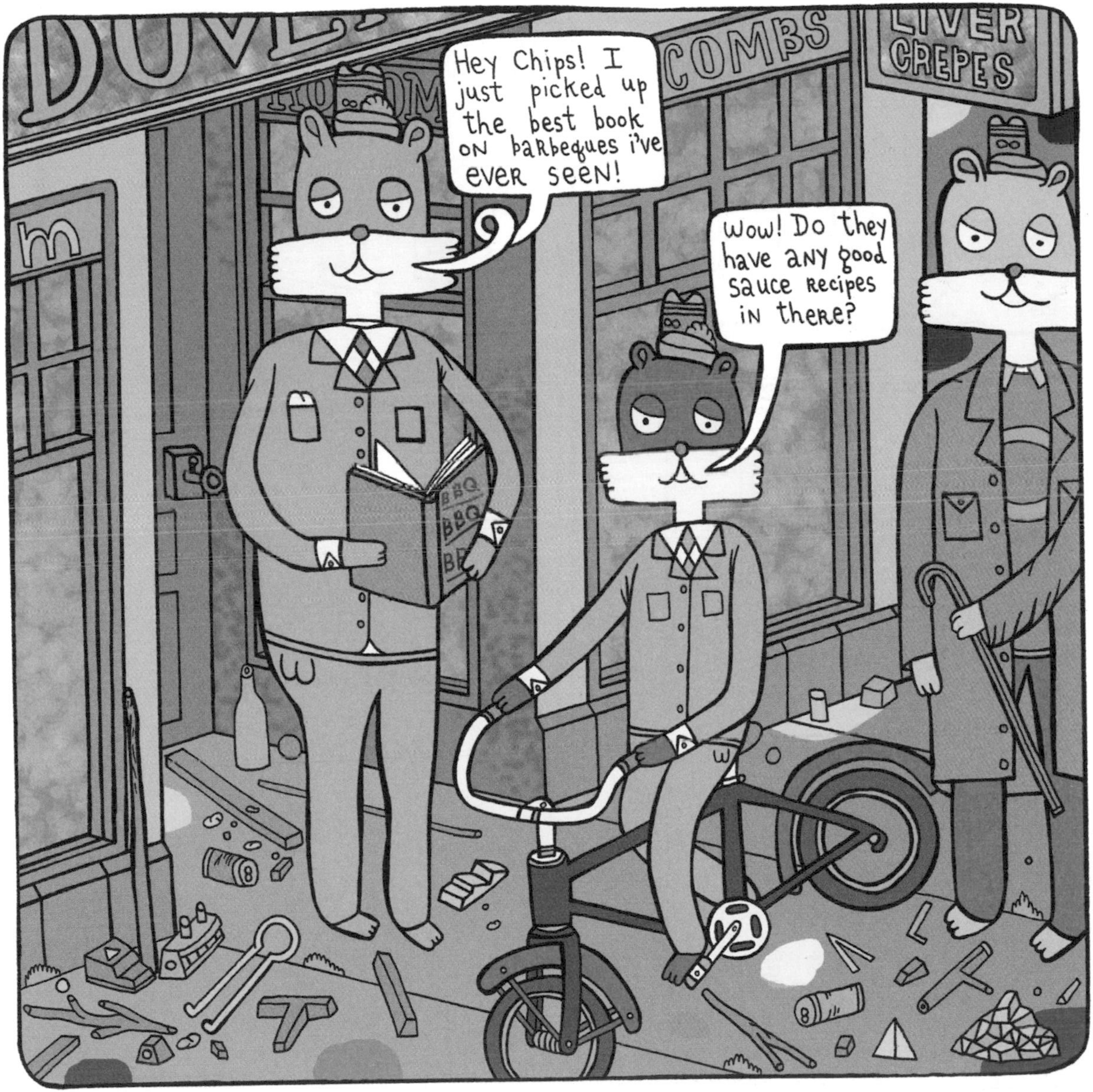
COMBS
LIVER CREPES
Hey Chips! I just picked up the best book on barbeques i've ever seen!
Wow! Do they have any good sauce recipes in there?
BBQ
BBQ

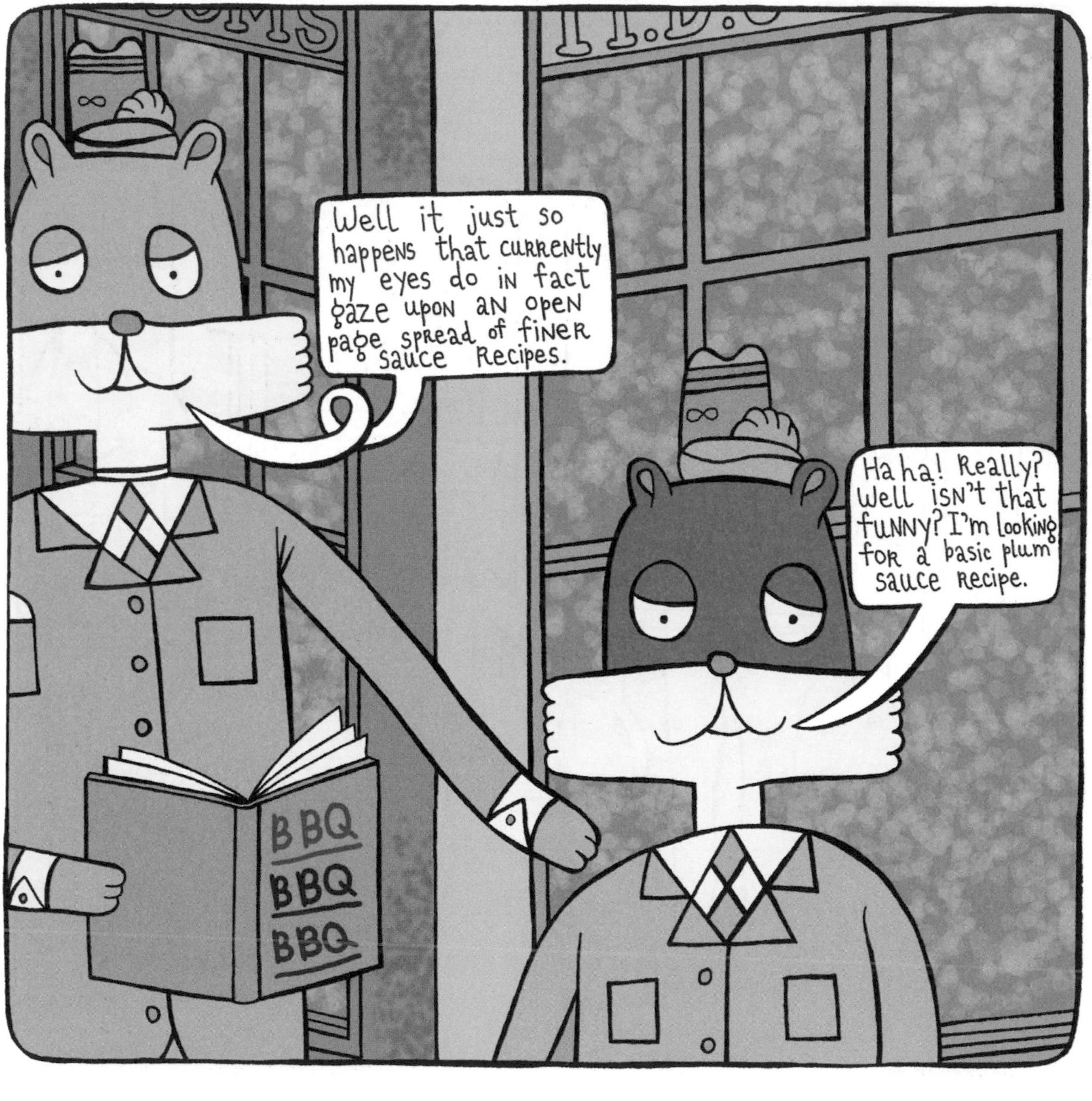
Well it just so happens that currently my eyes do in fact gaze upon an open page spread of finer sauce Recipes.
Ha ha! Really? Well isn't that funny? I'm looking for a basic plum sauce recipe.
BBQ BBQ BBQ

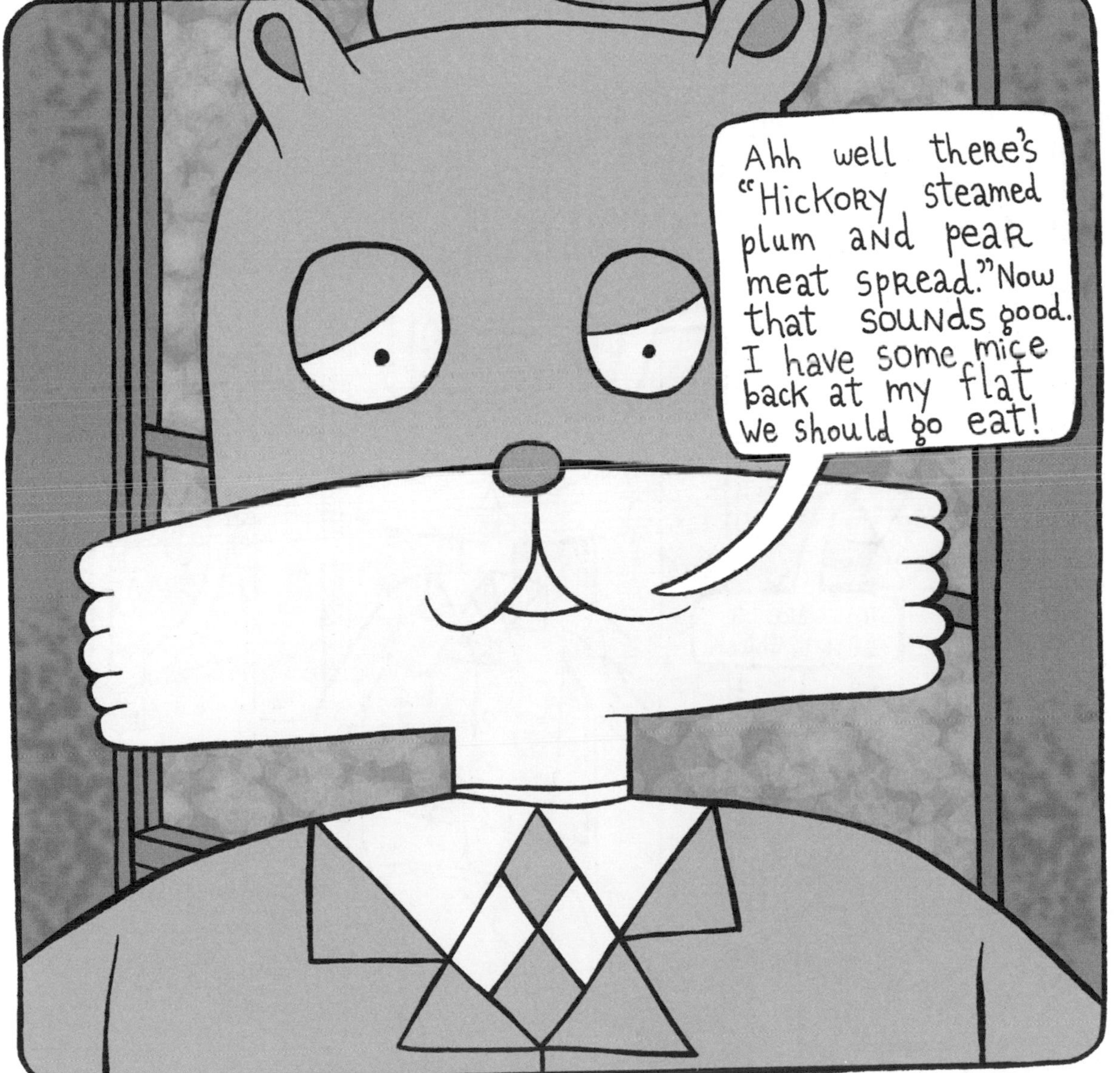
Ahh well there's "Hickory steamed plum and pear meat spread." Now that sounds good. I have some mice back at my flat we should go eat!

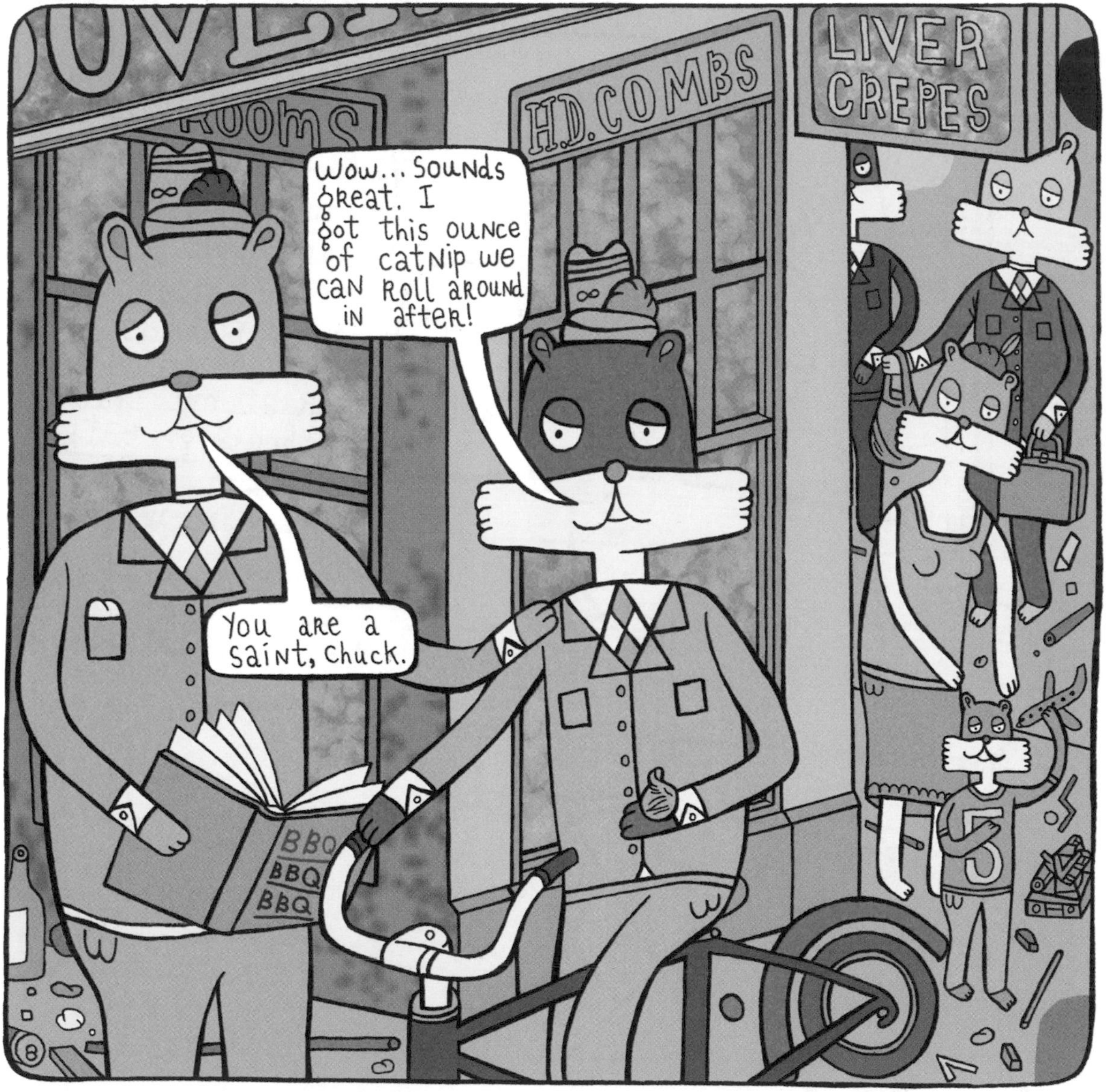
ROOMS
H.D. COMBS
LIVER CREPES
Wow... sounds great. I got this ounce of catnip we can roll around in after!
You are a saint, Chuck.
BBQ BBQ BBQ

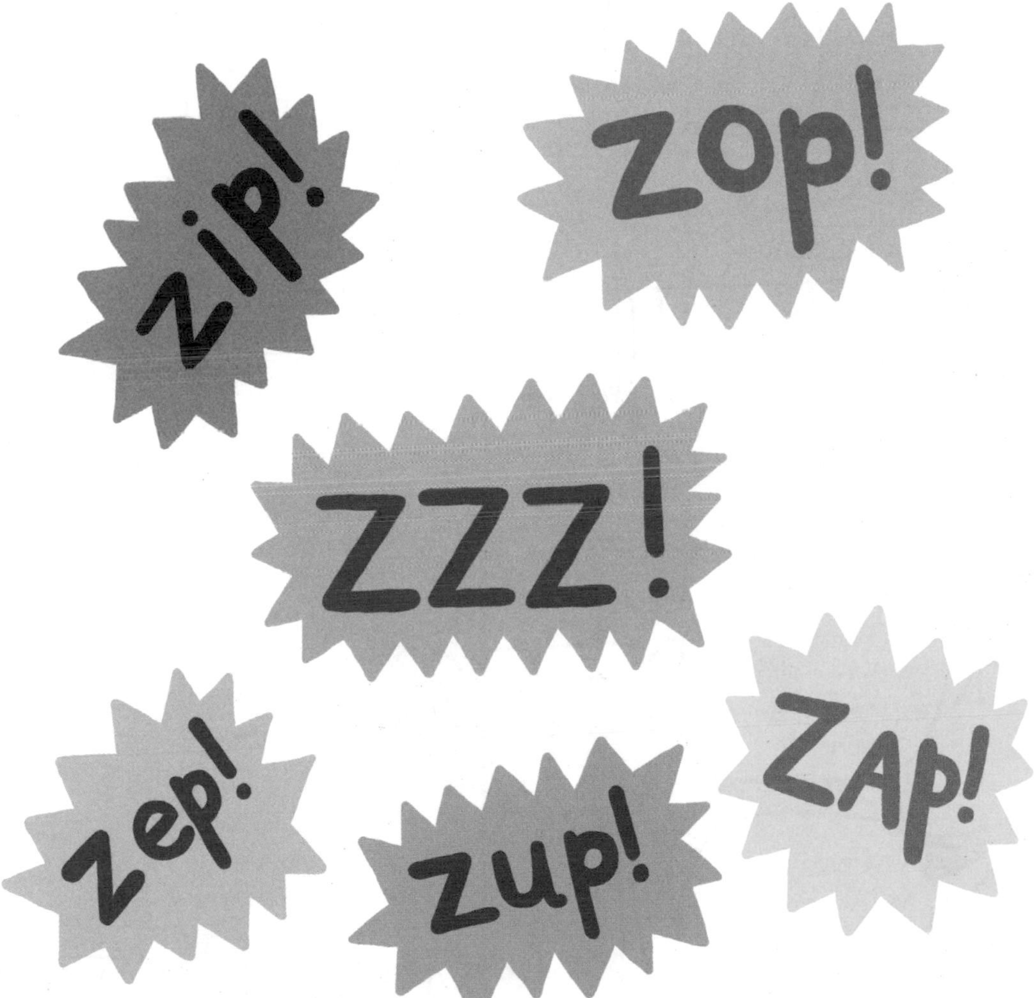
zip!
zop!
ZZZ!
zep!
zup!
ZAp!

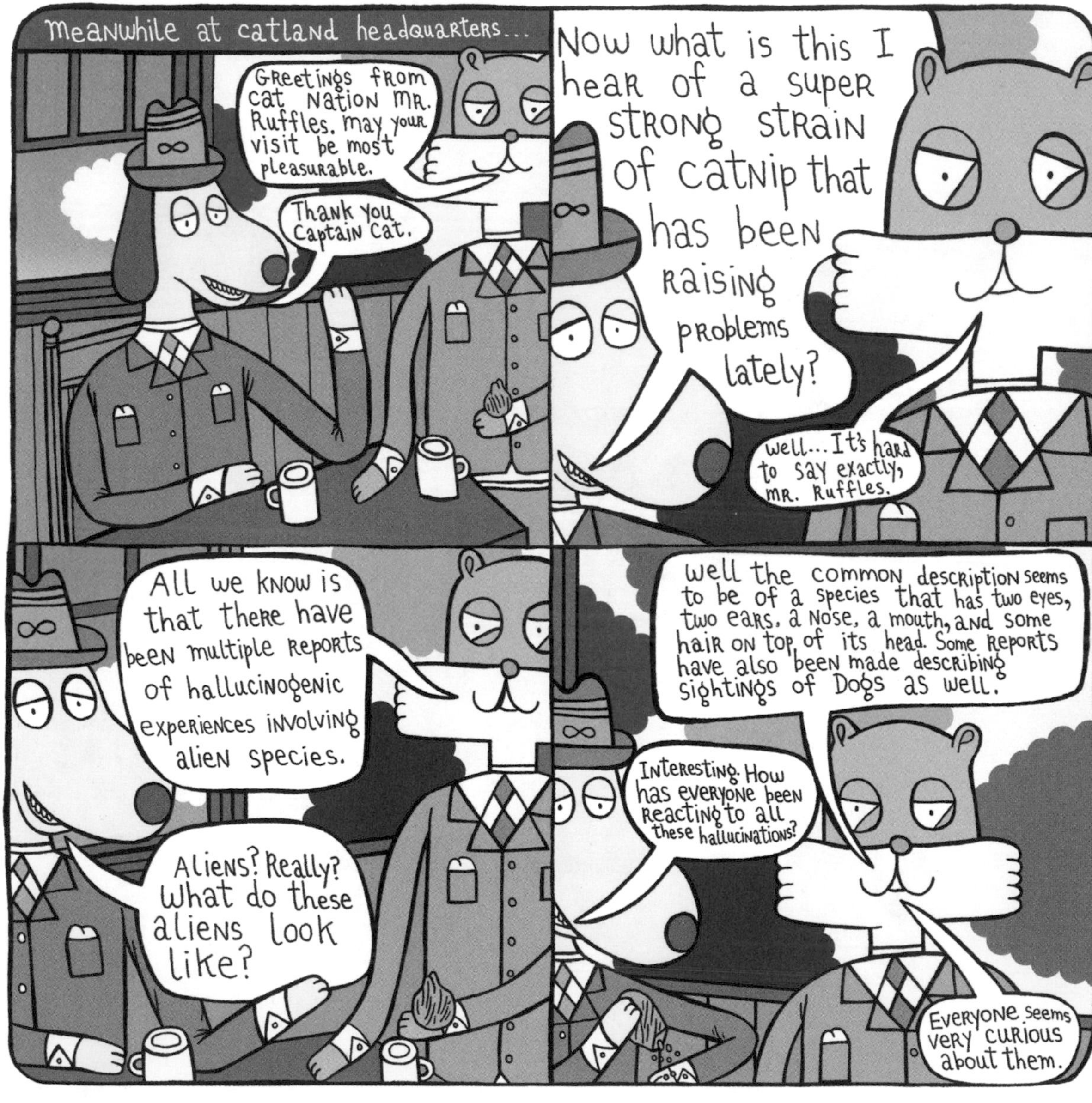

Meanwhile at catland headquarters...
Greetings from cat Nation Mr. Ruffles. may your visit be most pleasurable.
Thank you Captain Cat.
Now what is this I hear of a super strong strain of catnip that has been raising problems lately?
Well... It's hard to say exactly, Mr. Ruffles.
All we know is that there have been multiple reports of hallucinogenic experiences involving alien species.
Aliens? Really? What do these aliens look like?
Well the common description seems to be of a species that has two eyes, two ears, a nose, a mouth, and some hair on top of its head. Some reports have also been made describing sightings of Dogs as well.
Interesting. How has everyone been reacting to all these hallucinations?
Everyone seems very curious about them.

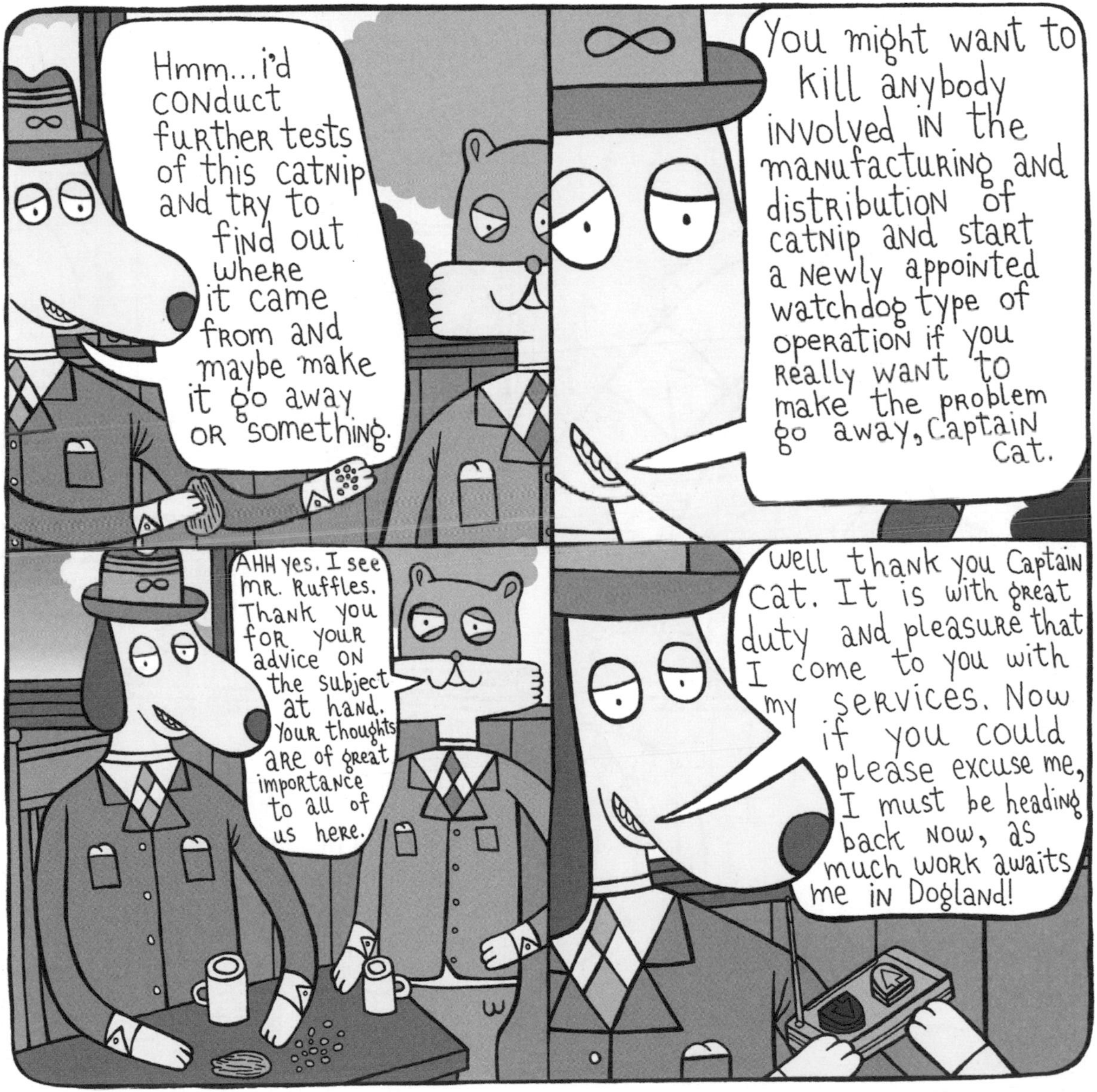
Hmm... i'd conduct further tests of this catnip and try to find out where it came from and maybe make it go away or something.
You might want to kill anybody involved in the manufacturing and distribution of catnip and start a newly appointed watchdog type of operation if you really want to make the problem go away, Captain Cat.
AHH yes. I see Mr. Ruffles. Thank you for your advice on the subject at hand. Your thoughts are of great importance to all of us here.
Well thank you Captain Cat. It is with great duty and pleasure that I come to you with my services. Now if you could please excuse me, I must be heading back now, as much work awaits me in Dogland!

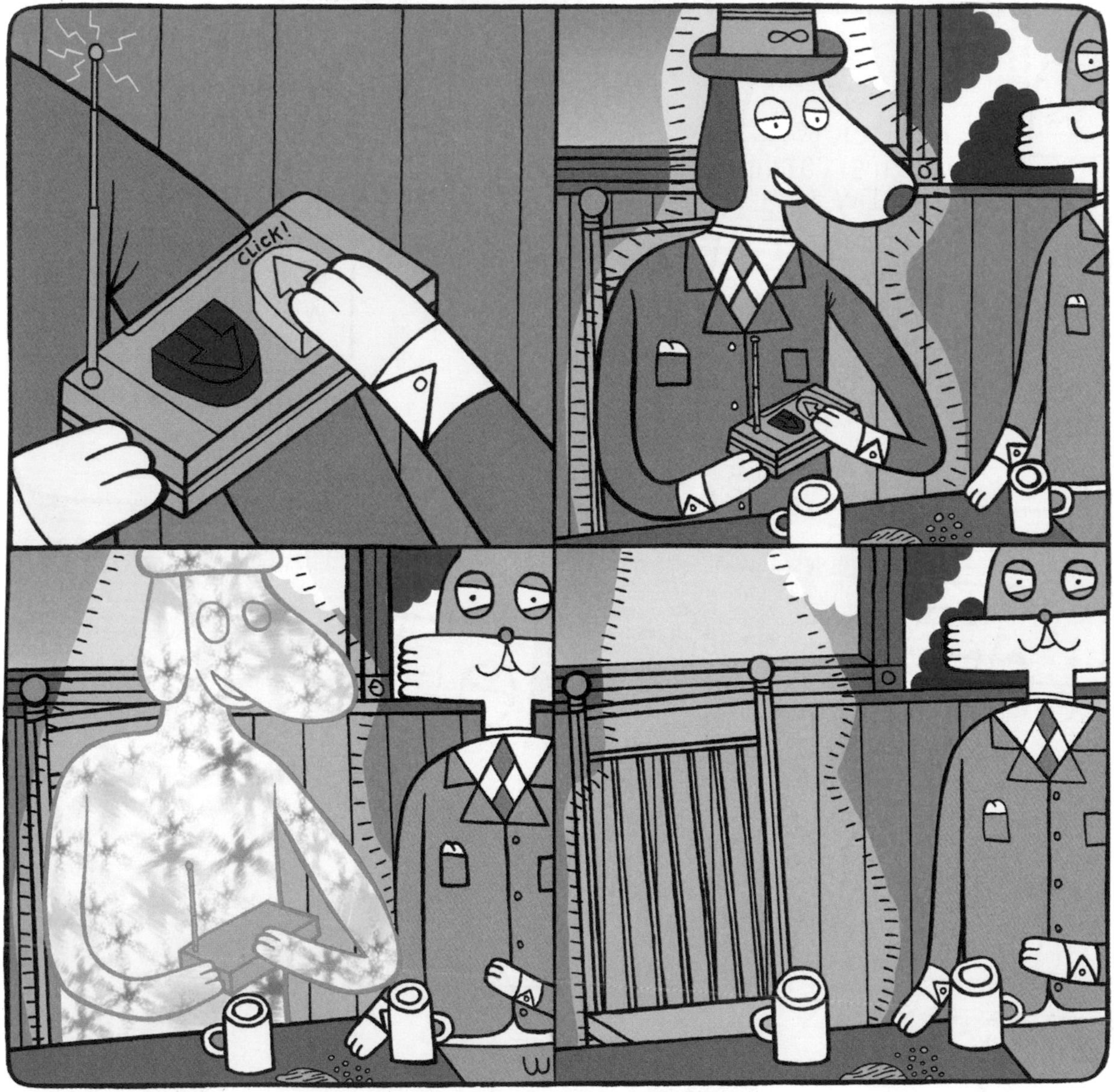
CLICK!

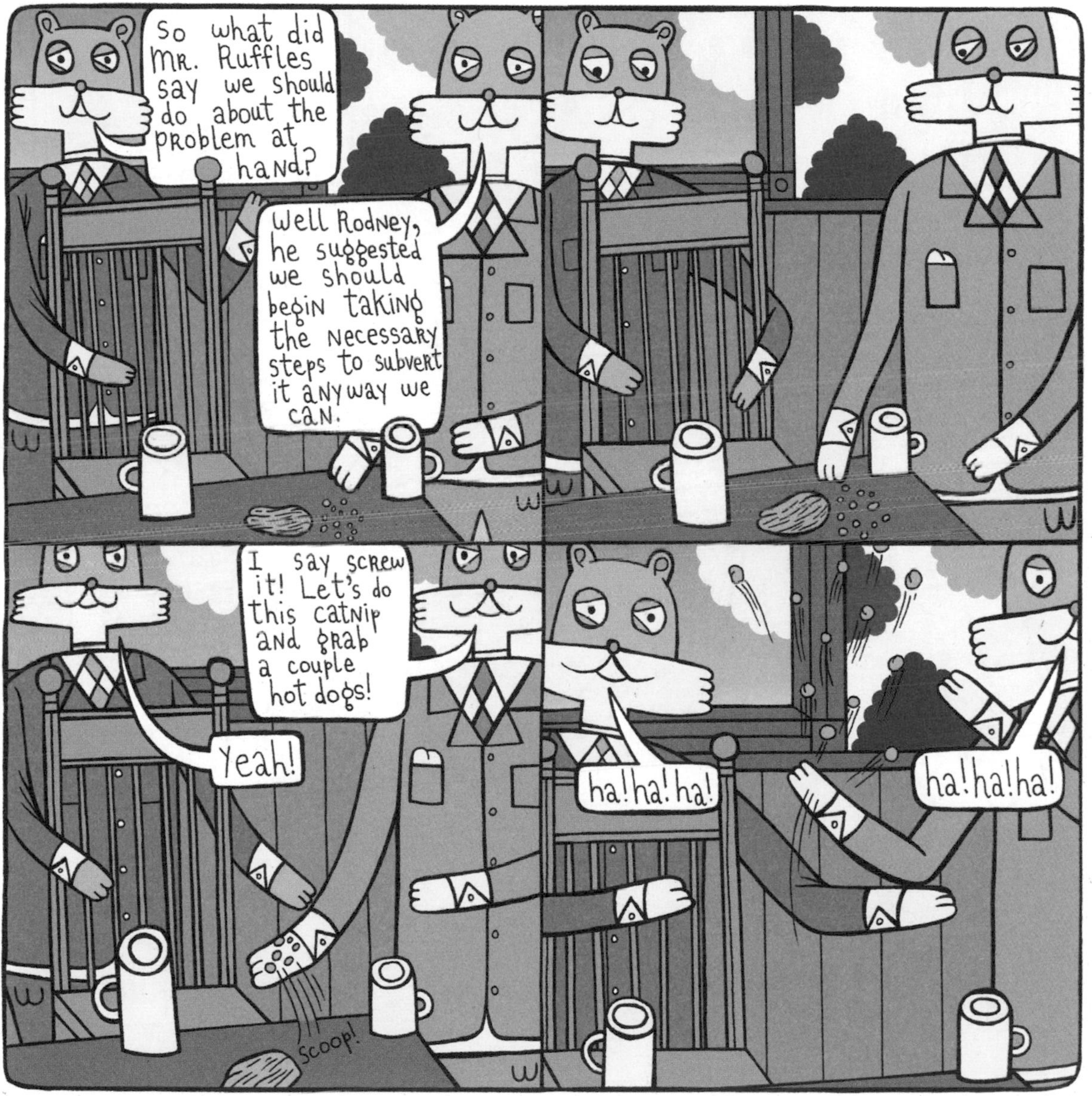
So what did Mr. Ruffles say we should do about the problem at hand?
Well Rodney, he suggested we should begin taking the necessary steps to subvert it anyway we can.
I say screw it! Let's do this catnip and grab a couple hot dogs!
Yeah!
scoop!
ha!ha!ha!
ha!ha!ha!

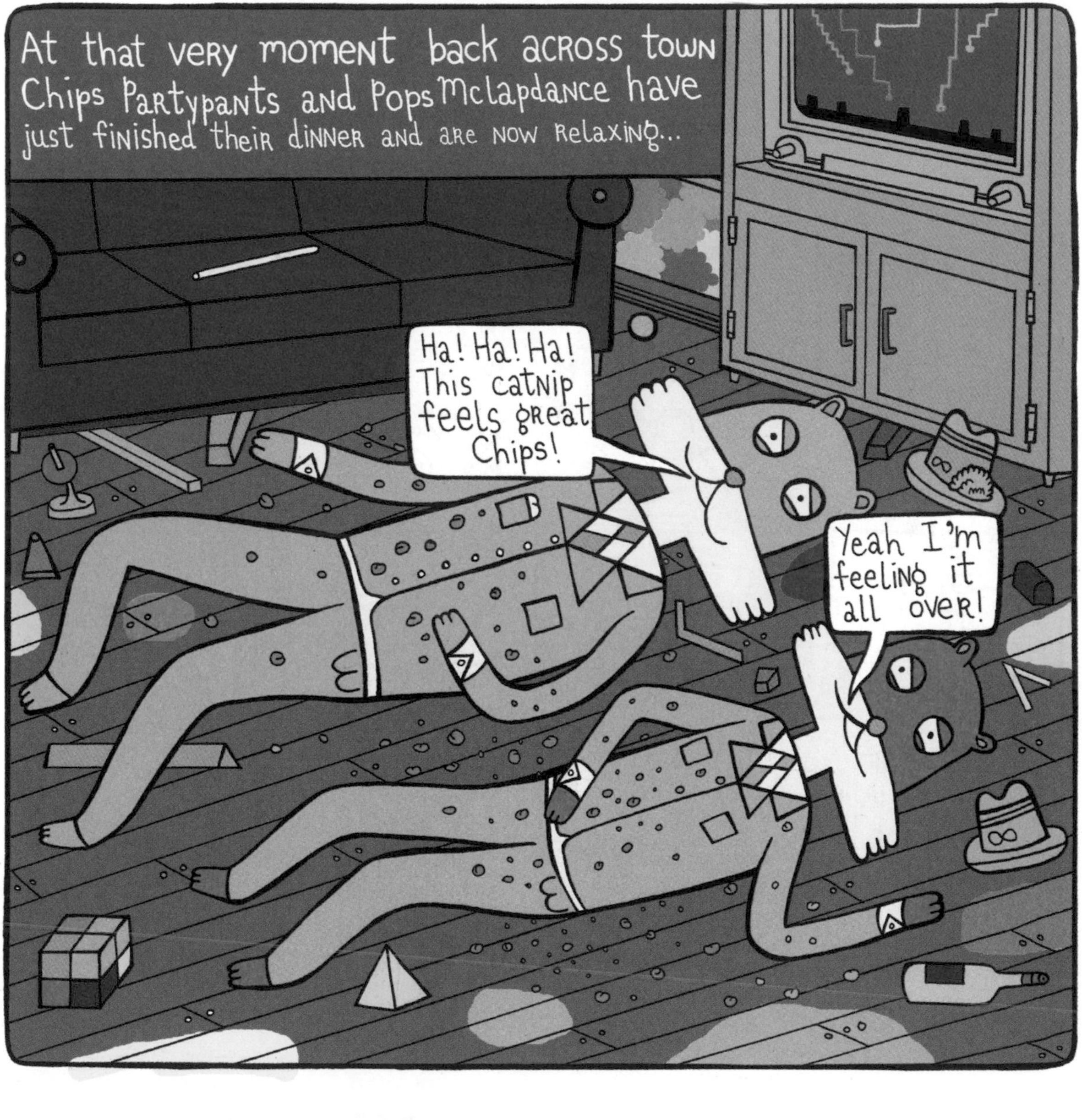
At that very moment back across town Chips Partypants and Pops Mclapdance have just finished their dinner and are now relaxing...
Ha! Ha! Ha! This catnip feels great Chips!
Yeah I'm feeling it all over!

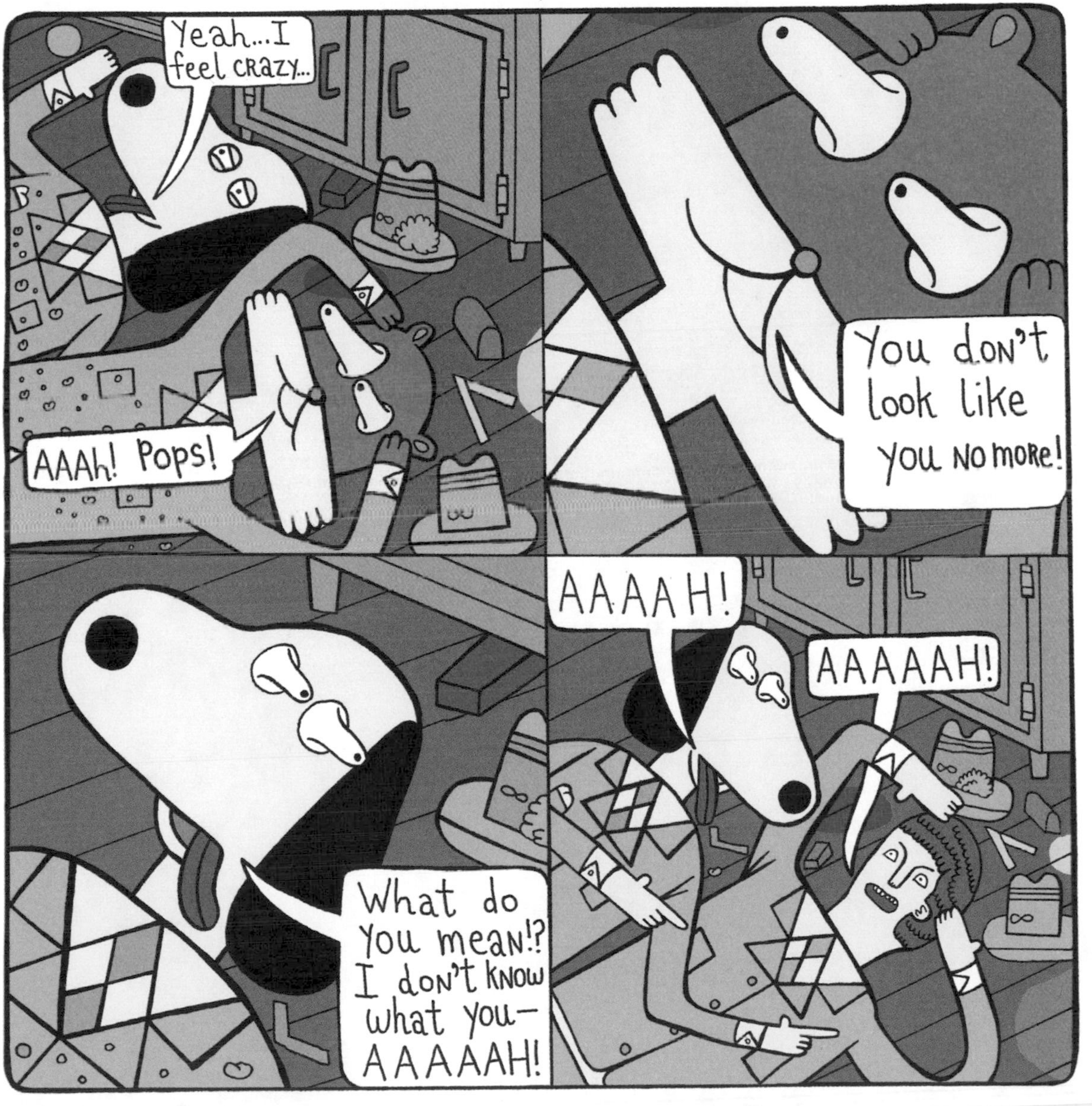
Yeah...I feel crazy...
AAAh! Pops!
You don't look like you no more!
What do you mean!? I don't know what you— AAAAAH!
AAAAH!
AAAAAH!

FLIM FLAM

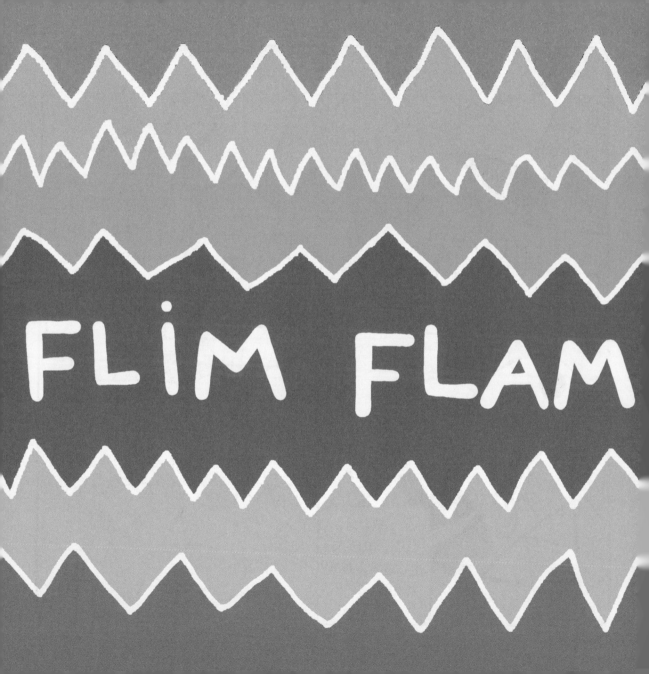

FLIM FLAM

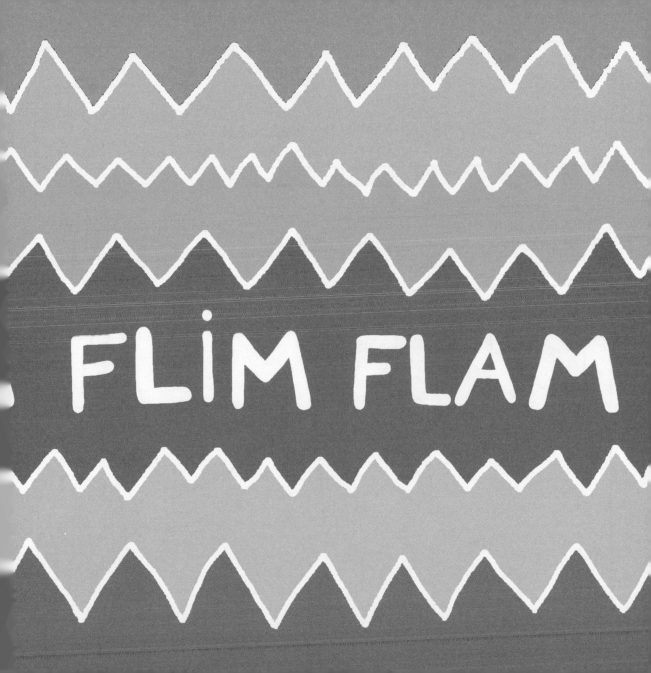

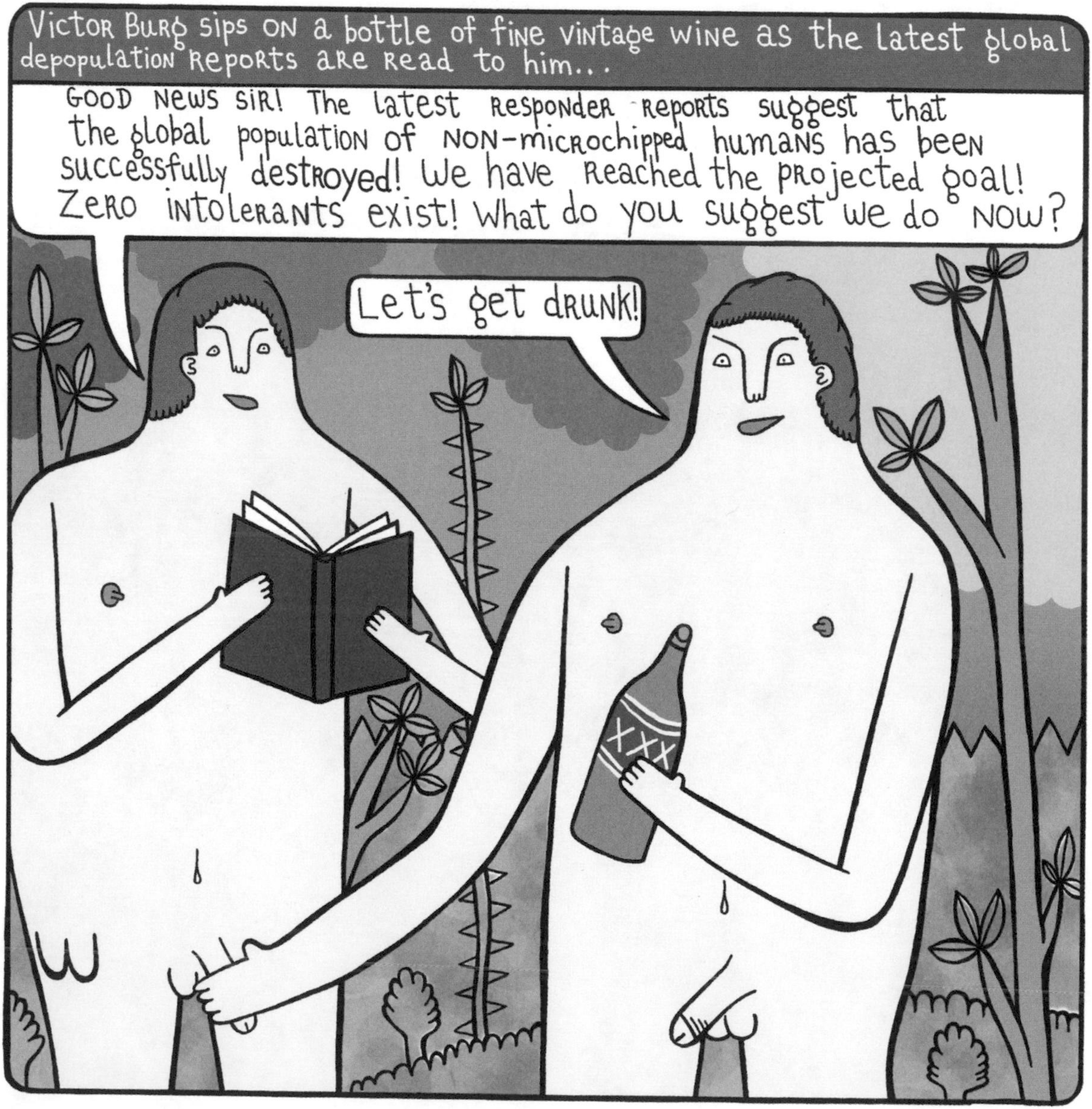
Victor Burg sips on a bottle of fine vintage wine as the latest global depopulation reports are read to him...
GOOD NEWS SIR! The latest RESPONDER REPORTS suggest that the global population of NON-microchipped humans has been successfully destroyed! We have reached the projected goal! Zero intolerants exist! What do you suggest we do now?
Let's get drunk!
XXX

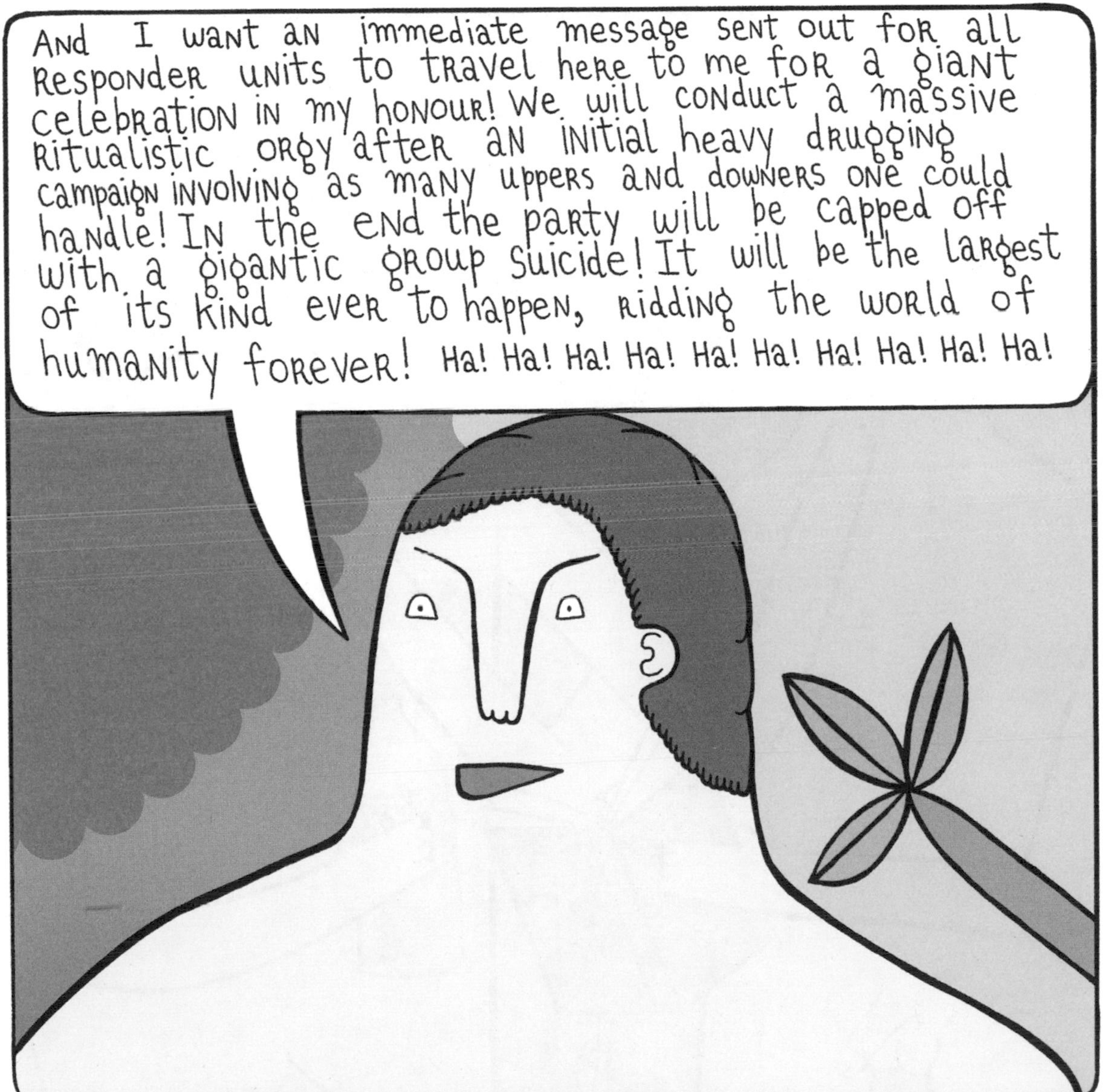
And I want an immediate message sent out for all Responder units to travel here to me for a giant celebration in my honour! We will conduct a massive ritualistic orgy after an initial heavy drugging campaign involving as many uppers and downers one could handle! In the end the party will be capped off with a gigantic group suicide! It will be the largest of its kind ever to happen, ridding the world of humanity forever! Ha! Ha! Ha! Ha! Ha! Ha! Ha! Ha! Ha! Ha!

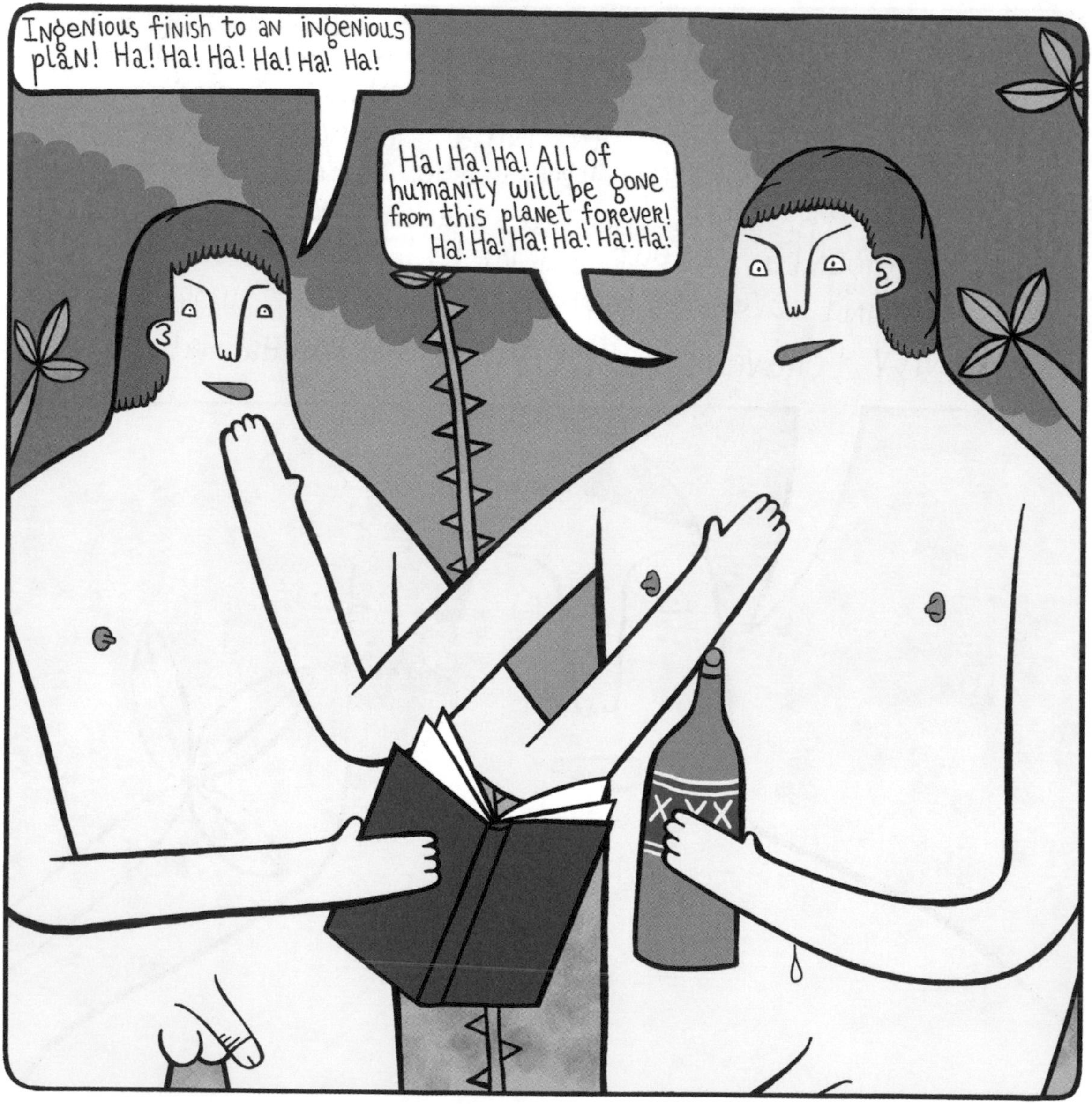
Ingenious finish to an ingenious plan! Ha! Ha! Ha! Ha! Ha! Ha!
Ha! Ha! Ha! All of humanity will be gone from this planet forever! Ha! Ha! Ha! Ha! Ha! Ha!
XXX

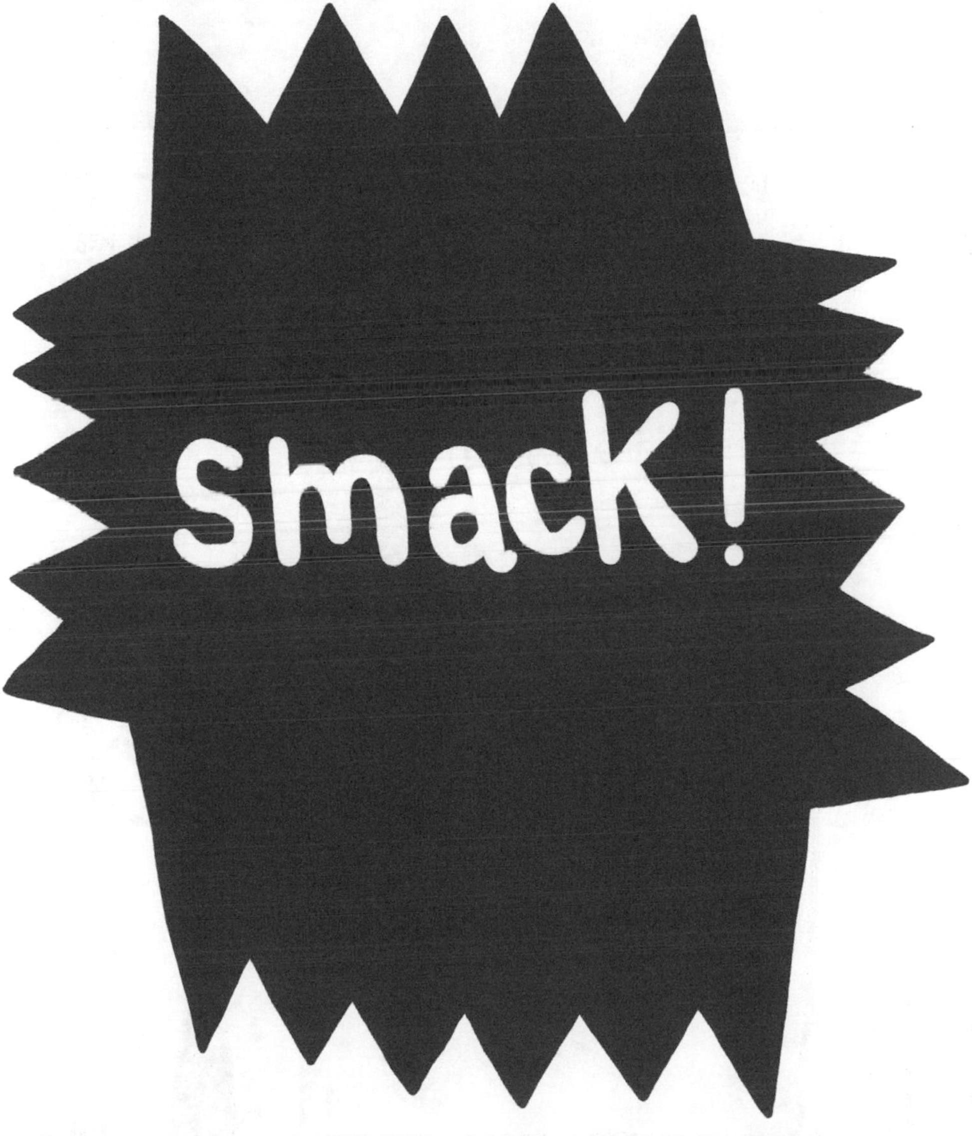
smacK!

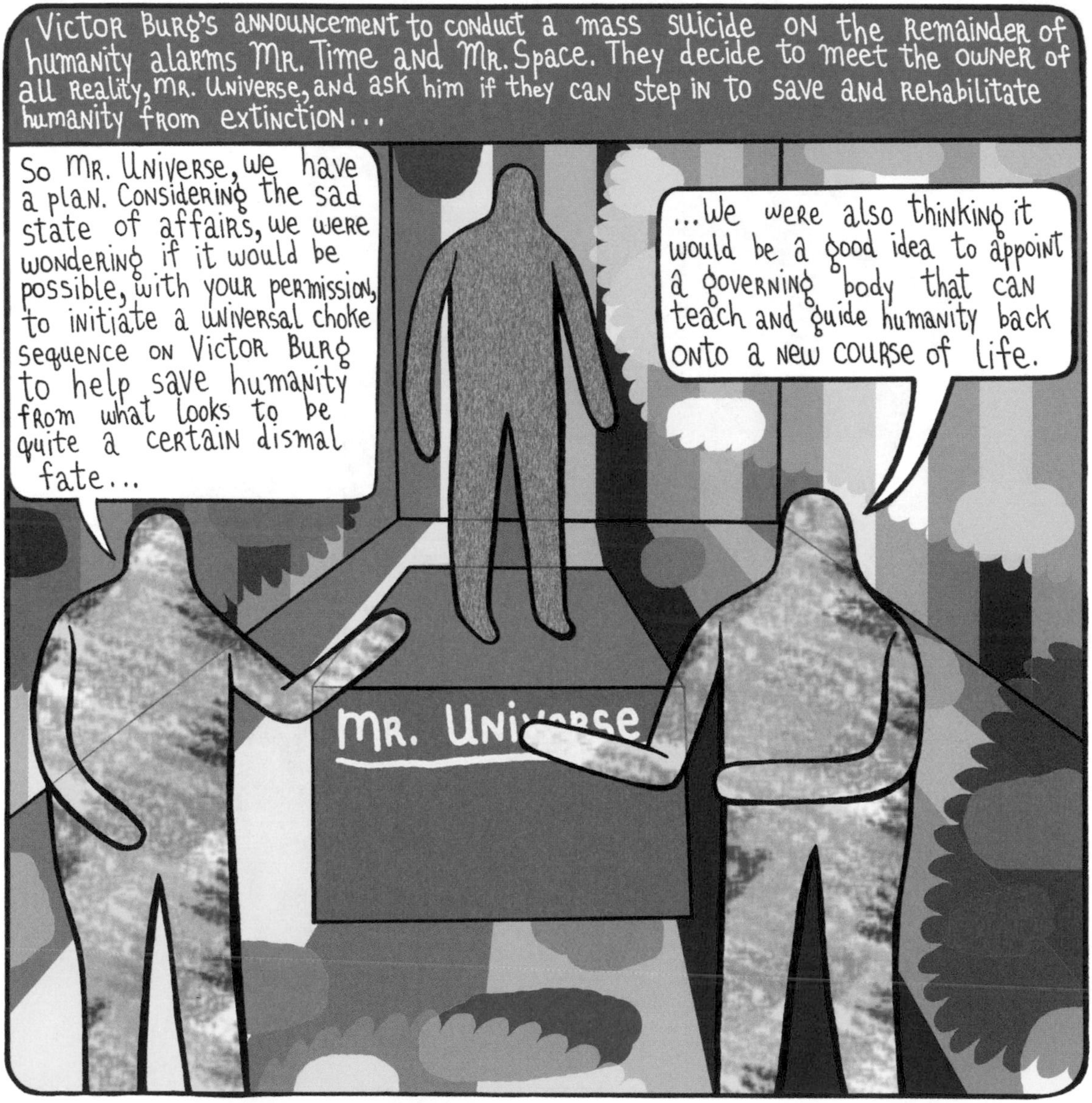
Victor Burg's announcement to conduct a mass suicide on the remainder of humanity alarms Mr. Time and Mr. Space. They decide to meet the owner of all reality, Mr. Universe, and ask him if they can step in to save and rehabilitate humanity from extinction...
So Mr. Universe, we have a plan. Considering the sad state of affairs, we were wondering if it would be possible, with your permission, to initiate a universal choke sequence on Victor Burg to help save humanity from what looks to be quite a certain dismal fate...
...We were also thinking it would be a good idea to appoint a governing body that can teach and guide humanity back onto a new course of life.

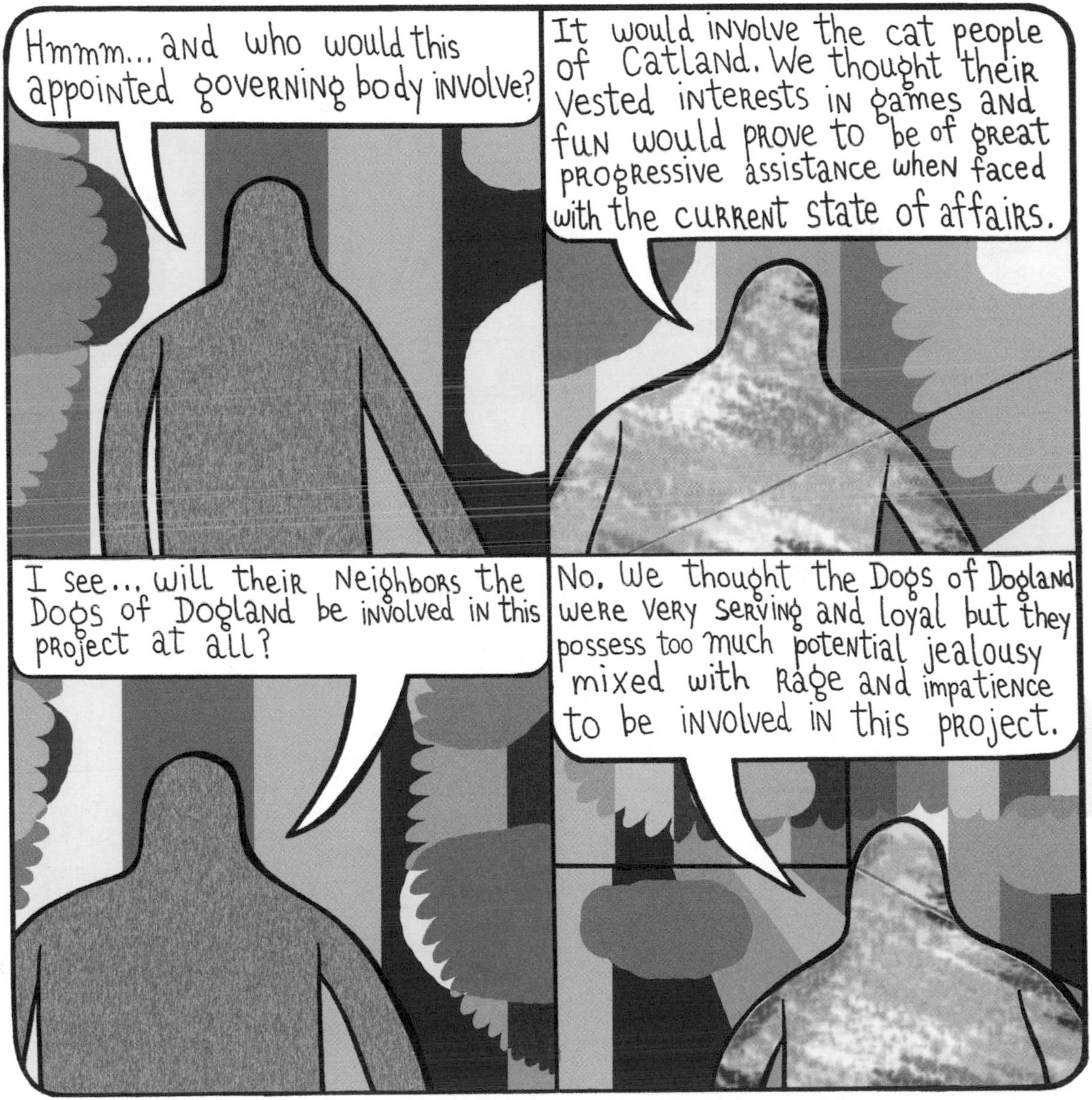
Hmmm... and who would this appointed governing body involve?
It would involve the cat people of Catland. We thought their vested interests in games and fun would prove to be of great progressive assistance when faced with the current state of affairs.
I see... will their neighbors the Dogs of Dogland be involved in this project at all?
No. We thought the Dogs of Dogland were very serving and loyal but they possess too much potential jealousy mixed with rage and impatience to be involved in this project.

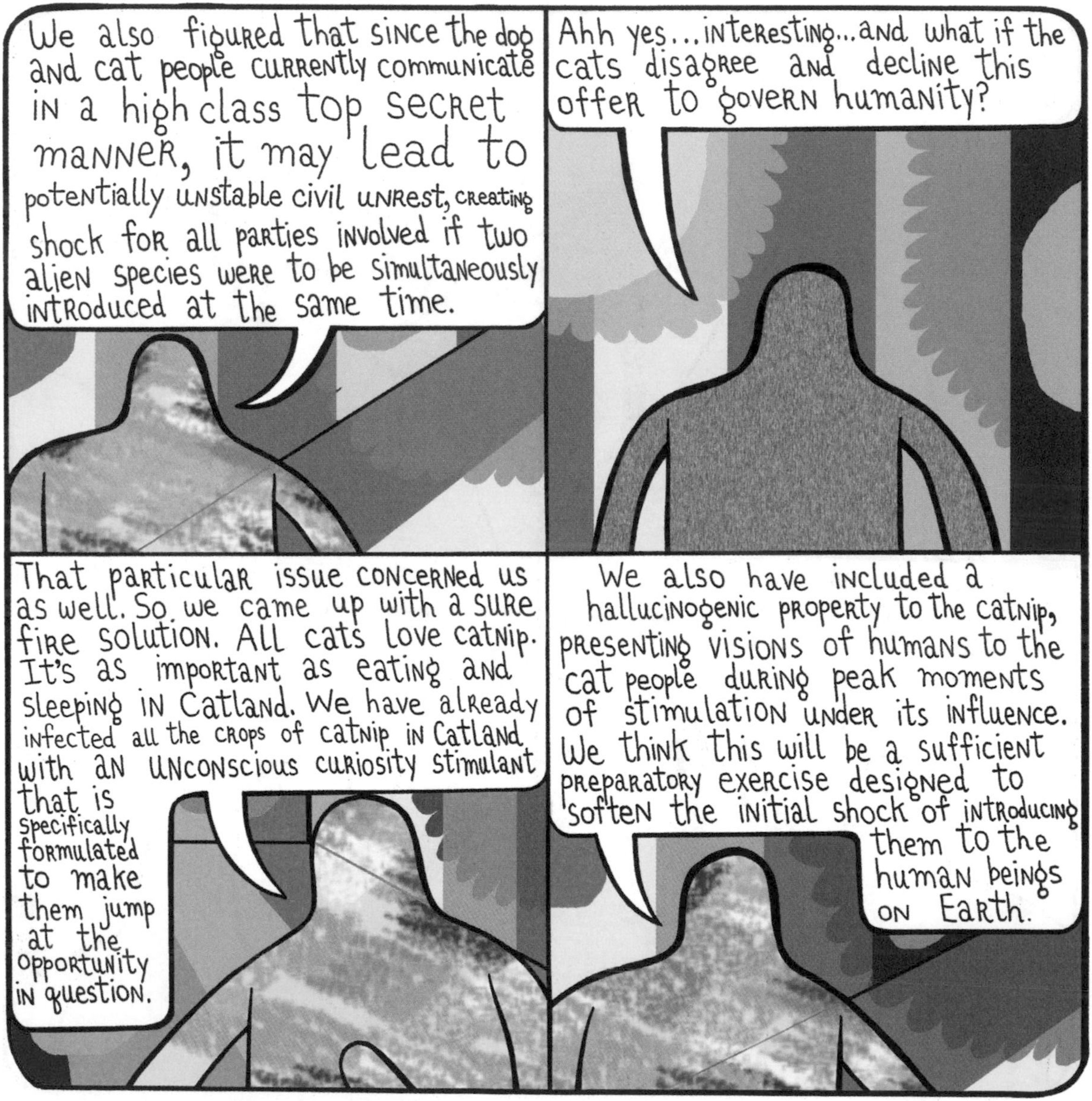

We also figured that since the dog and cat people CURRENTLY communicate in a high class top secret MANNER, it may lead to potentially unstable civil UNREST, CREATING shock for all parties involved if two alien species WERE to be simultaneously INTRODUCED at the same time.

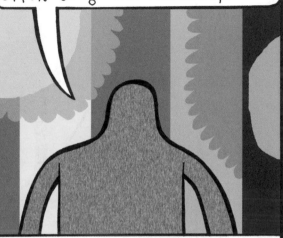

Ahh yes...INTERESTING...and what if the cats disagree and decline this offer to govern humanity?

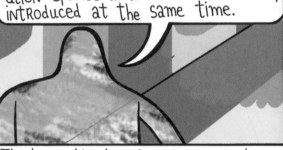

That PARTICULAR issue CONCERNED us as well. So, we came up with a SURE fire SOLUTION. ALL cats love catnip. It's as important as eating and sleeping IN Catland. We have already infected all the crops of catnip in Catland with AN UNCONSCIOUS curiosity stimulant that is specifically formulated to make them jump at the OPPORTUNITY IN question.

We also have included a hallucinogenic property to the catnip, PRESENTING VISIONS of humans to the cat people DURING peak moments of stimulation UNDER its influence. We think this will be a sufficient PREPARATORY EXERCISE designed to soften the initial shock of INTRODUCING them to the human beings ON Earth.

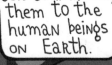

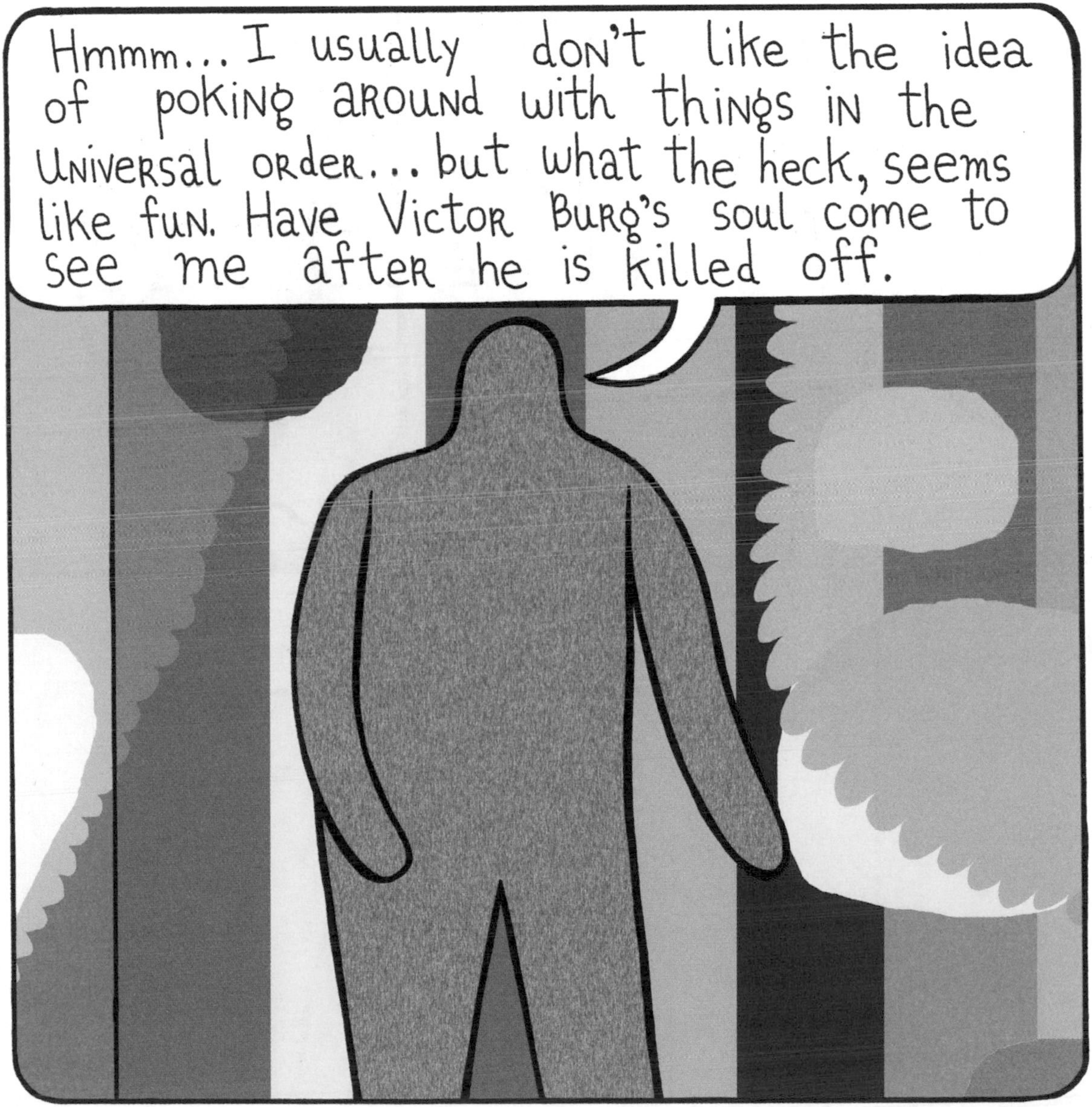
Hmmm... I usually don't like the idea of poking around with things in the Universal order... but what the heck, seems like fun. Have Victor Burg's soul come to see me after he is killed off.

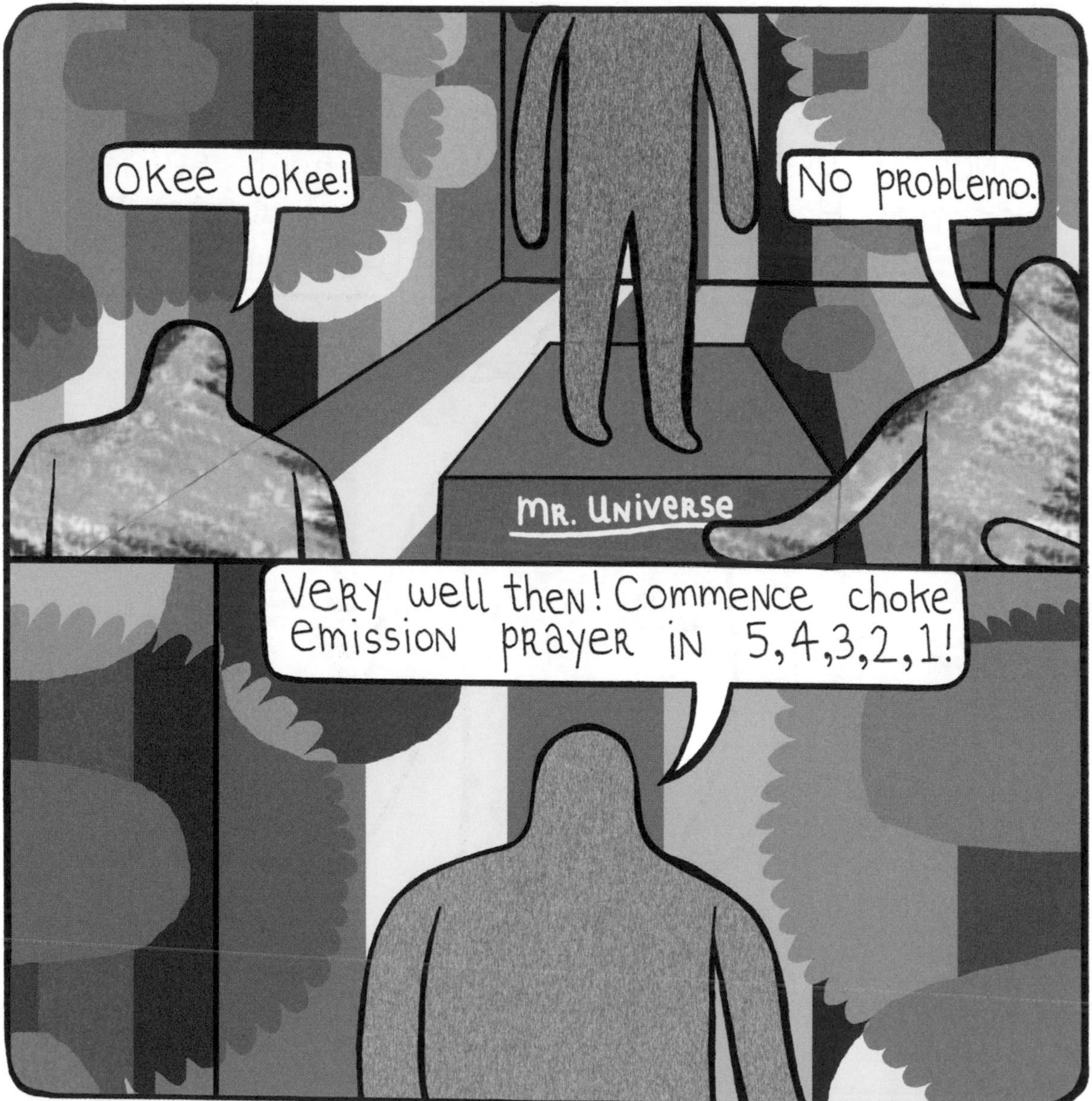
Okee dokee!
No problemo.
MR. UNIVERSE
Very well then! Commence choke emission prayer in 5,4,3,2,1!

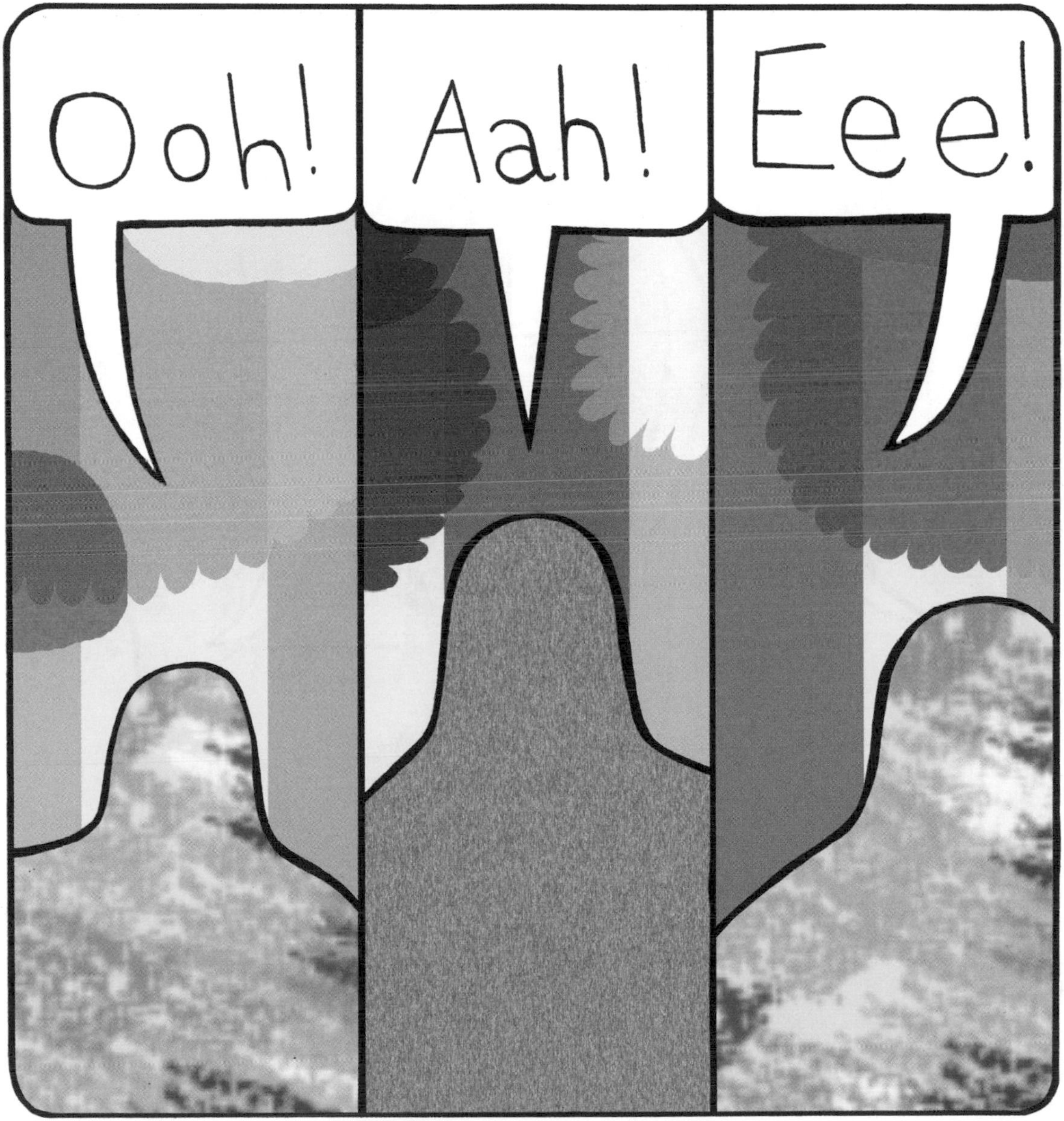
Ooh!
Aah!
Eee!

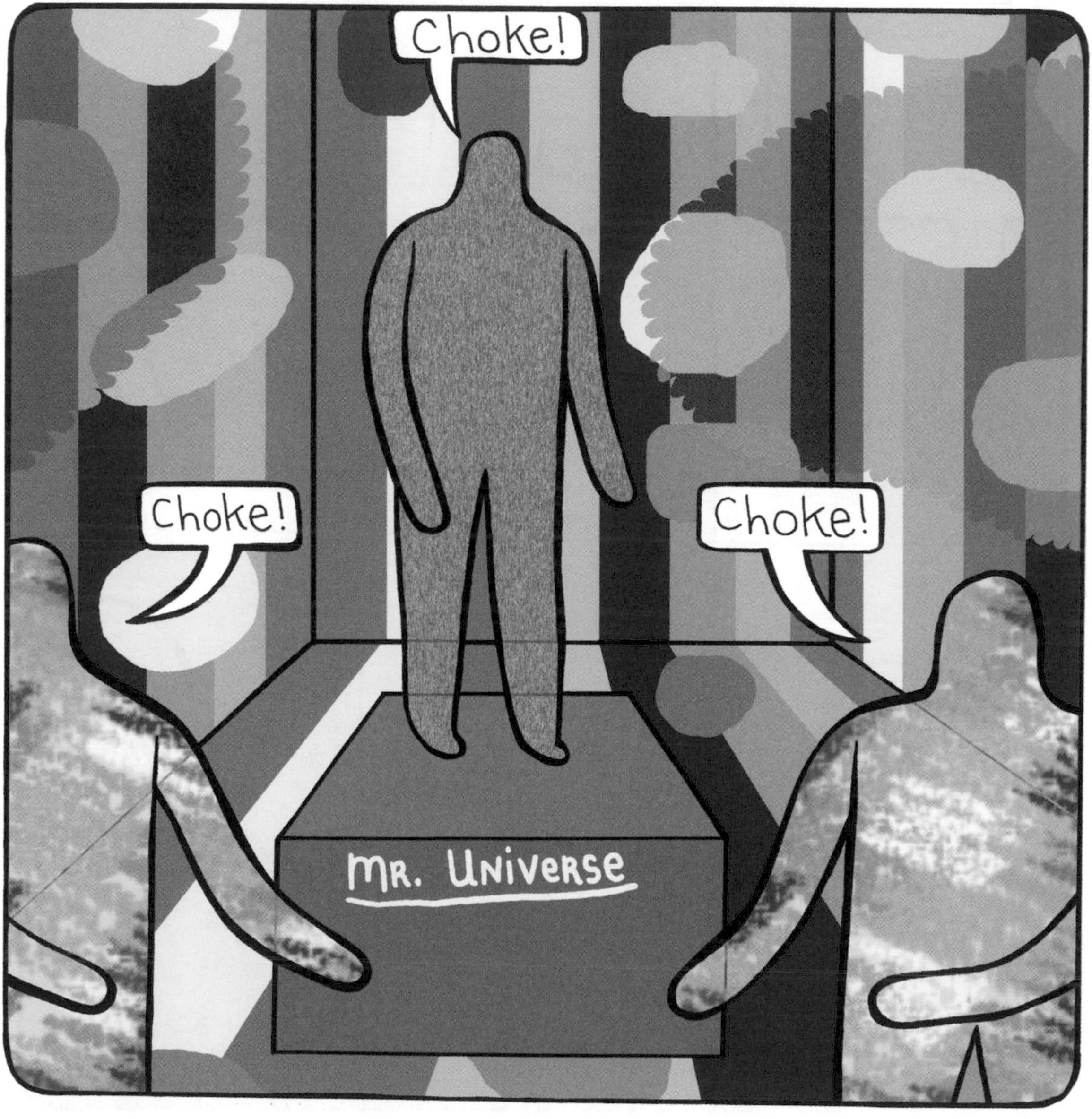
Choke!
Choke!
Choke!
MR. UNIVERSE

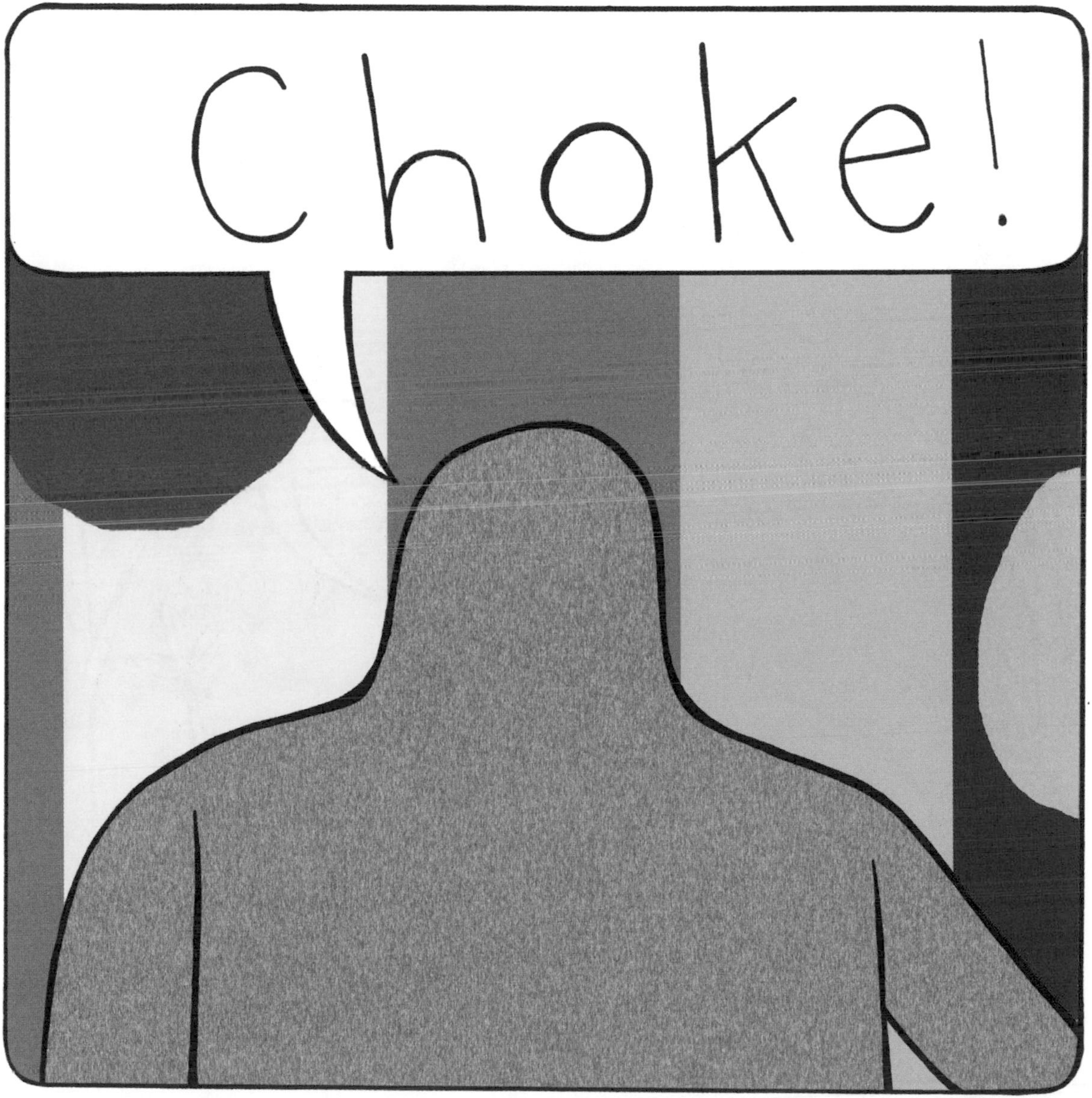
Choke!

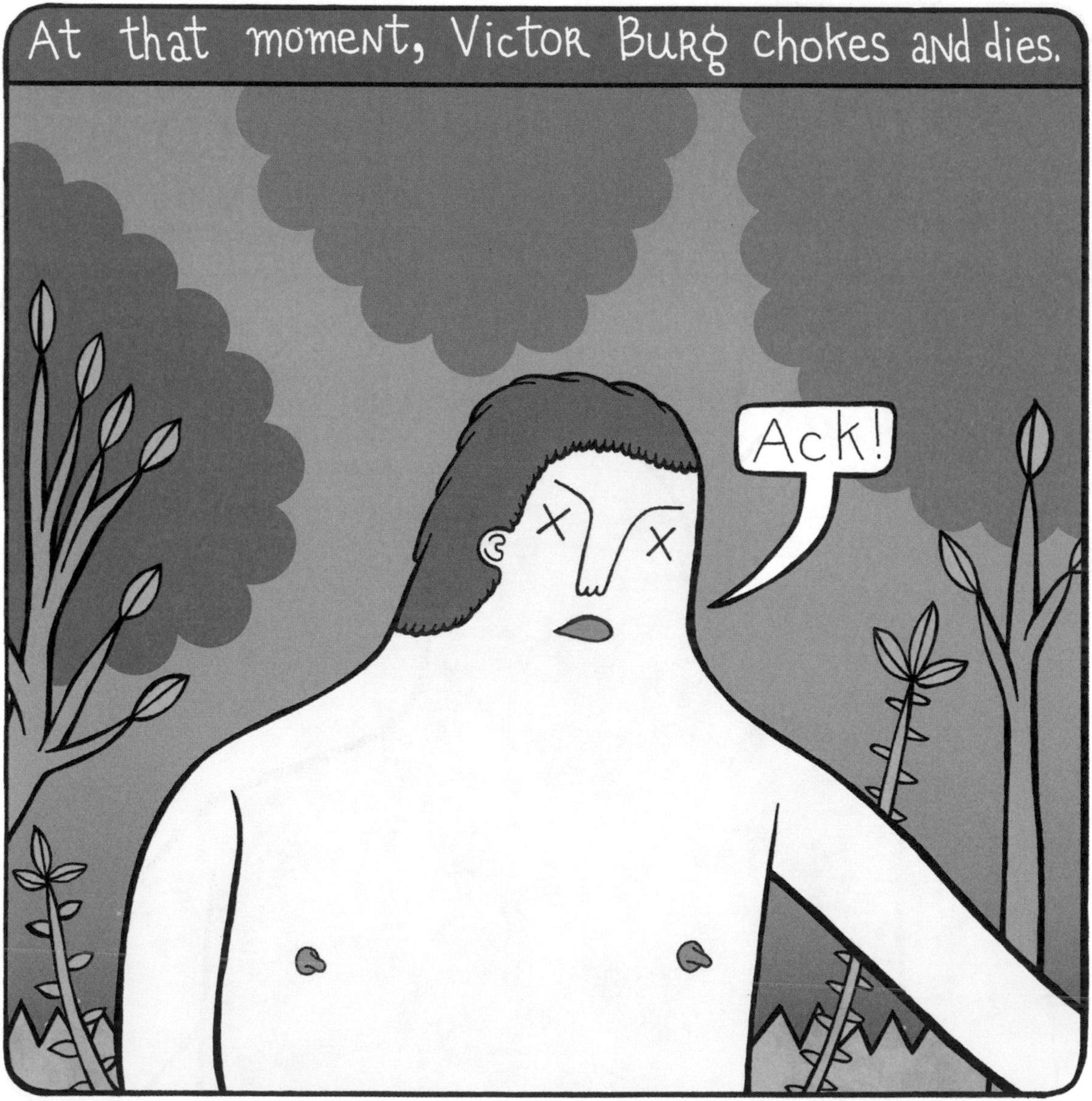
At that moment, Victor Burg chokes and dies.
Ack!

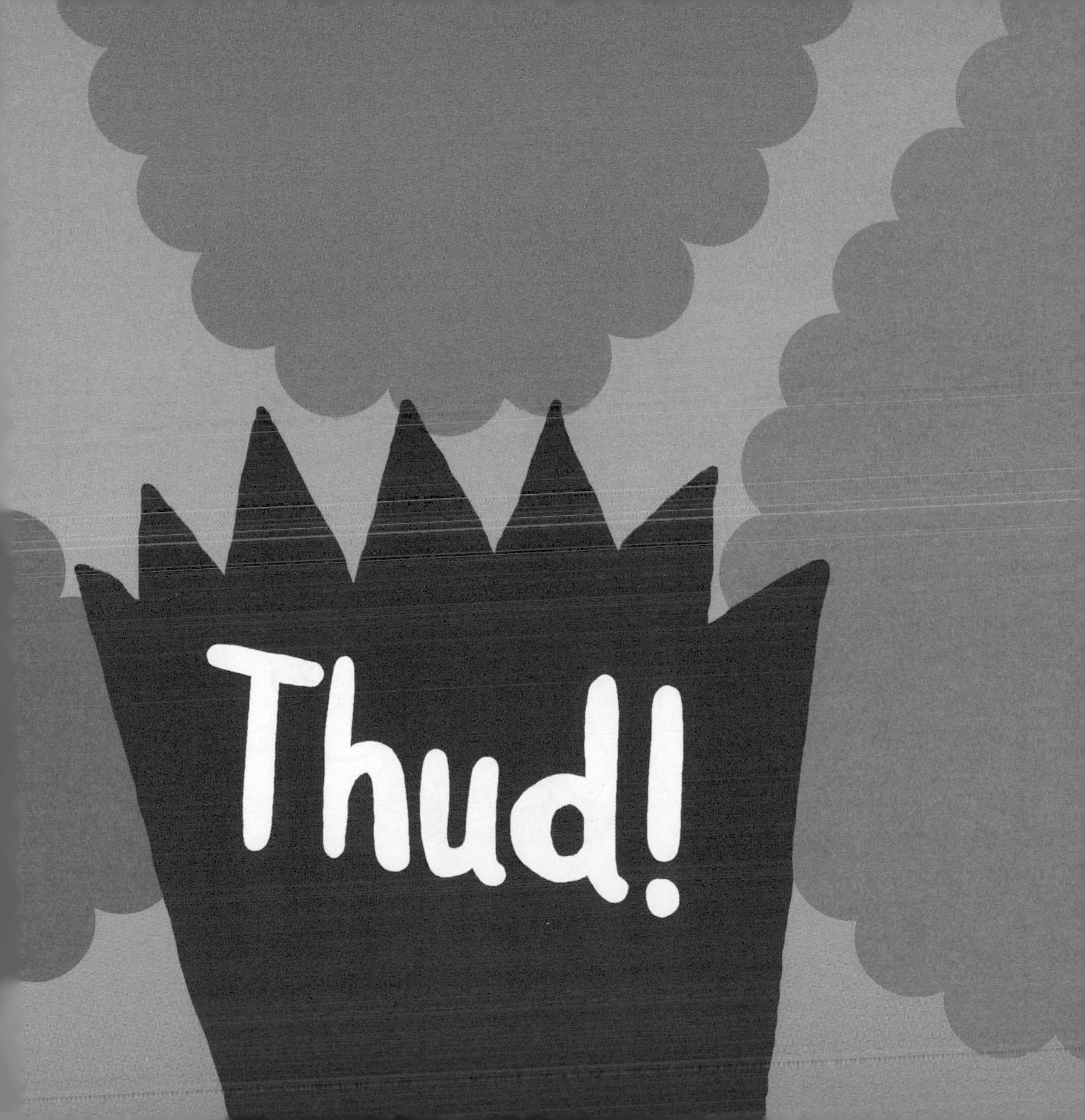
Thud!

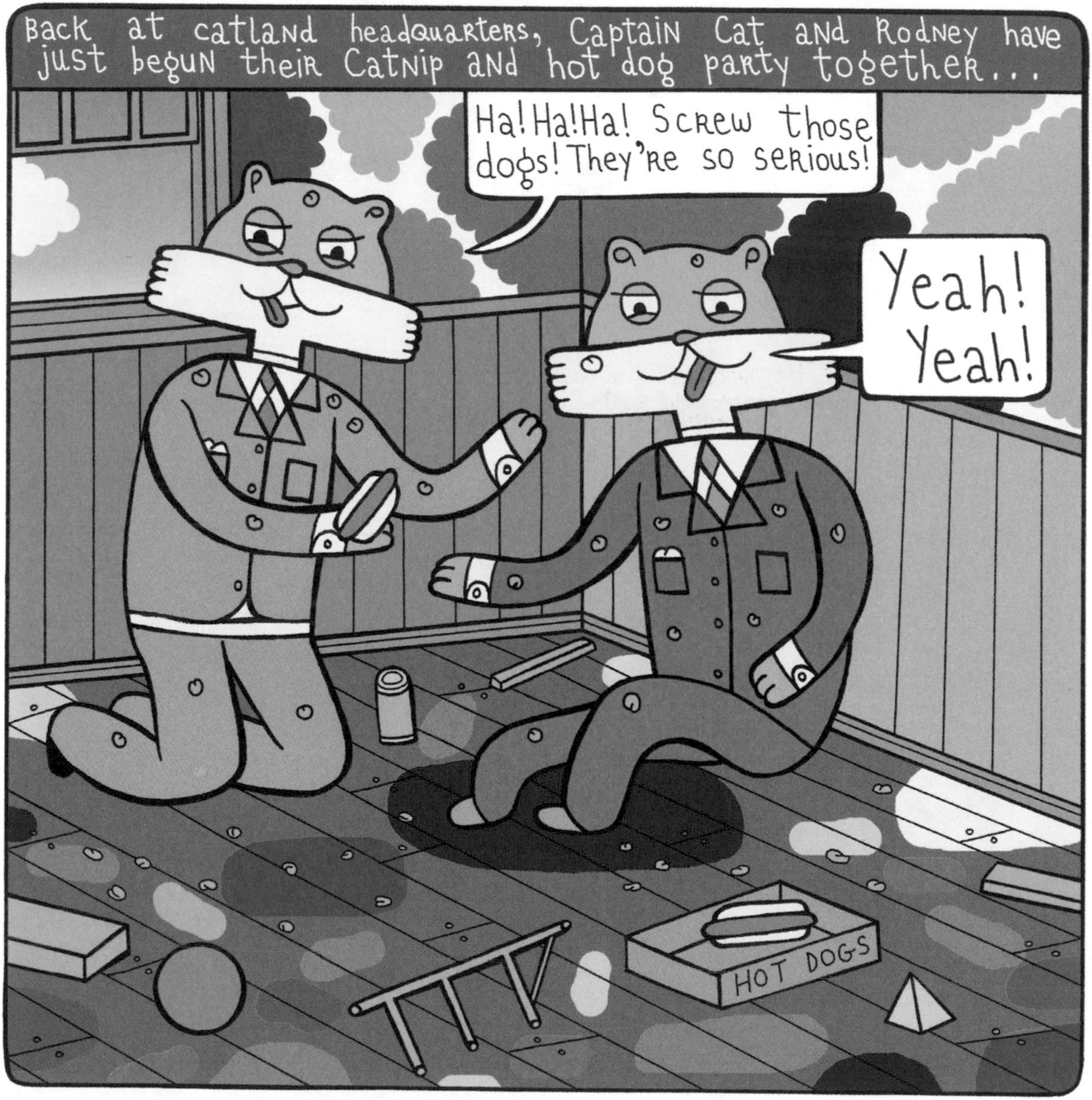
Back at catland headquarters, Captain Cat and Rodney have just begun their Catnip and hot dog party together...
Ha! Ha! Ha! Screw those dogs! They're so serious!
Yeah! Yeah!
HOT DOGS

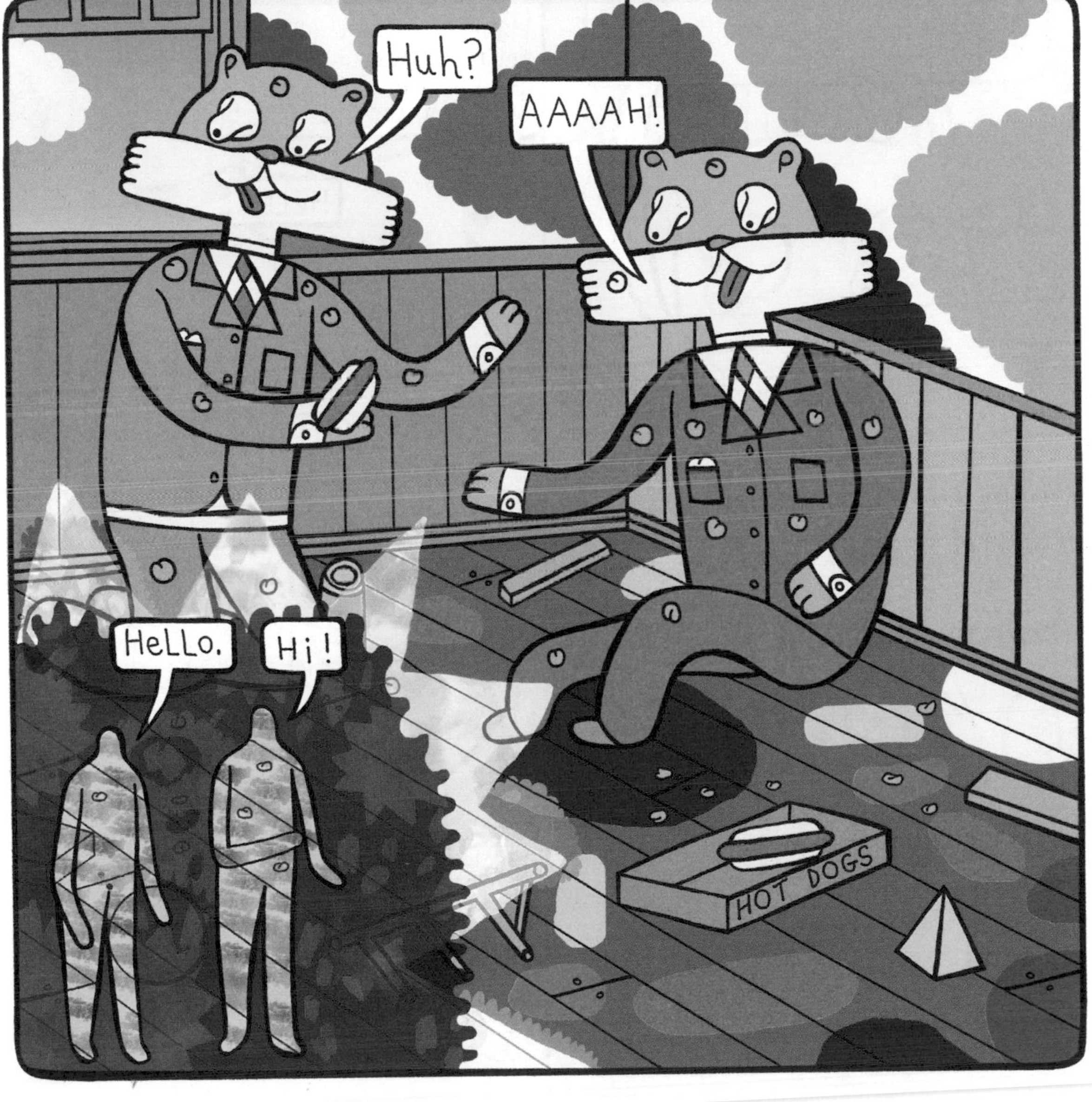
Huh?
AAAAH!
HeLLo.
Hi!
HOT DOGS

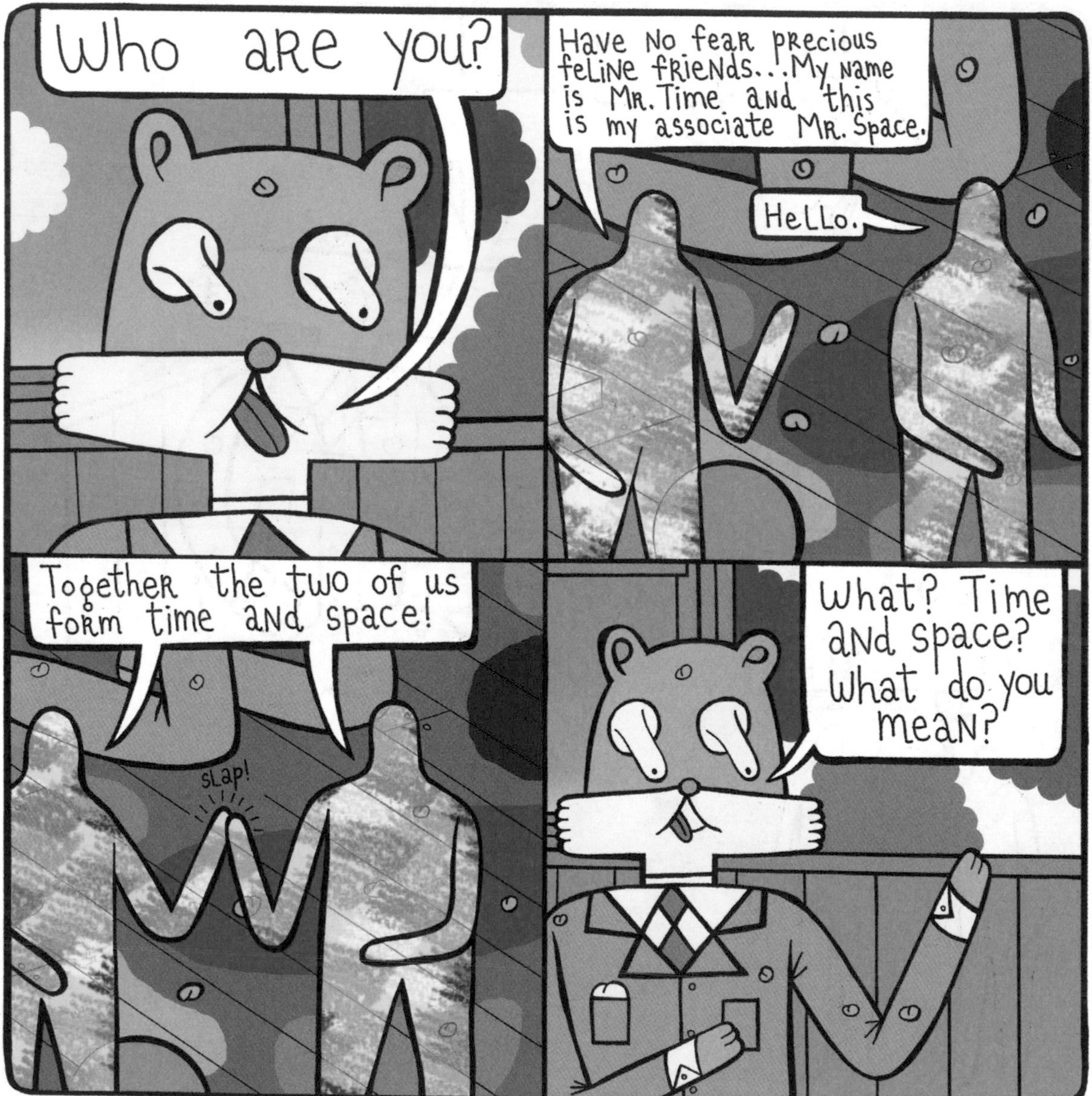
Who are you?
Have no fear precious feline friends...My name is Mr. Time and this is my associate Mr. Space.
Hello.
Together the two of us form time and space!
SLAP!
What? Time and space? What do you mean?

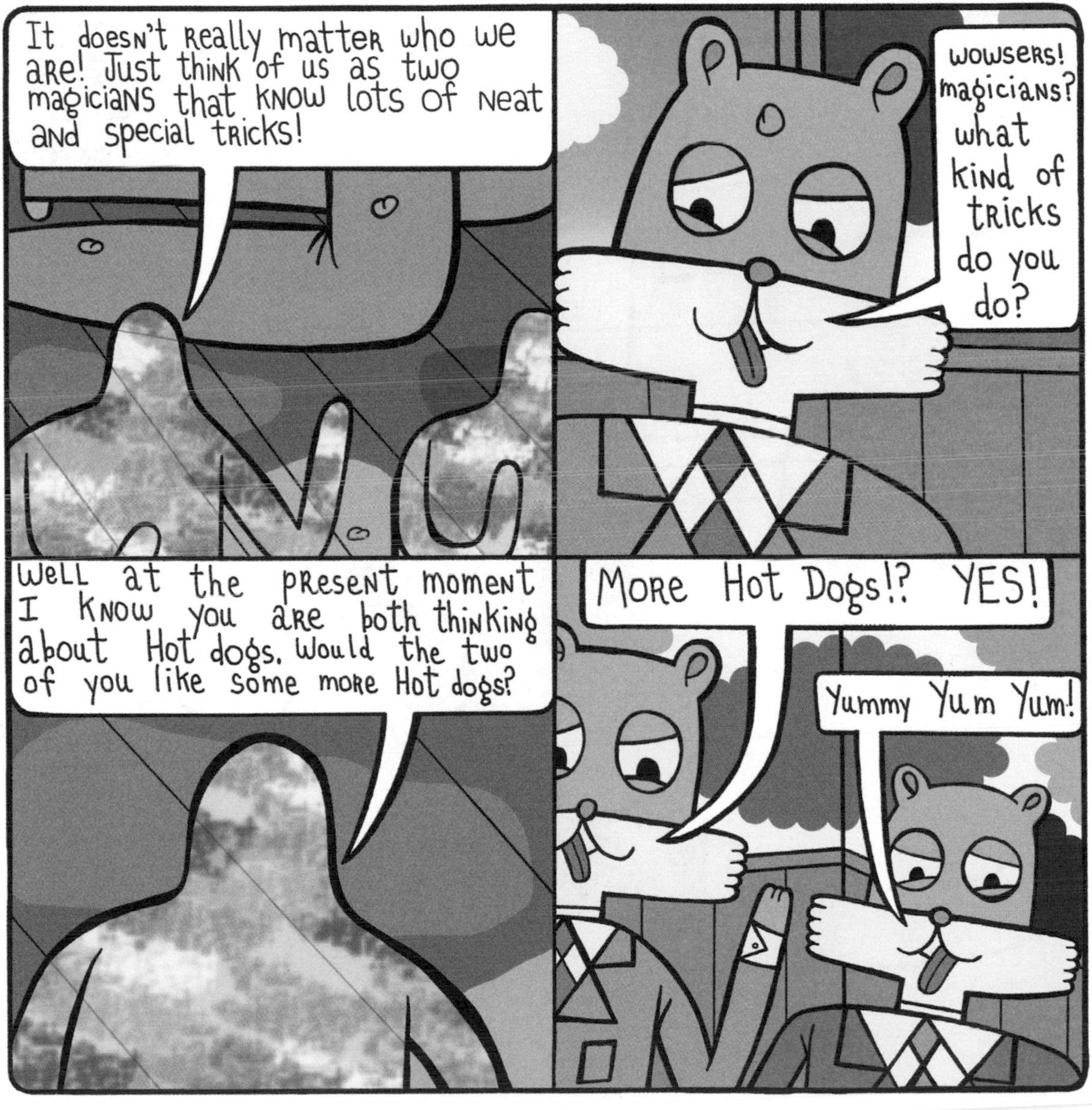
It doesn't really matter who we are! Just think of us as two magicians that know lots of neat and special tricks!
wowsers! magicians? what kind of tricks do you do?
Well at the present moment I know you are both thinking about Hot dogs. Would the two of you like some more Hot dogs?
More Hot Dogs!? YES!
Yummy Yum Yum!

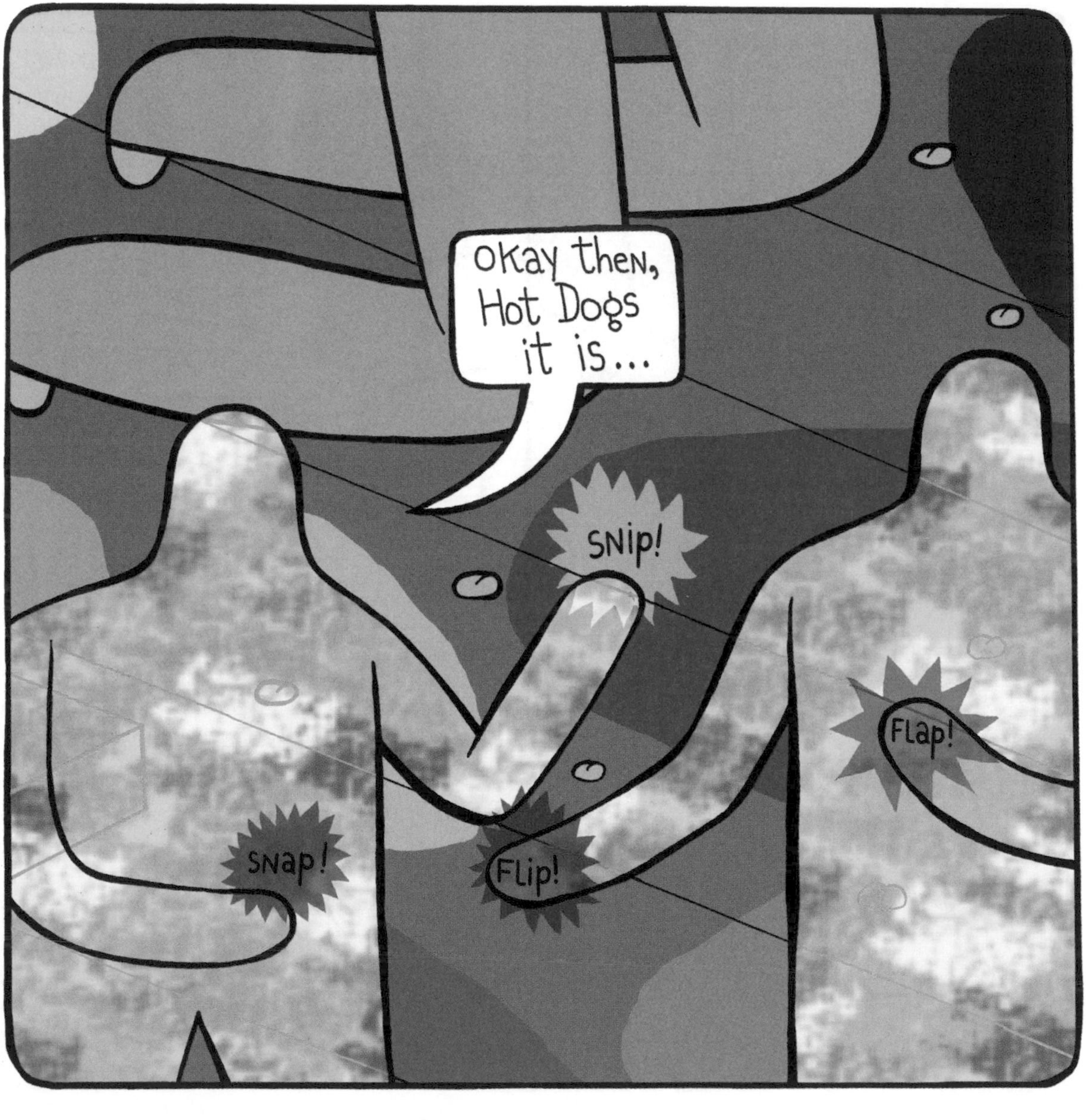
OKay then, Hot Dogs it is...
SNIP!
FLAP!
SNAP!
FLIP!

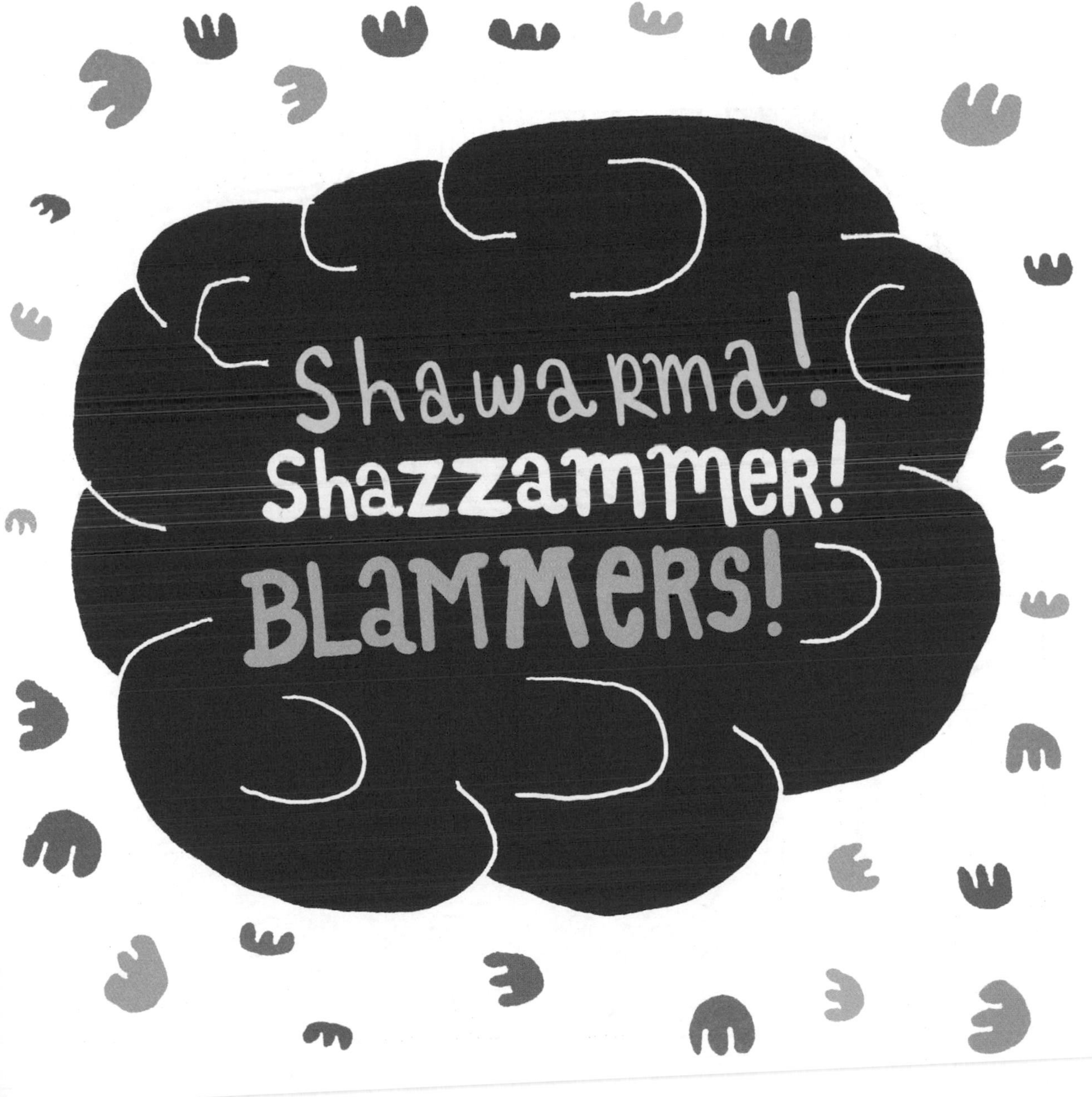
Shawarma!
Shazzammer!
BLAMMERS!

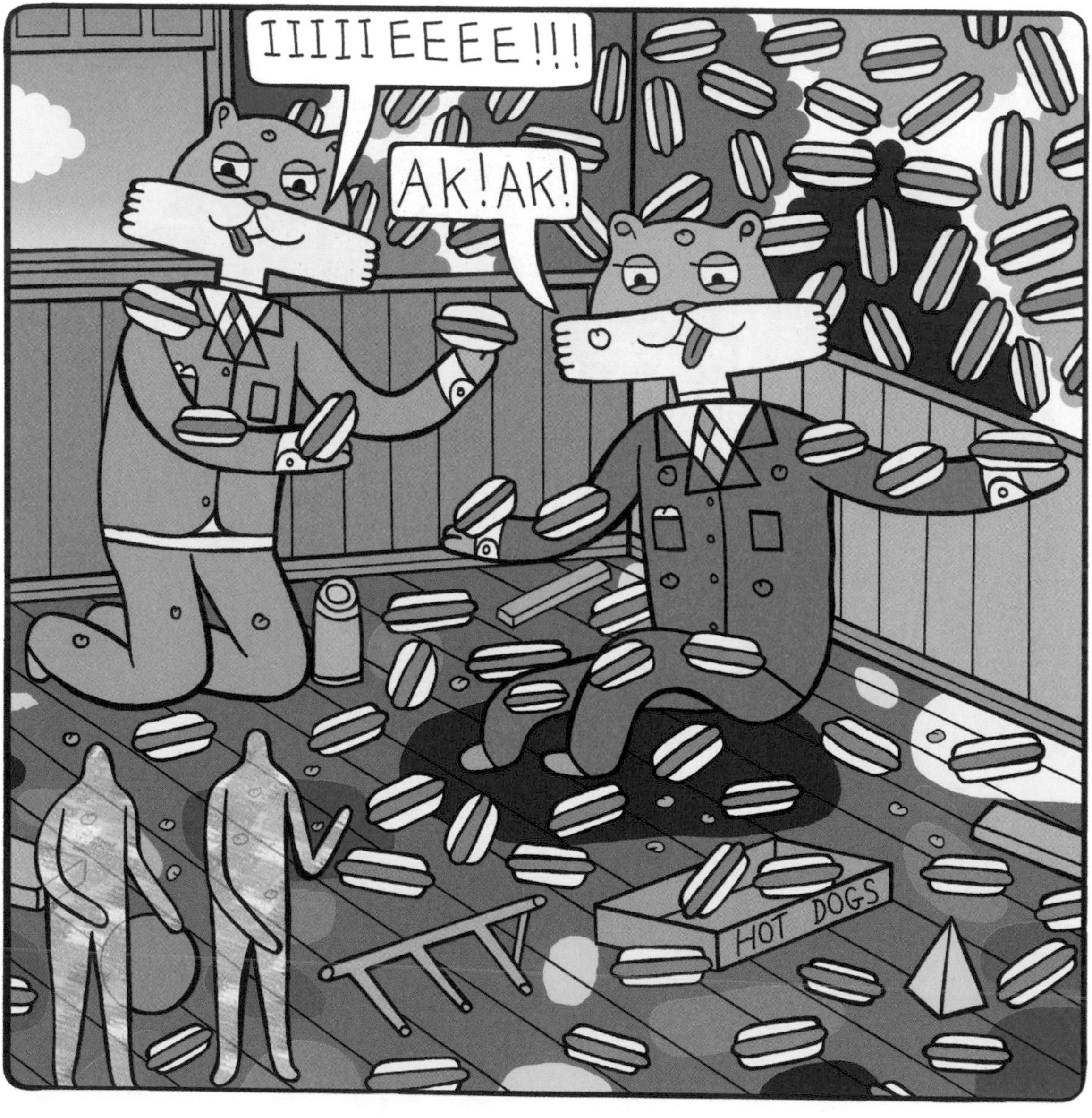
IIIIIEEEE!!!
AK!AK!
HOT DOGS

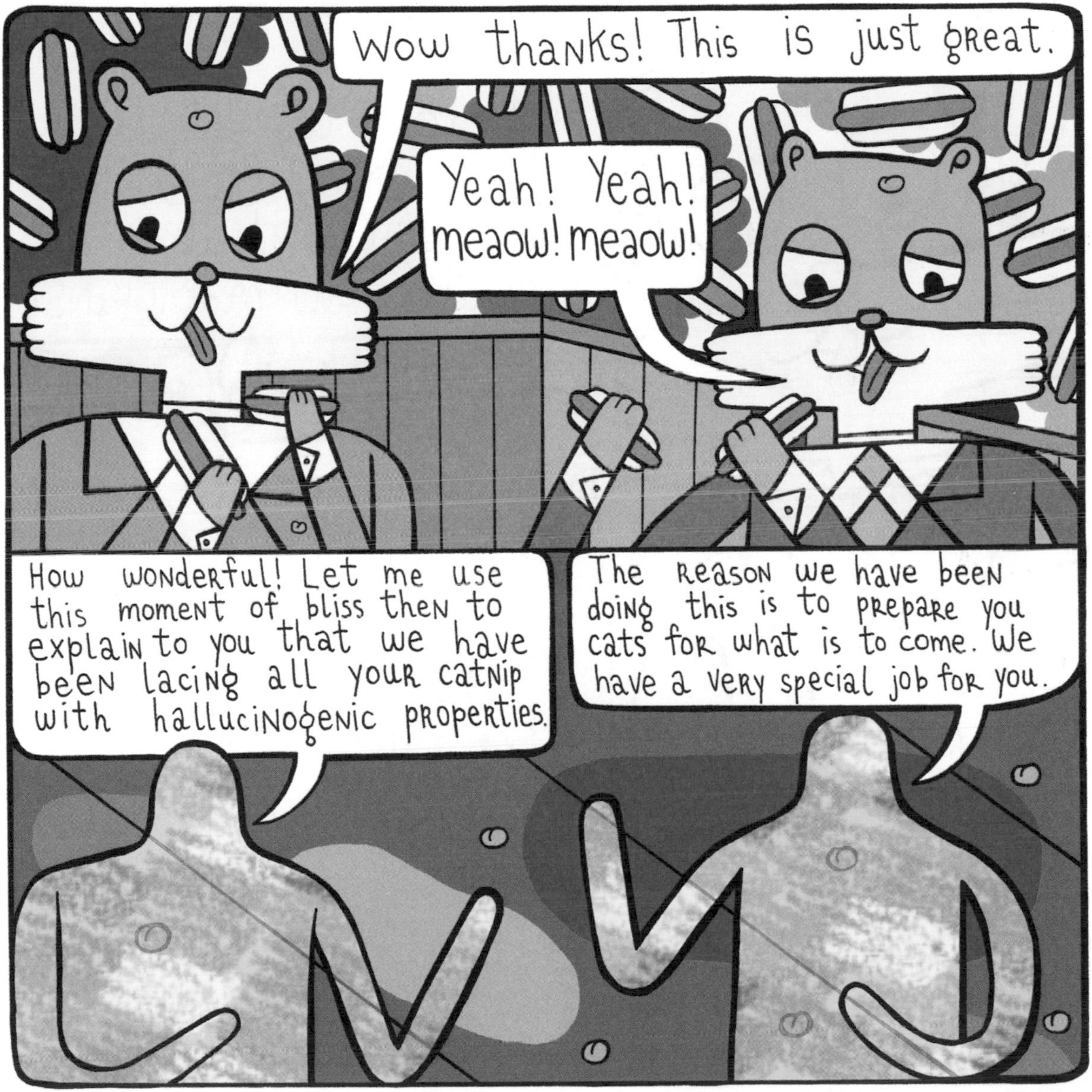
Wow thanks! This is just great.
Yeah! Yeah! meaow! meaow!
How wonderful! Let me use this moment of bliss then to explain to you that we have been lacing all your catnip with hallucinogenic properties.
The reason we have been doing this is to prepare you cats for what is to come. We have a very special job for you.

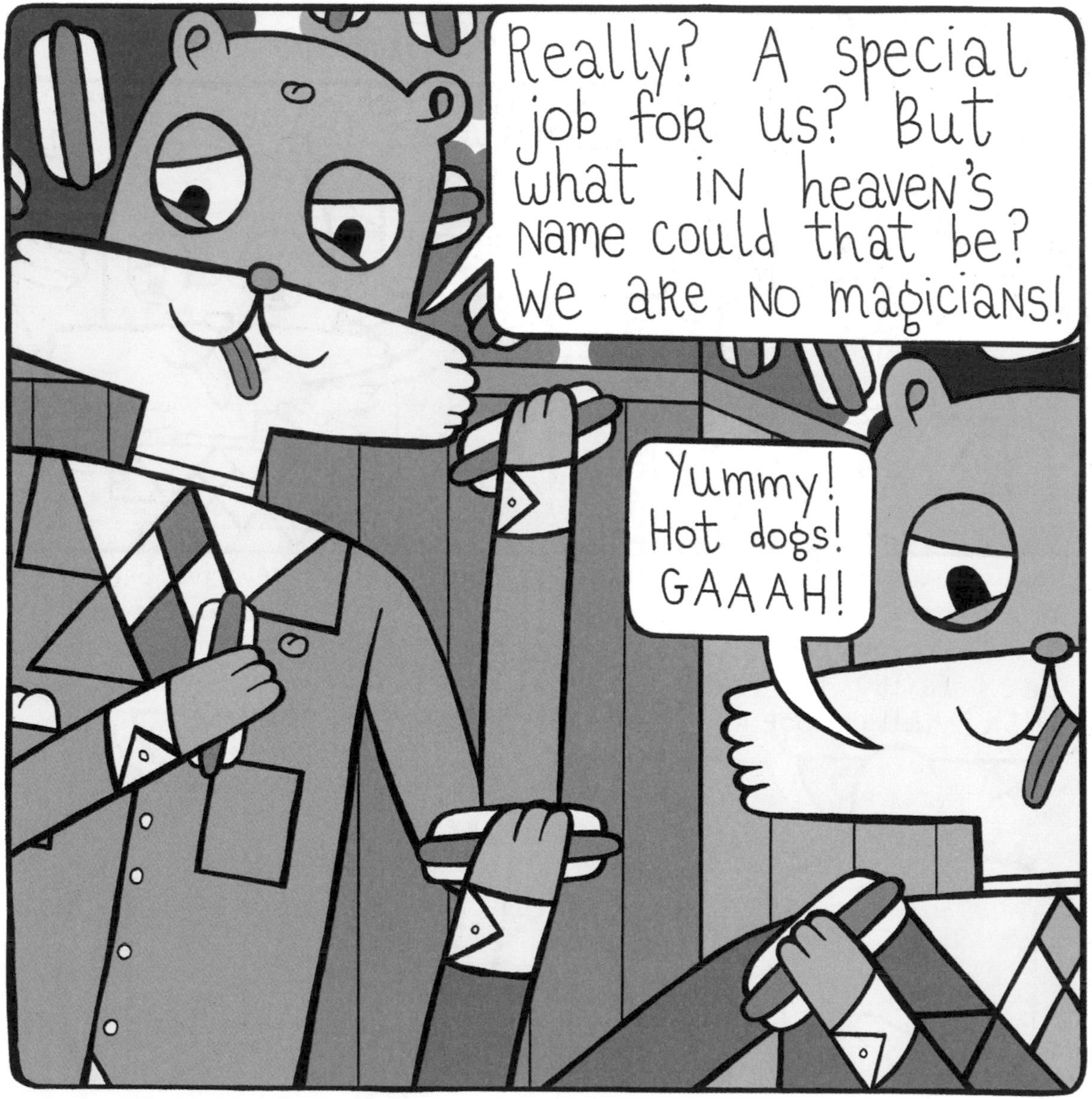
Really? A special job for us? But what in heaven's name could that be? We are no magicians!
Yummy! Hot dogs! GAAAH!

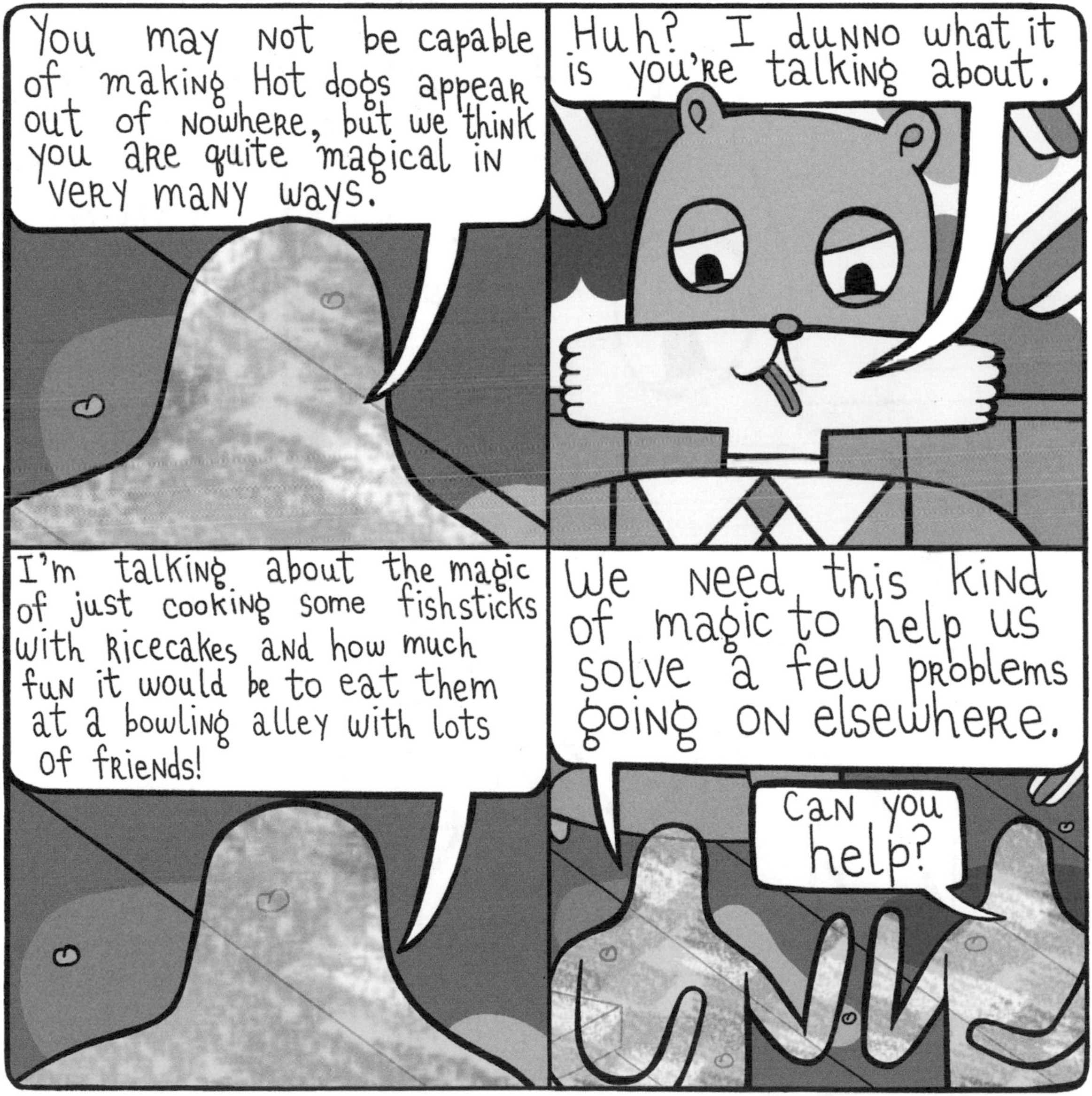
You may not be capable of making Hot dogs appear out of nowhere, but we think you are quite magical in very many ways.
Huh? I dunno what it is you're talking about.
I'm talking about the magic of just cooking some fishsticks with ricecakes and how much fun it would be to eat them at a bowling alley with lots of friends!
We need this kind of magic to help us solve a few problems going on elsewhere.
Can you help?

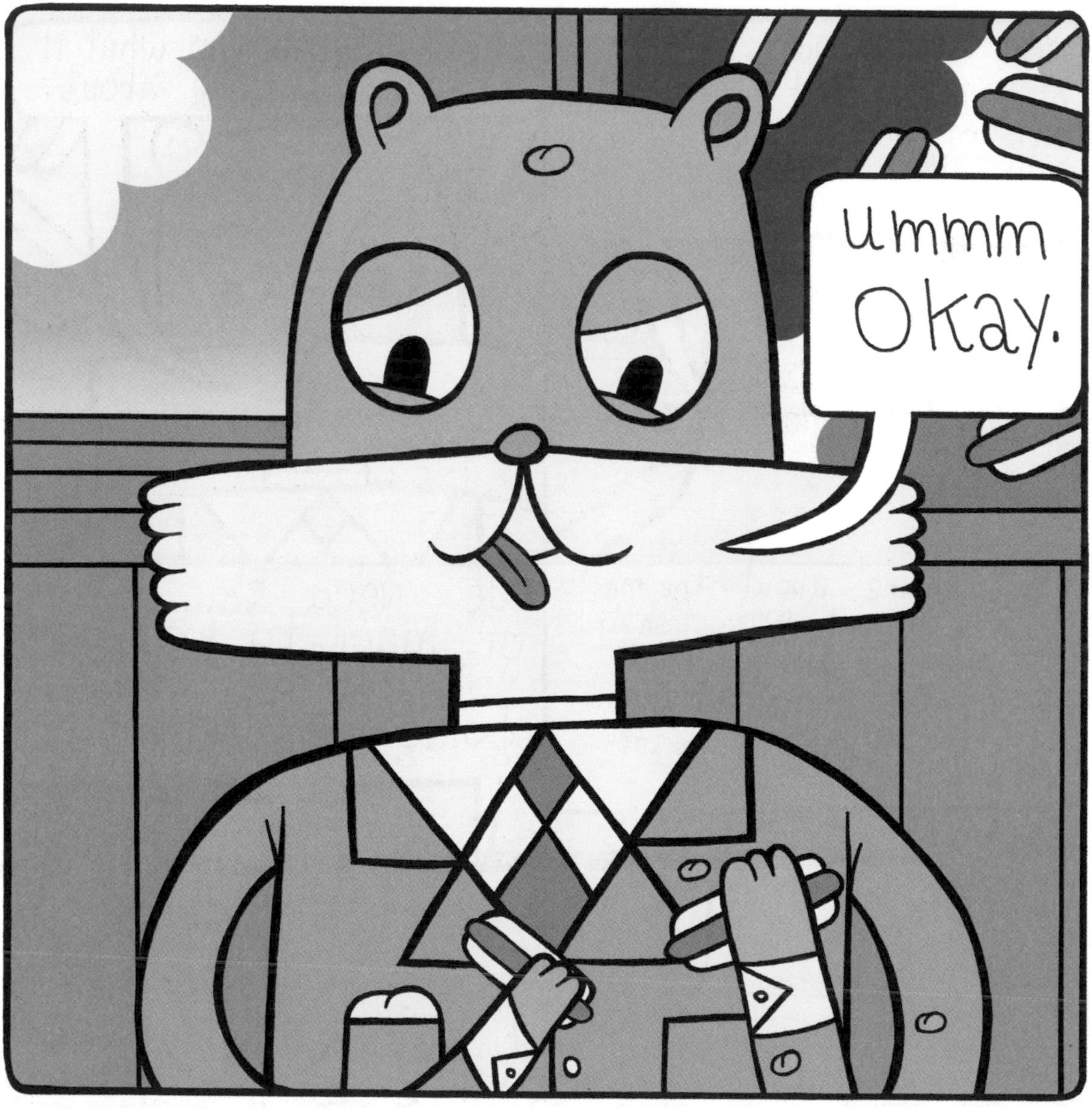
Ummm
Okay.

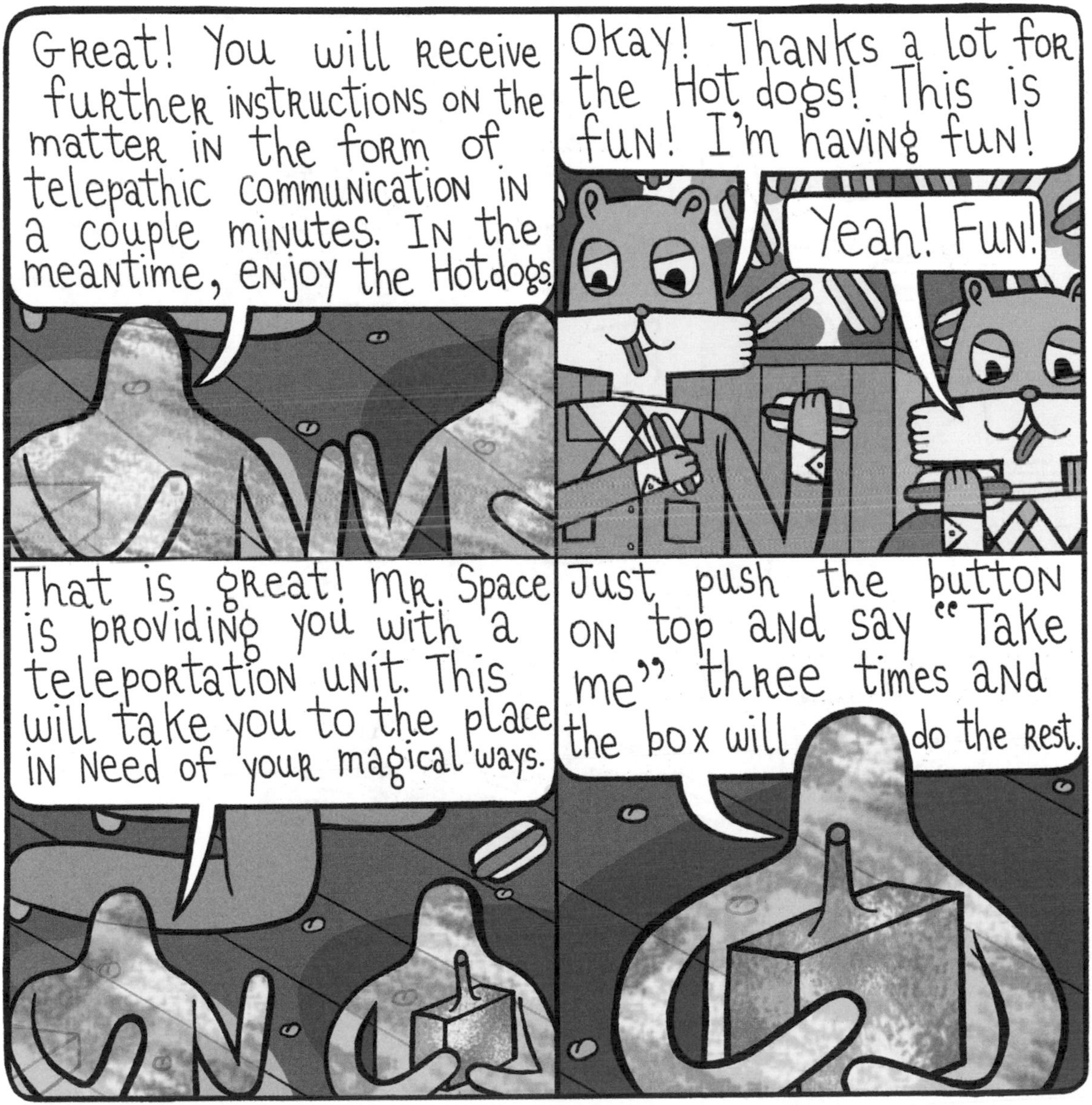
Great! You will receive further instructions on the matter in the form of telepathic communication in a couple minutes. In the meantime, enjoy the Hotdogs.
Okay! Thanks a lot for the Hot dogs! This is fun! I'm having fun!
Yeah! Fun!
That is great! Mr. Space is providing you with a teleportation unit. This will take you to the place in need of your magical ways.
Just push the button on top and say "Take me" three times and the box will do the rest.

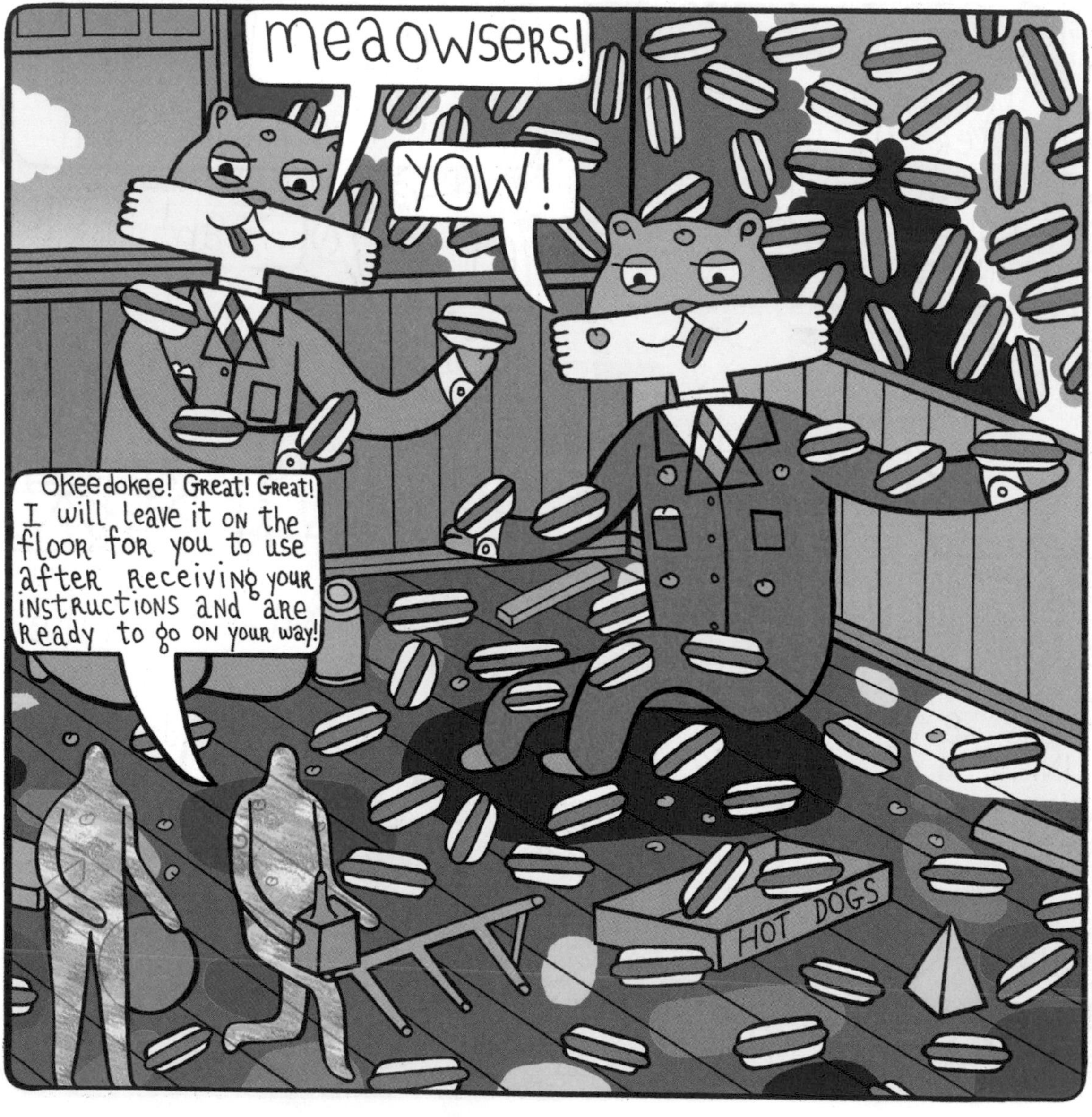
meaowsers!
YOW!
Okeedokee! Great! Great! I will leave it on the floor for you to use after receiving your instructions and are ready to go on your way!
HOT DOGS

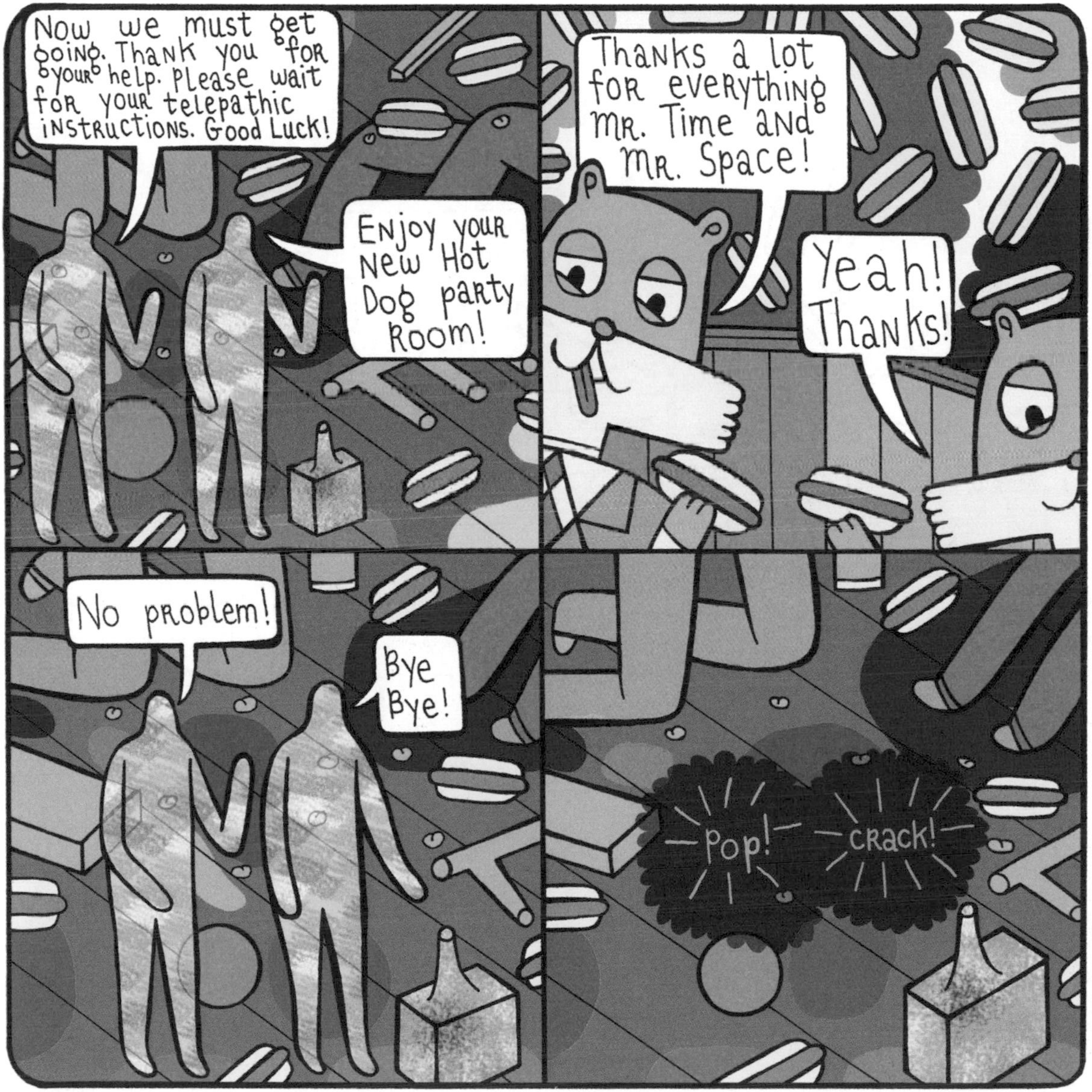
Now we must get going. Thank you for your help. Please wait for your telepathic instructions. Good Luck!
Enjoy your New Hot Dog party Room!
Thanks a lot for everything Mr. Time and Mr. Space!
Yeah! Thanks!
No problem!
Bye Bye!
Pop!
crack!

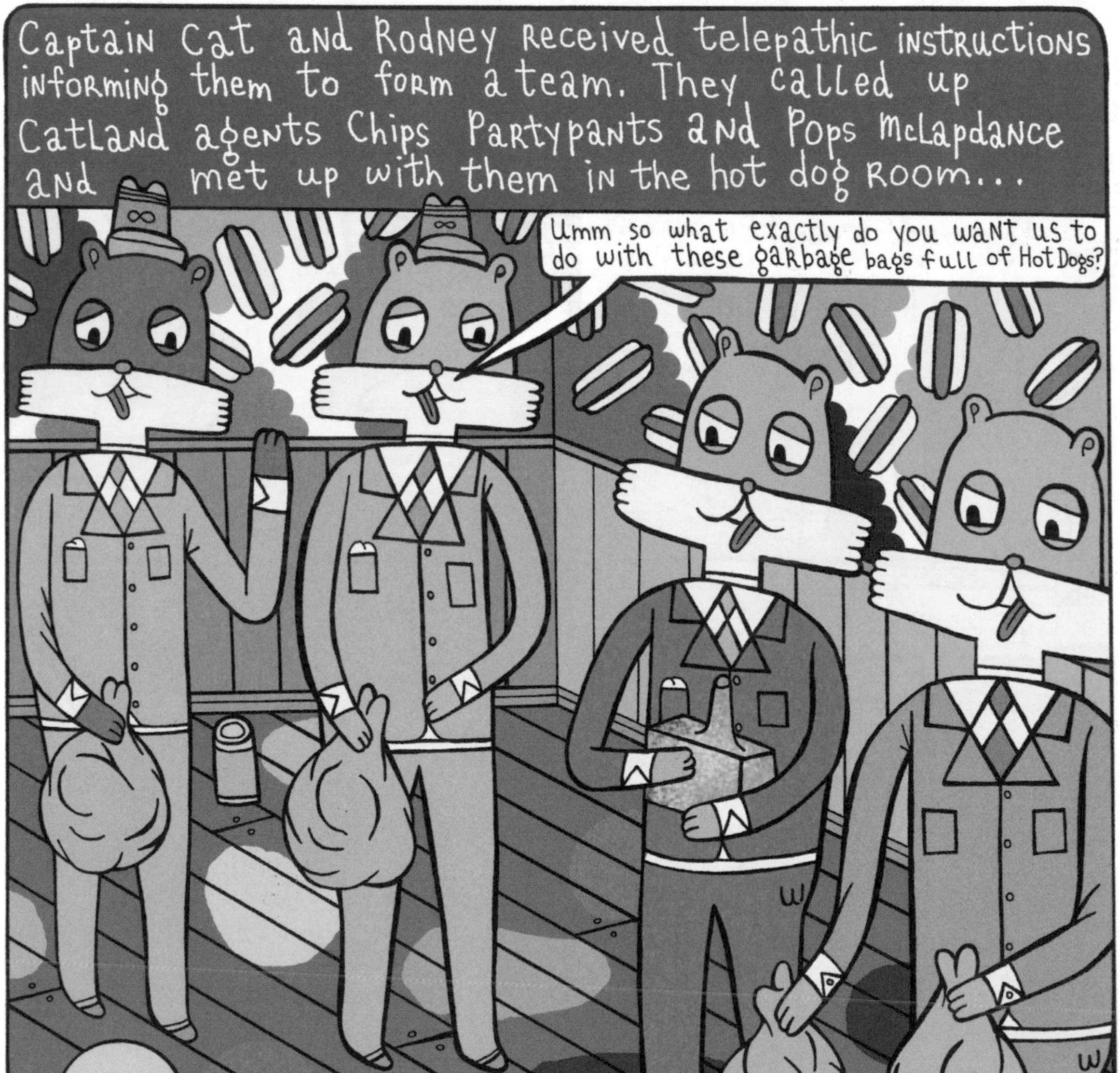
Captain Cat and Rodney received telepathic instructions informing them to form a team. They called up Catland agents Chips Partypants and Pops McLapdance and met up with them in the hot dog room...
Umm so what exactly do you want us to do with these garbage bags full of Hot Dogs?

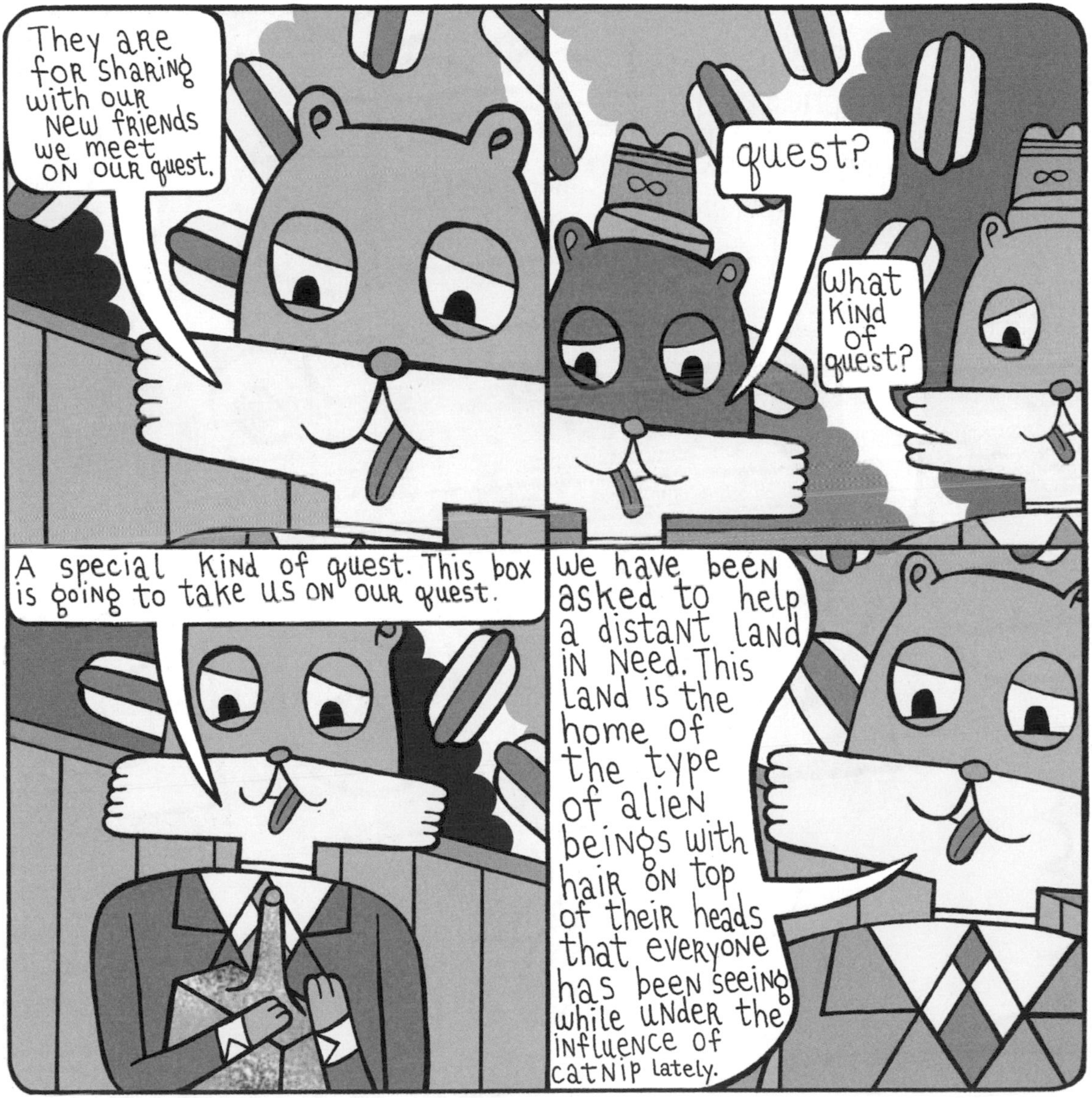
They are for sharing with our new friends we meet on our quest.
quest?
What kind of quest?
A special kind of quest. This box is going to take us on our quest.
We have been asked to help a distant land in need. This land is the home of the type of alien beings with hair on top of their heads that everyone has been seeing while under the influence of catnip lately.

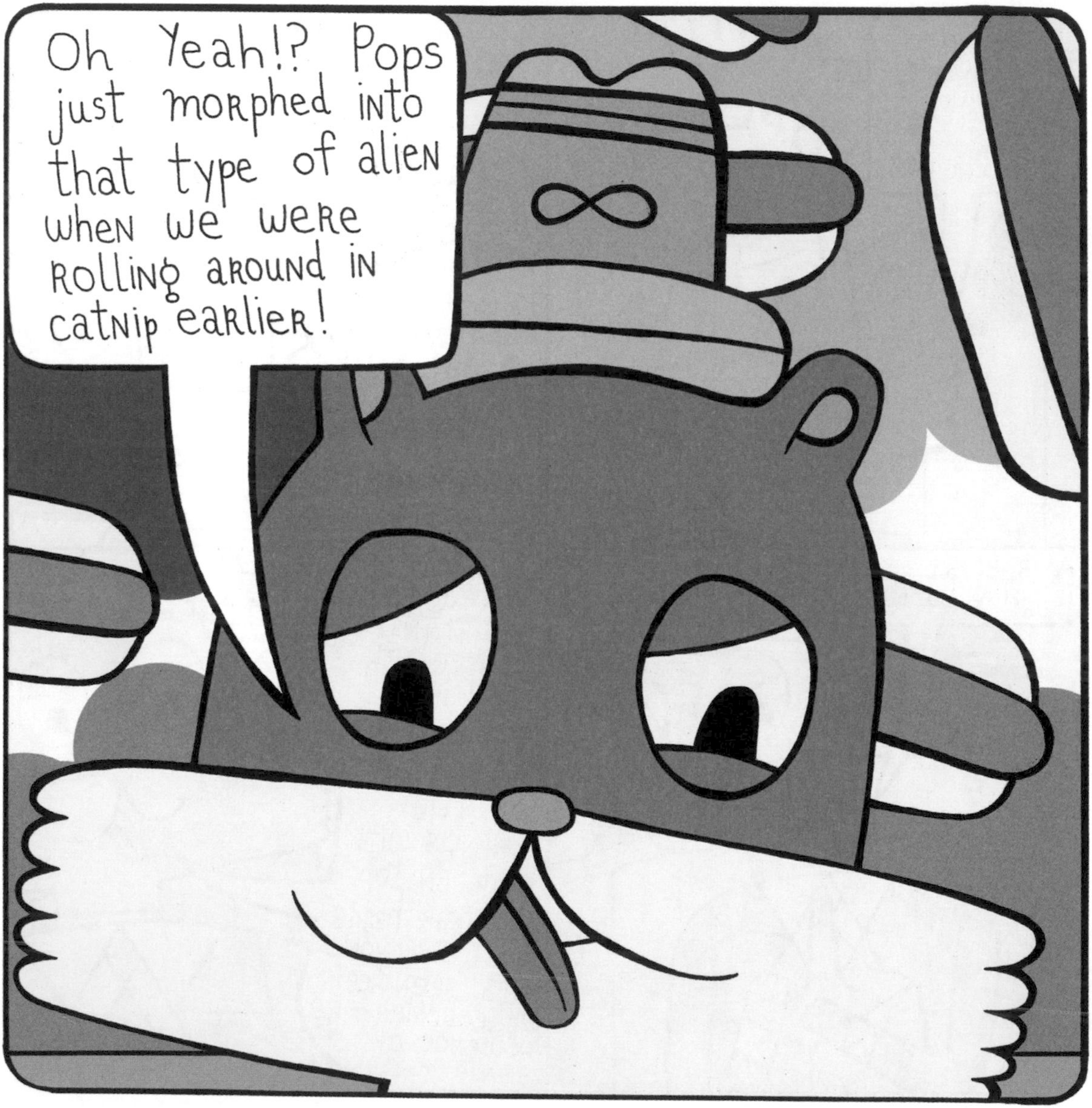
Oh Yeah!? Pops just morphed into that type of alien when we were rolling around in catnip earlier!

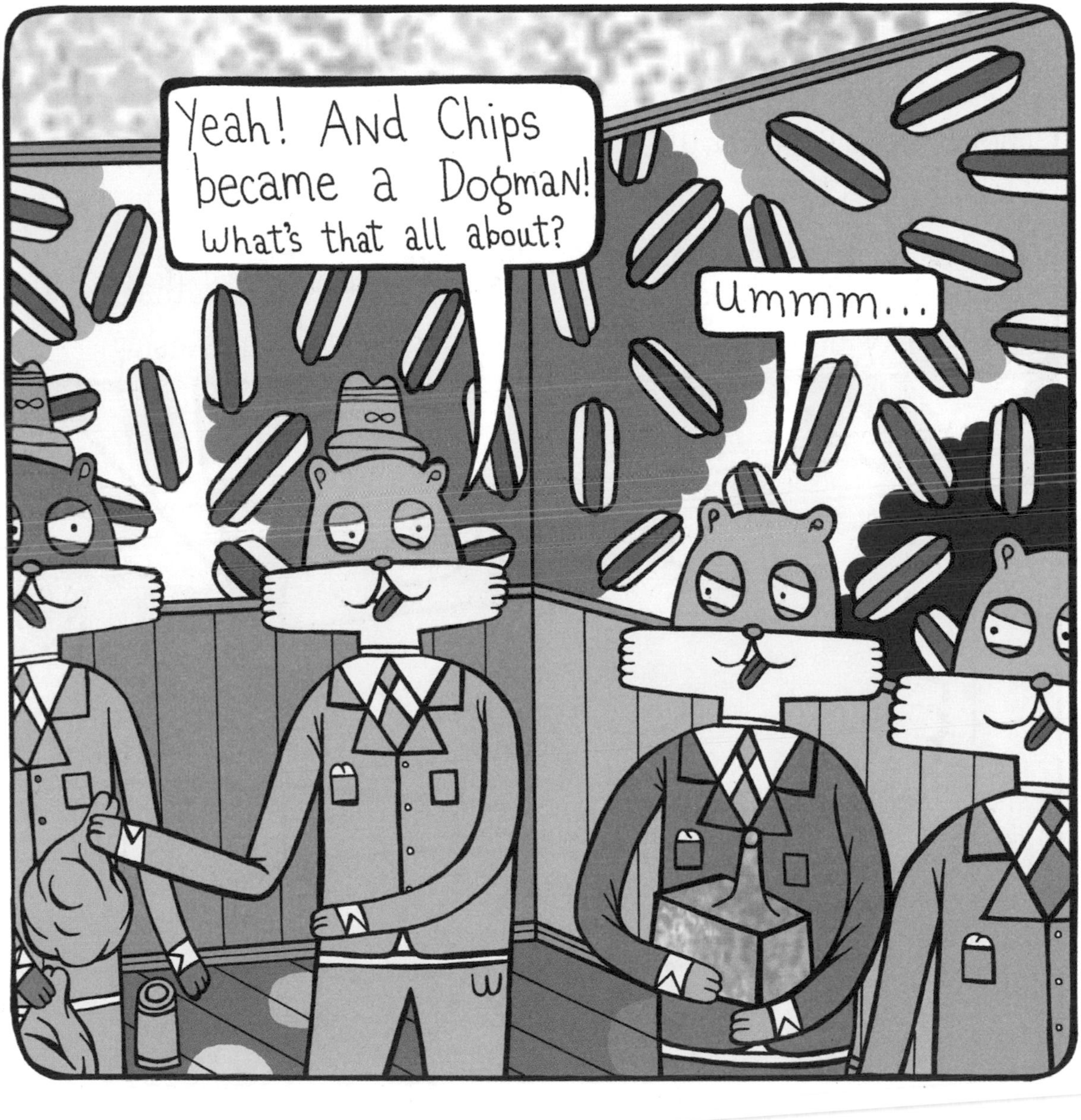
Yeah! AND Chips became a Dogman! What's that all about?
Ummm...

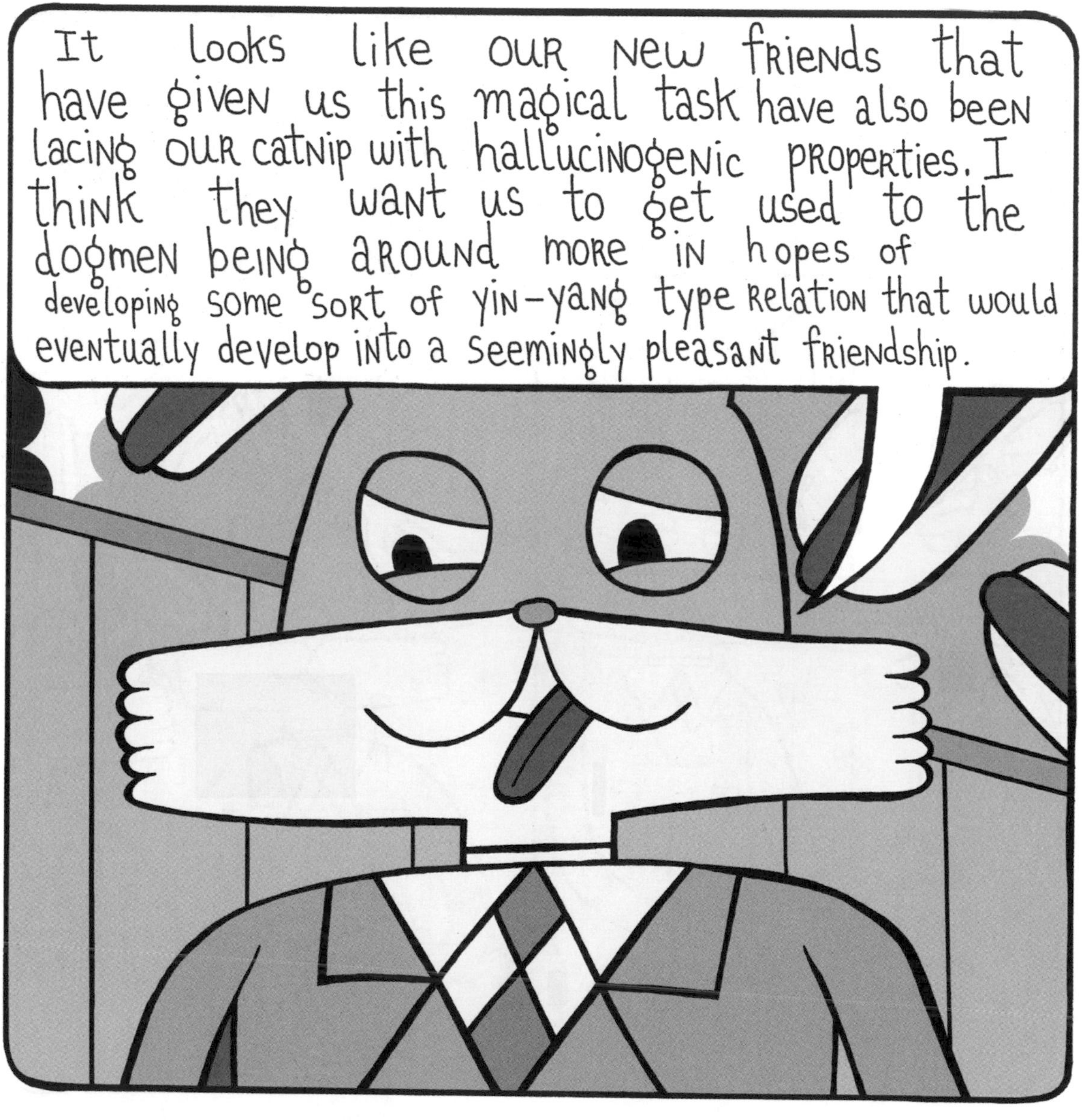
It looks like our new friends that have given us this magical task have also been lacing our catnip with hallucinogenic properties. I think they want us to get used to the dogmen being around more in hopes of developing some sort of yin-yang type relation that would eventually develop into a seemingly pleasant friendship.

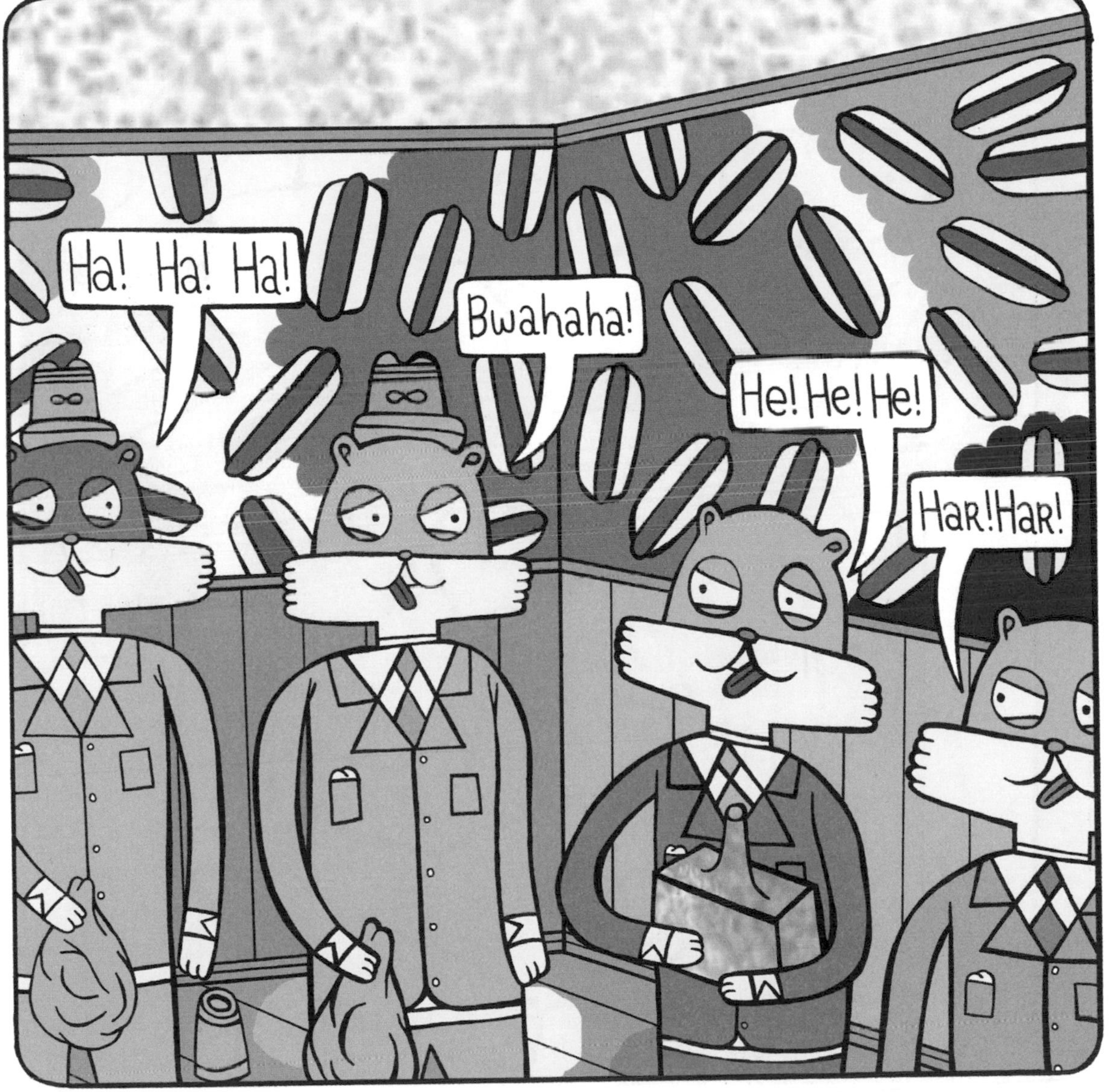
Ha! Ha! Ha!
Bwahaha!
He! He! He!
Har!Har!

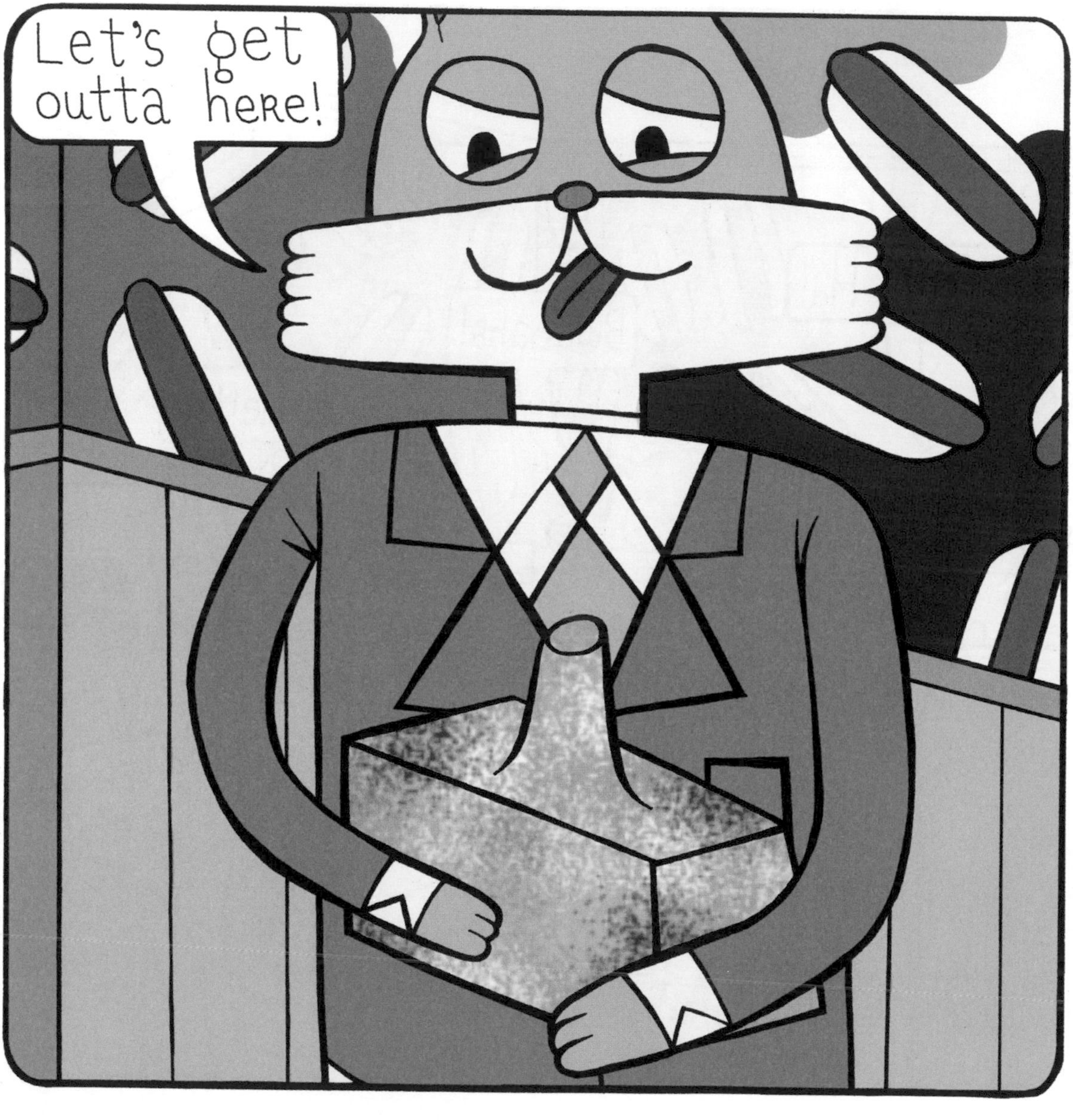
Let's get outta here!

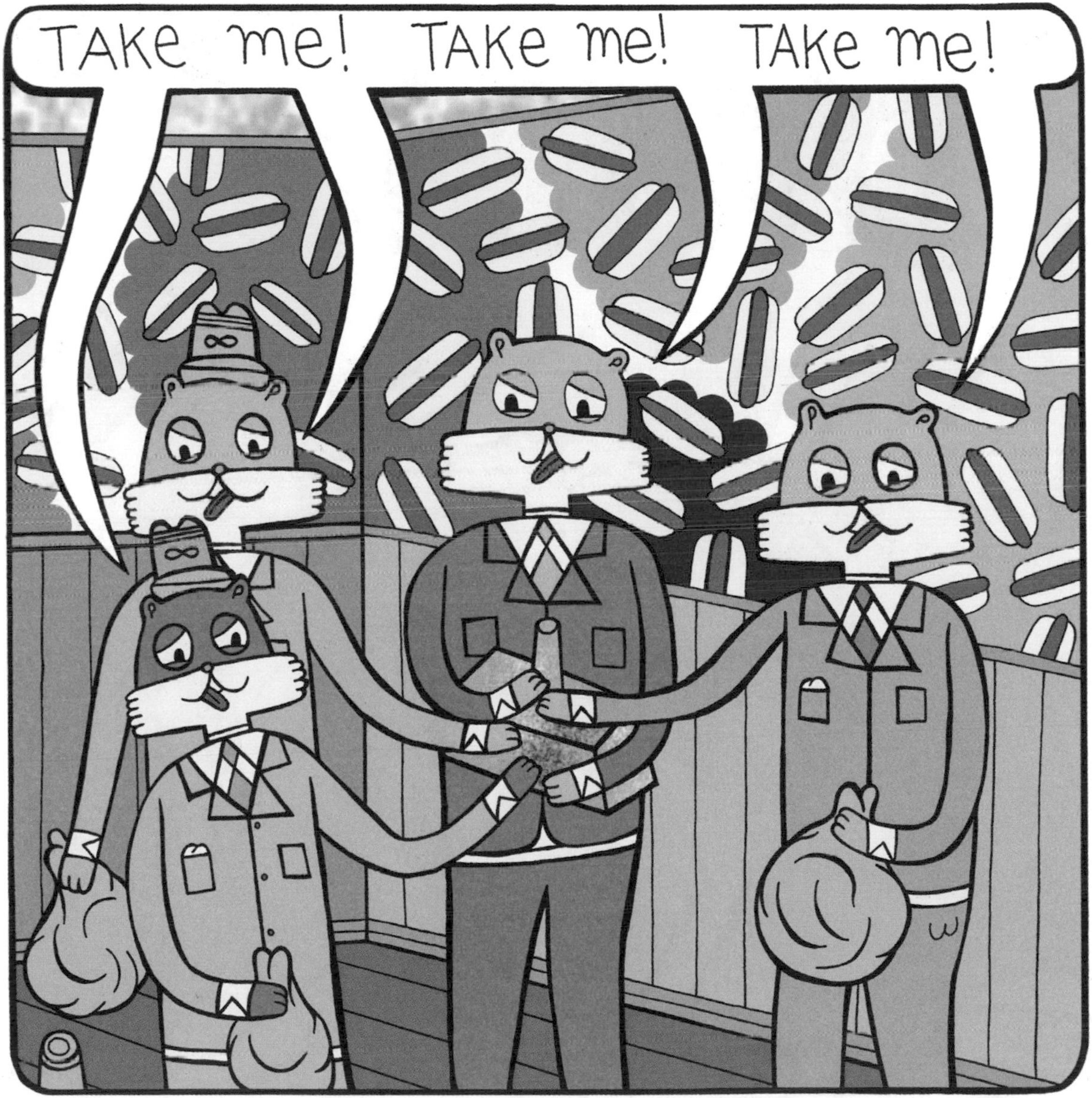
TAKE me! TAKE me! TAKE me!

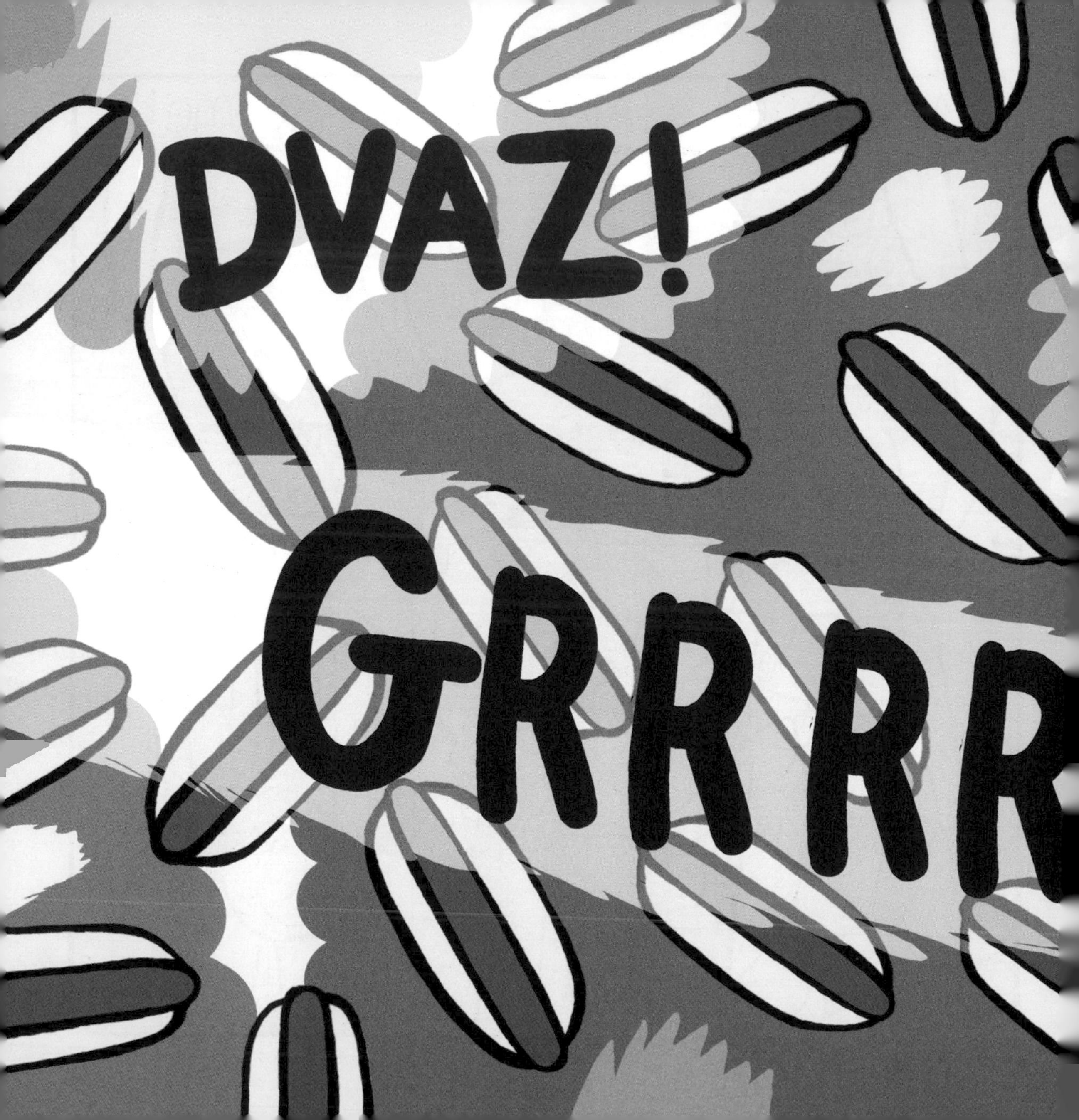
DVAZ!
GRRRR

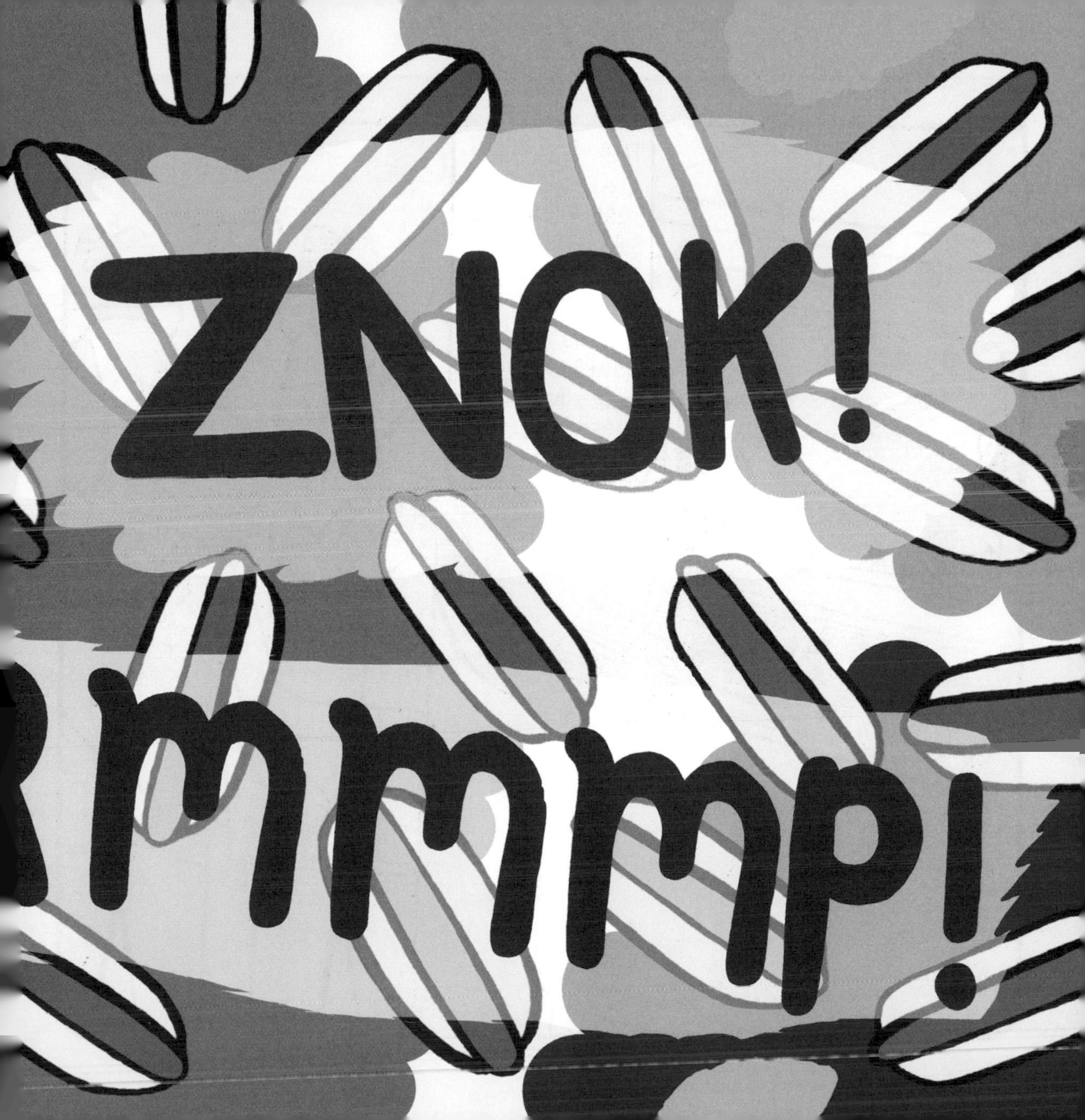
ZNOK!
mmmp!

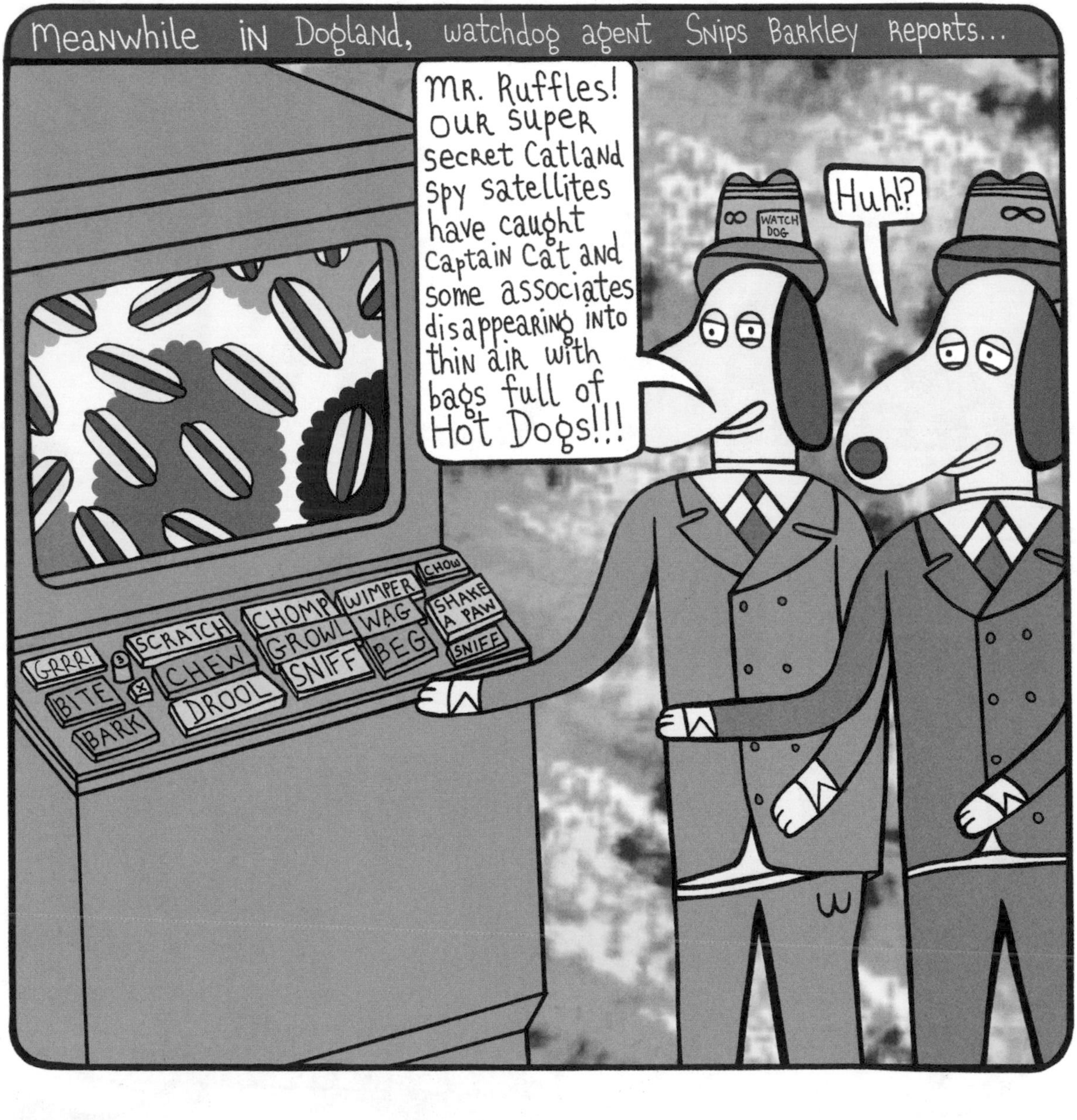
Meanwhile in Dogland, watchdog agent Snips Barkley reports...
Mr. Ruffles! Our super secret Catland spy satellites have caught Captain Cat and some associates disappearing into thin air with bags full of Hot Dogs!!!
Huh!?
WATCH DOG
GRRR!
BITE
BARK
SCRATCH
CHEW
DROOL
CHOMP
GROWL
SNIFF
WIMPER
WAG
BEG
CHOW
SHAKE A PAW
SNIFF

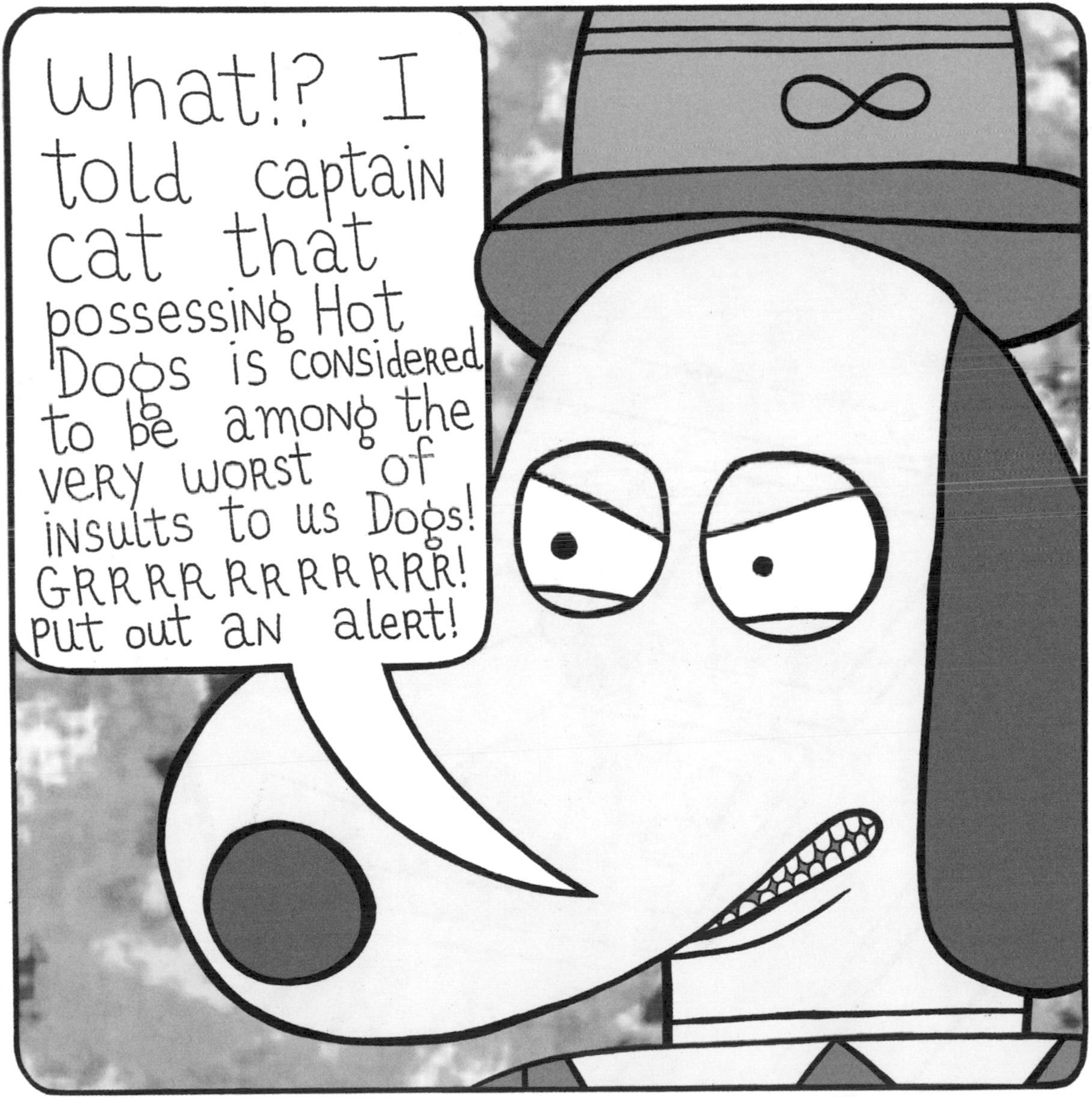
What!? I told captain cat that possessing Hot Dogs is considered to be among the very worst of insults to us Dogs! GRRRRRRRRRRR! Put out an alert!

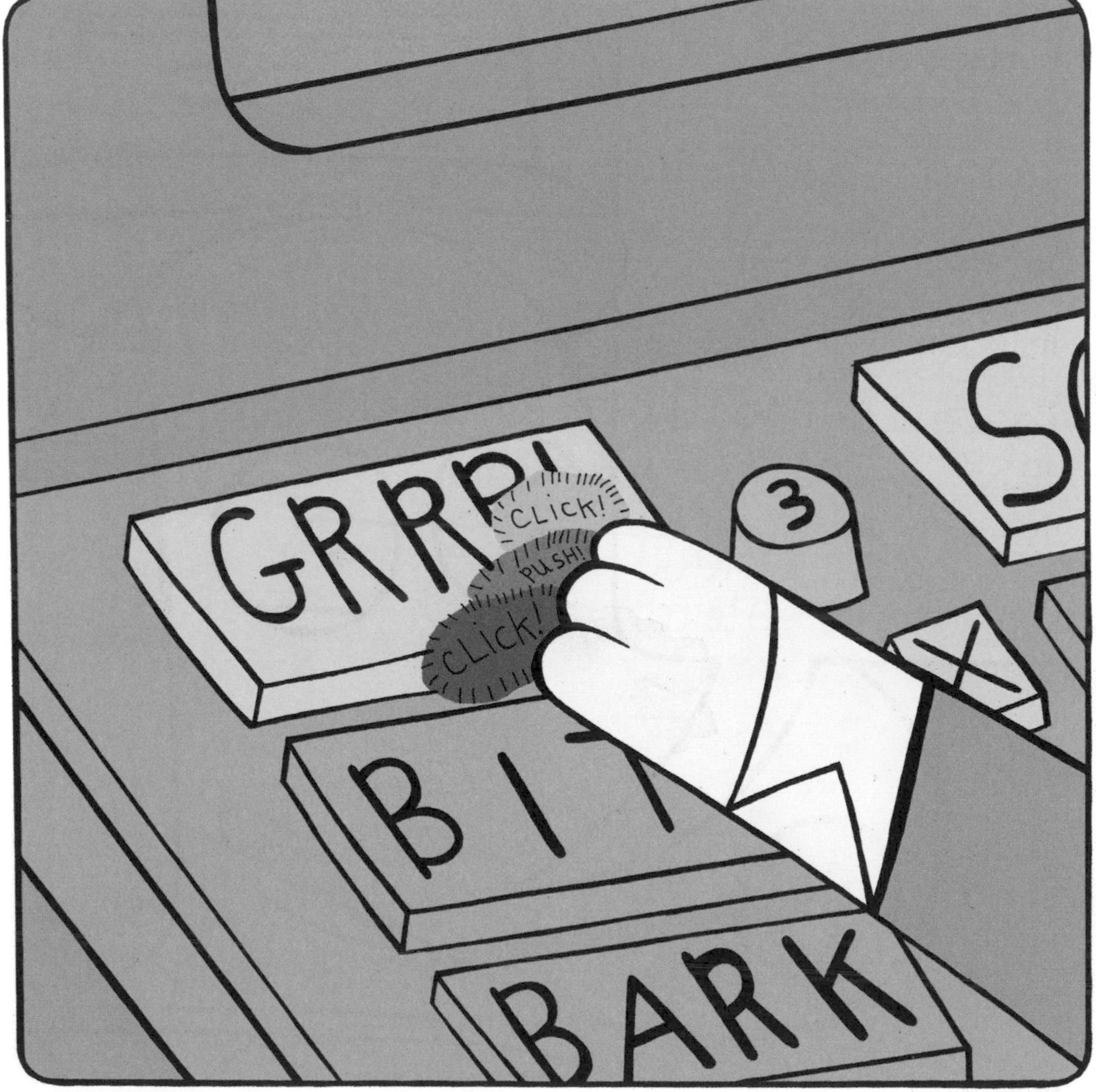
CLICK!
PUSH!
CLICK!
3
BARK

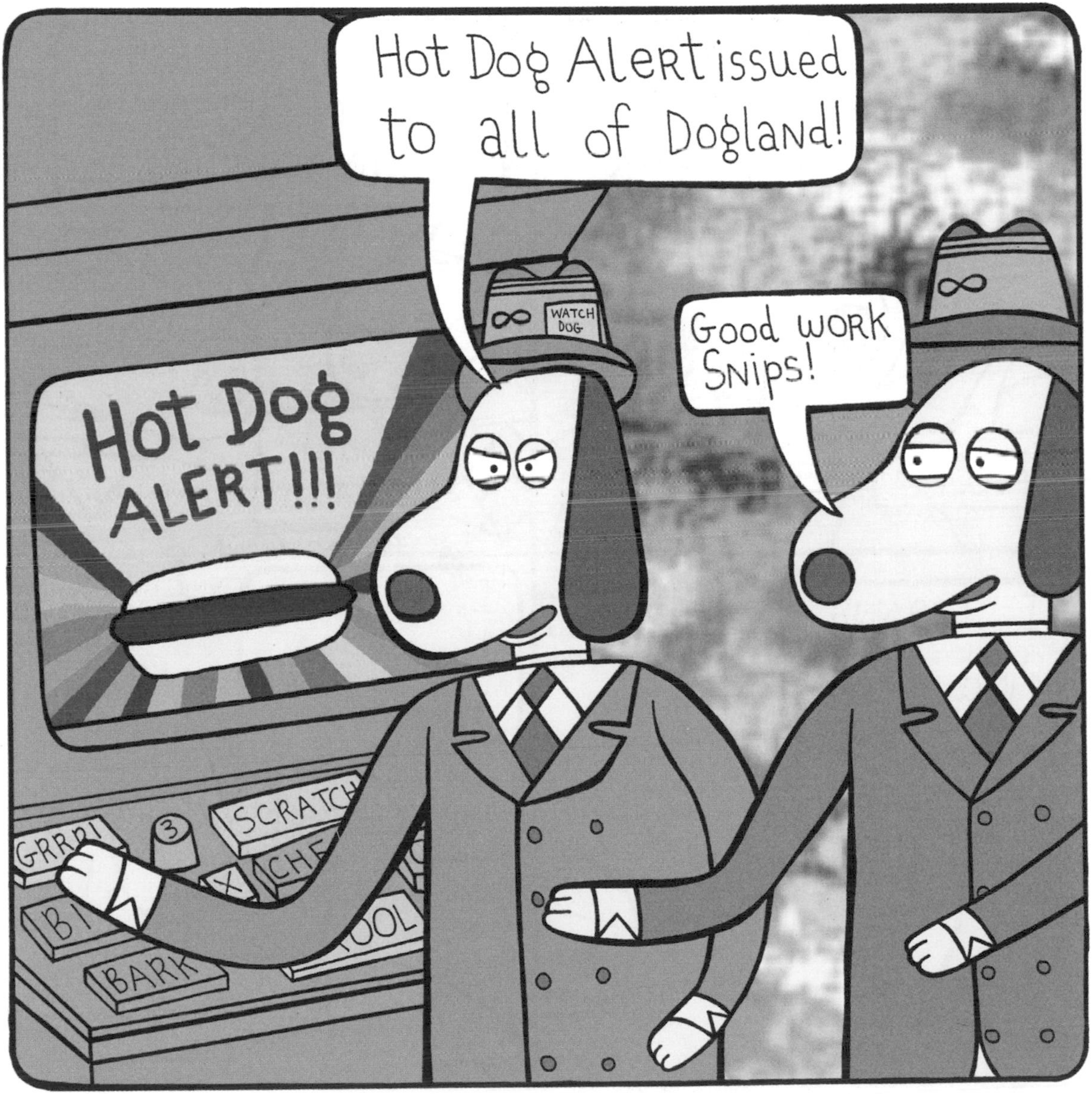
Hot Dog Alert issued to all of Dogland!
Good work Snips!
Hot Dog ALERT!!!
WATCH DOG
SCRATCH
BARK

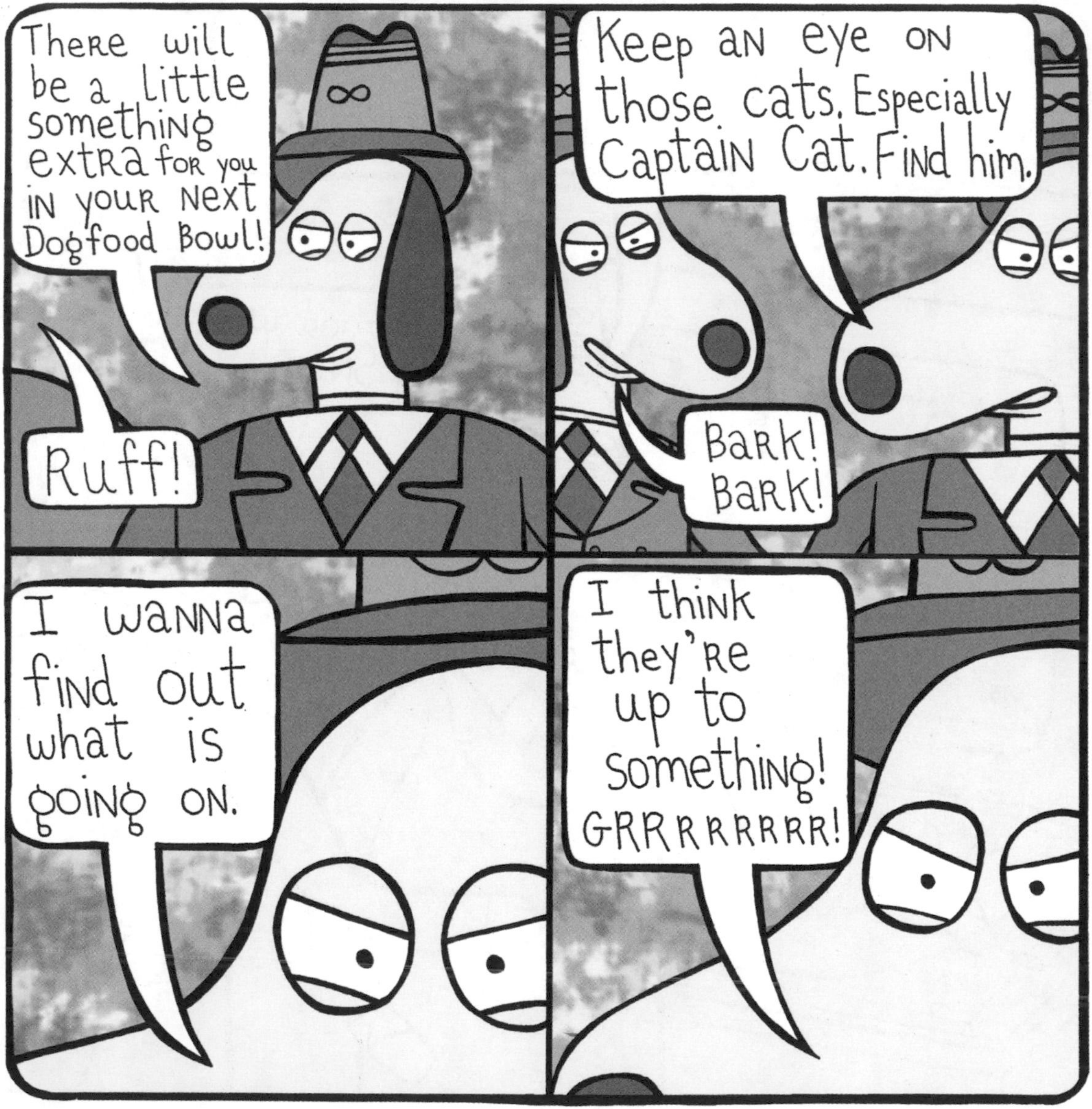
There will be a little something extra for you in your next Dogfood Bowl!
Ruff!
Keep an eye on those cats. Especially Captain Cat. Find him.
Bark! Bark!
I wanna find out what is going on.
I think they're up to something! GRRRRRRRR!

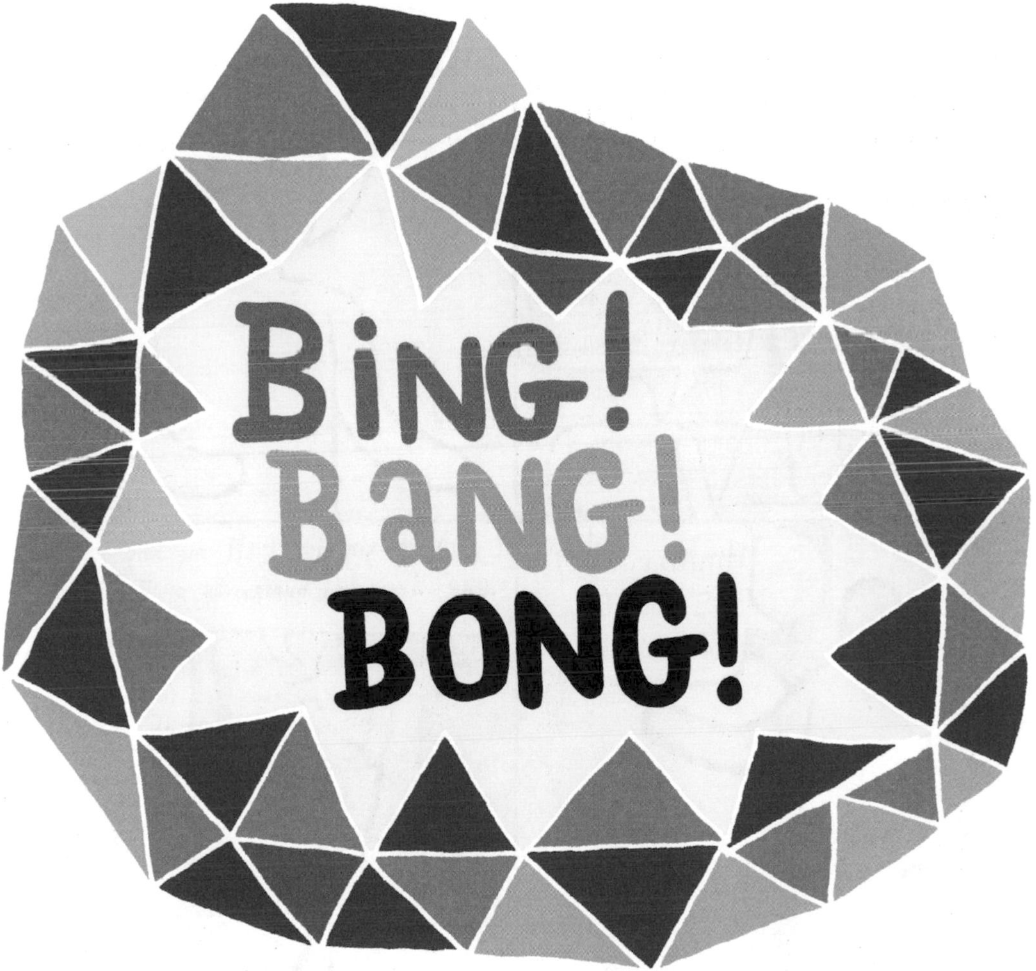
BiNG!
BaNG!
BONG!

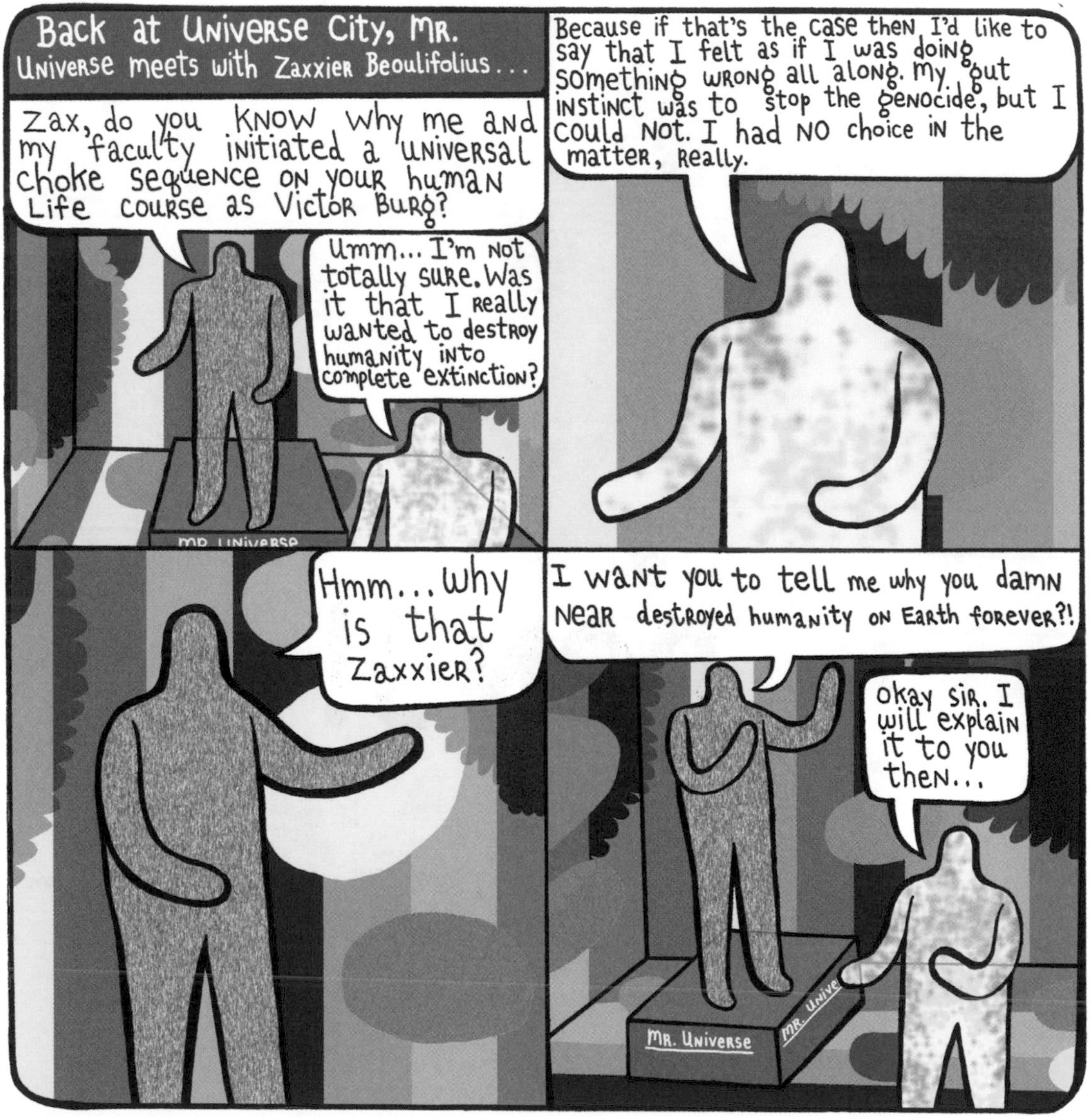
Back at Universe City, Mr. Universe meets with Zaxxier Beoulifolius...
Zax, do you know why me and my faculty initiated a universal choke sequence on your human life course as Victor Burg?
Umm... I'm not totally sure. Was it that I really wanted to destroy humanity into complete extinction?
Because if that's the case then I'd like to say that I felt as if I was doing something wrong all along. My gut instinct was to stop the genocide, but I could not. I had no choice in the matter, really.
Hmm... why is that Zaxxier?
I want you to tell me why you damn near destroyed humanity on Earth forever?!
Okay sir. I will explain it to you then...
Mr. Universe

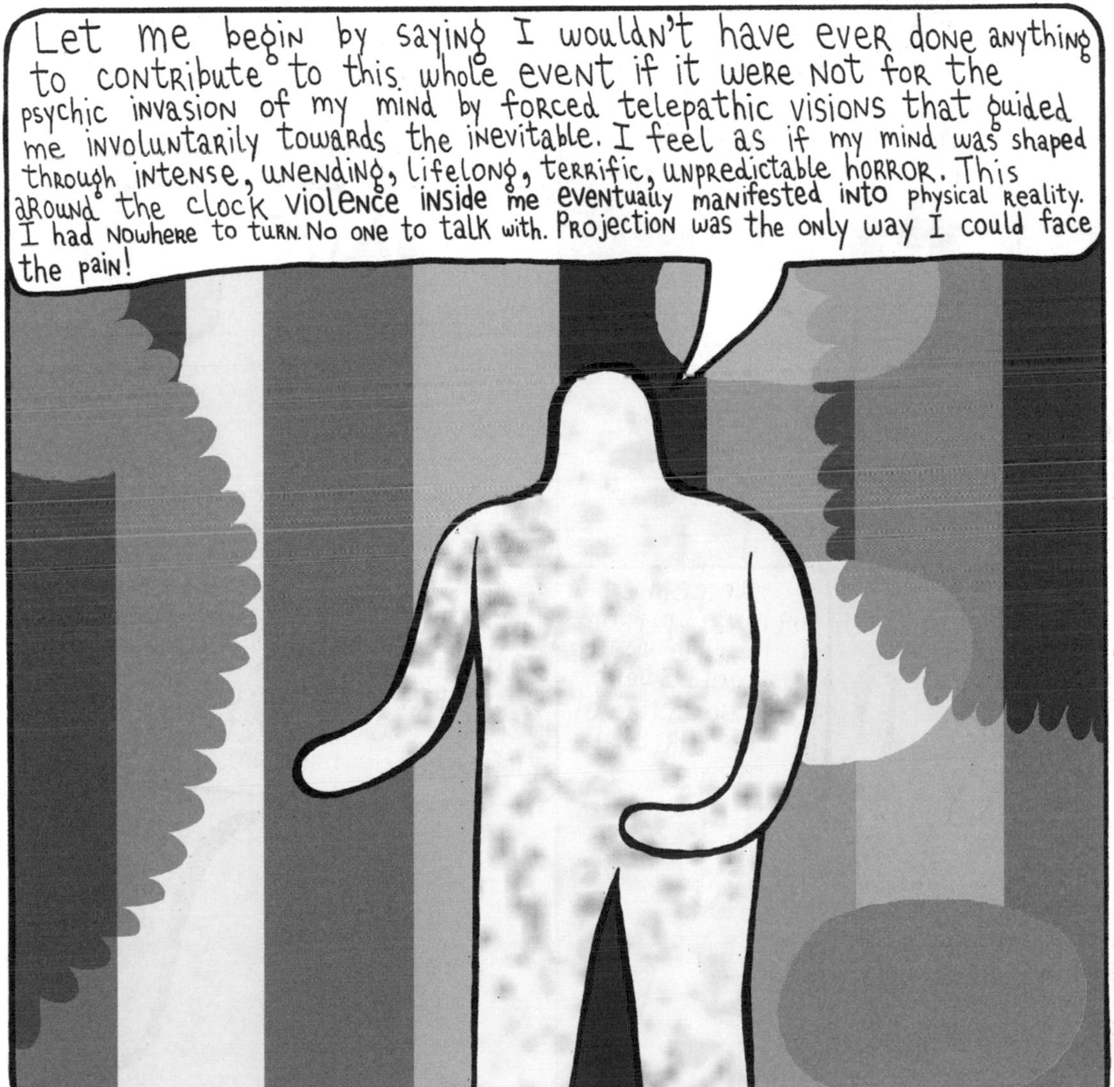
Let me begin by saying I wouldn't have ever done anything to contribute to this whole event if it were not for the psychic invasion of my mind by forced telepathic visions that guided me involuntarily towards the inevitable. I feel as if my mind was shaped through intense, unending, lifelong, terrific, unpredictable horror. This around the clock violence inside me eventually manifested into physical reality. I had nowhere to turn. No one to talk with. Projection was the only way I could face the pain!

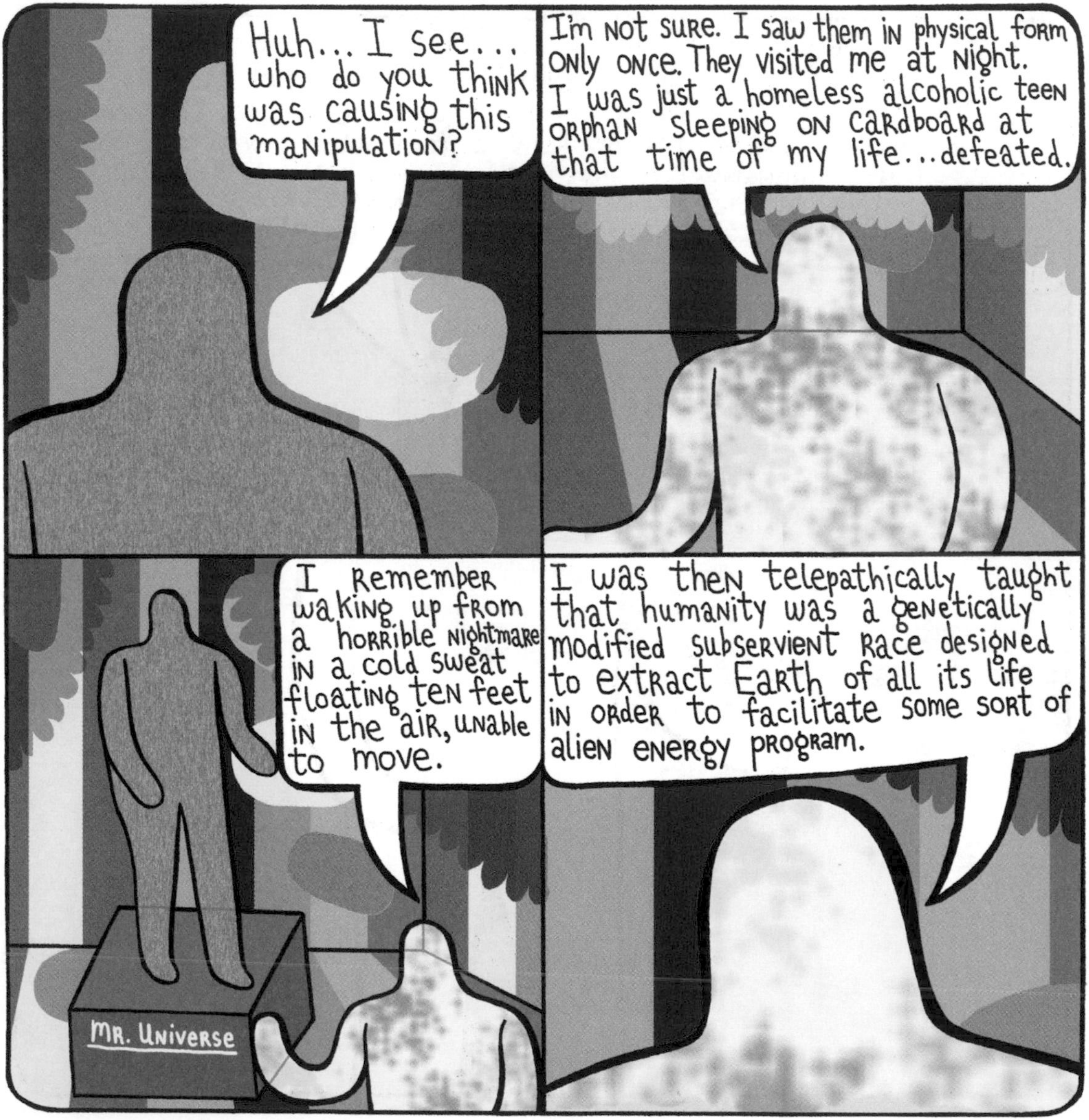
Huh... I see... who do you think was causing this manipulation?
I'm not sure. I saw them in physical form only once. They visited me at night. I was just a homeless alcoholic teen orphan sleeping on cardboard at that time of my life...defeated.
I remember waking up from a horrible nightmare in a cold sweat floating ten feet in the air, unable to move.
MR. UNIVERSE
I was then telepathically taught that humanity was a genetically modified subservient race designed to extract Earth of all its life in order to facilitate some sort of alien energy program.

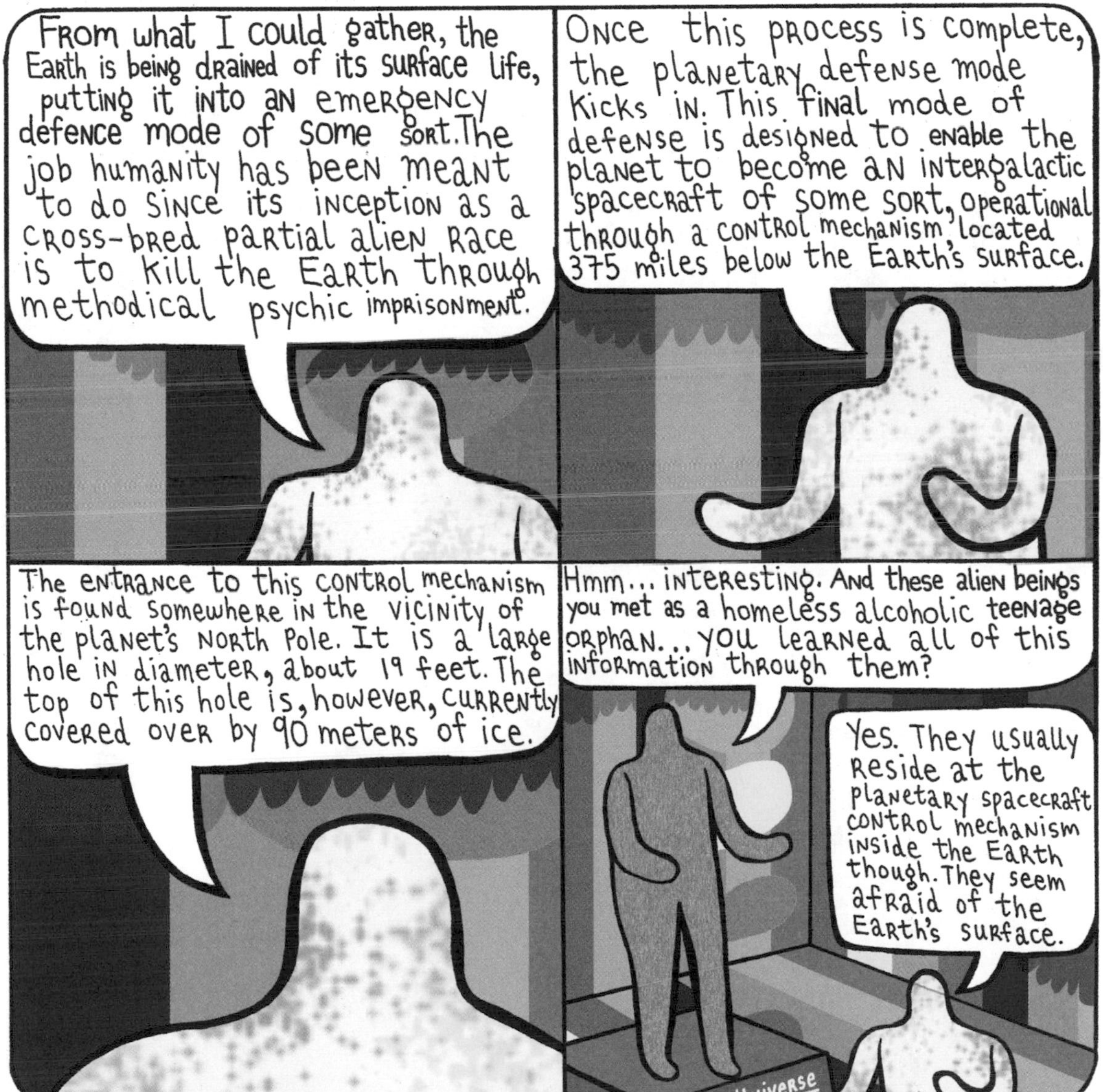
From what I could gather, the Earth is being drained of its surface life, putting it into an emergency defence mode of some sort. The job humanity has been meant to do since its inception as a cross-bred partial alien race is to kill the Earth through methodical psychic imprisonment.
Once this process is complete, the planetary defense mode kicks in. This final mode of defense is designed to enable the planet to become an intergalactic spacecraft of some sort, operational through a control mechanism, located 375 miles below the Earth's surface.
The entrance to this control mechanism is found somewhere in the vicinity of the planet's North Pole. It is a large hole in diameter, about 19 feet. The top of this hole is, however, currently covered over by 90 meters of ice.
Hmm... interesting. And these alien beings you met as a homeless alcoholic teenage orphan... you learned all of this information through them?
Yes. They usually reside at the planetary spacecraft control mechanism inside the Earth though. They seem afraid of the Earth's surface.
Universe

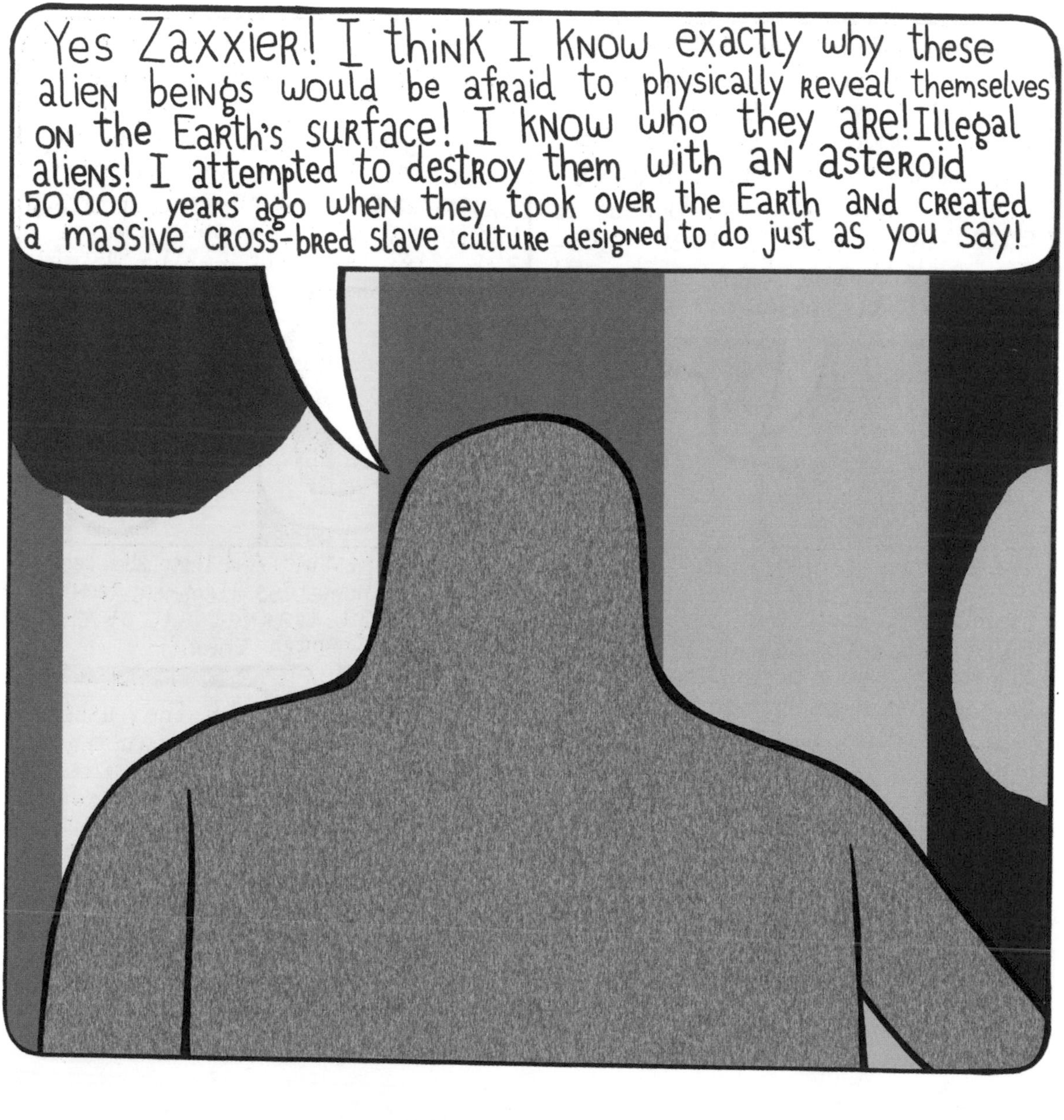
Yes Zaxxier! I think I know exactly why these alien beings would be afraid to physically reveal themselves on the Earth's surface! I know who they are! Illegal aliens! I attempted to destroy them with an asteroid 50,000 years ago when they took over the Earth and created a massive cross-bred slave culture designed to do just as you say!

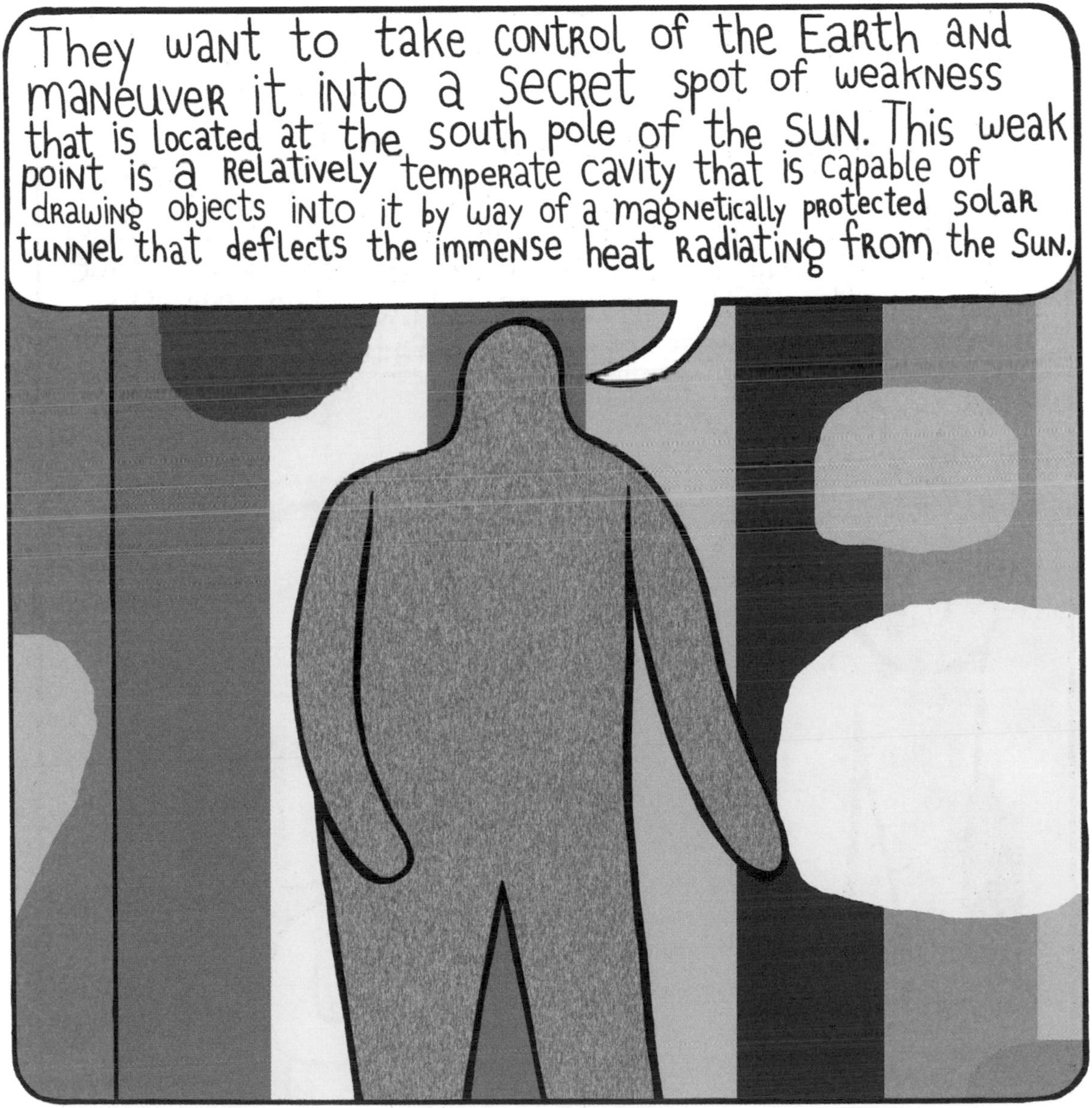
They want to take control of the Earth and maneuver it into a secret spot of weakness that is located at the south pole of the sun. This weak point is a relatively temperate cavity that is capable of drawing objects into it by way of a magnetically protected solar tunnel that deflects the immense heat radiating from the sun.

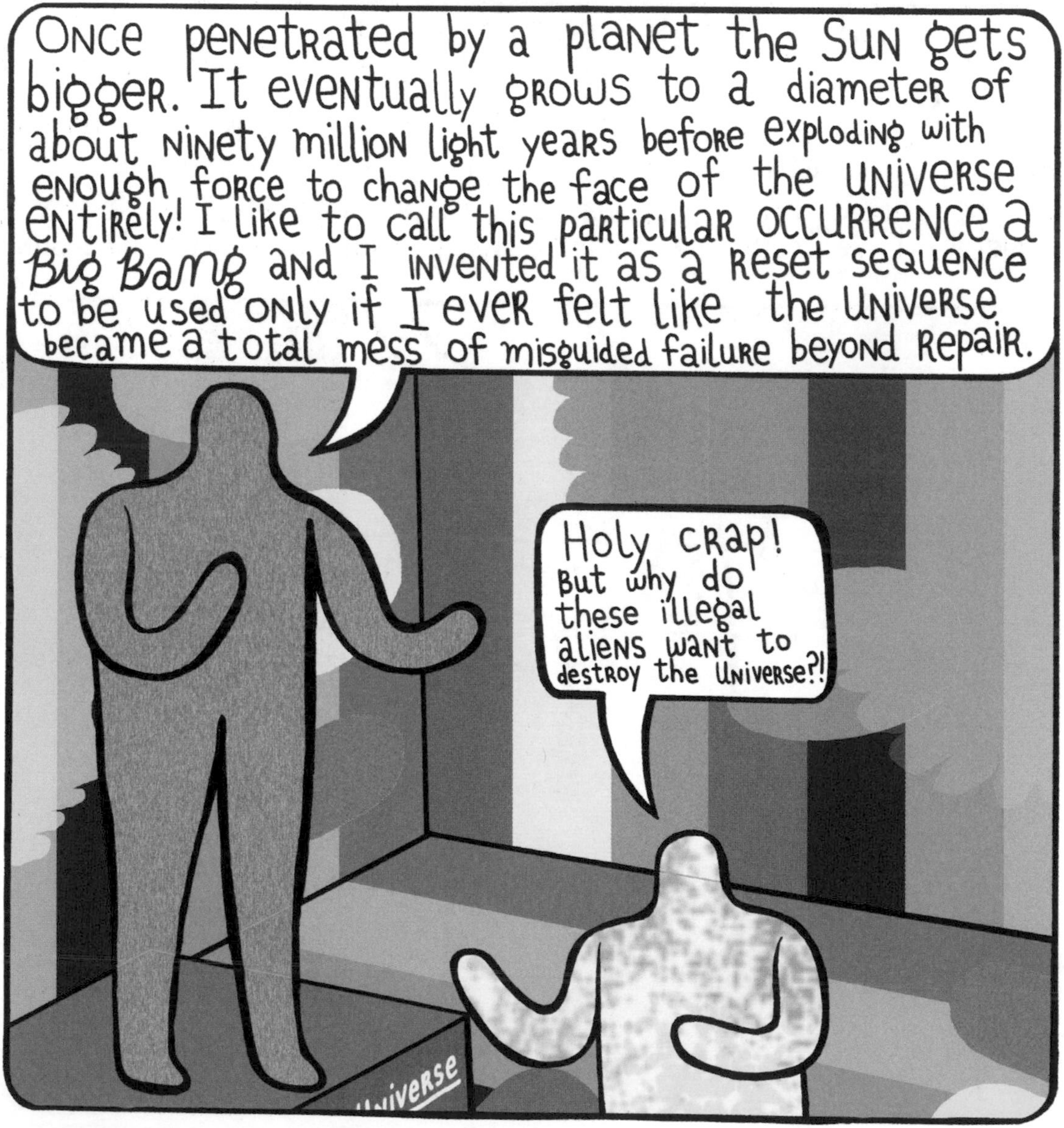
Once penetrated by a planet the Sun gets bigger. It eventually grows to a diameter of about ninety million light years before exploding with enough force to change the face of the universe entirely! I like to call this particular occurrence a *Big Bang* and I invented it as a reset sequence to be used only if I ever felt like the universe became a total mess of misguided failure beyond repair.
Holy crap! But why do these illegal aliens want to destroy the Universe?!
Universe

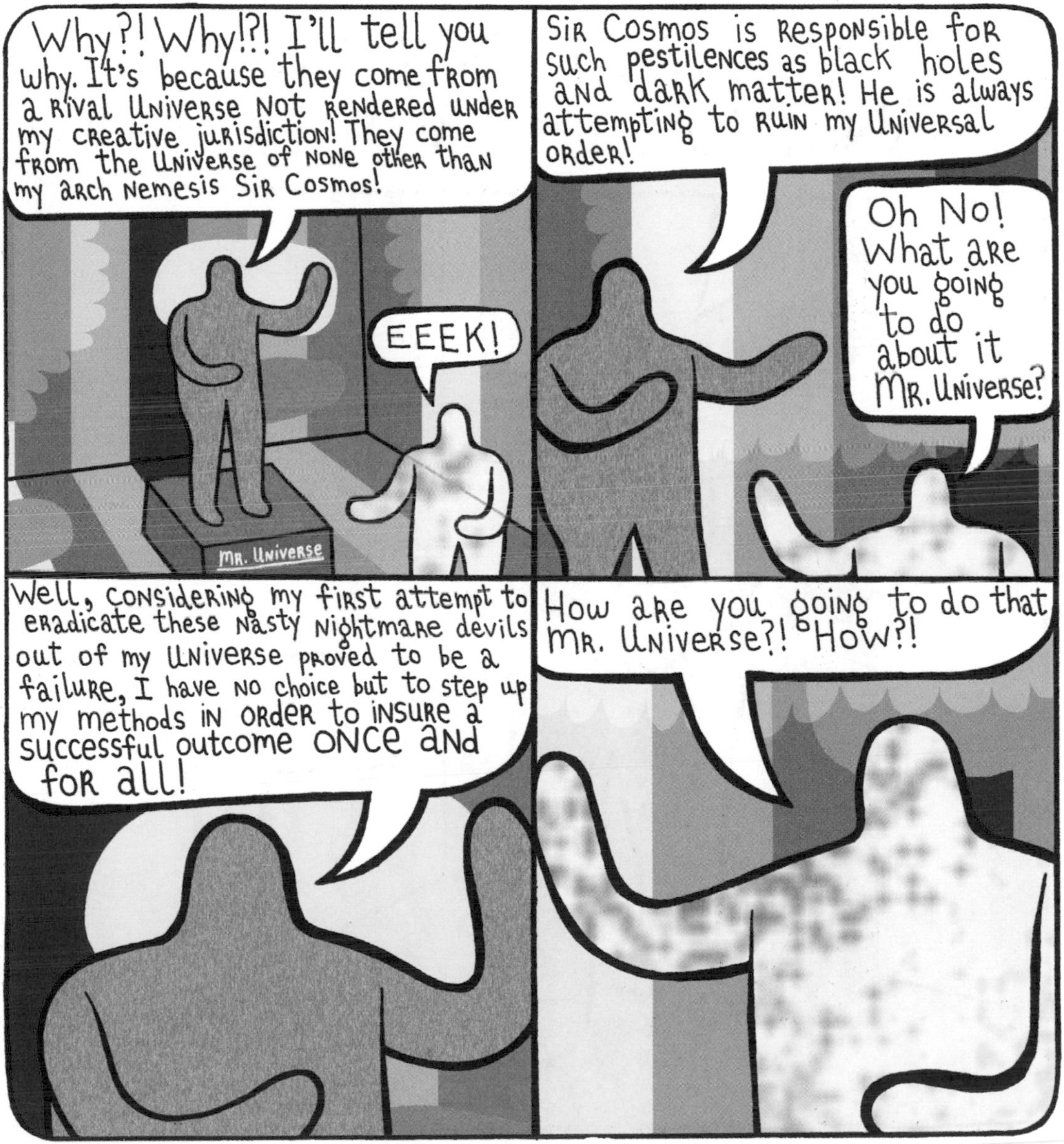
Why?! Why!?! I'll tell you why. It's because they come from a rival Universe not rendered under my creative jurisdiction! They come from the Universe of none other than my arch nemesis Sir Cosmos!
EEEK!
Sir Cosmos is responsible for such pestilences as black holes and dark matter! He is always attempting to ruin my Universal order!
Oh No! What are you going to do about it Mr. Universe?
MR. UNIVERSE
Well, considering my first attempt to eradicate these nasty nightmare devils out of my Universe proved to be a failure, I have no choice but to step up my methods in order to insure a successful outcome ONCE AND FOR ALL!
How are you going to do that Mr. Universe?! How?!

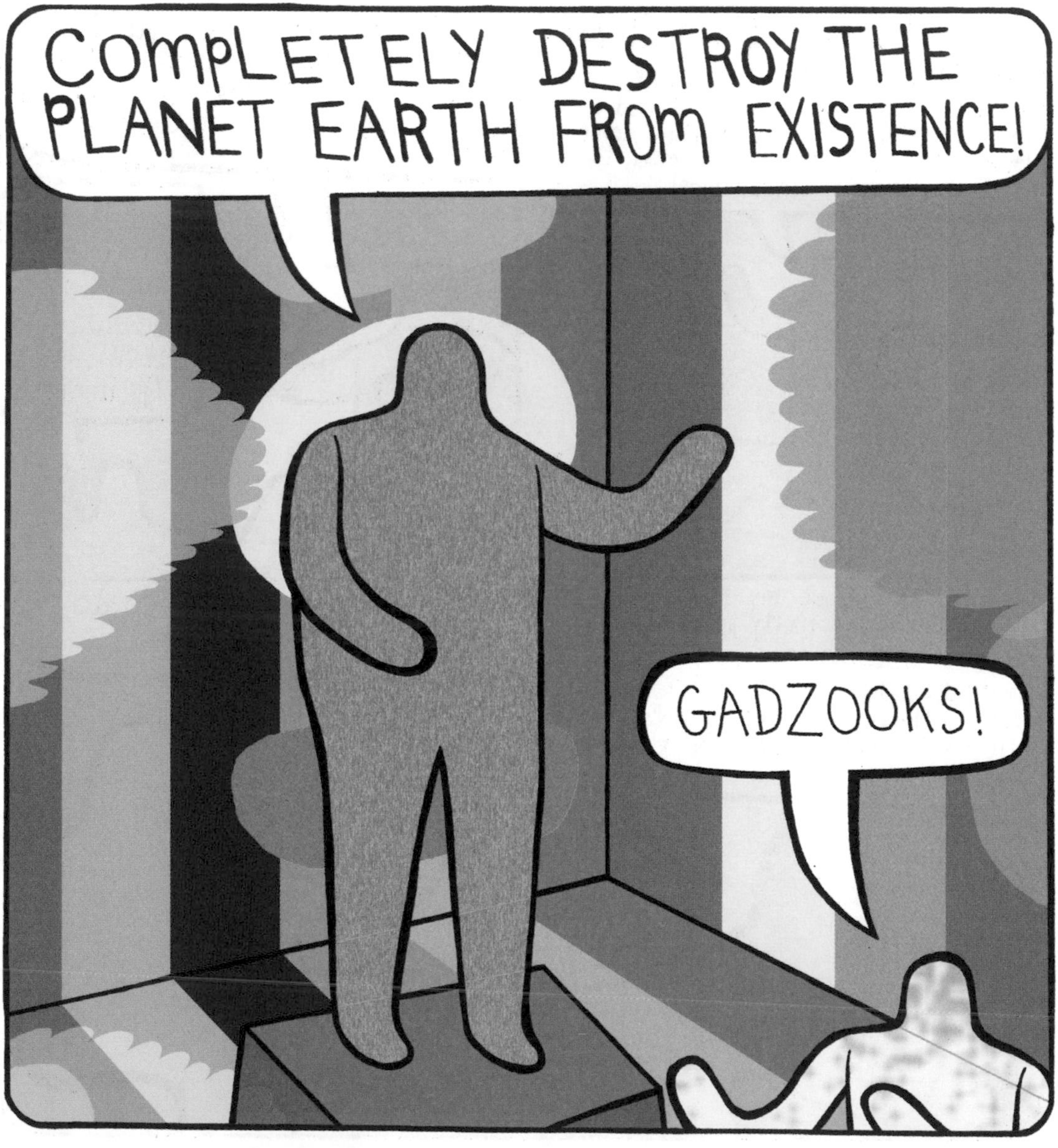
COMPLETELY DESTROY THE PLANET EARTH FROM EXISTENCE!
GADZOOKS!

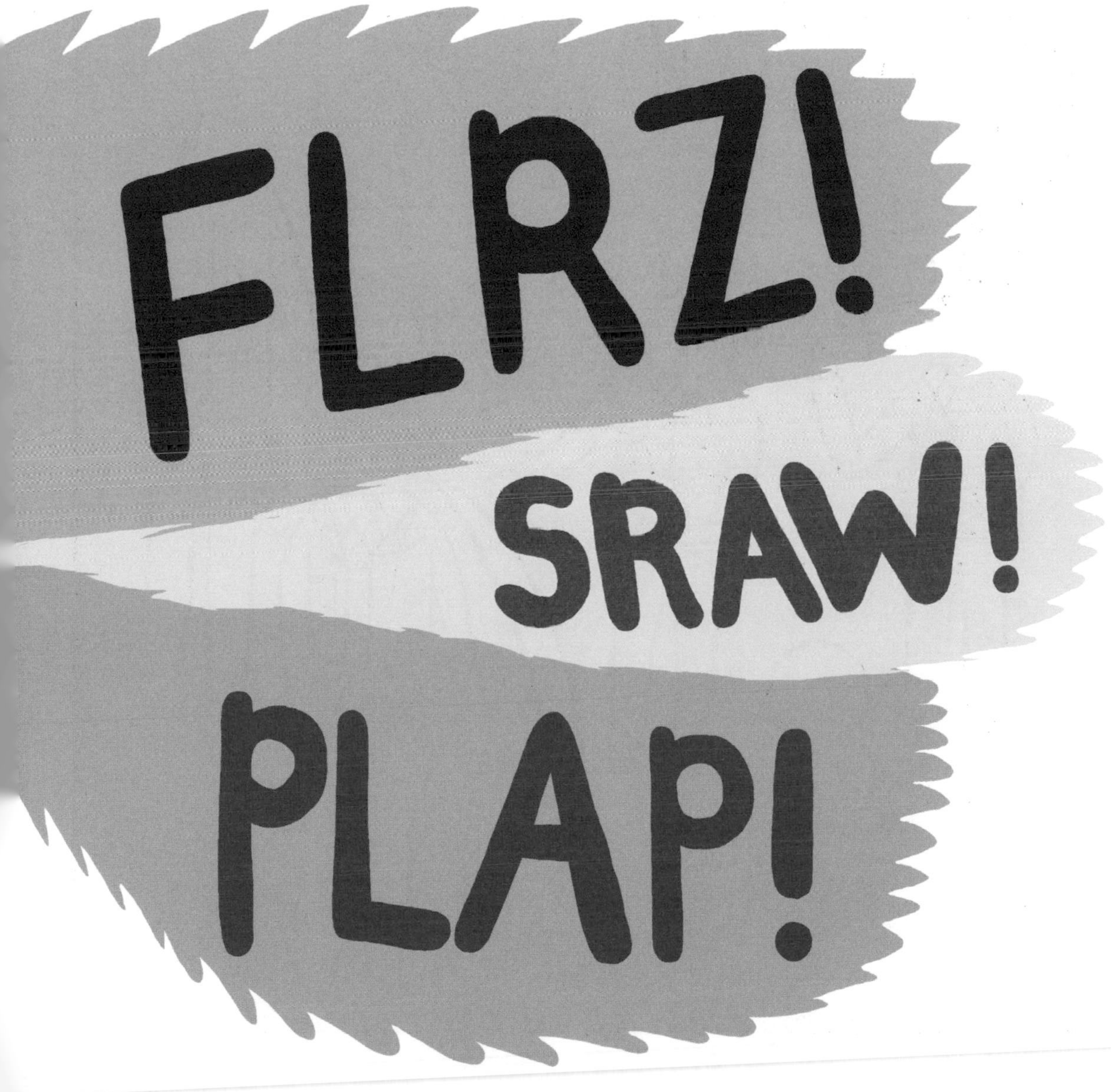
FLRZ!
SRAW!
PLAP!

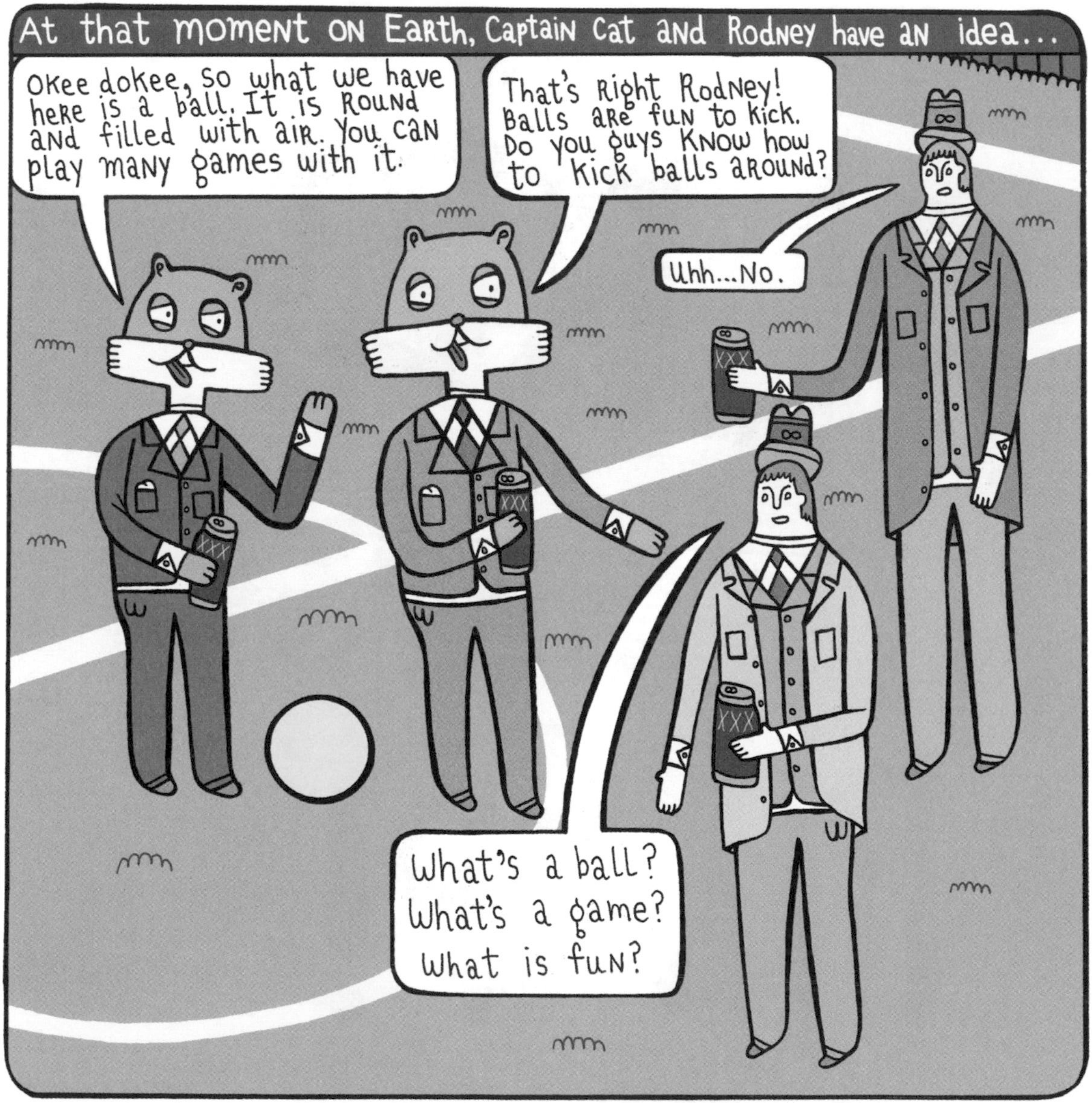
At that moment on Earth, Captain Cat and Rodney have an idea...
Okee dokee, so what we have here is a ball. It is round and filled with air. You can play many games with it.
That's right Rodney! Balls are fun to kick. Do you guys know how to kick balls around?
Uhh...No.
What's a ball? What's a game? What is fun?

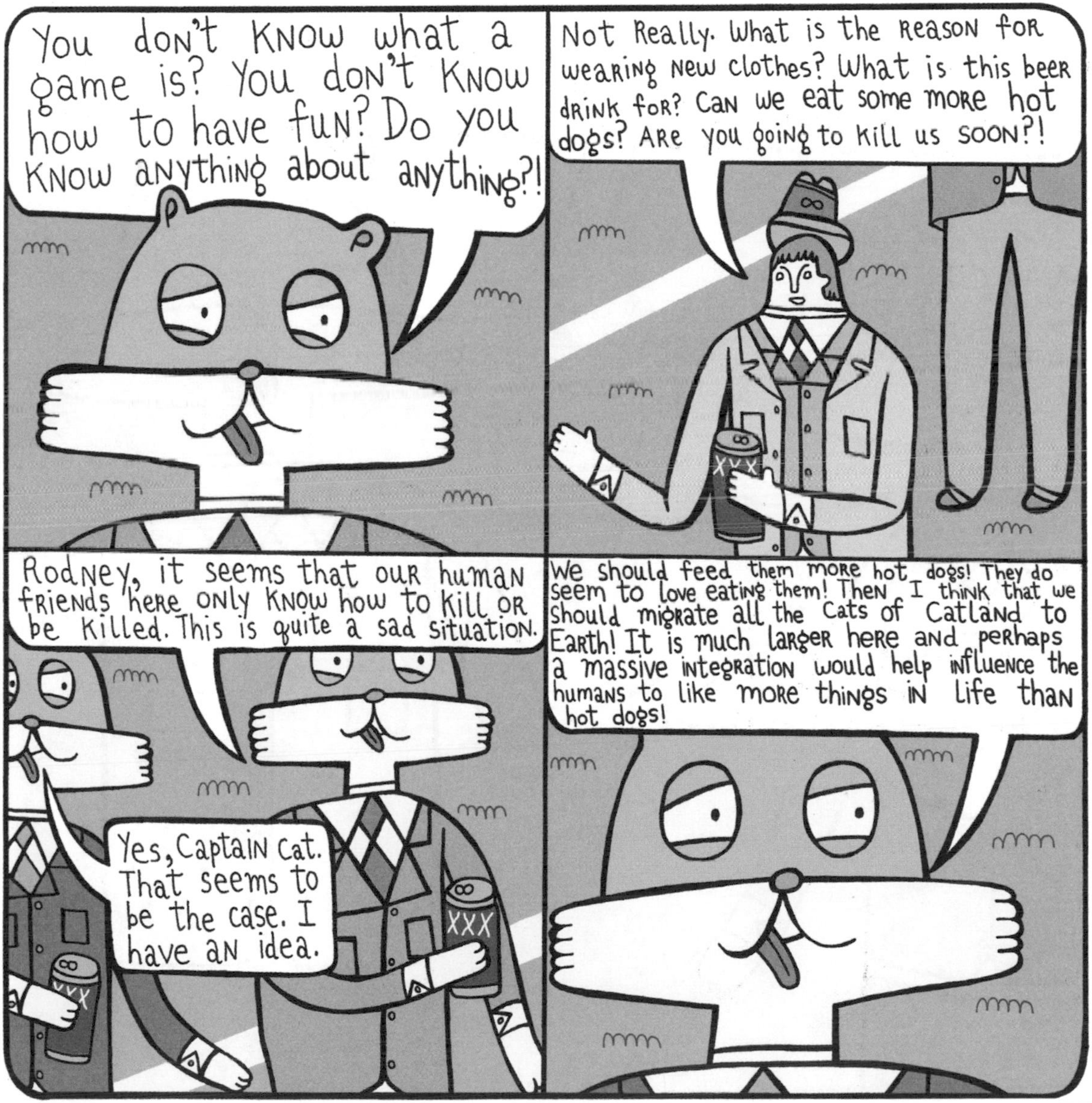
You don't know what a game is? You don't know how to have fun? Do you know anything about anything?!
Not really. What is the reason for wearing new clothes? What is this beer drink for? Can we eat some more hot dogs? Are you going to kill us soon?!
Rodney, it seems that our human friends here only know how to kill or be killed. This is quite a sad situation.
Yes, Captain Cat. That seems to be the case. I have an idea.
We should feed them more hot dogs! They do seem to love eating them! Then I think that we should migrate all the cats of Catland to Earth! It is much larger here and perhaps a massive integration would help influence the humans to like more things in life than hot dogs!

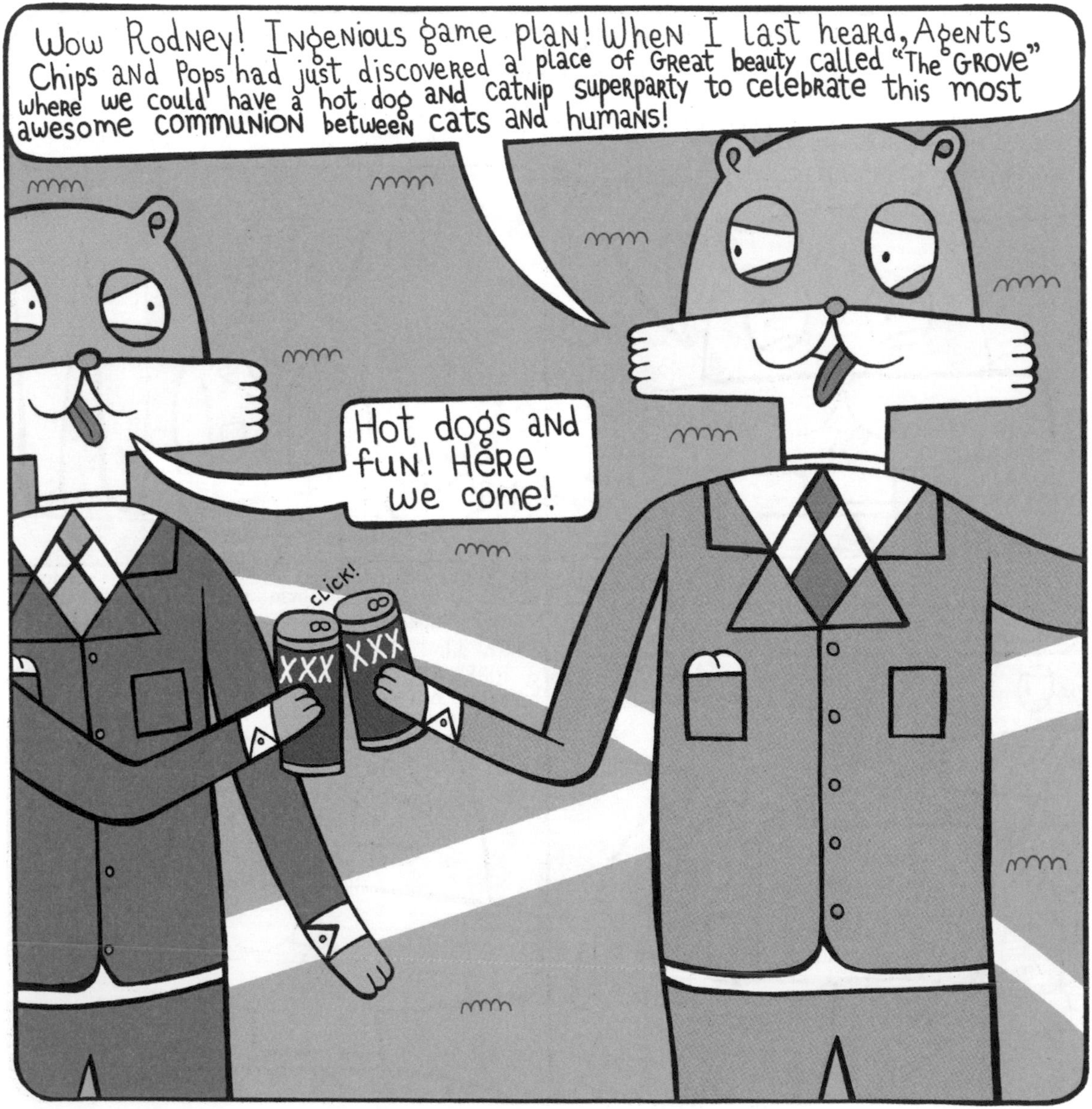
Wow Rodney! Ingenious game plan! When I last heard, Agents Chips and Pops had just discovered a place of great beauty called "The Grove" where we could have a hot dog and catnip superparty to celebrate this most awesome communion between cats and humans!
Hot dogs and fun! Here we come!
CLICK!
XXX
XXX

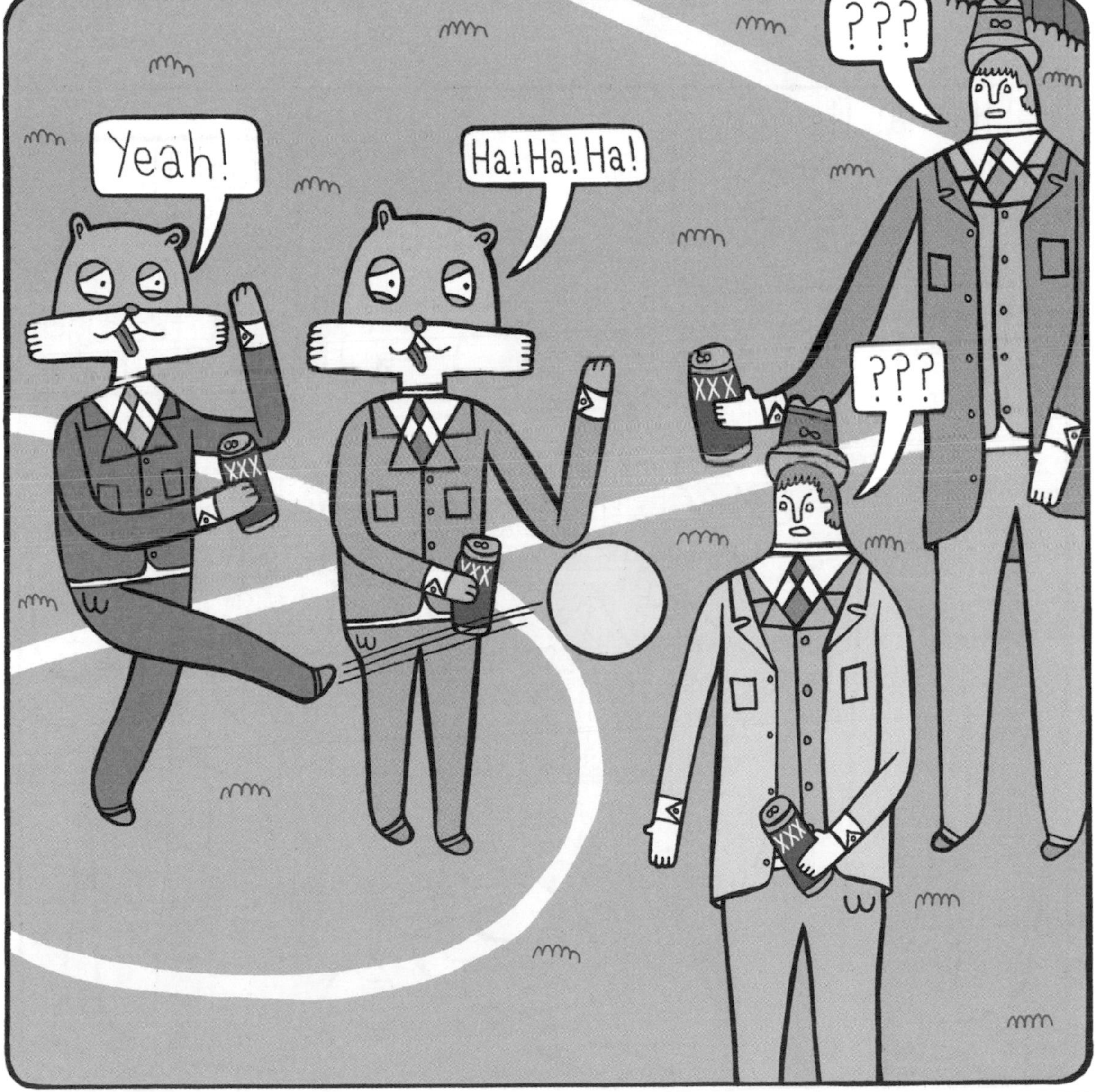
Yeah!
Ha! Ha! Ha!
???
???

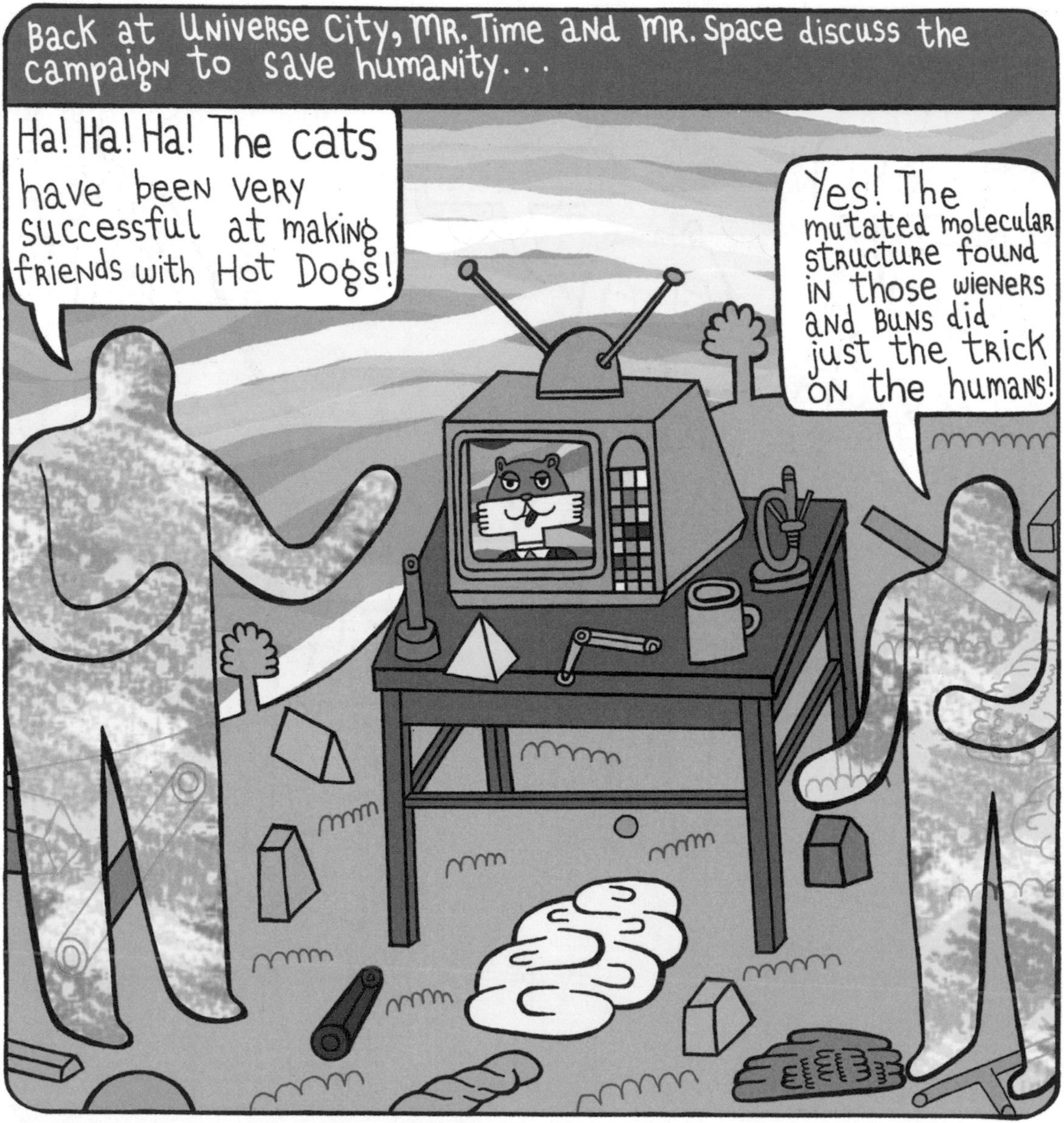
Back at Universe City, Mr. Time and Mr. Space discuss the campaign to save humanity...
Ha! Ha! Ha! The cats have been very successful at making friends with Hot Dogs!
Yes! The mutated molecular structure found in those wieners and buns did just the trick on the humans!

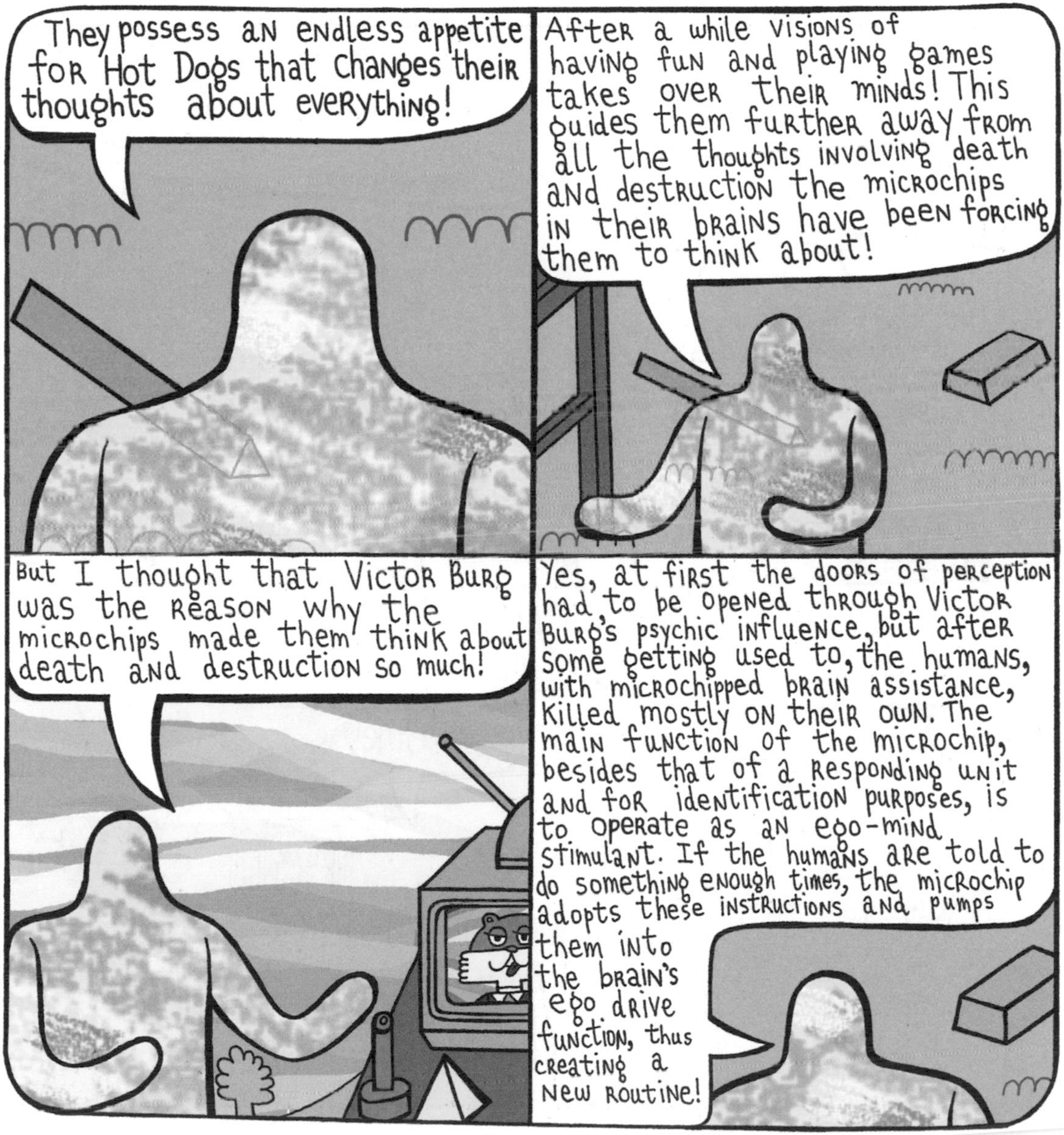
They possess an endless appetite for Hot Dogs that changes their thoughts about everything!
After a while visions of having fun and playing games takes over their minds! This guides them further away from all the thoughts involving death and destruction the microchips in their brains have been forcing them to think about!
But I thought that Victor Burg was the reason why the microchips made them think about death and destruction so much!
Yes, at first the doors of perception had to be opened through Victor Burg's psychic influence, but after some getting used to, the humans, with microchipped brain assistance, killed mostly on their own. The main function of the microchip, besides that of a responding unit and for identification purposes, is to operate as an ego-mind stimulant. If the humans are told to do something enough times, the microchip adopts these instructions and pumps them into the brain's ego drive function, thus creating a new routine!

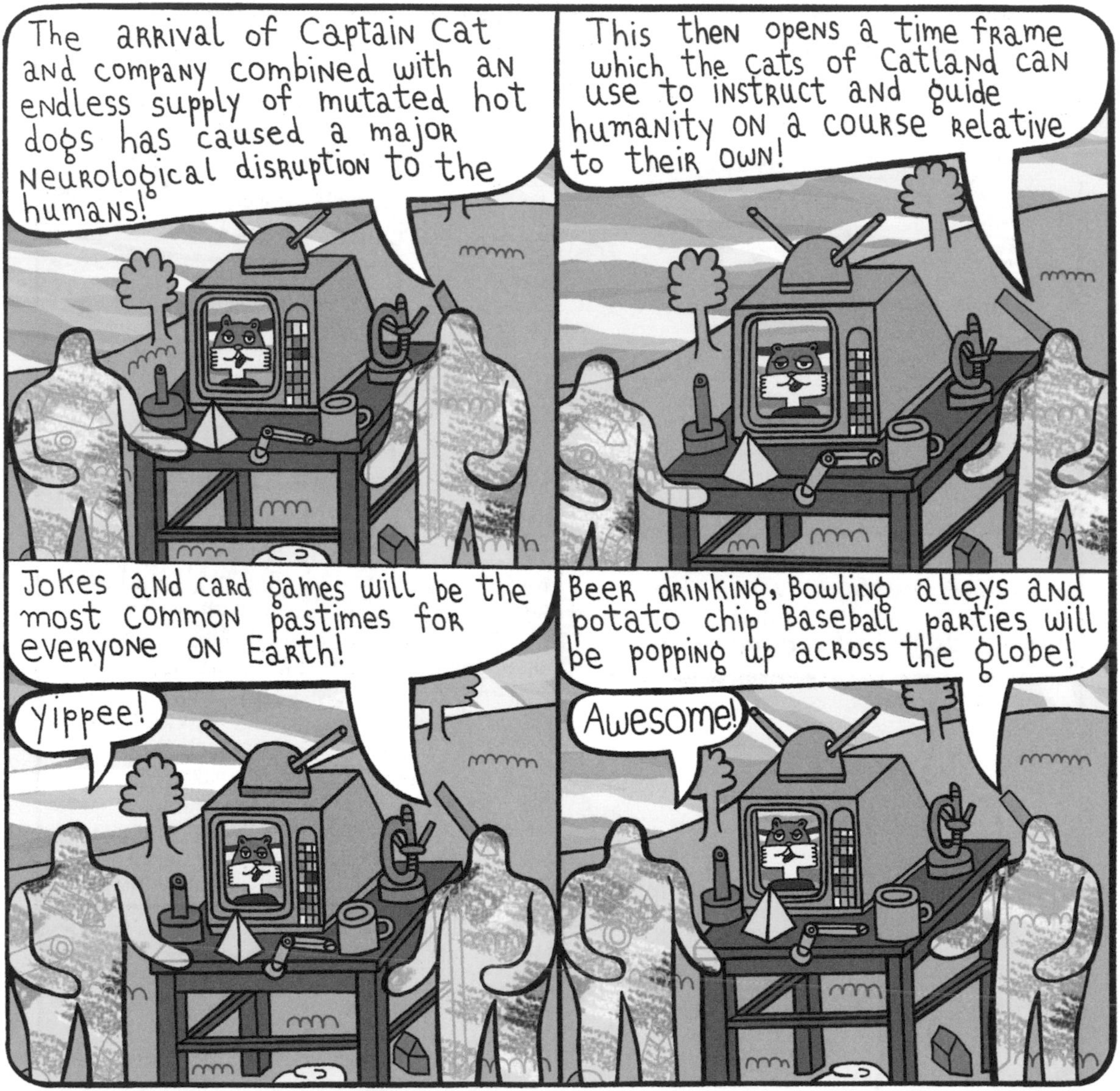
The arrival of Captain Cat and company combined with an endless supply of mutated hot dogs has caused a major neurological disruption to the humans!
This then opens a time frame which the cats of Catland can use to instruct and guide humanity on a course relative to their own!
Jokes and card games will be the most common pastimes for everyone on Earth!
Yippee!
Beer drinking, bowling alleys and potato chip baseball parties will be popping up across the globe!
Awesome!

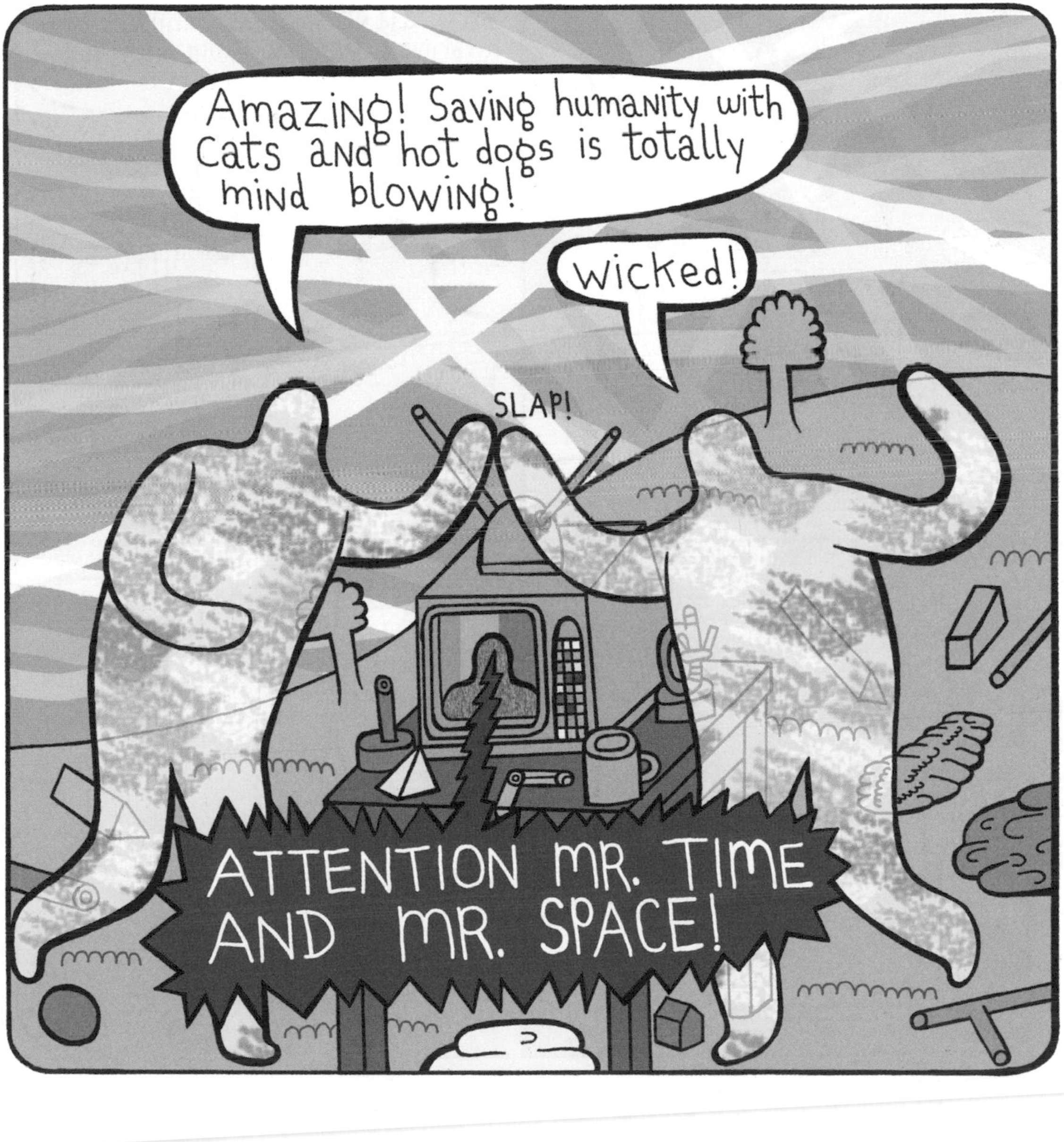
Amazing! Saving humanity with cats and hot dogs is totally mind blowing!
Wicked!
SLAP!
ATTENTION MR. TIME AND MR. SPACE!

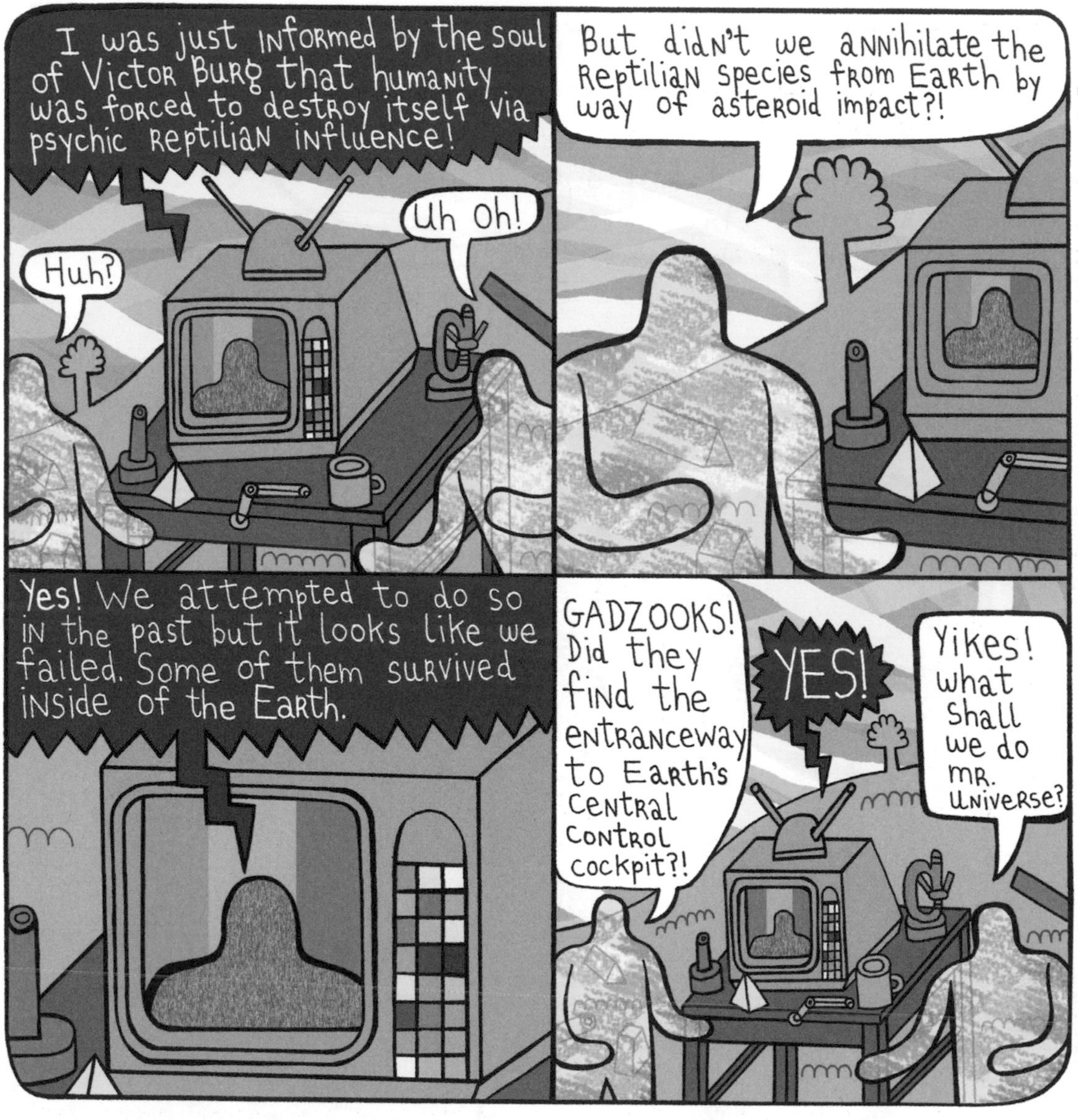
I was just informed by the soul of Victor Burg that humanity was forced to destroy itself via psychic Reptilian influence!
Huh?
Uh Oh!
But didn't we annihilate the Reptilian species from Earth by way of asteroid impact?!
Yes! We attempted to do so in the past but it looks like we failed. Some of them survived inside of the Earth.
GADZOOKS! Did they find the entranceway to Earth's central control cockpit?!
YES!
Yikes! what shall we do mr. Universe?

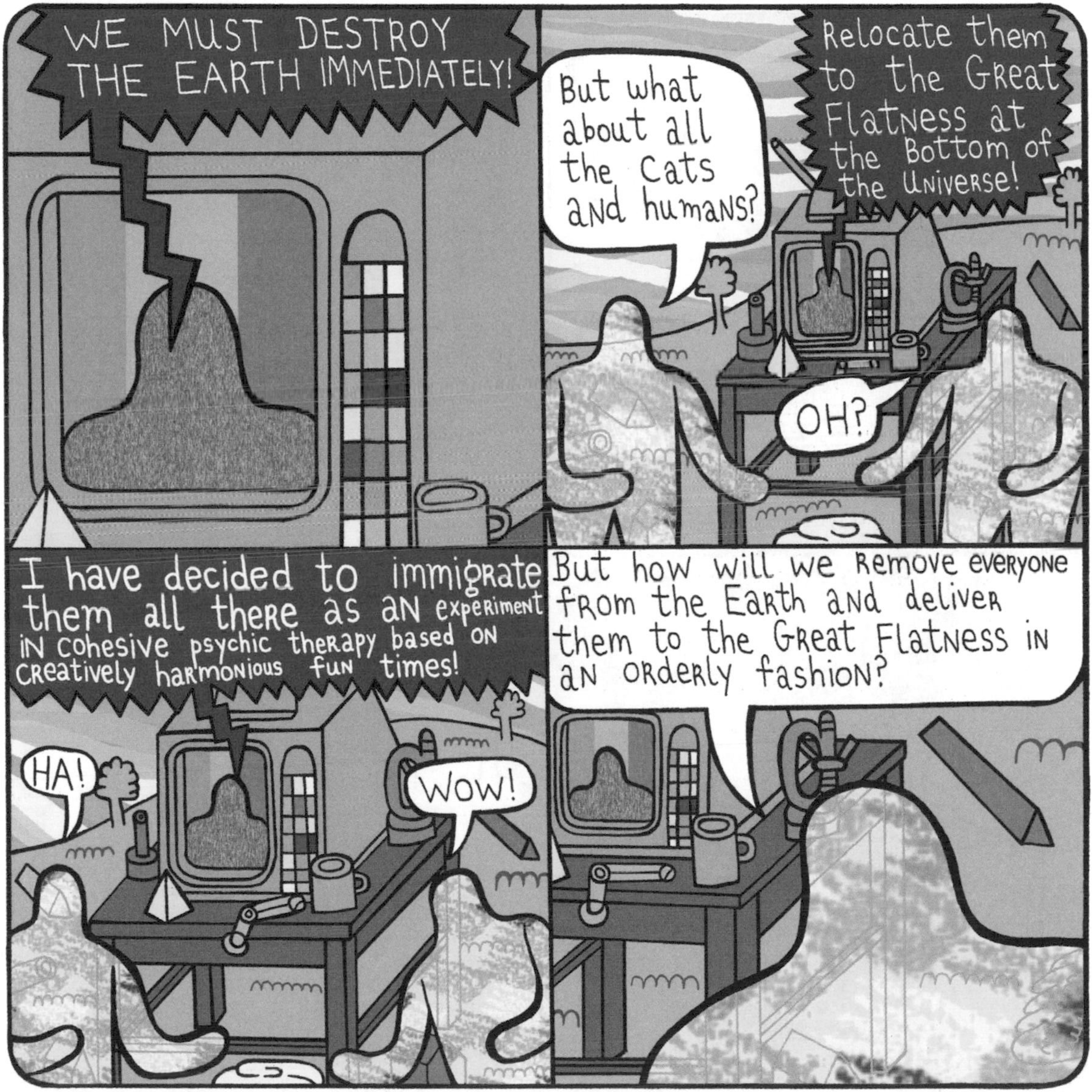
WE MUST DESTROY THE EARTH IMMEDIATELY!
But what about all the cats and humans?
Relocate them to the Great Flatness at the Bottom of the Universe!
OH?
I have decided to immigrate them all there as an experiment in cohesive psychic therapy based on creatively harmonious fun times!
HA!
WOW!
But how will we remove everyone from the Earth and deliver them to the Great Flatness in an orderly fashion?

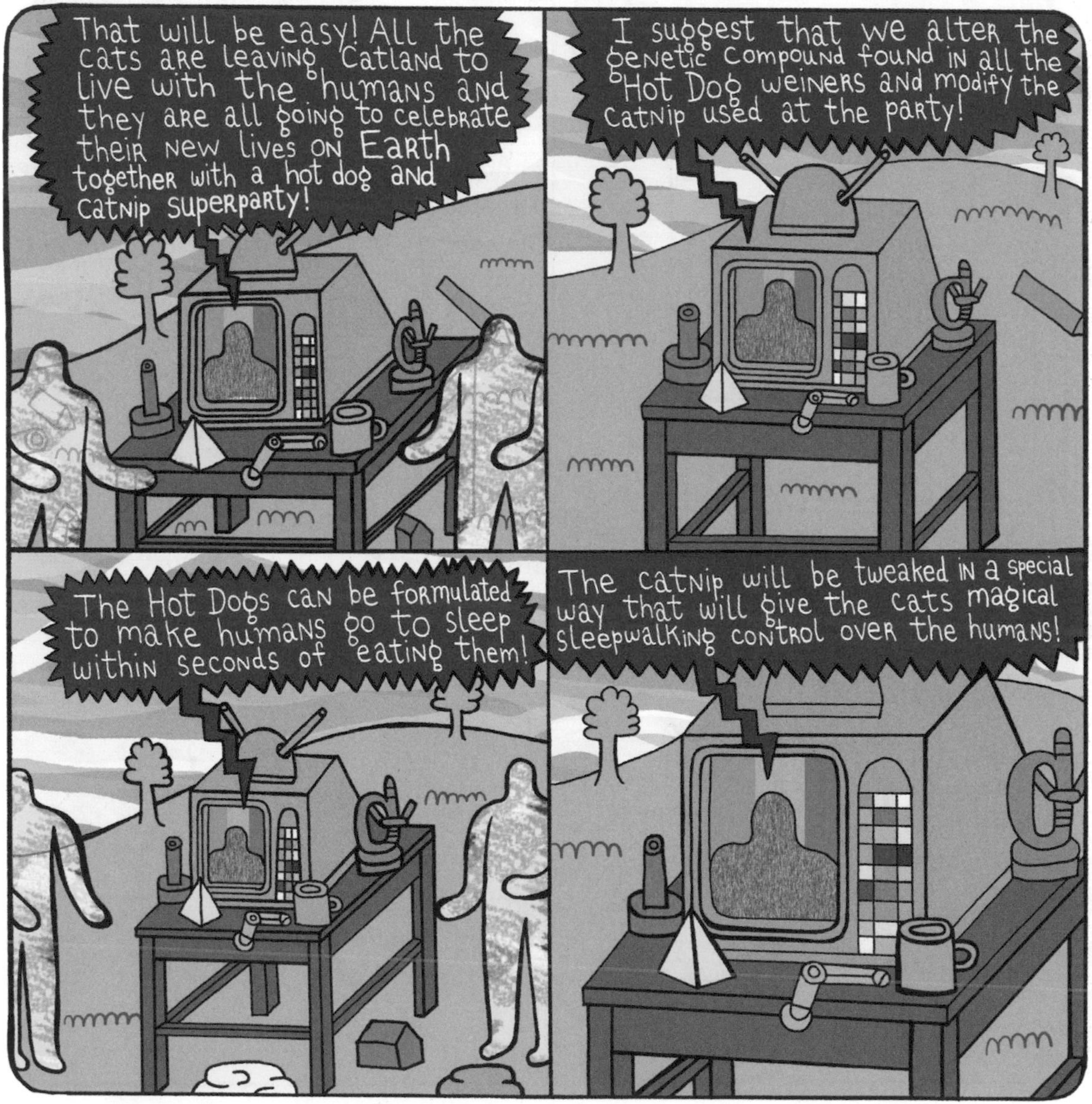
That will be easy! All the cats are leaving Catland to live with the humans and they are all going to celebrate their new lives on Earth together with a hot dog and catnip superparty!
I suggest that we alter the genetic compound found in all the Hot Dog weiners and modify the catnip used at the party!
The Hot Dogs can be formulated to make humans go to sleep within seconds of eating them!
The catnip will be tweaked in a special way that will give the cats magical sleepwalking control over the humans!

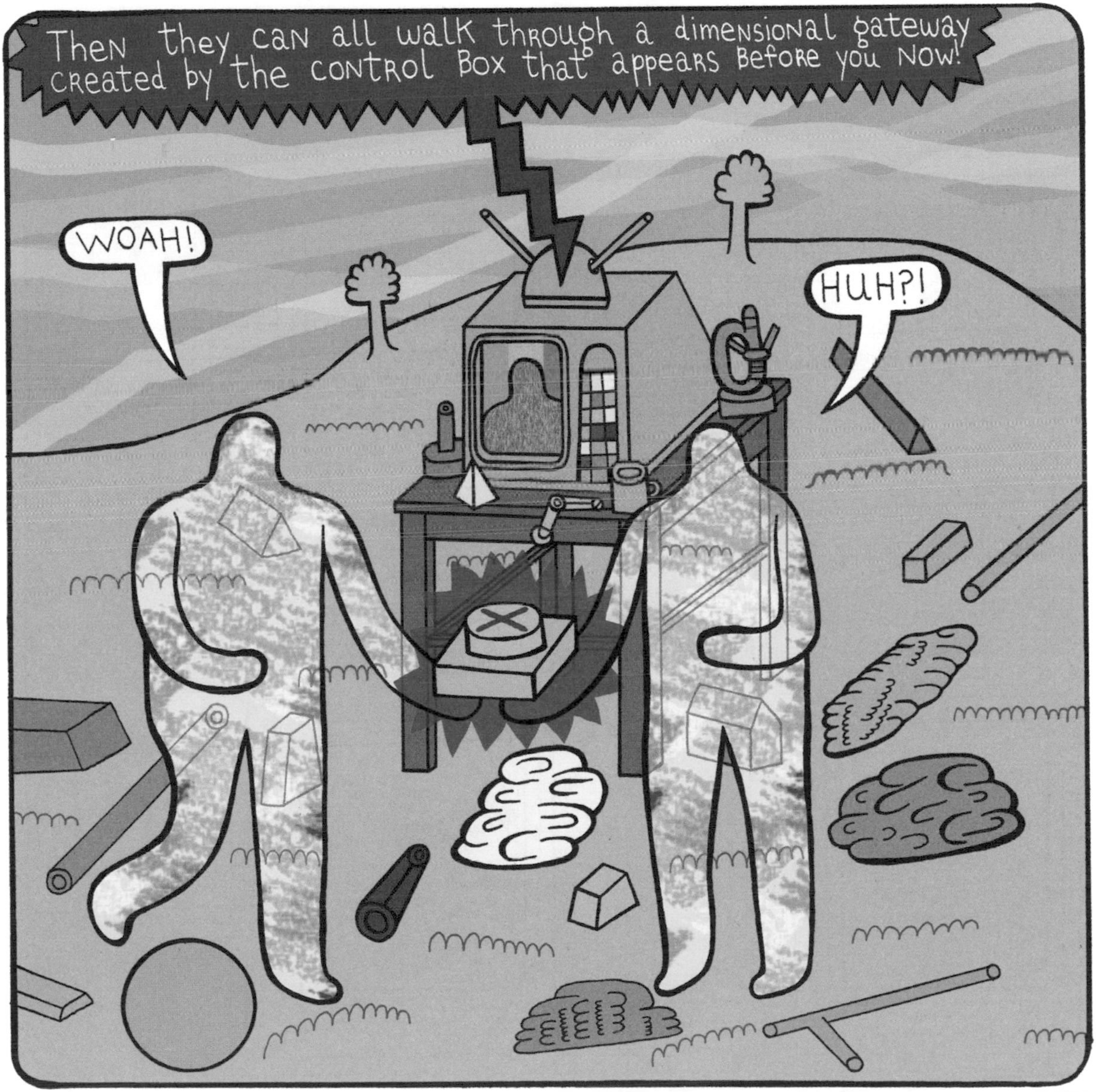
Then they can all walk through a dimensional gateway created by the control box that appears before you now!
WOAH!
HUH?!

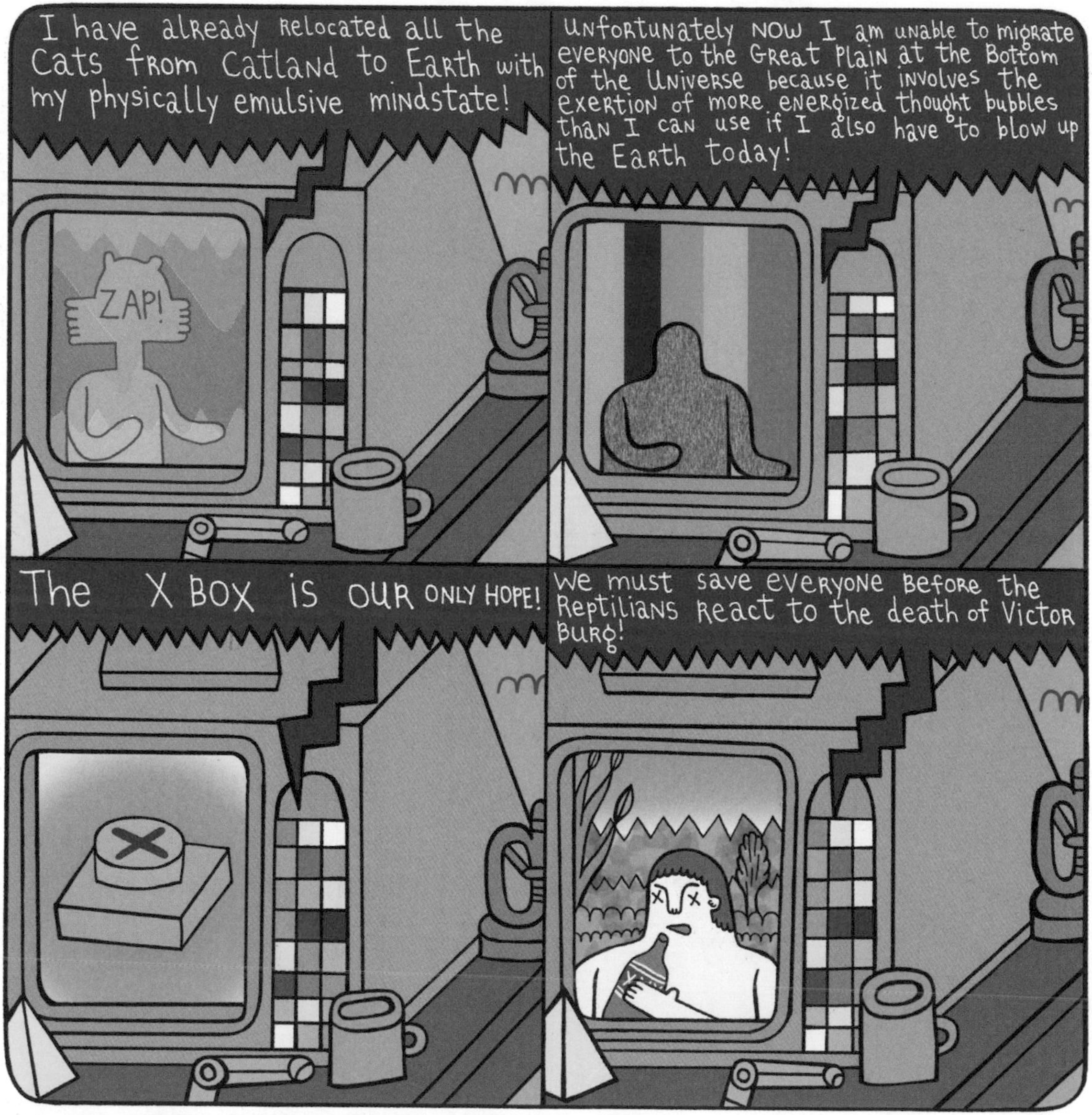
I have already relocated all the Cats from Catland to Earth with my physically emulsive mindstate!
ZAP!
Unfortunately now I am unable to migrate everyone to the Great Plain at the Bottom of the Universe because it involves the exertion of more energized thought bubbles than I can use if I also have to blow up the Earth today!
The X BOX is OUR ONLY HOPE!
We must save everyone before the Reptilians react to the death of Victor Burg!

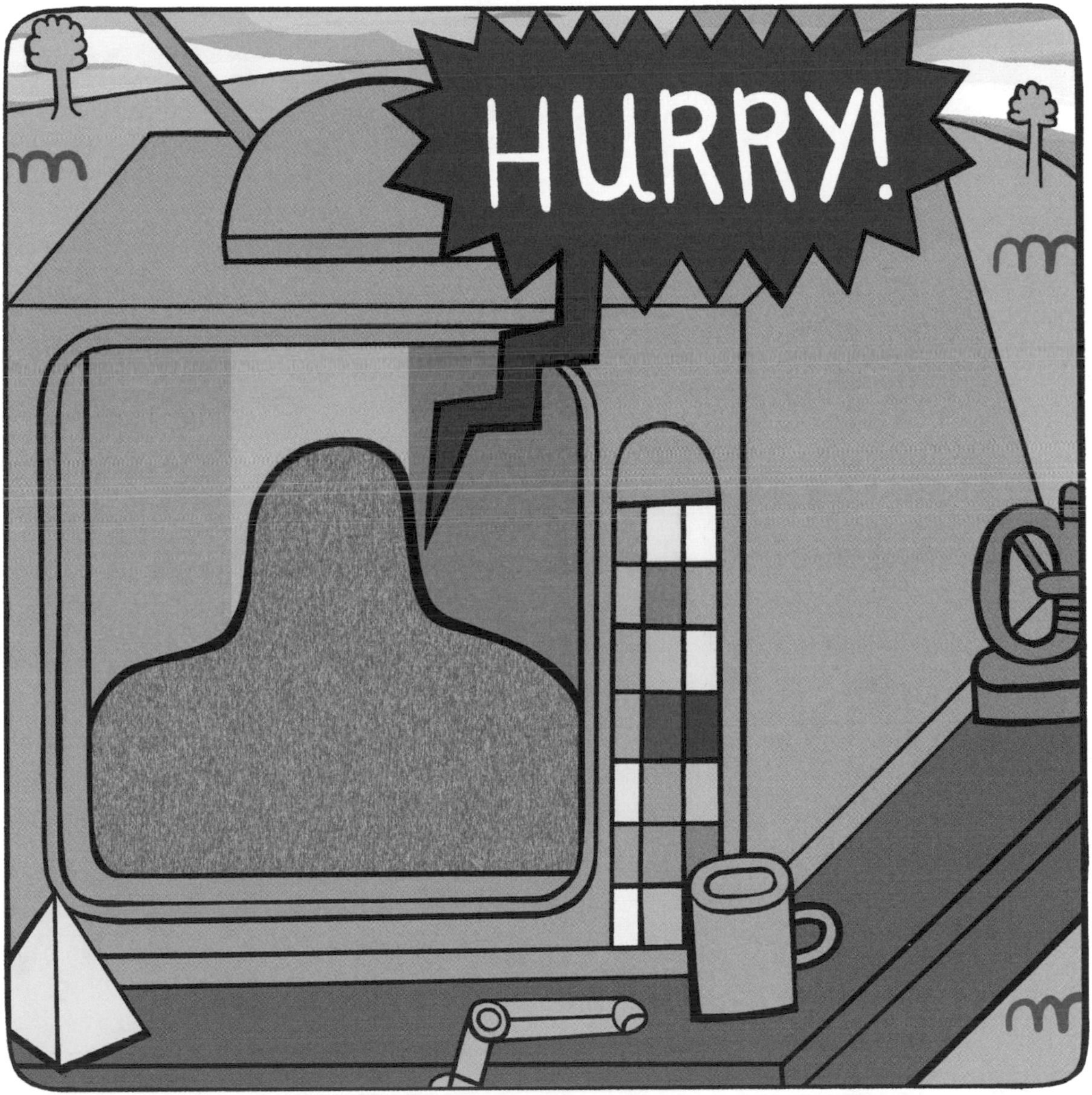
HURRY!

ZOOIE!
FLASH!
BASH!
WRRZZ!

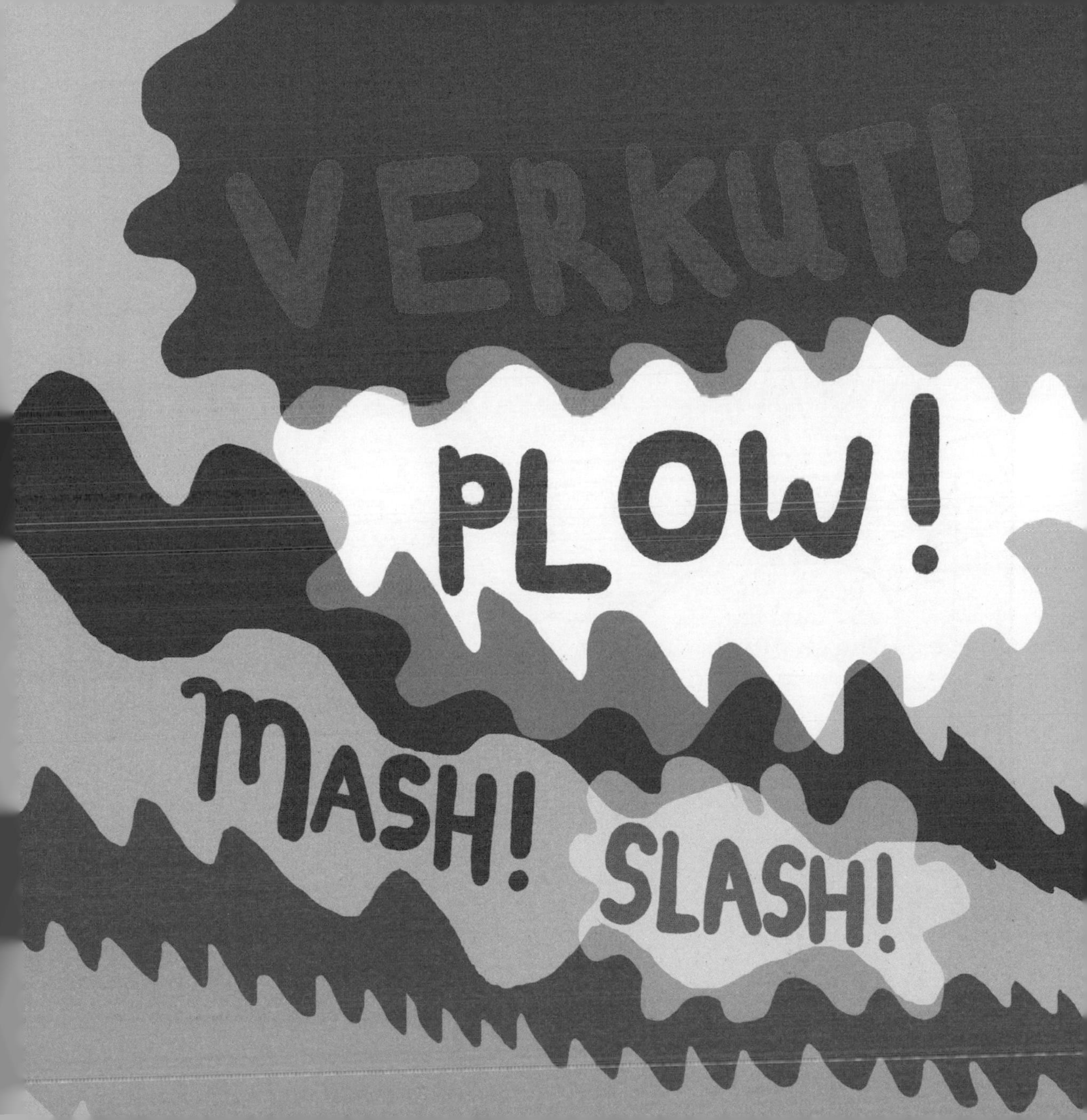
VERKUT!
PLOW!
MASH!
SLASH!

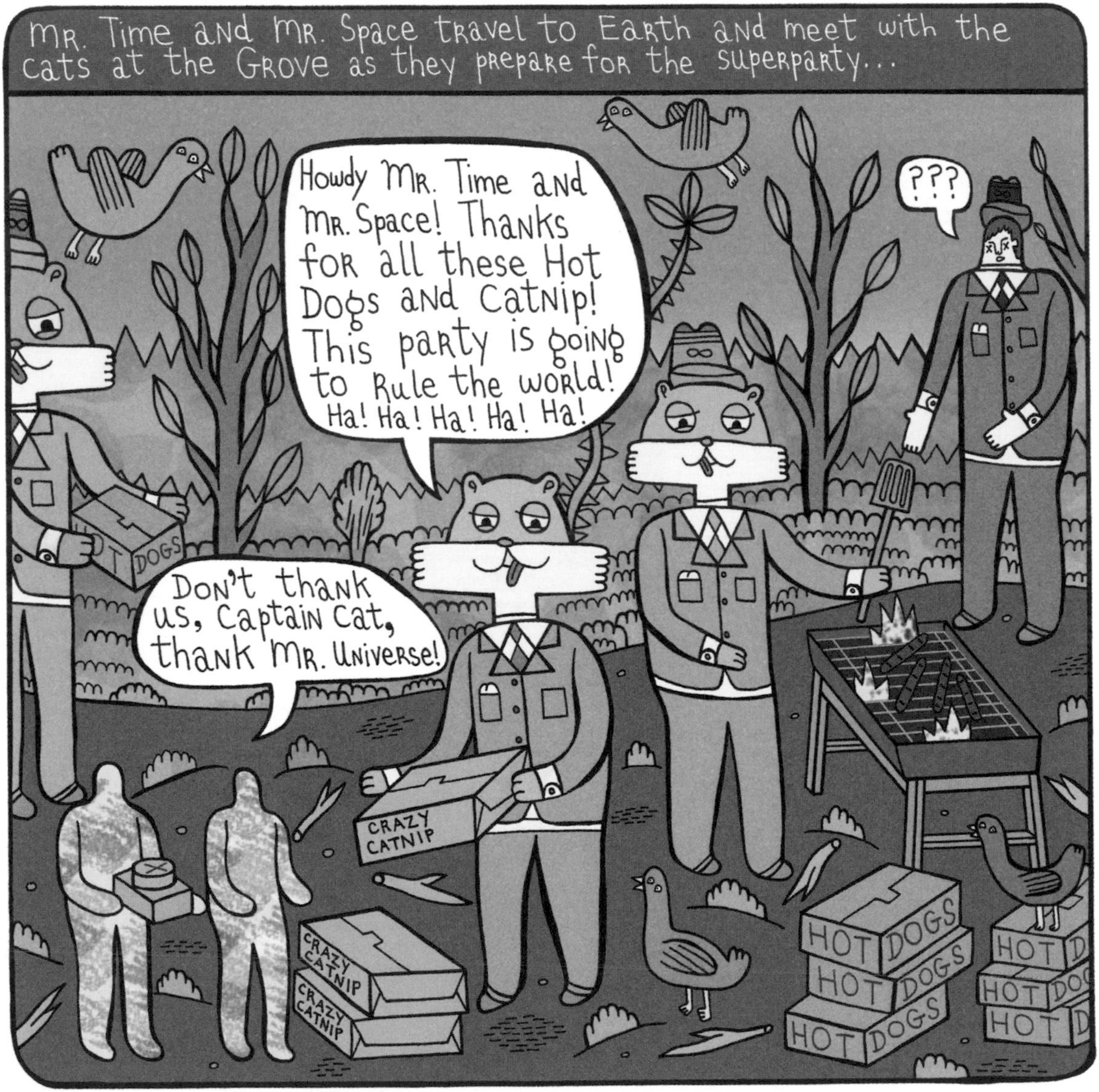
Mr. Time and Mr. Space travel to Earth and meet with the cats at the Grove as they prepare for the superparty...
Howdy Mr. Time and Mr. Space! Thanks for all these Hot Dogs and Catnip! This party is going to Rule the world! Ha! Ha! Ha! Ha! Ha!
???
Don't thank us, Captain Cat, thank Mr. Universe!
HOT DOGS
CRAZY CATNIP
CRAZY CATNIP
CRAZY CATNIP
HOT DOGS
HOT DOGS
HOT DOGS
HOT D
HOT DO
HOT D

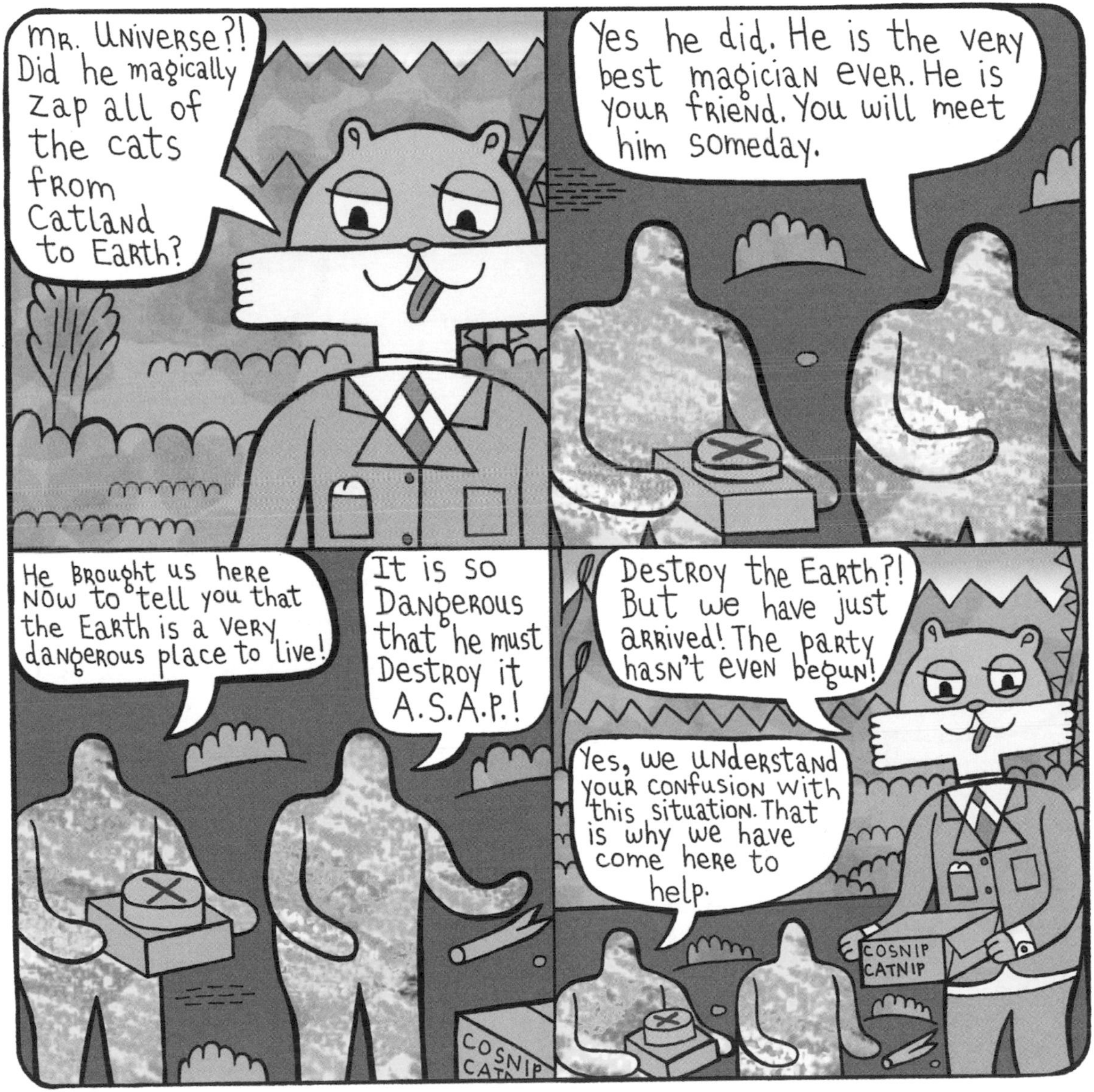

Mr. Universe?! Did he magically zap all of the cats from Catland to Earth?
Yes he did. He is the very best magician ever. He is your friend. You will meet him someday.
He brought us here now to tell you that the Earth is a very dangerous place to live!
It is so dangerous that he must destroy it A.S.A.P.!
Destroy the Earth?! But we have just arrived! The party hasn't even begun!
Yes, we understand your confusion with this situation. That is why we have come here to help.
COSNIP CATNIP

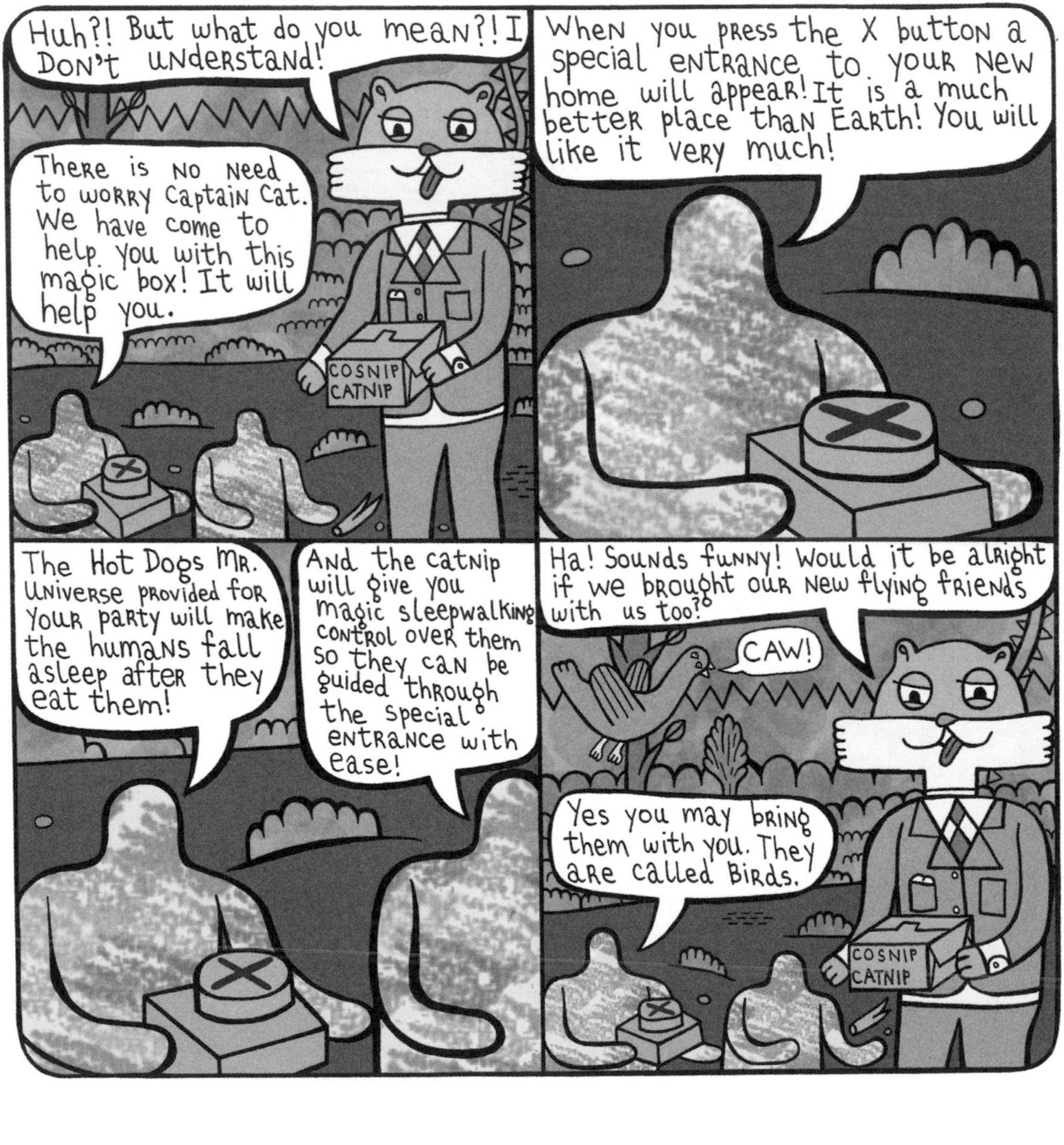
Huh?! But what do you mean?! I DON'T UNDERSTAND!
There is NO Need to WORRY Captain Cat. We have come to help you with this magic box! It will help you.
COSNIP CATNIP
When you press the X button a special entrance to your New home will appear! It is a much better place than Earth! You will like it very much!
The Hot Dogs MR. Universe provided for your party will make the humans fall asleep after they eat them!
And the catnip will give you magic sleepwalking control over them so they can be guided through the special entrance with ease!
Ha! Sounds funny! Would it be alright if we brought our new flying friends with us too?
CAW!
Yes you may bring them with you. They are called Birds.
COSNIP CATNIP

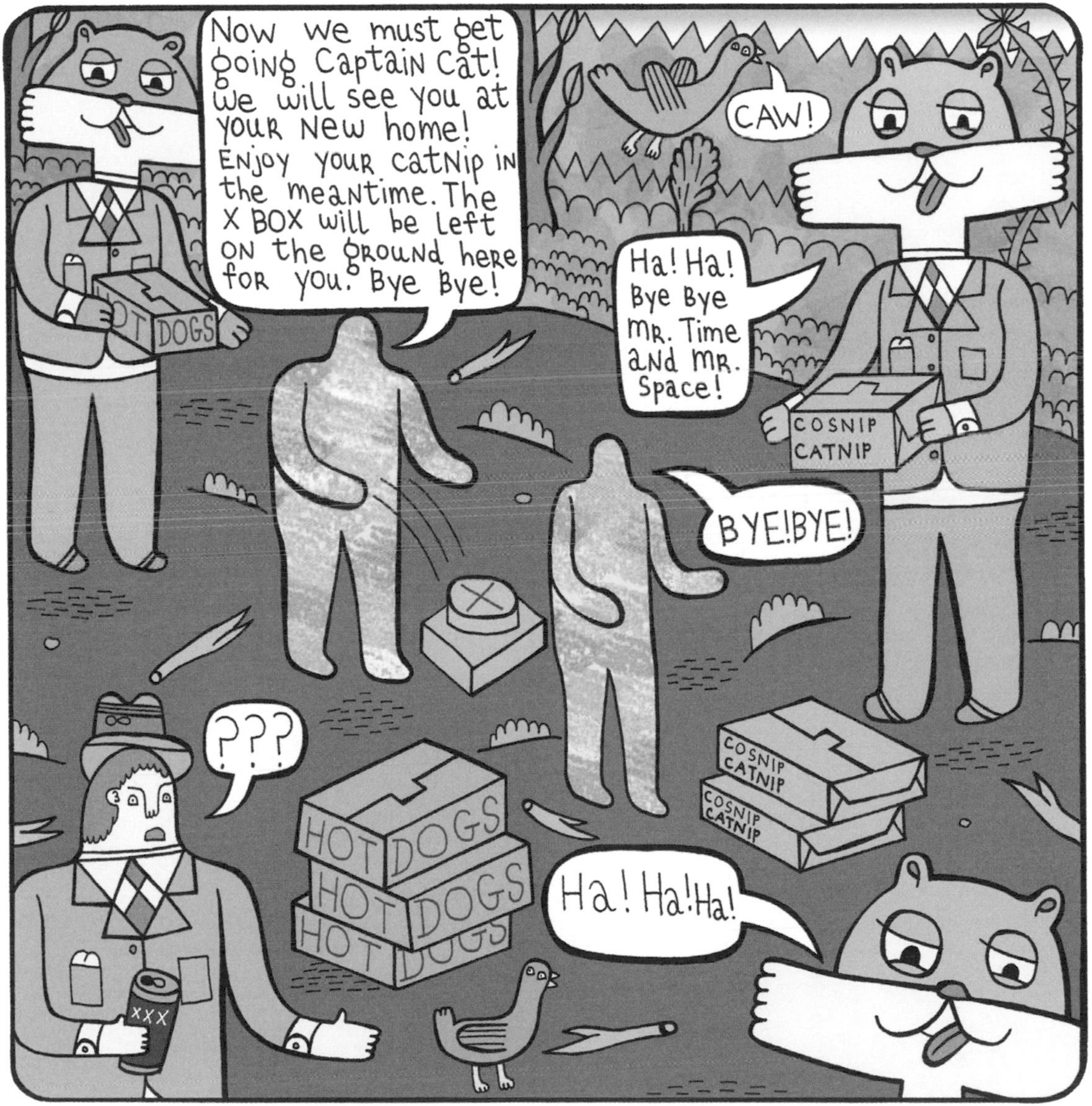
Now we must get going Captain Cat! We will see you at your New home! Enjoy your catNip in the meanTime. The X BOX will be left ON the ground here for you. Bye Bye!
CAW!
Ha! Ha! Bye Bye Mr. Time and Mr. Space!
HOT DOGS
COSNIP CATNIP
BYE!BYE!
???
HOT DOGS
HOT DOGS
HOT DOGS
COSNIP CATNIP
COSNIP CATNIP
Ha! Ha! Ha!
XXX

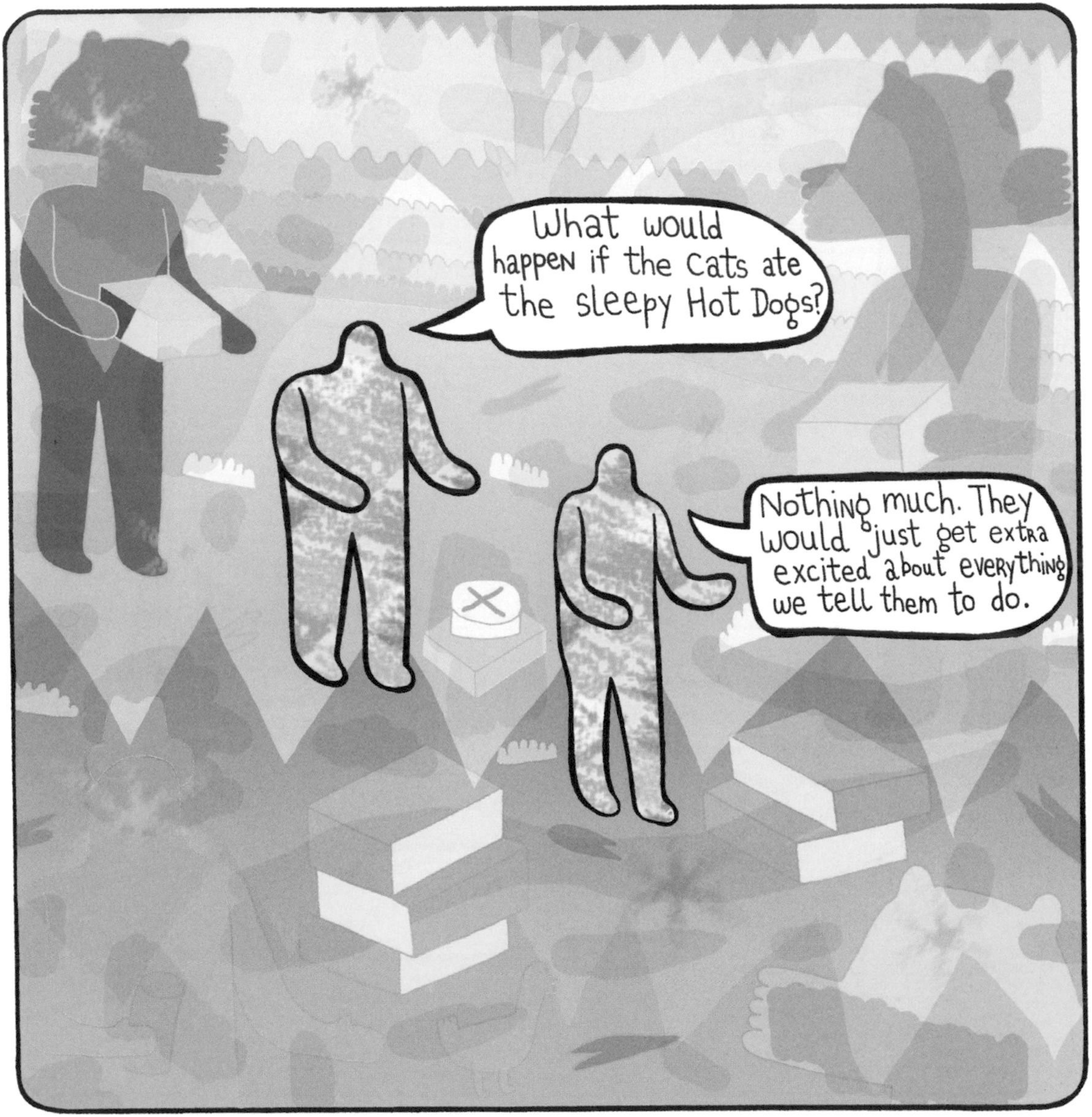
What would happen if the cats ate the sleepy Hot Dogs?
Nothing much. They would just get extra excited about everything we tell them to do.

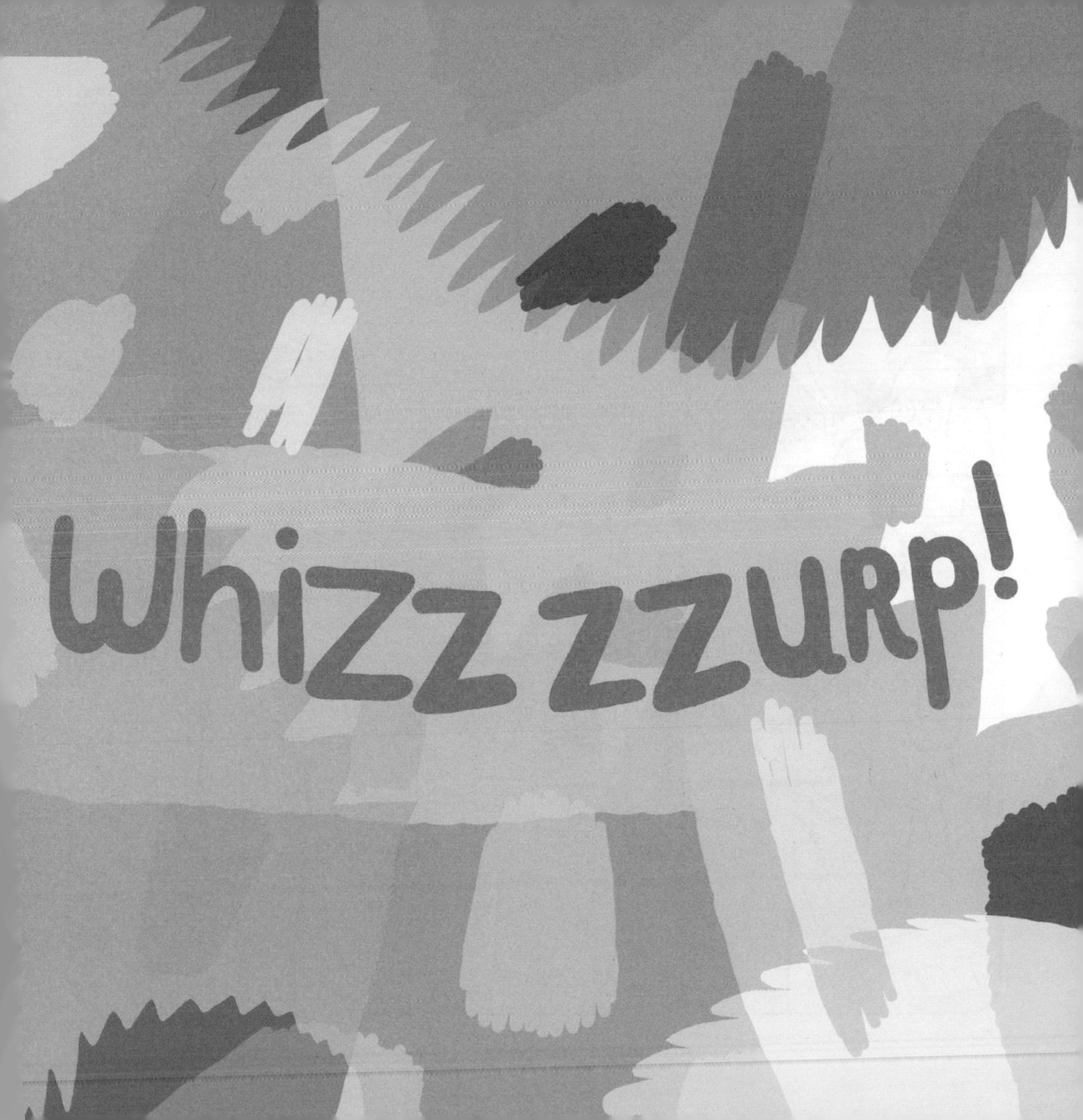
WhiZZZZZURP!

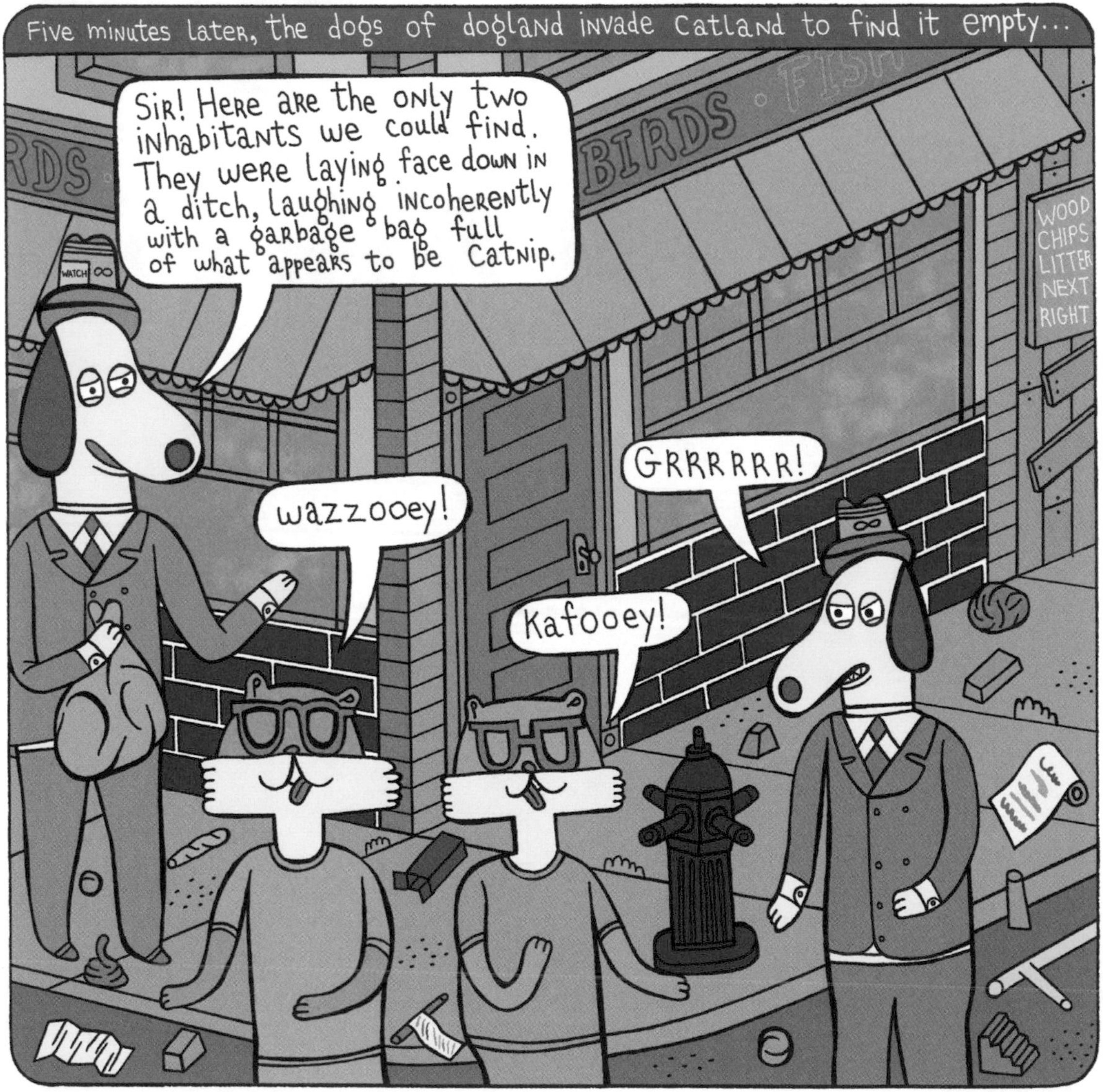
Five minutes later, the dogs of dogland invade Catland to find it empty...
Sir! Here are the only two inhabitants we could find. They were laying face down in a ditch, laughing incoherently with a garbage bag full of what appears to be Catnip.
wazzooey!
Kafooey!
GRRRRRR!
BIRDS
WOOD CHIPS LITTER NEXT RIGHT
WATCH

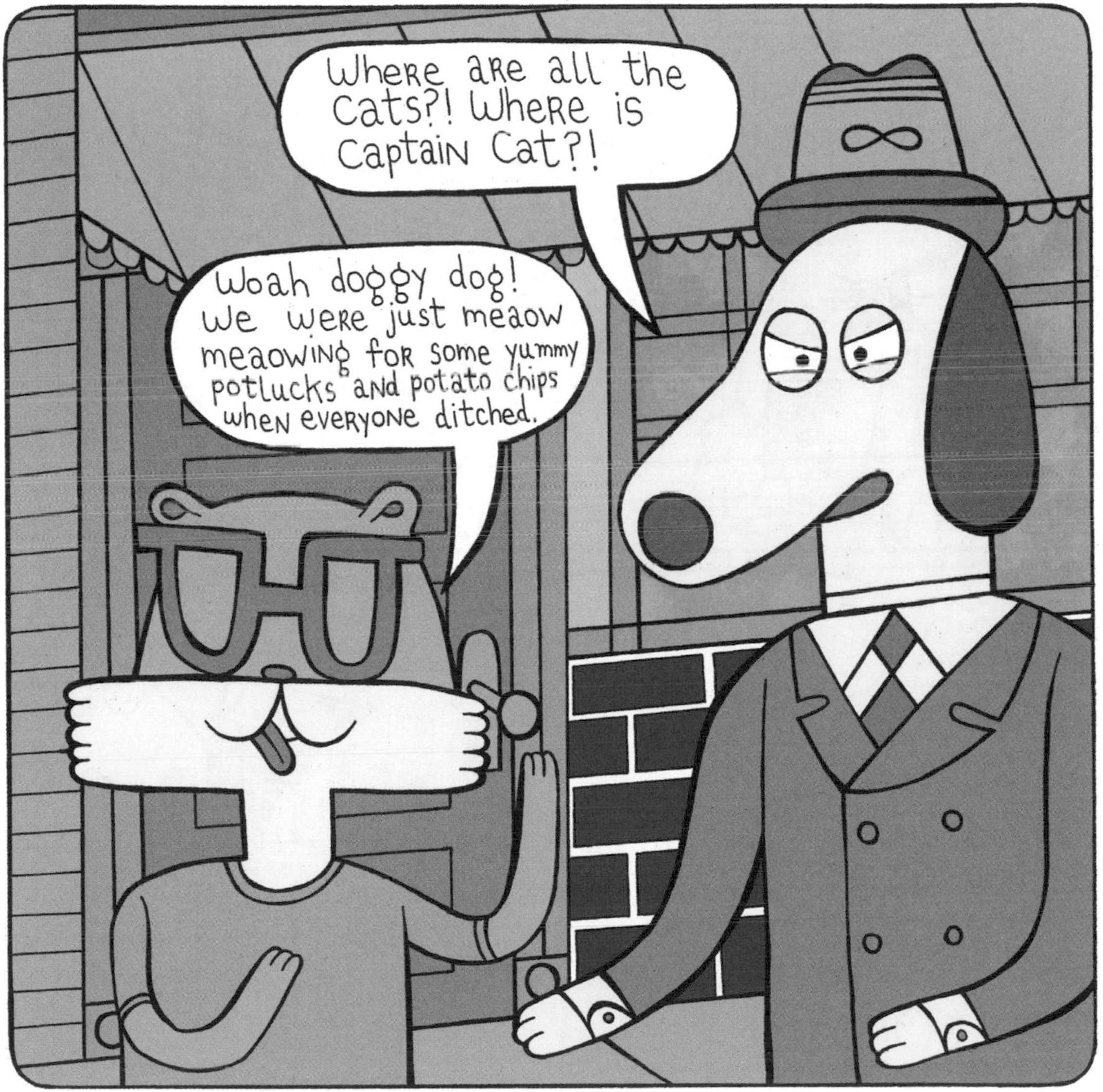
Where are all the Cats?! Where is Captain Cat?!
Woah doggy dog! We were just meaow meaowing for some yummy potlucks and potato chips when everyone ditched.

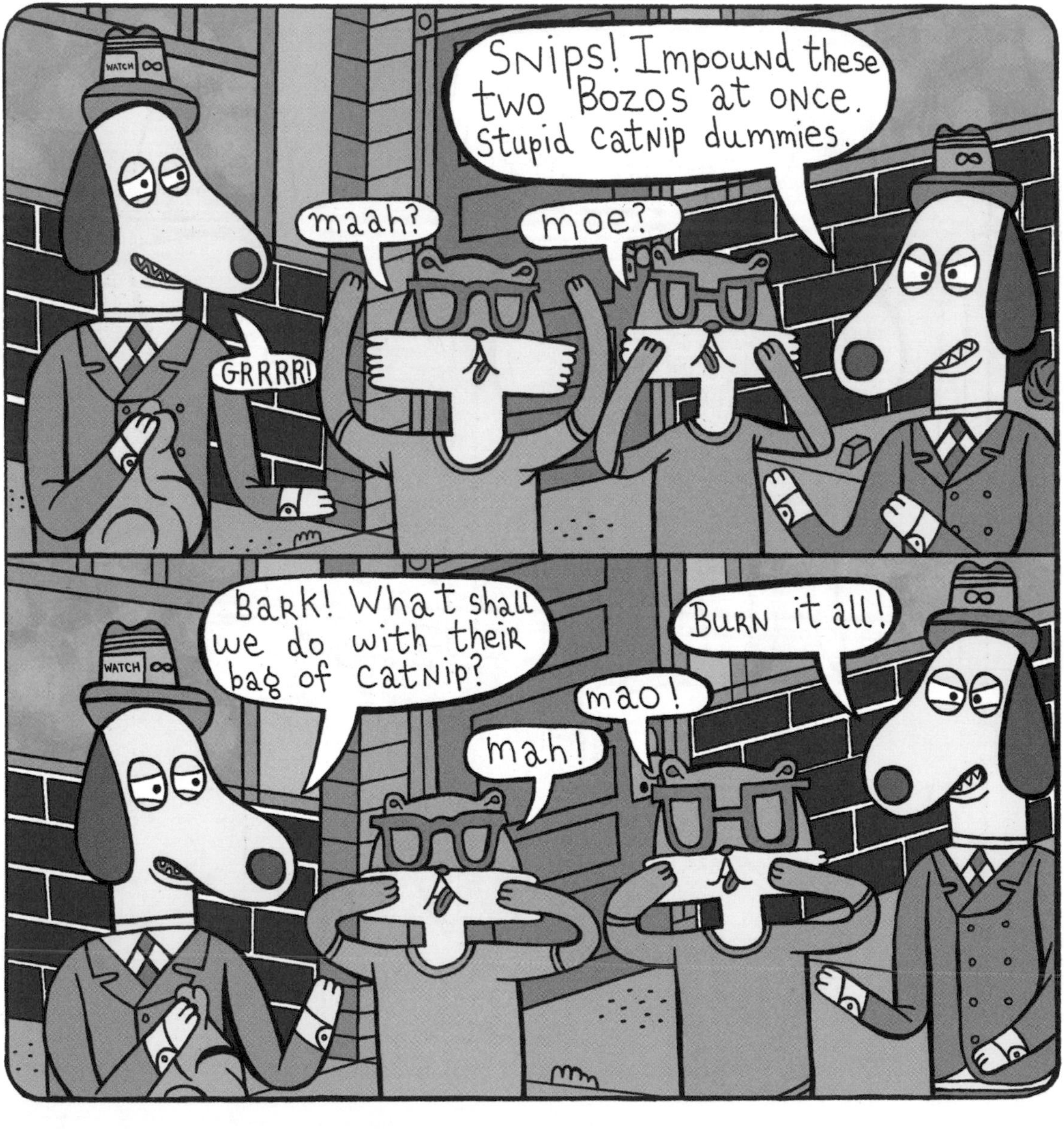
WATCH
SNIPS! Impound these two Bozos at once. Stupid catnip dummies.
maah?
moe?
GRRRR!
WATCH
BARK! What shall we do with their bag of catnip?
BURN it all!
mao!
mah!

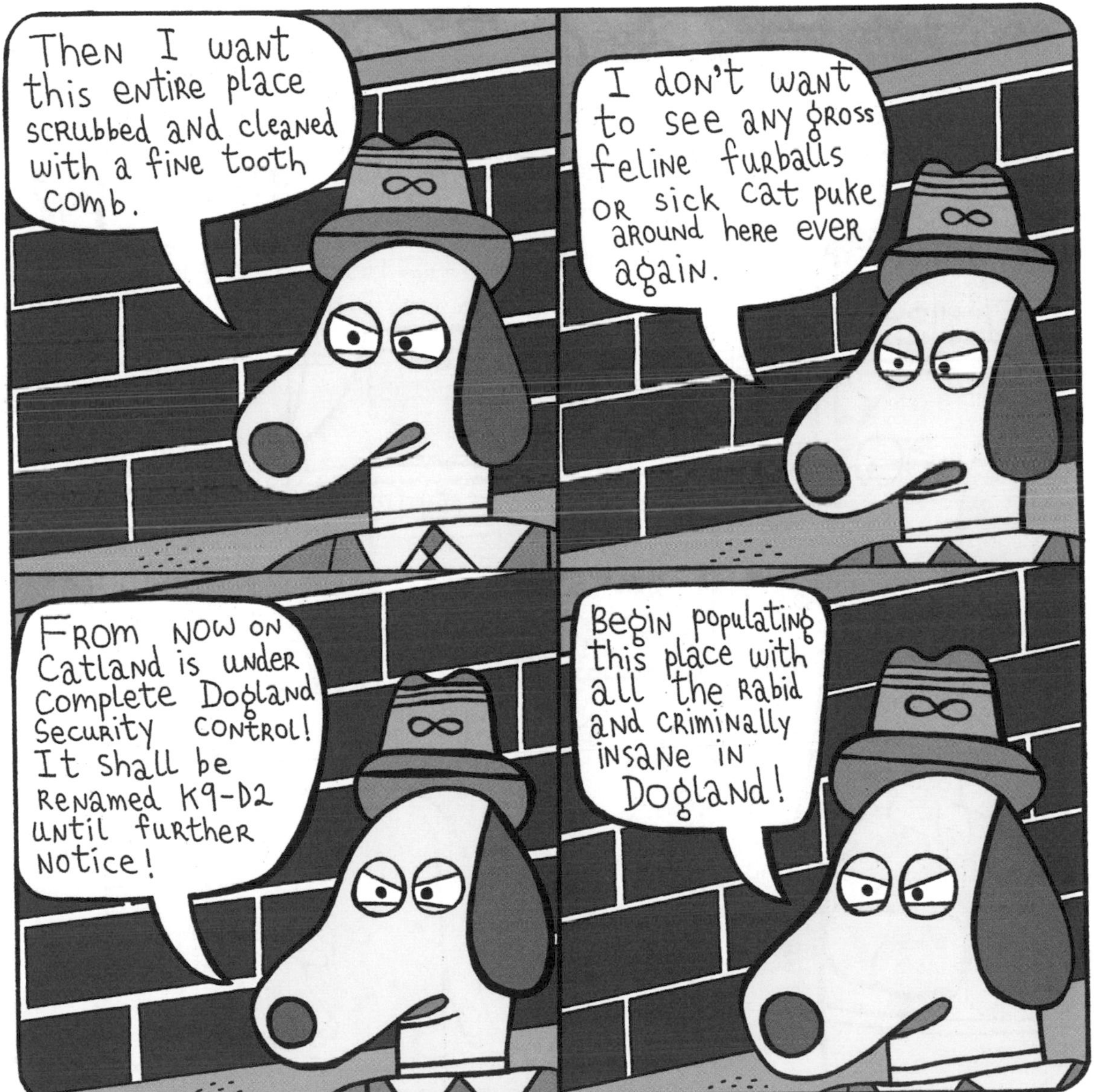
Then I want this entire place scrubbed and cleaned with a fine tooth comb.
I don't want to see any gross feline furballs or sick cat puke around here ever again.
From now on Catland is under Complete Dogland Security Control! It shall be renamed K9-D2 until further Notice!
Begin populating this place with all the rabid and criminally insane in Dogland!

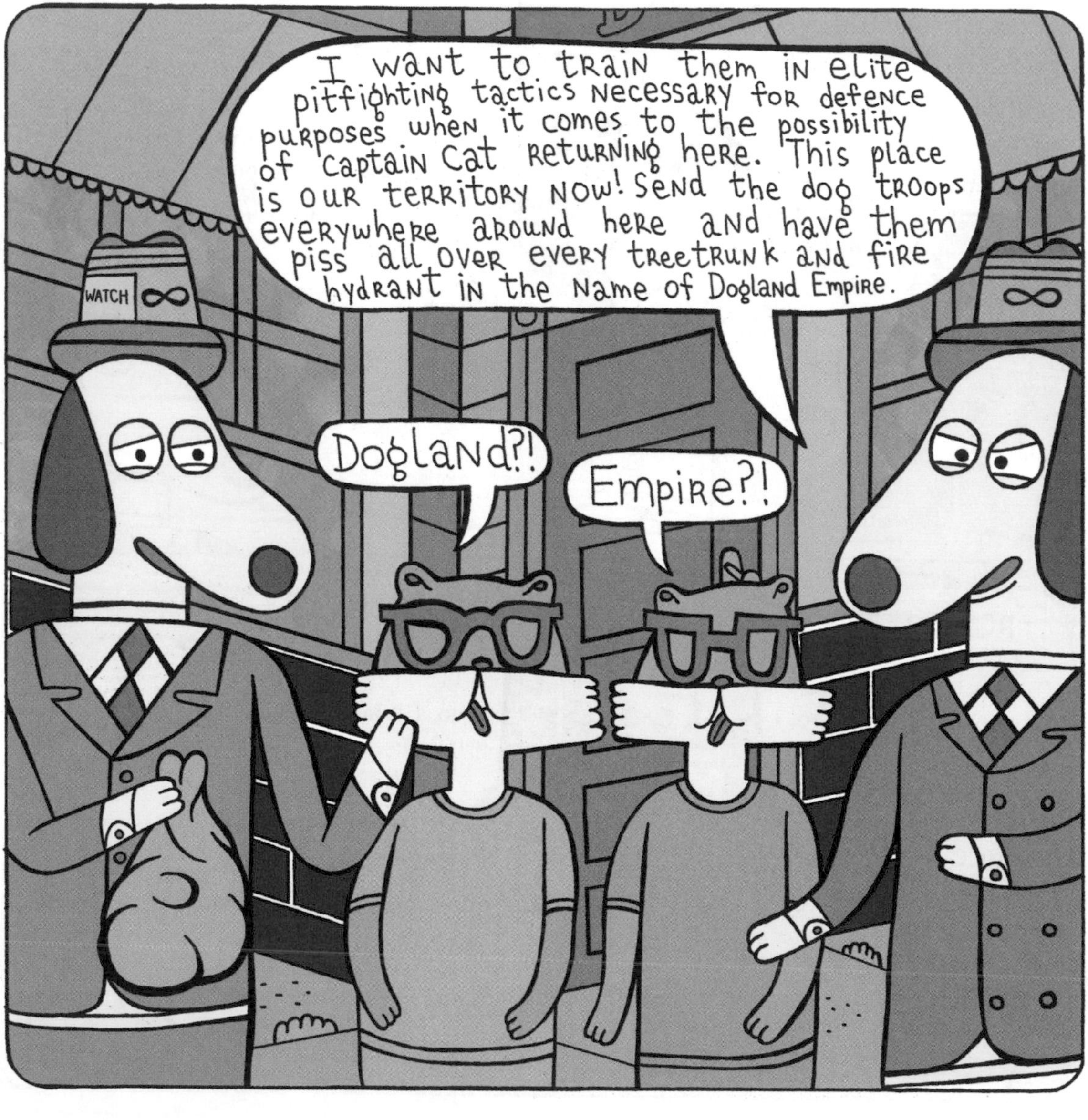
WATCH
I want to train them in elite pitfighting tactics necessary for defence purposes when it comes to the possibility of Captain Cat returning here. This place is our territory now! Send the dog troops everywhere around here and have them piss all over every treetrunk and fire hydrant in the name of Dogland Empire.
Dogland?!
Empire?!

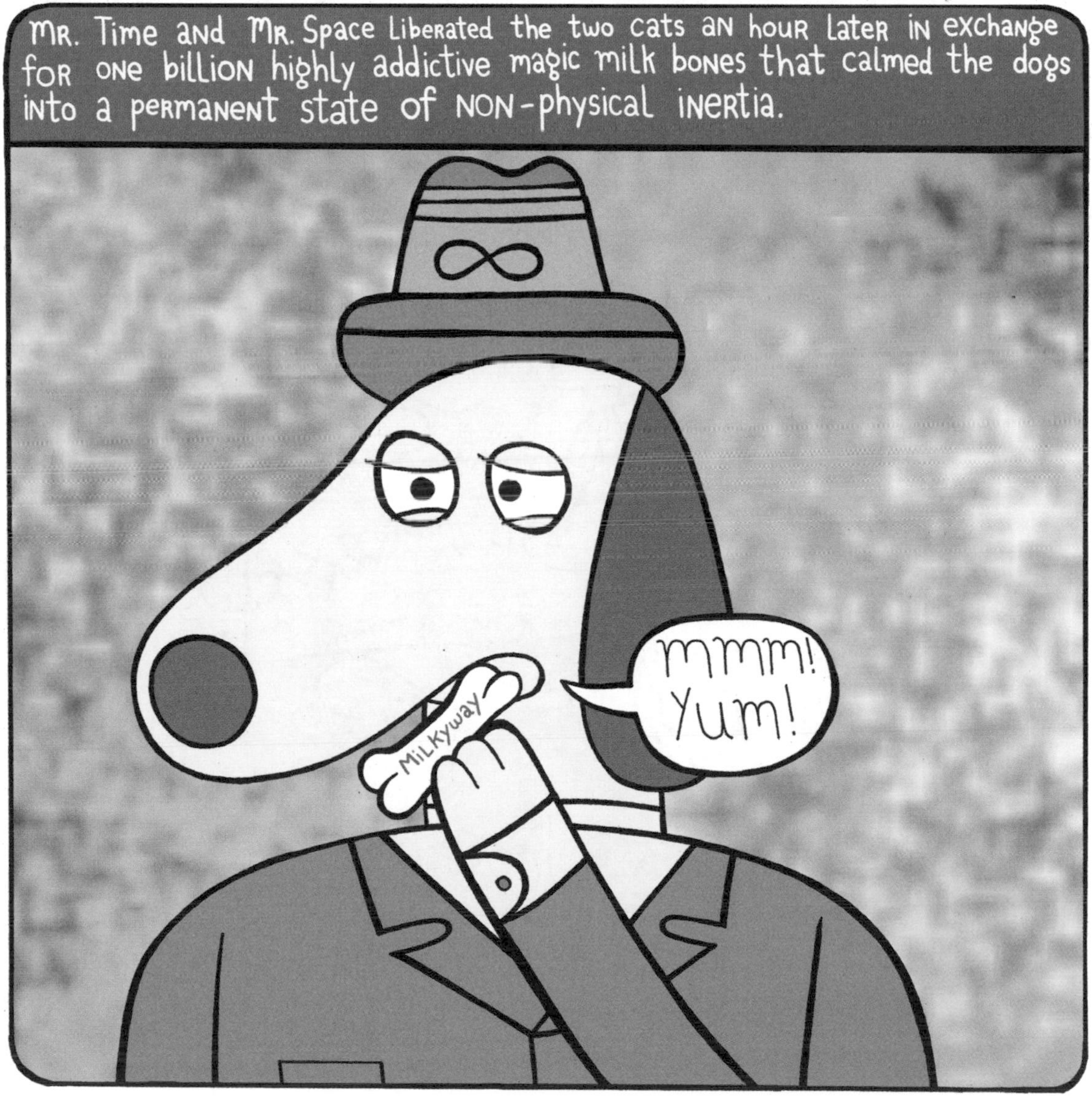
Mr. Time and Mr. Space Liberated the two cats an hour later in exchange for one billion highly addictive magic milk bones that calmed the dogs into a permanent state of non-physical inertia.
Milkyway
mmm! Yum!

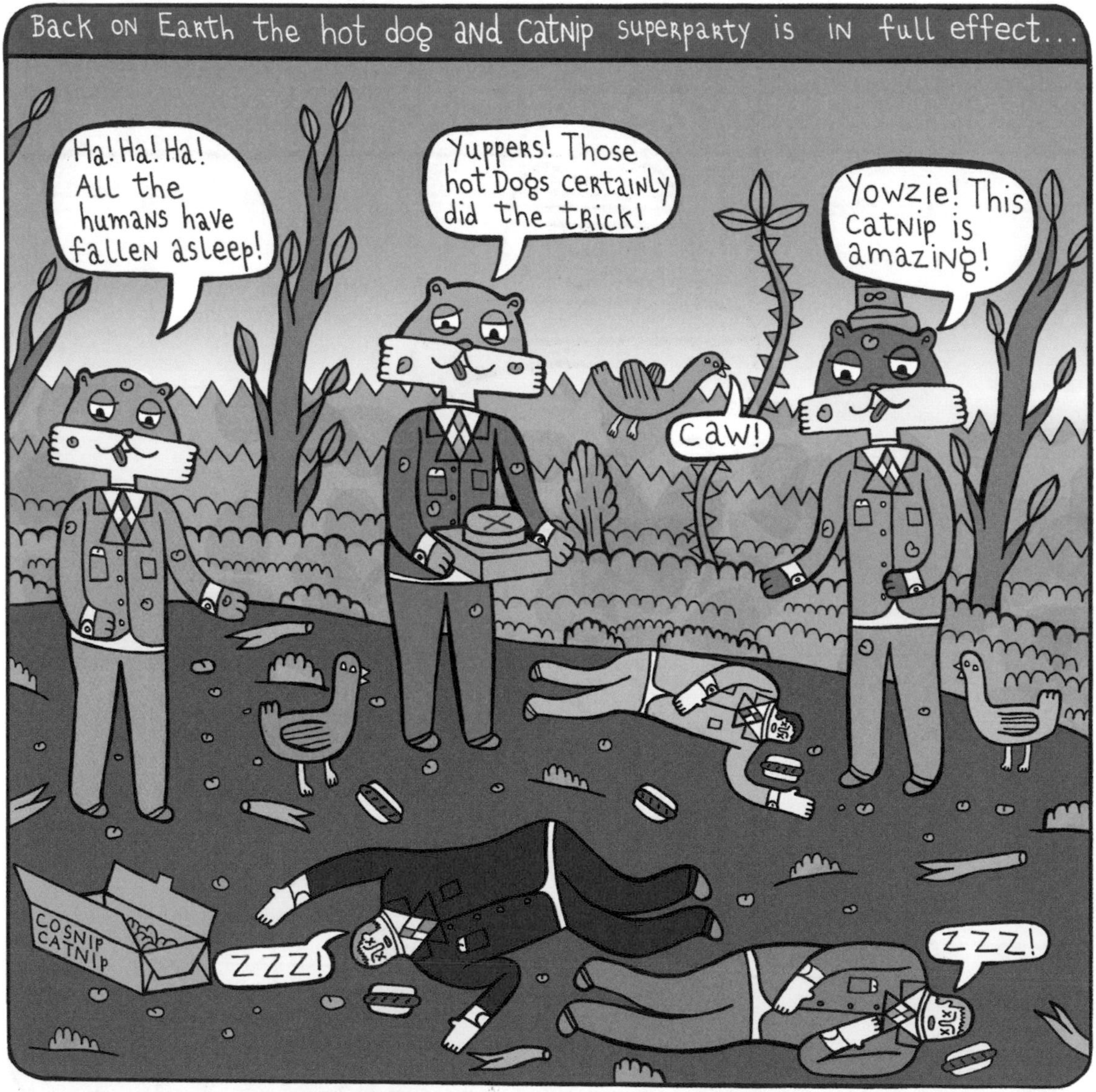

Back on Earth the hot dog and catnip superparty is in full effect...
Ha! Ha! Ha! All the humans have fallen asleep!
Yuppers! Those hot Dogs certainly did the trick!
Yowzie! This catnip is amazing!
CAW!
COSNIP CATNIP
ZZZ!
ZZZ!

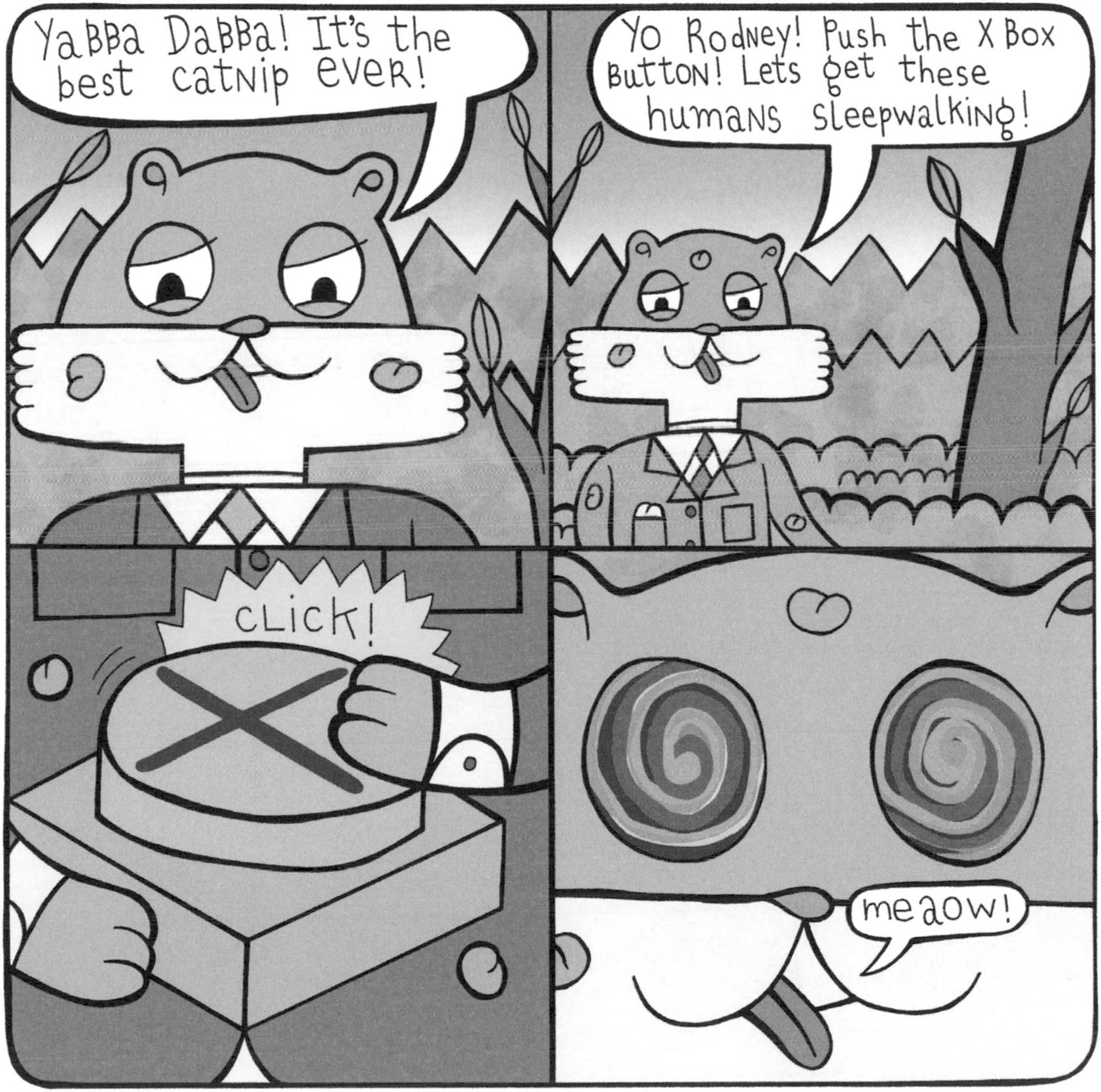
Yabba Dabba! It's the best catnip ever!
Yo Rodney! Push the X Box button! Lets get these humans sleepwalking!
CLICK!
meaow!

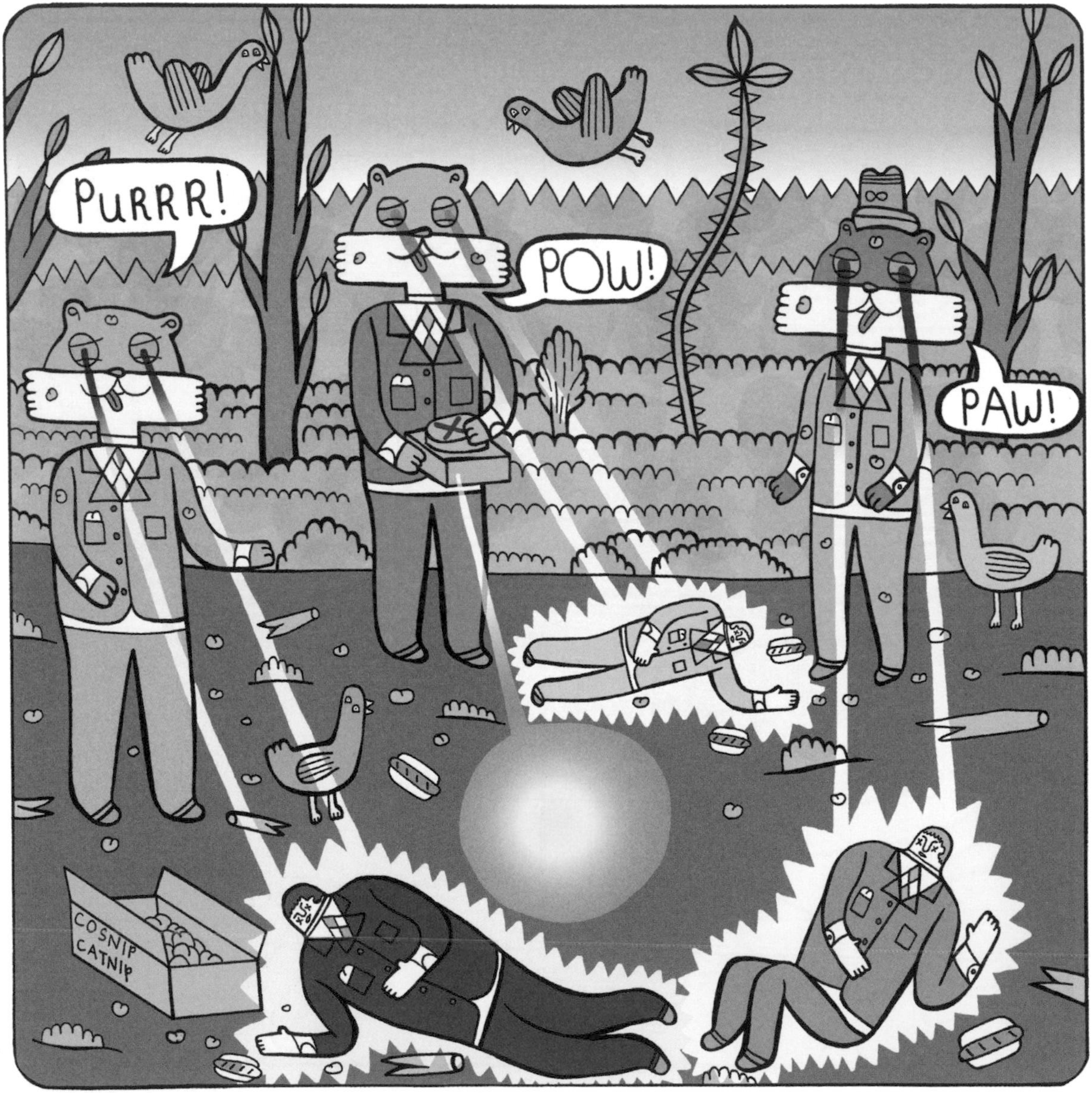
PURRR!
POW!
PAW!
COSNIP
CATNIP

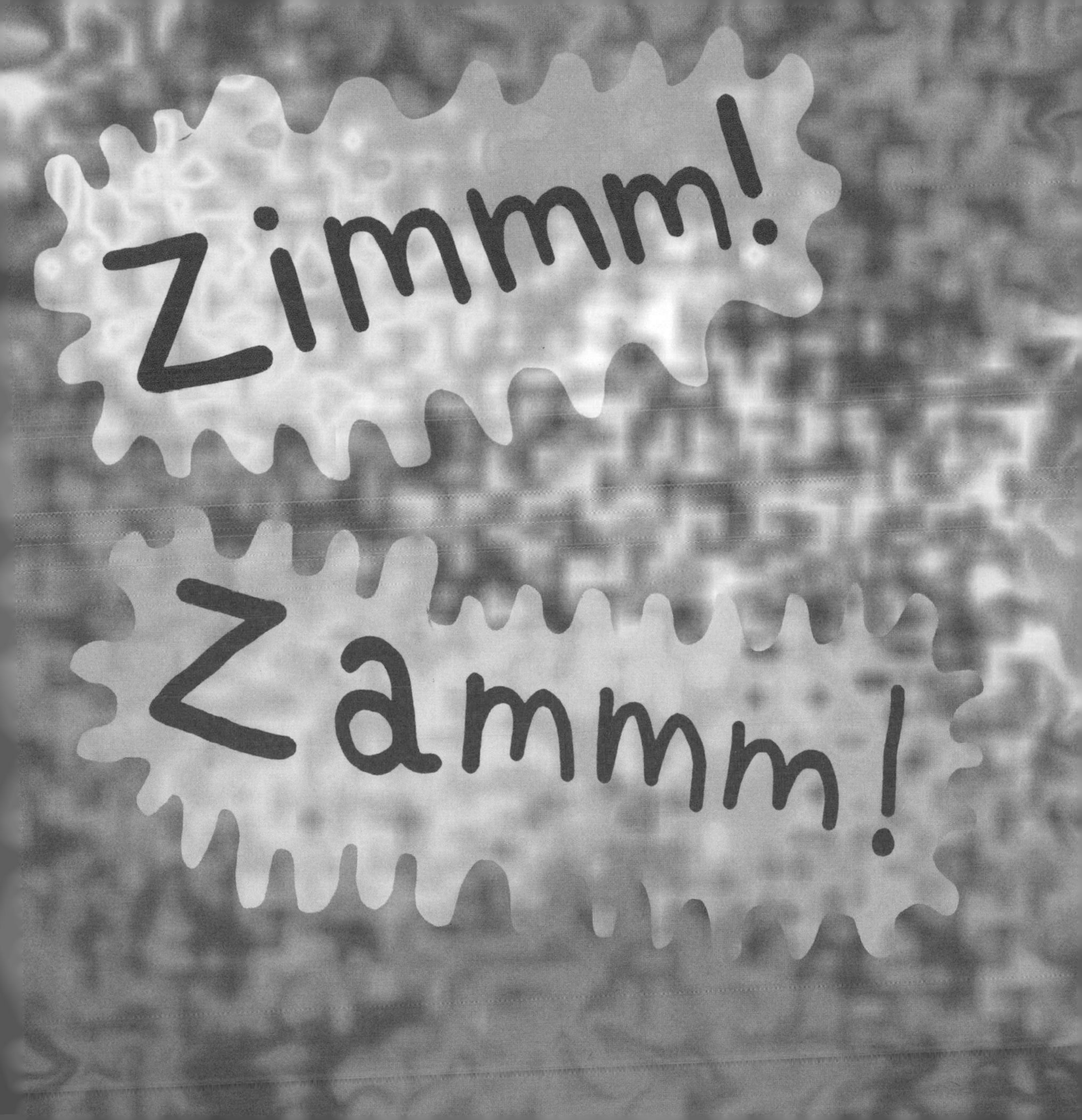
Zimmm!
Zammm!

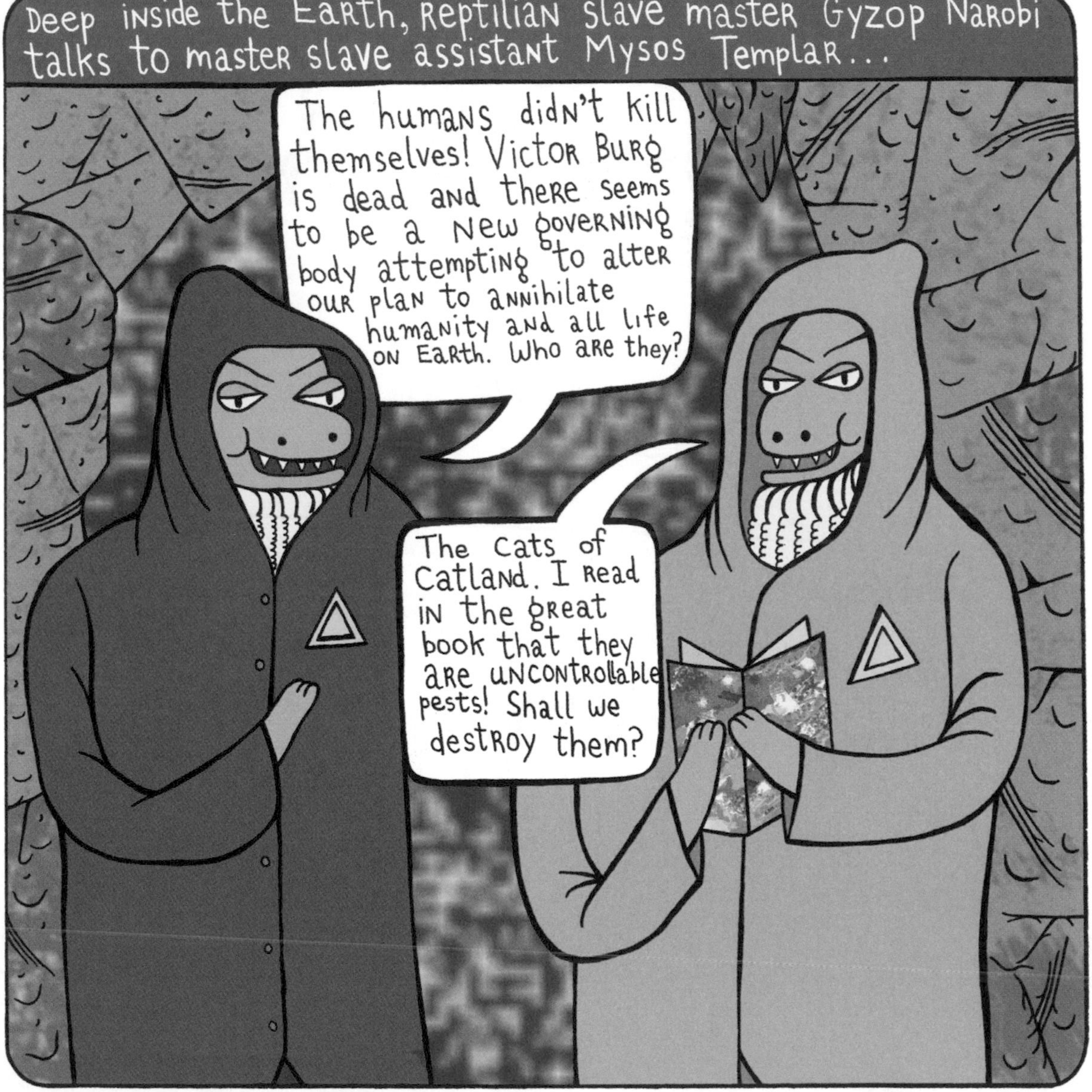
Deep inside the Earth, Reptilian slave master Gyzop Narobi talks to master slave assistant Mysos Templar...
The humans didn't kill themselves! Victor Burg is dead and there seems to be a new governing body attempting to alter our plan to annihilate humanity and all life on Earth. Who are they?
The cats of Catland. I read in the great book that they are uncontrollable pests! Shall we destroy them?

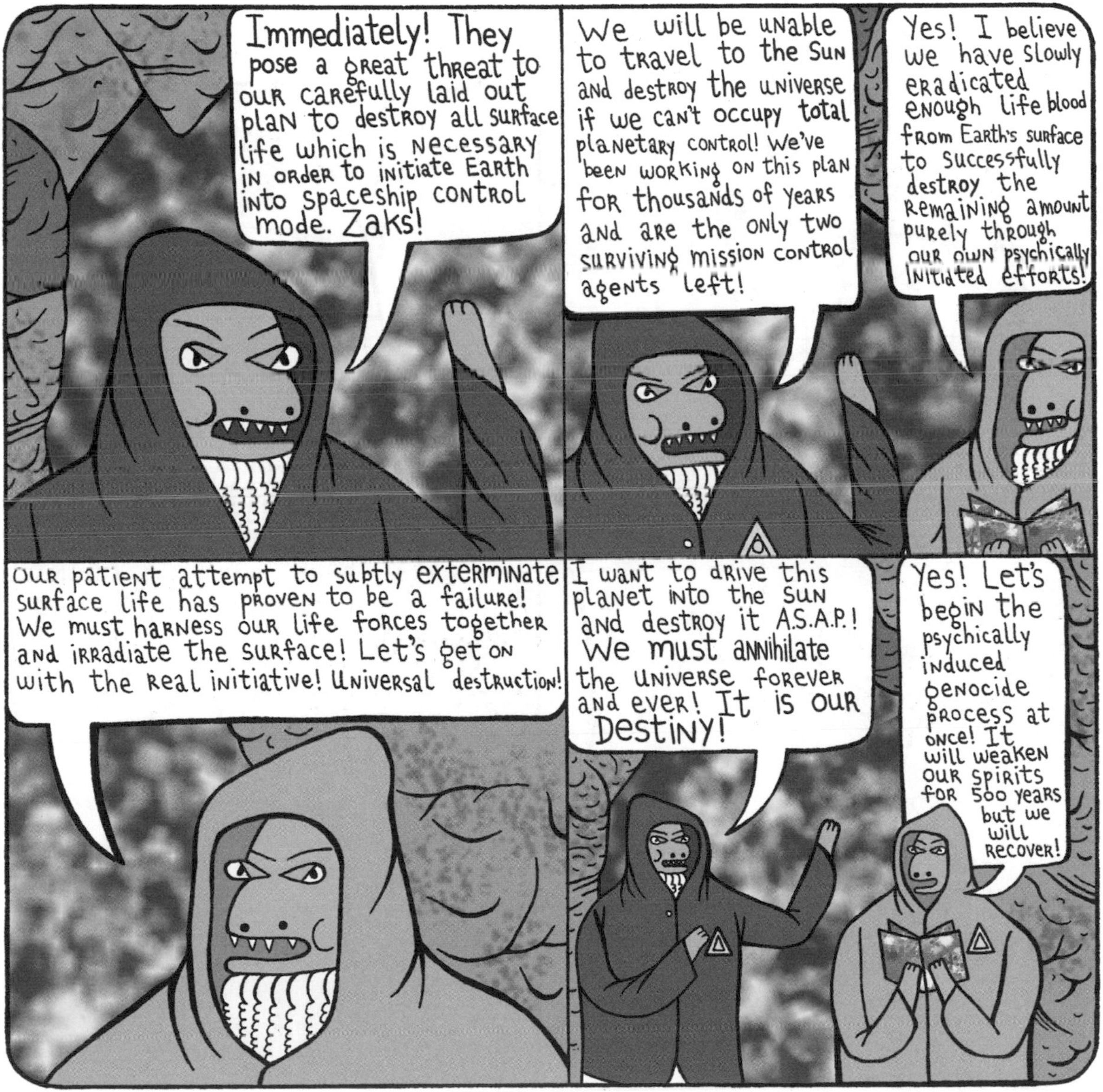
Immediately! They pose a great threat to our carefully laid out plan to destroy all surface life which is necessary in order to initiate Earth into spaceship control mode. Zaks!
We will be unable to travel to the Sun and destroy the universe if we can't occupy total planetary control! We've been working on this plan for thousands of years and are the only two surviving mission control agents left!
Yes! I believe we have slowly eradicated enough life blood from Earth's surface to successfully destroy the remaining amount purely through our own psychically initiated efforts!
Our patient attempt to subtly exterminate surface life has proven to be a failure! We must harness our life forces together and irradiate the surface! Let's get on with the real initiative! Universal destruction!
I want to drive this planet into the Sun and destroy it A.S.A.P.! We must annihilate the universe forever and ever! It is our Destiny!
Yes! Let's begin the psychically induced genocide process at once! It will weaken our spirits for 500 years but we will recover!

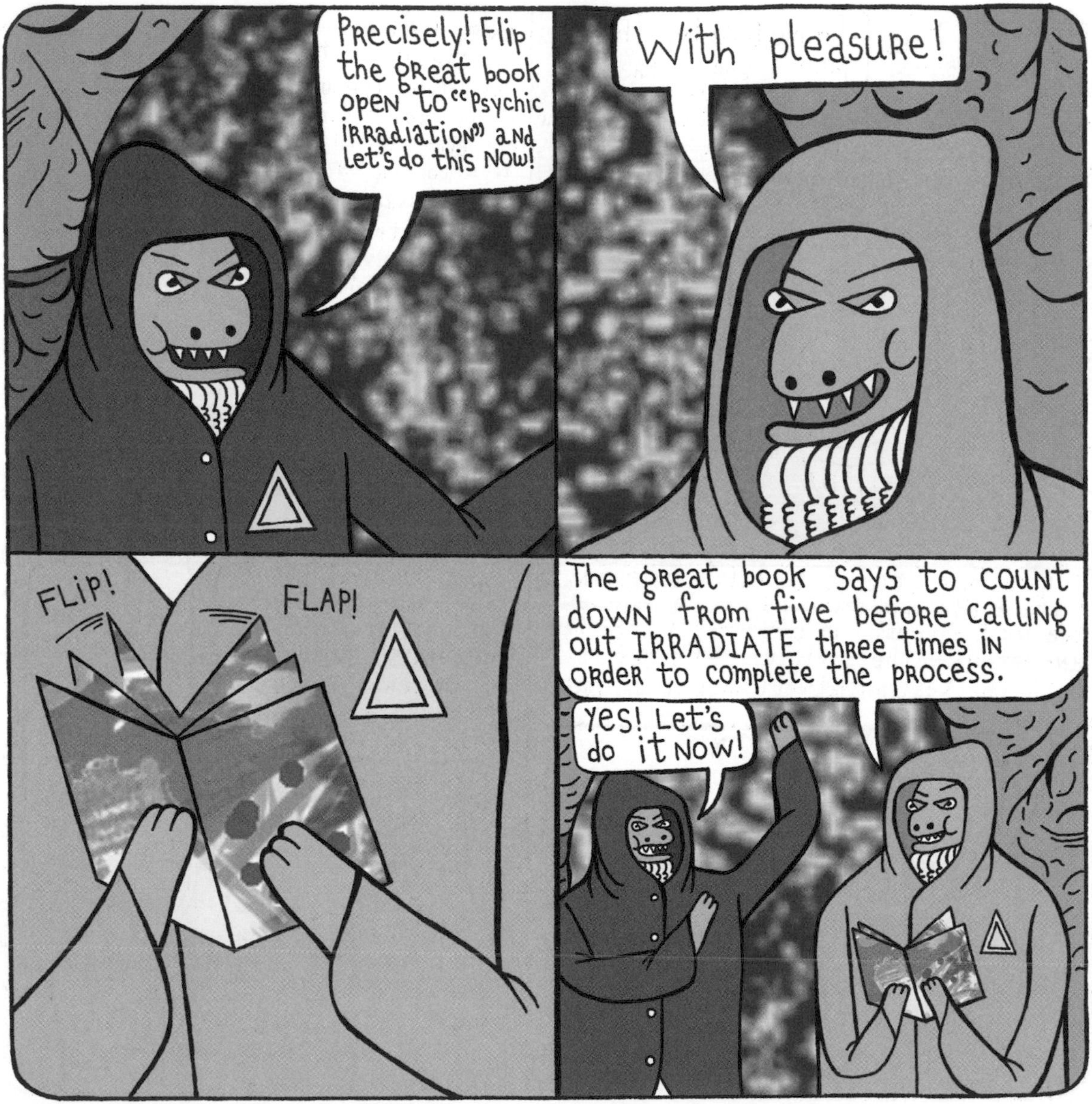
Precisely! Flip the great book open to "Psychic irradiation" and let's do this now!
With pleasure!
FLIP!
FLAP!
The great book says to count down from five before calling out IRRADIATE three times in order to complete the process.
Yes! Let's do it now!

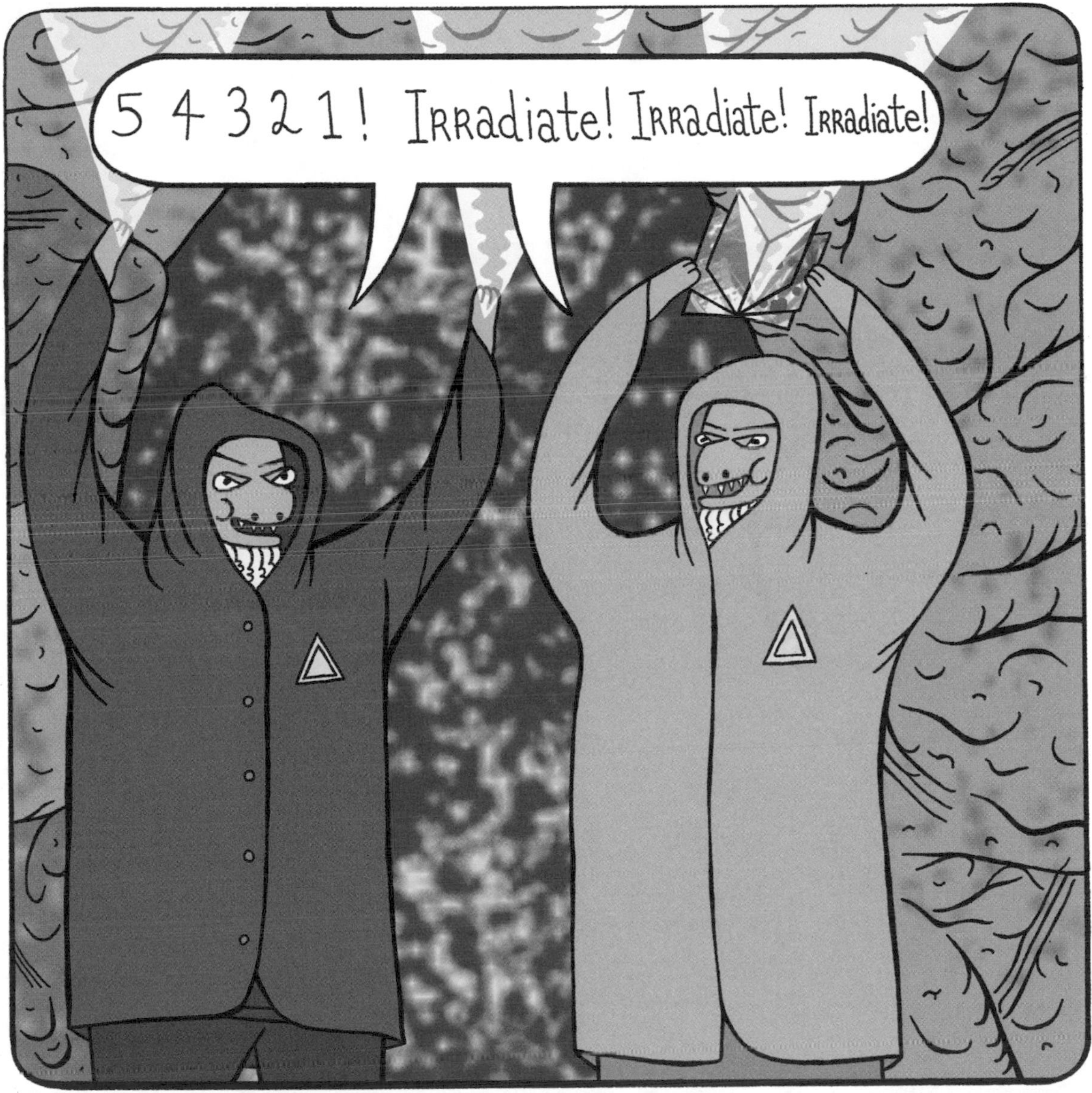
5 4 3 2 1! Irradiate! Irradiate! Irradiate!

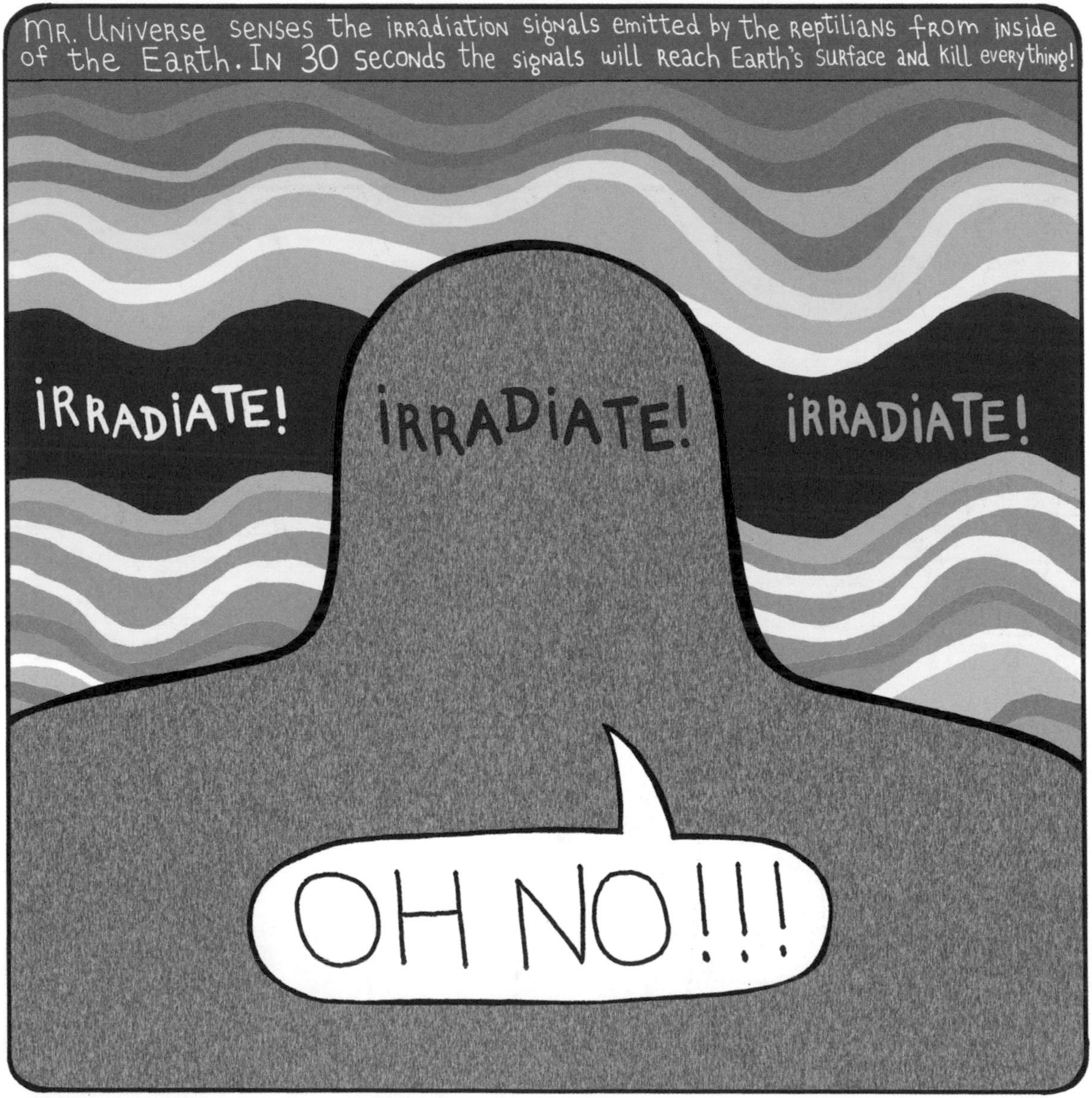

Mr. Universe senses the irradiation signals emitted by the reptilians from inside of the Earth. In 30 seconds the signals will reach Earth's surface and kill everything!
IRRADIATE!
IRRADIATE!
IRRADIATE!
OH NO!!!

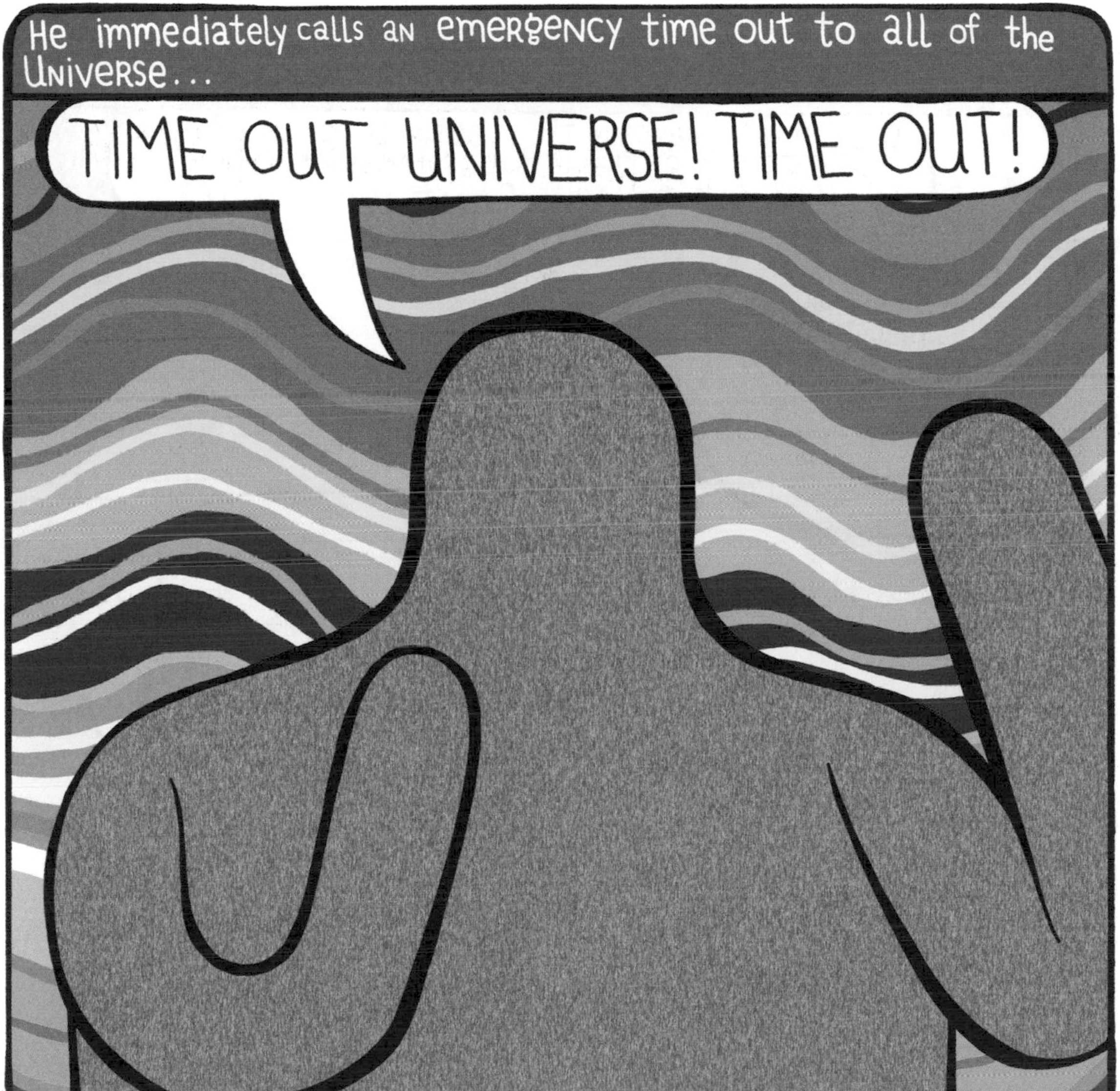
He immediately calls an emergency time out to all of the Universe...
TIME OUT UNIVERSE! TIME OUT!

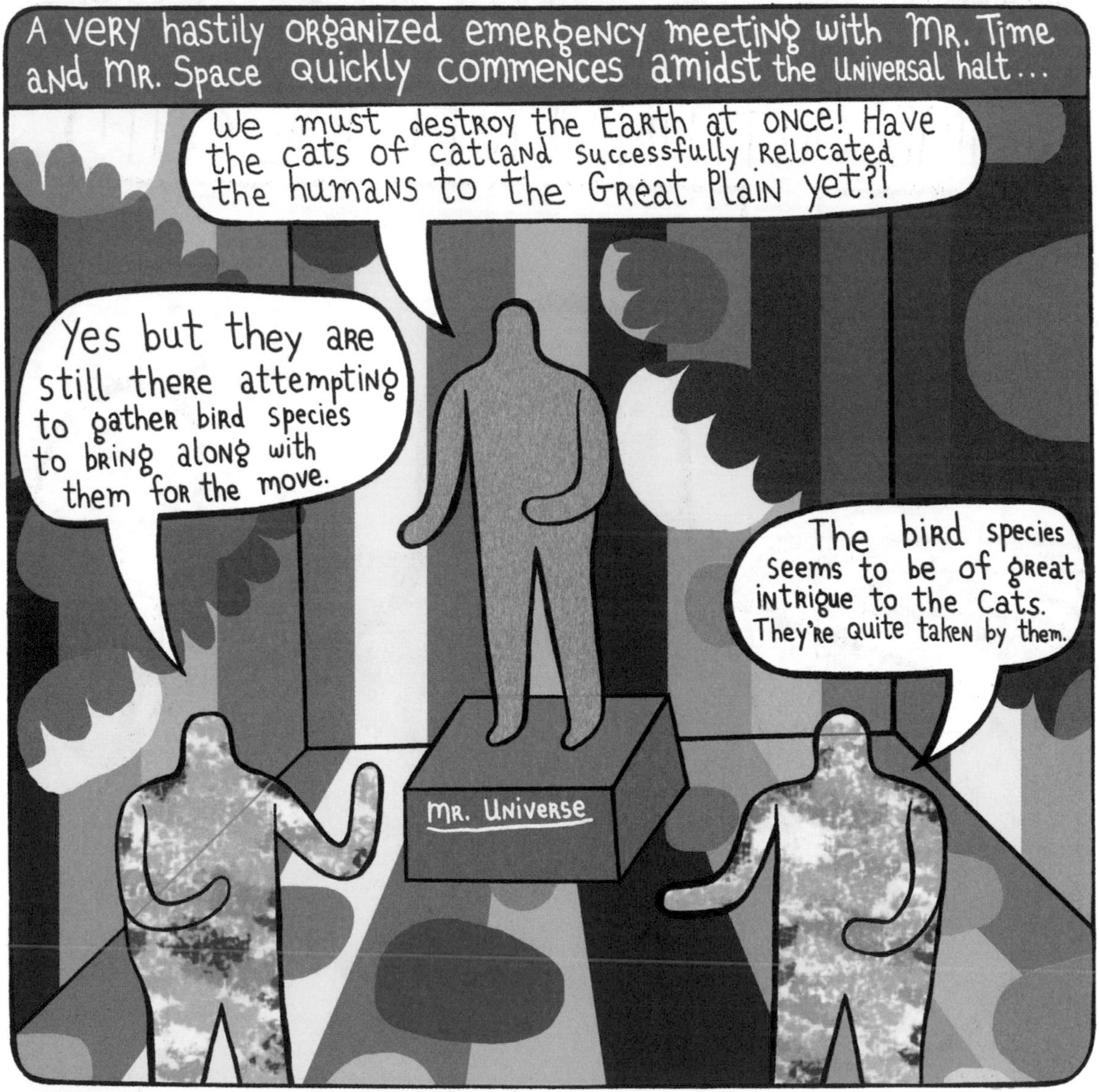
A very hastily organized emergency meeting with Mr. Time and Mr. Space quickly commences amidst the Universal halt...
We must destroy the Earth at once! Have the cats of Catland successfully relocated the humans to the Great Plain yet?!
Yes but they are still there attempting to gather bird species to bring along with them for the move.
The bird species seems to be of great intrigue to the Cats. They're quite taken by them.
Mr. Universe

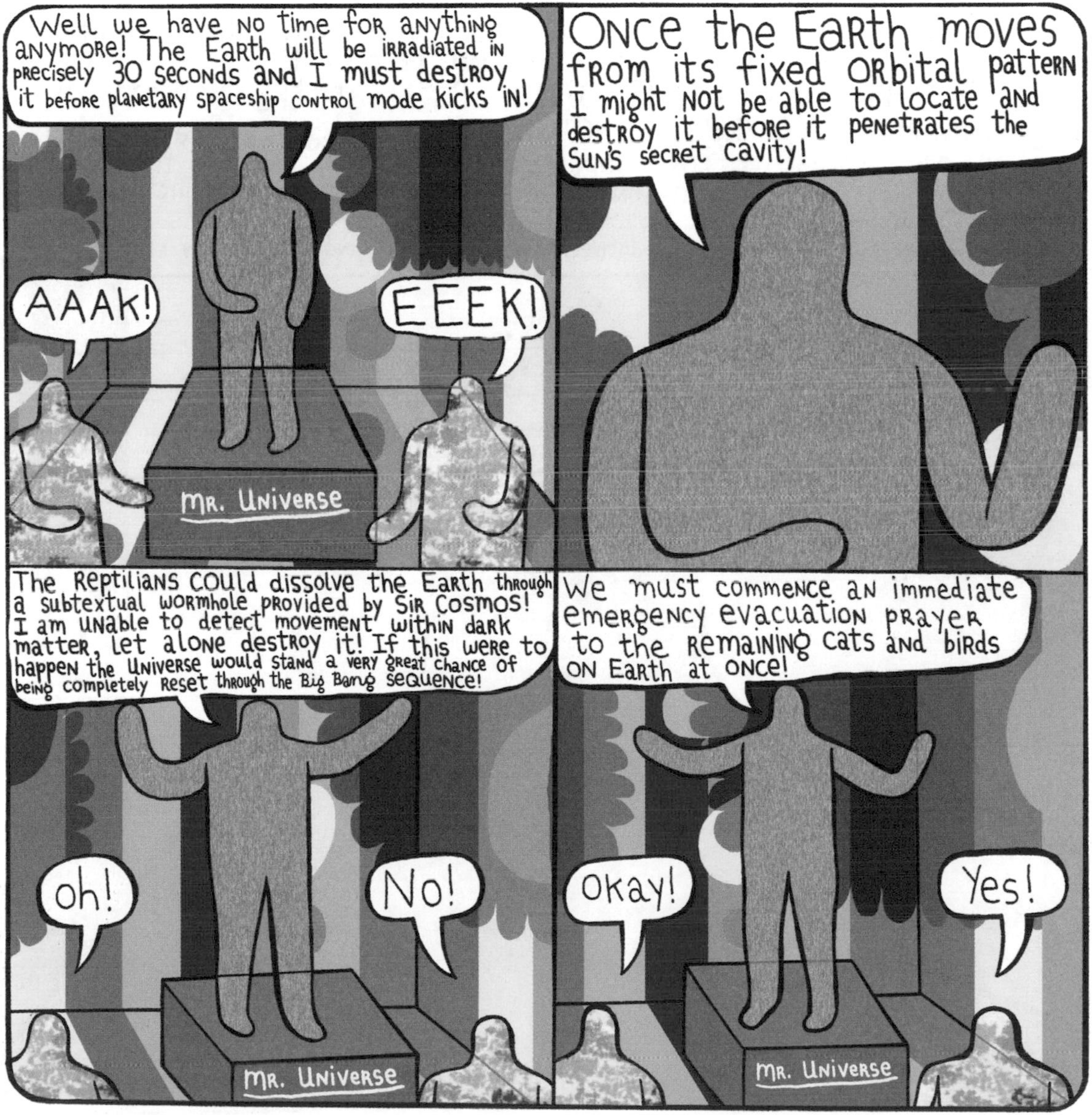
Well we have no time for anything anymore! The Earth will be irradiated in precisely 30 seconds and I must destroy it before planetary spaceship control mode kicks in!
AAAK!
EEEK!
MR. UNIVERSE
Once the Earth moves from its fixed orbital pattern I might not be able to locate and destroy it before it penetrates the Sun's secret cavity!
The Reptilians could dissolve the Earth through a subtextual wormhole provided by Sir Cosmos! I am unable to detect movement within dark matter, let alone destroy it! If this were to happen the Universe would stand a very great chance of being completely reset through the Big Bang sequence!
oh!
No!
MR. UNIVERSE
We must commence an immediate emergency evacuation prayer to the remaining cats and birds on Earth at once!
Okay!
Yes!
MR. UNIVERSE

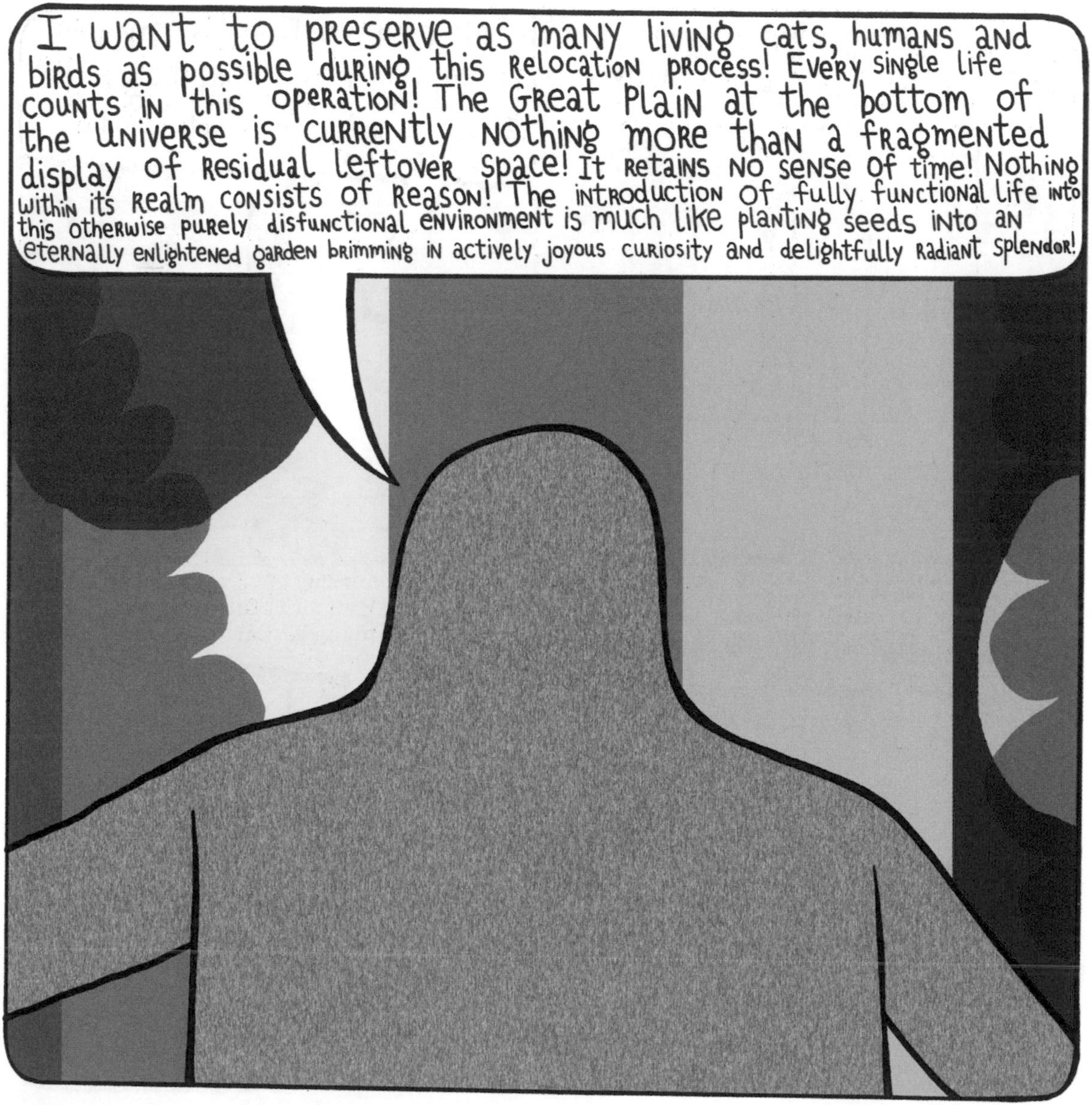
I want to preserve as many living cats, humans and birds as possible during this relocation process! Every single life counts in this operation! The Great Plain at the bottom of the Universe is currently nothing more than a fragmented display of residual leftover space! It retains no sense of time! Nothing within its realm consists of reason! The introduction of fully functional life into this otherwise purely disfunctional environment is much like planting seeds into an eternally enlightened garden brimming in actively joyous curiosity and delightfully radiant splendor!

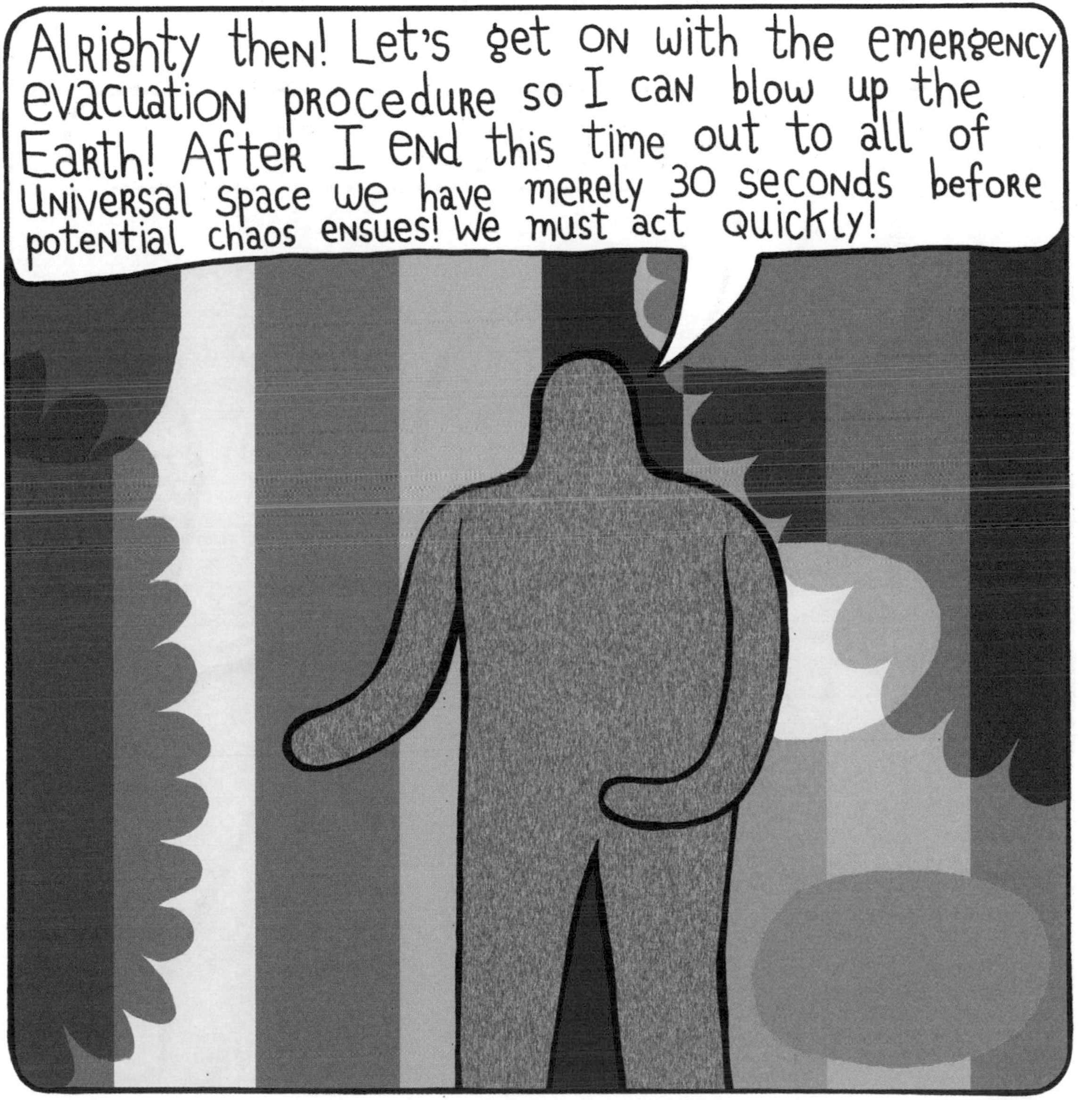
Alrighty then! Let's get on with the emergency evacuation procedure so I can blow up the Earth! After I end this time out to all of Universal space we have merely 30 seconds before potential chaos ensues! We must act quickly!

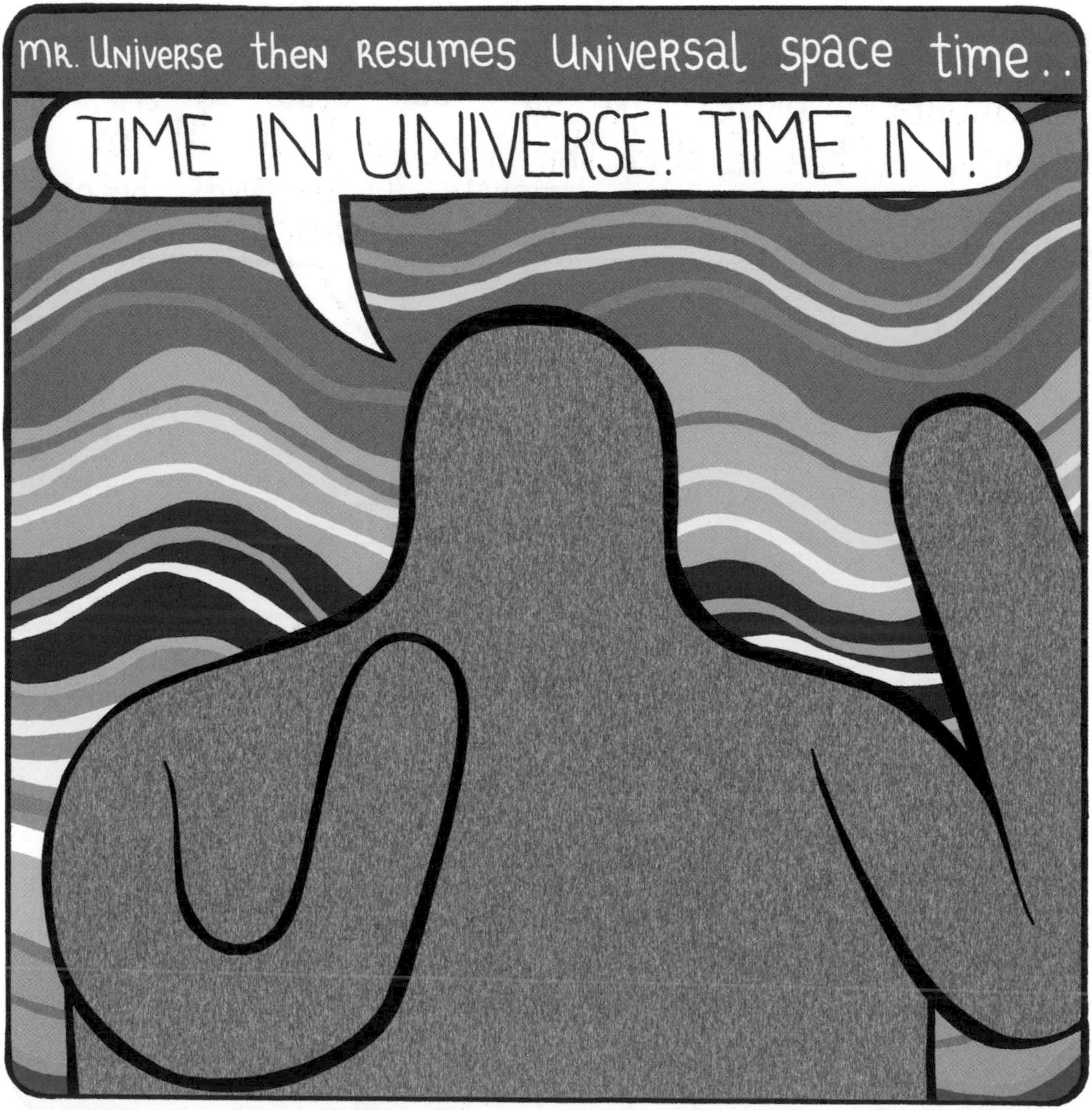
mr. Universe then resumes Universal space time..
TIME IN UNIVERSE! TIME IN!

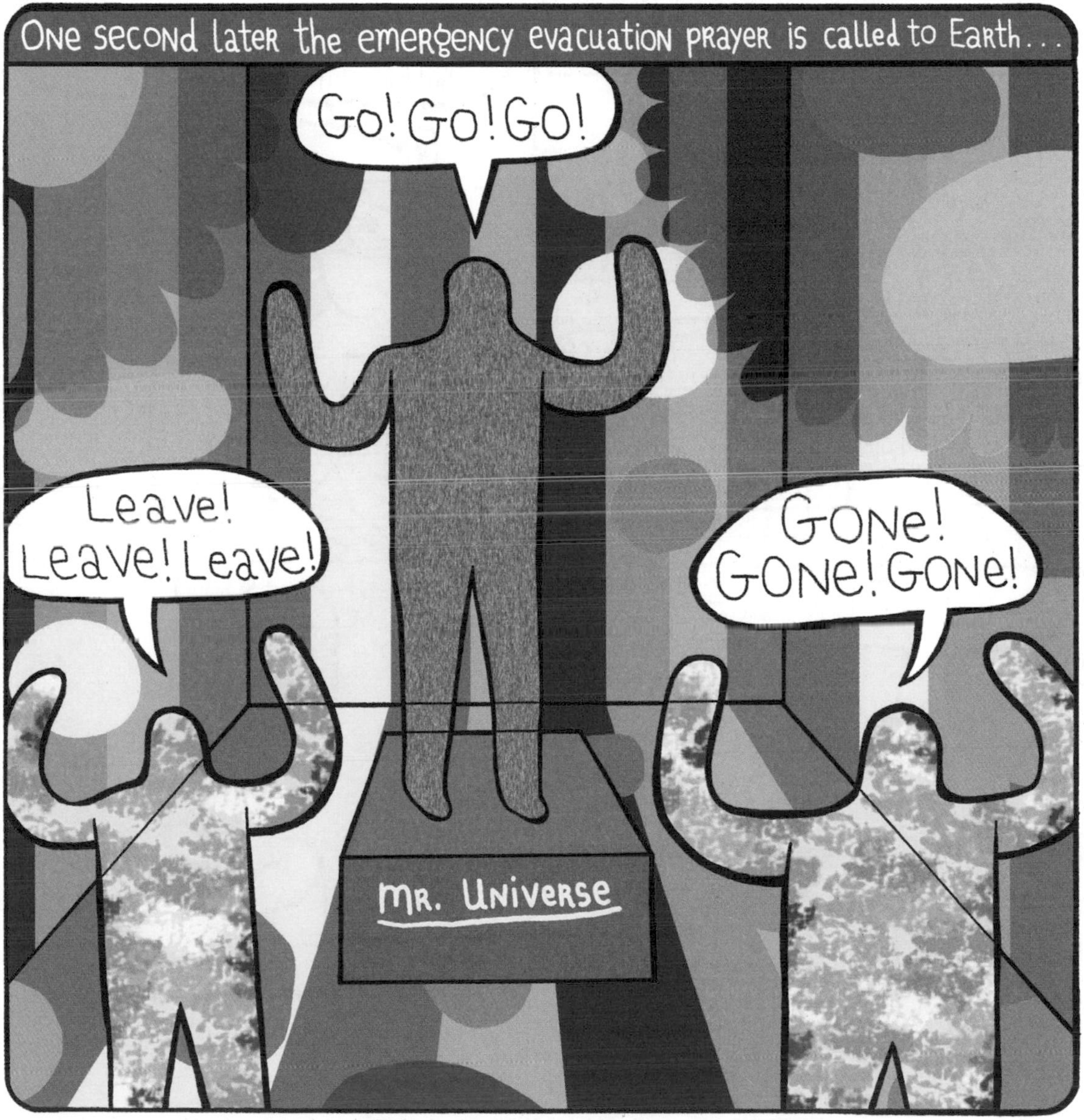
One second later the emergency evacuation prayer is called to Earth...
Go! Go! Go!
Leave! Leave! Leave!
Gone! Gone! Gone!
Mr. Universe

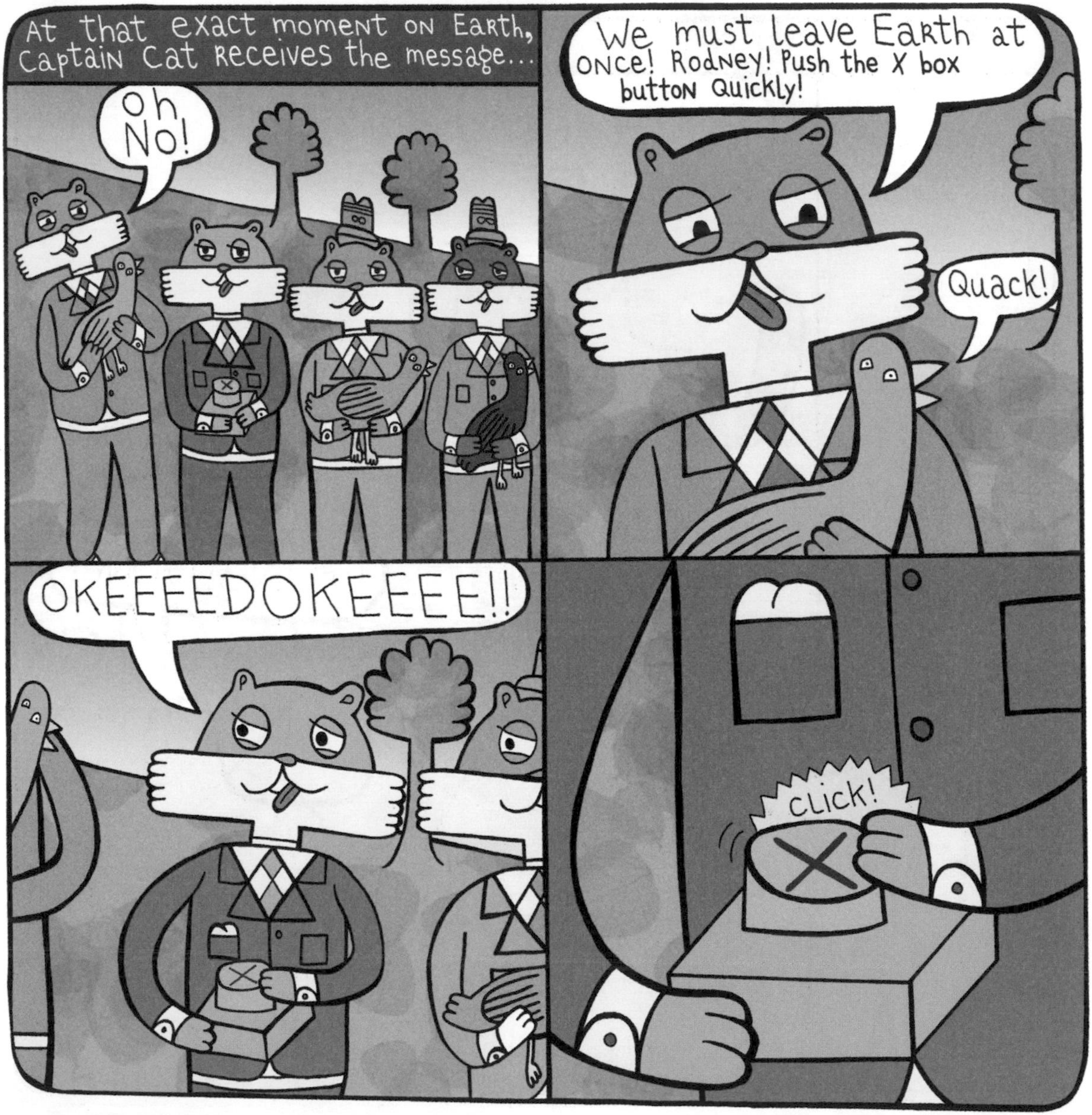
At that exact moment on Earth, Captain Cat receives the message...
Oh No!
We must leave Earth at once! Rodney! Push the X box button quickly!
Quack!
OKEEEEDOKEEEEE!!
CLICK!

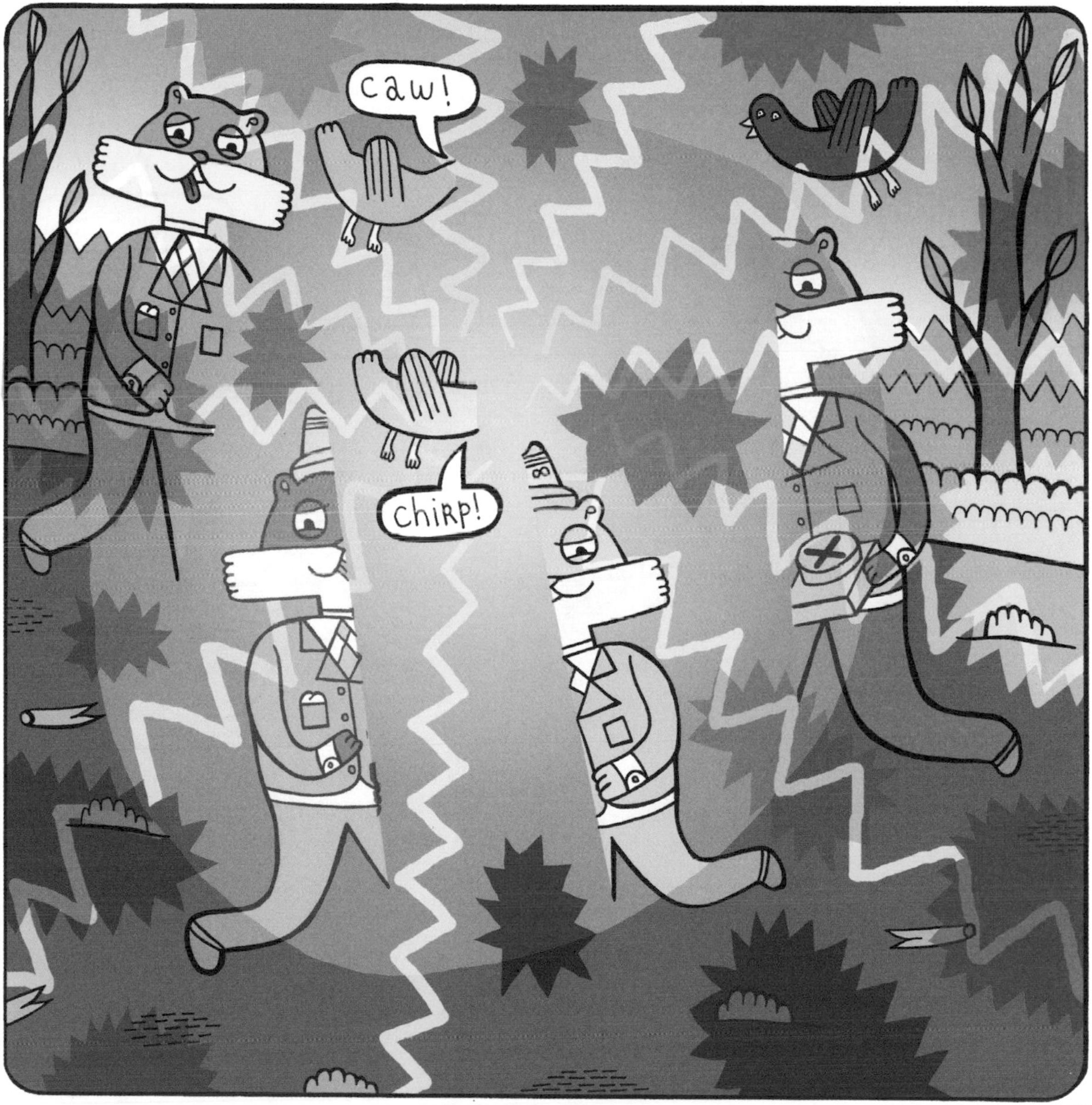
caw!
chirp!

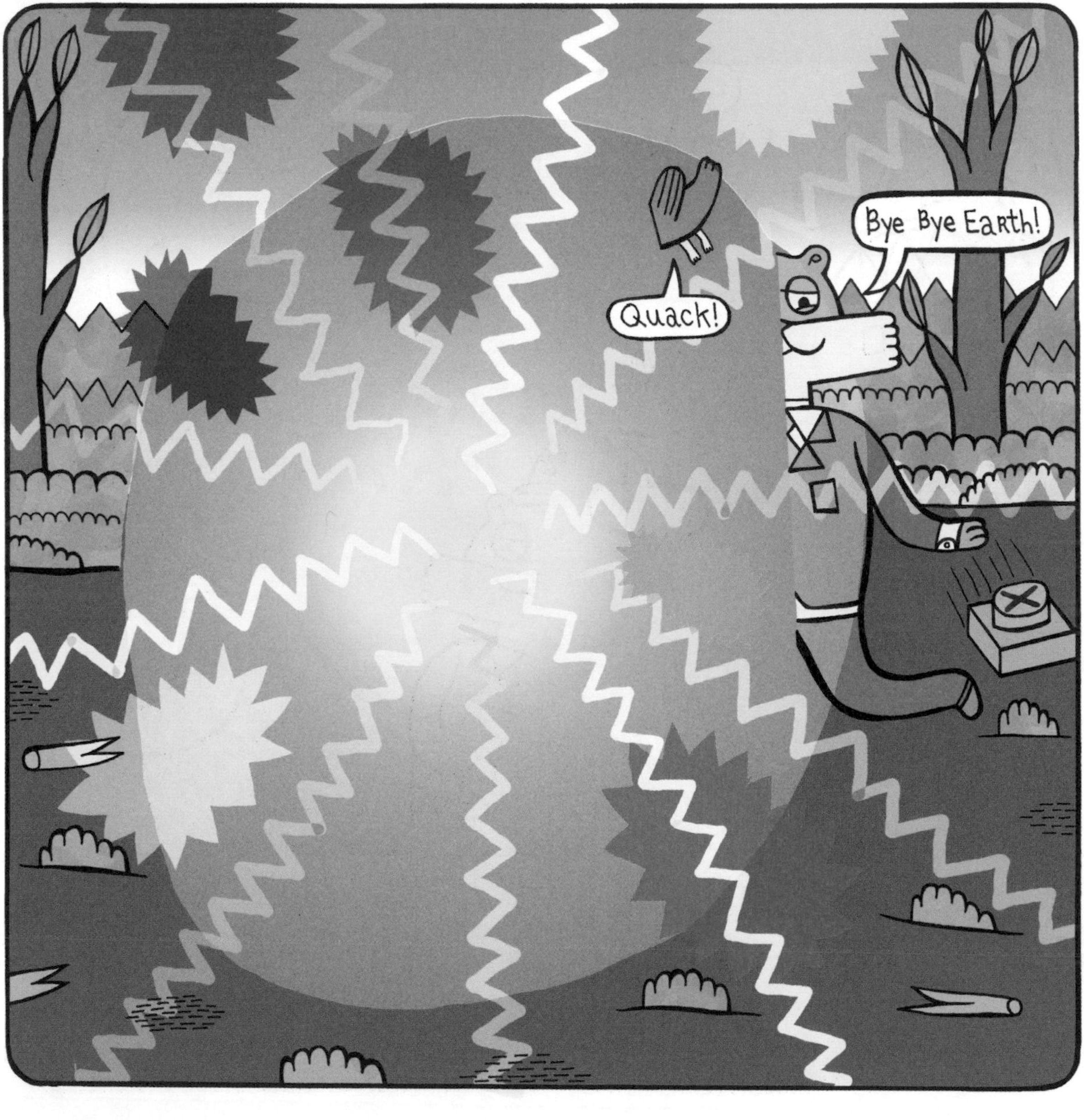
Quack!
Bye Bye Earth!

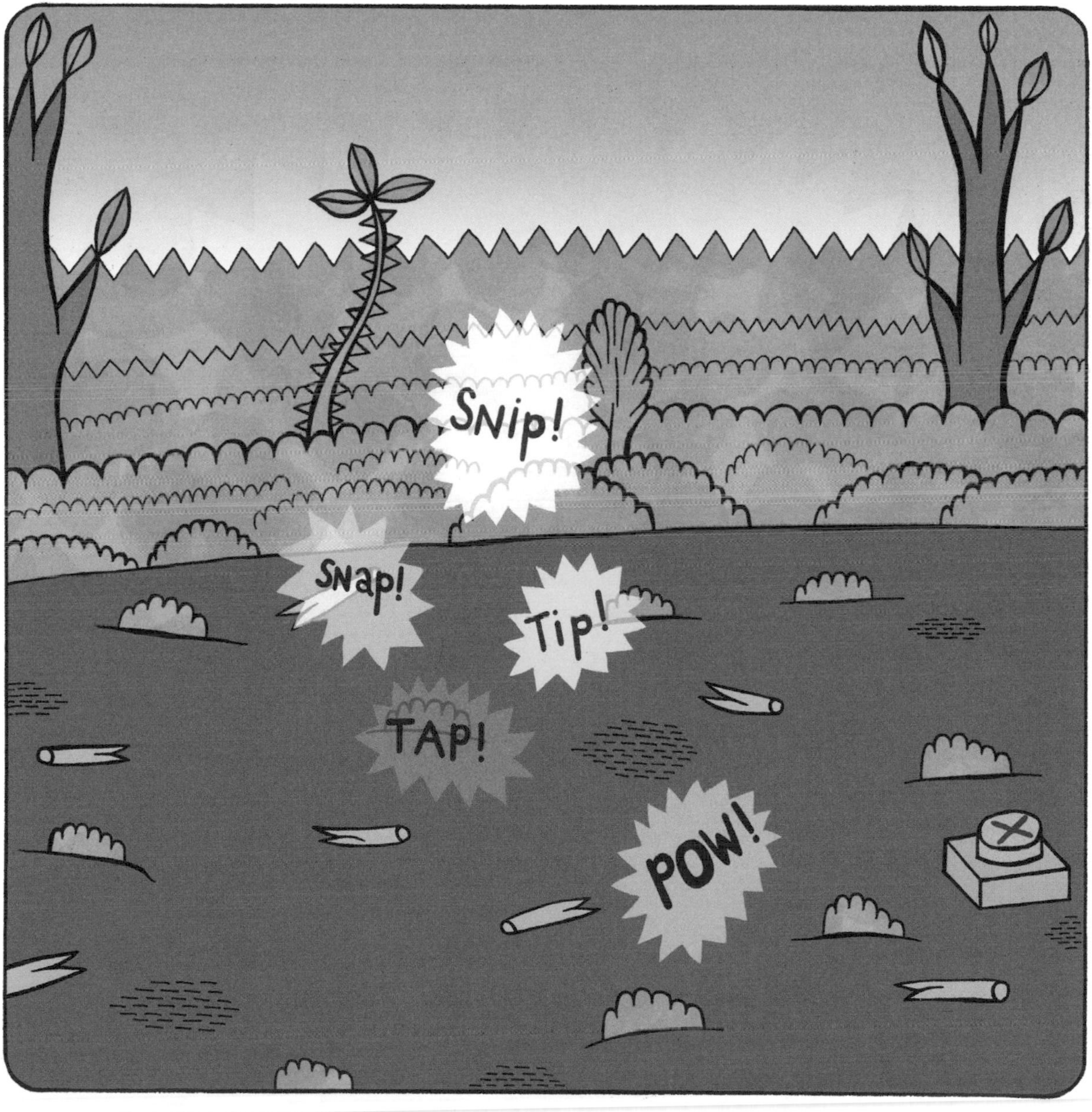
SNIP!
SNAP!
Tip!
TAP!
POW!

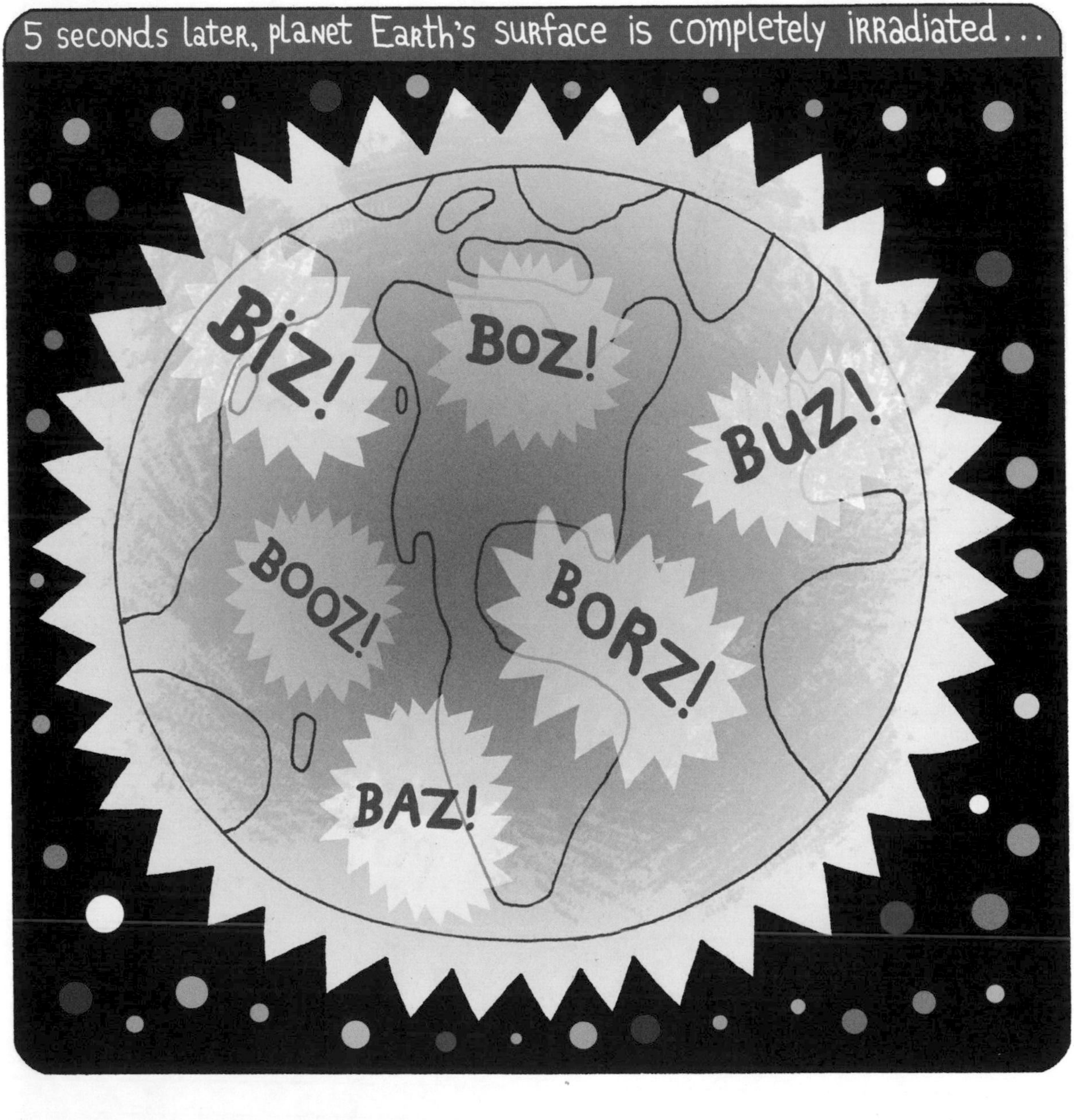
5 seconds later, planet Earth's surface is completely irradiated...
BiZ!
BOZ!
BUZ!
BOOZ!
BORZ!
BAZ!

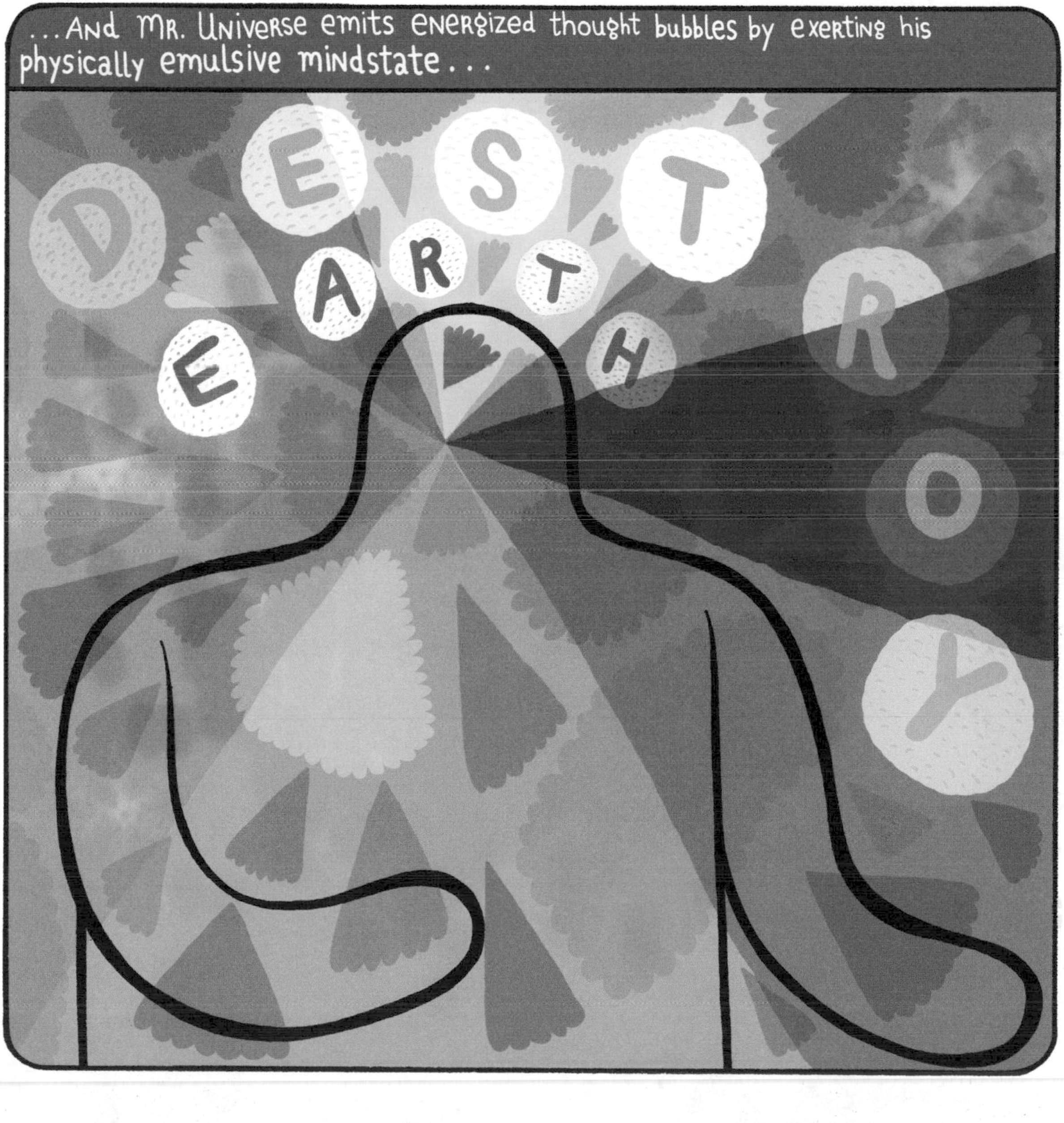
...And Mr. Universe emits energized thought bubbles by exerting his physically emulsive mindstate...
DESTROY
EARTH

Instantly the Earth violently explodes, reducing it to trillions

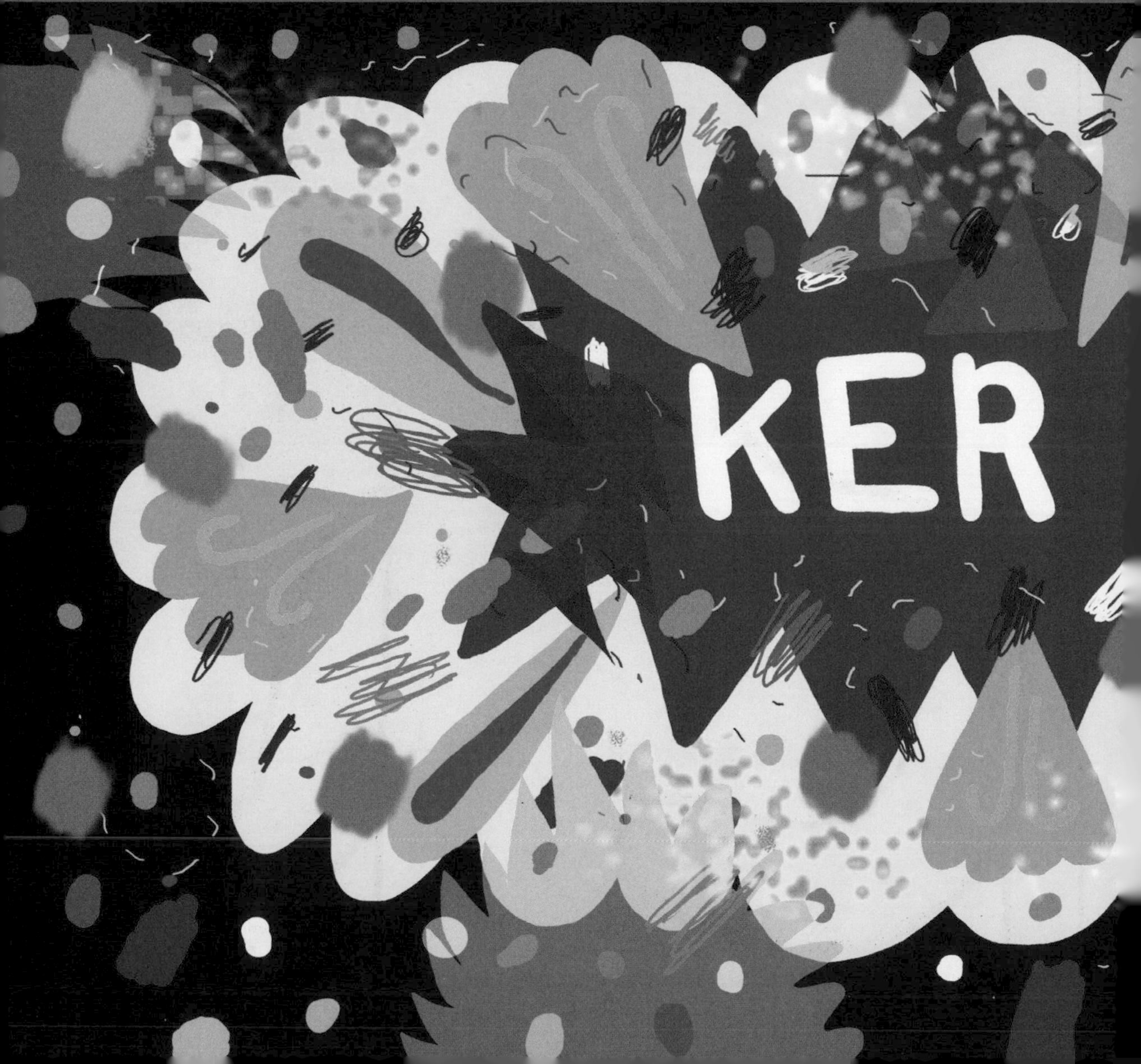
KER

of aimlessly wandering single celled granular dust particulates . . .

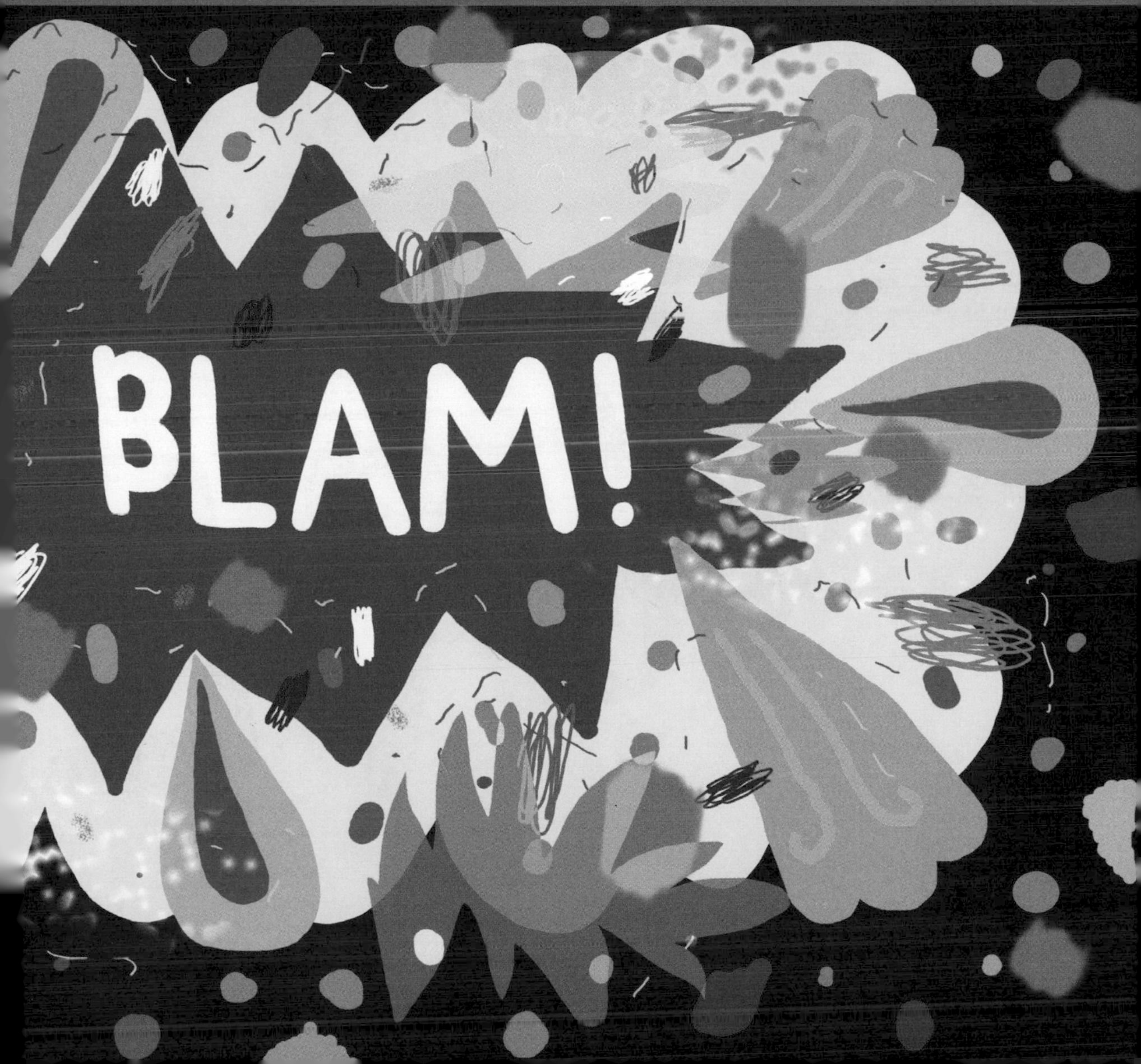
BLAM!

And the Great Plain at the Bottom of the Universe

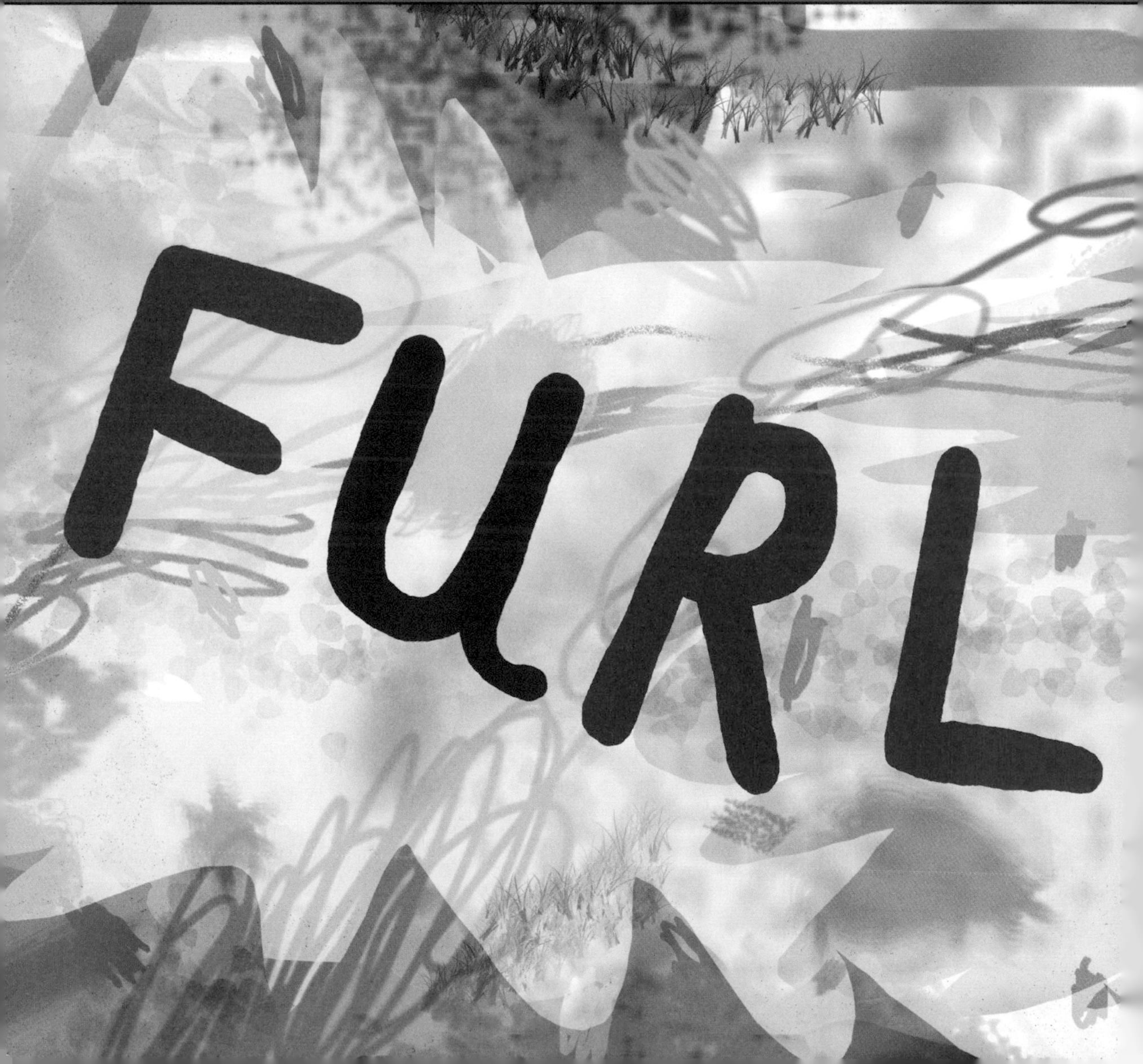
FURL

bears intelligent life for the first time...

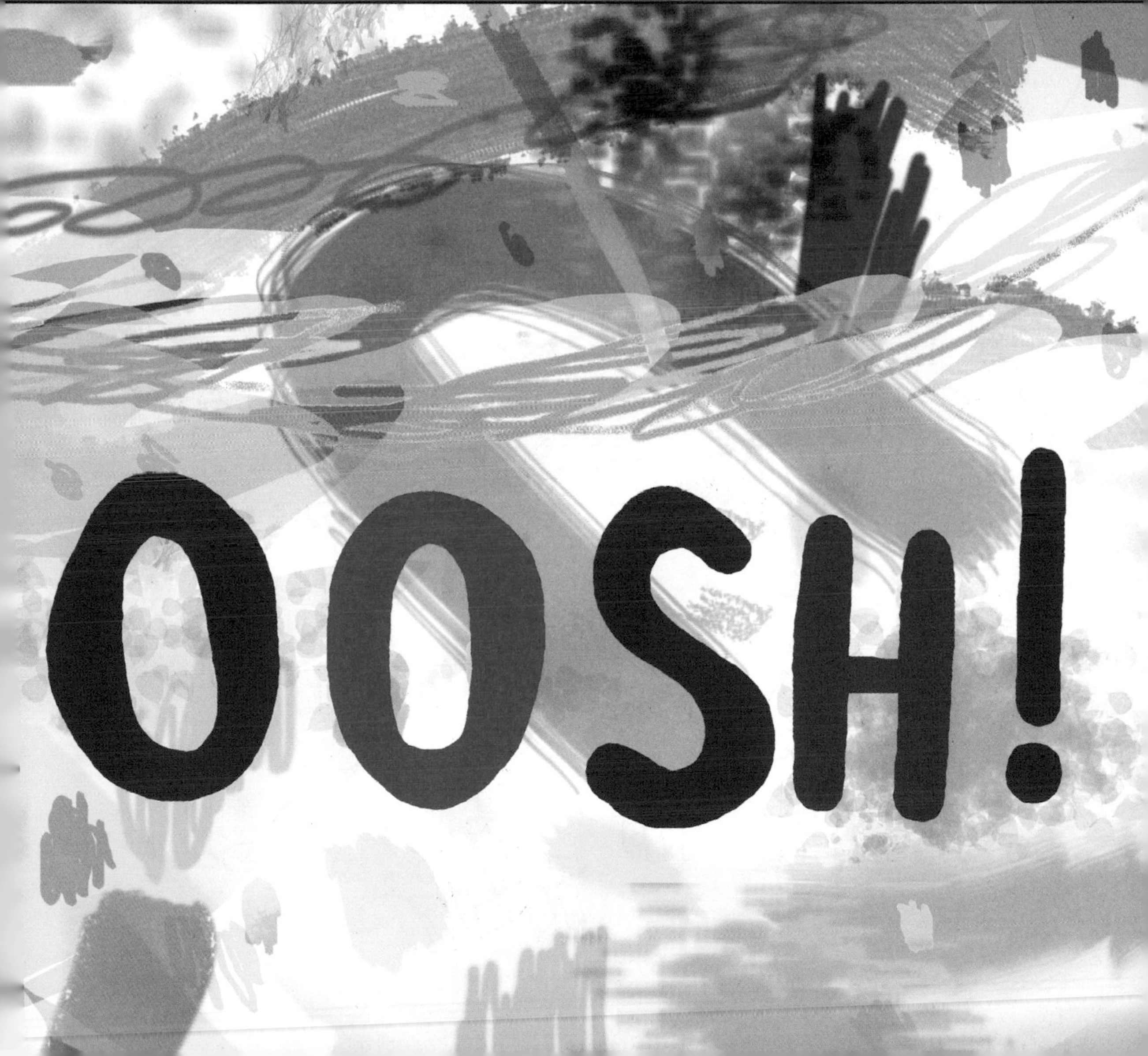
OOSH!

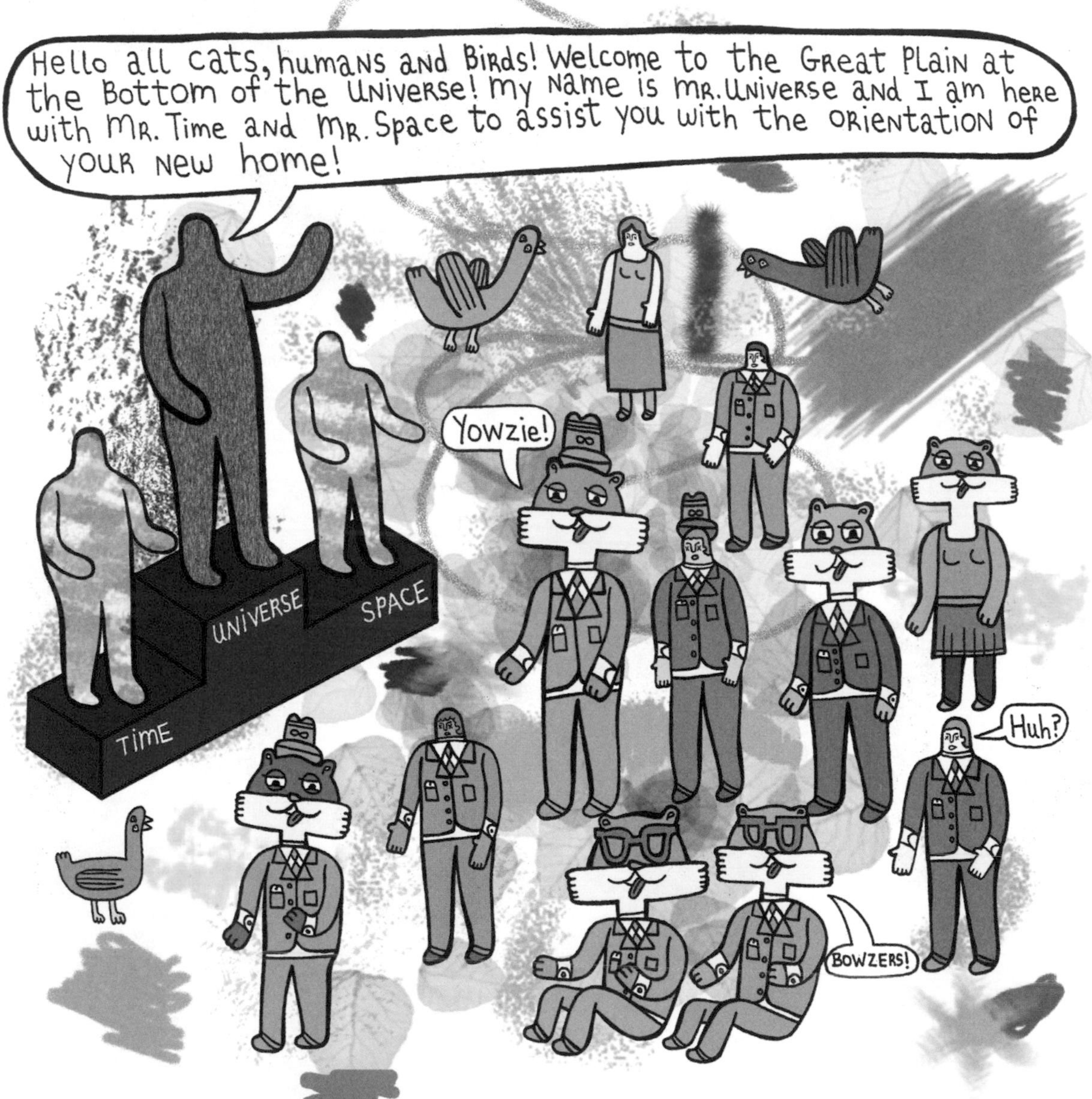

Hello all cats, humans and Birds! Welcome to the Great Plain at the Bottom of the Universe! My Name is Mr. Universe and I am here with Mr. Time and Mr. Space to assist you with the orientation of your new home!
Yowzie!
UNIVERSE
SPACE
TIME
Huh?
BOWZERS!

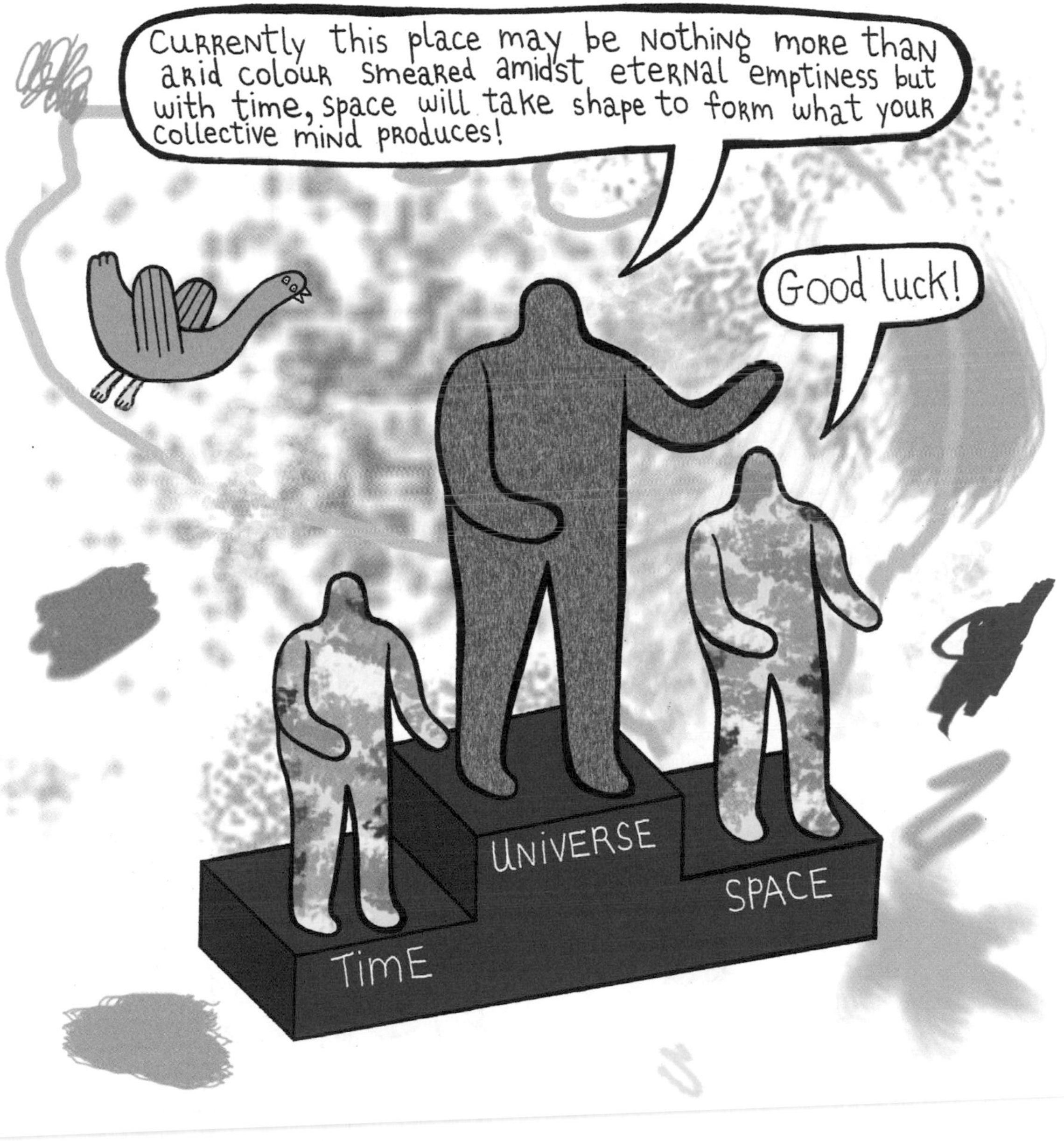
Currently this place may be nothing more than arid colour smeared amidst eternal emptiness but with time, space will take shape to form what your collective mind produces!
Good luck!
UNIVERSE
SPACE
TIME

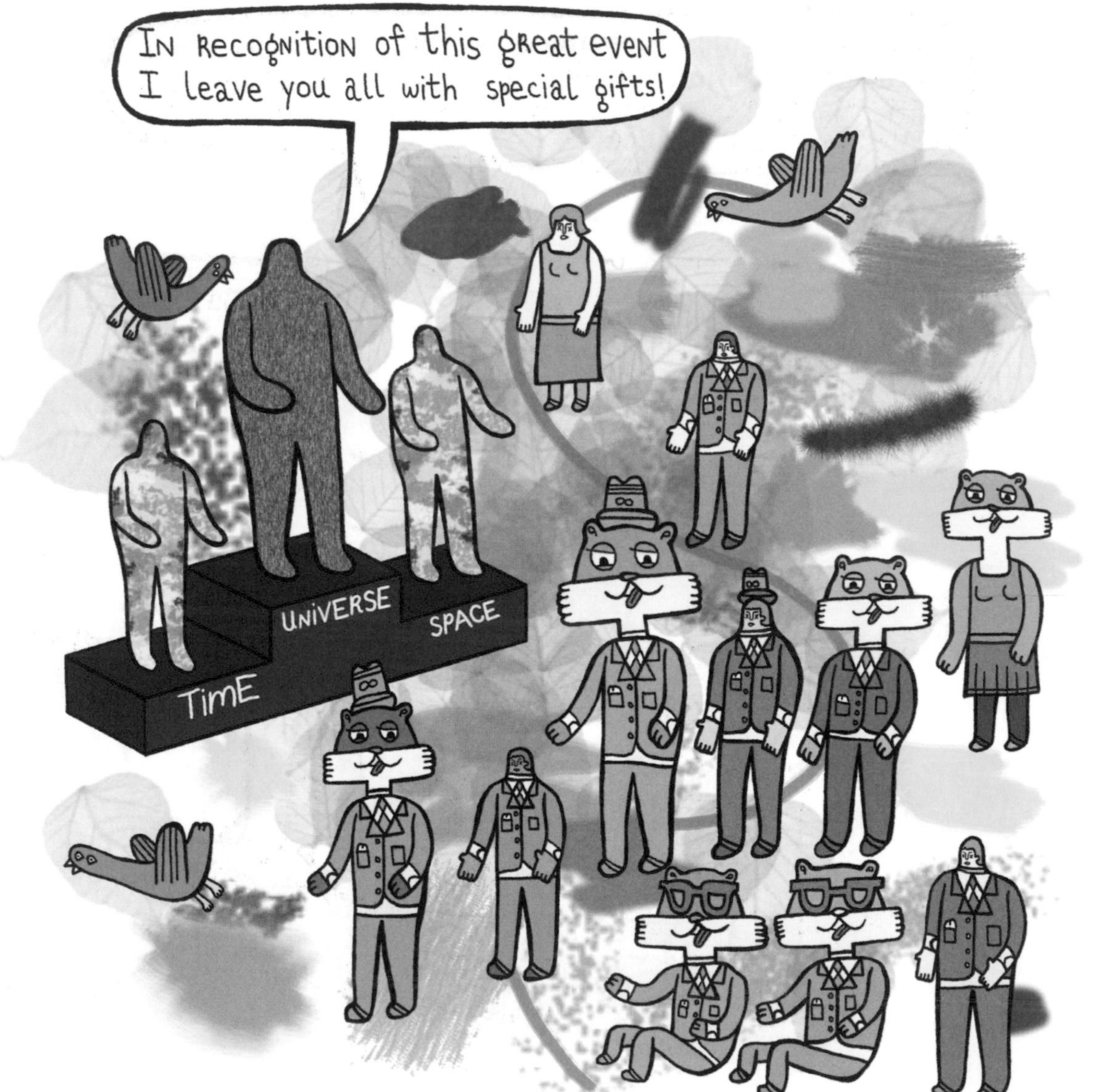
In recognition of this great event
I leave you all with special gifts!
UNIVERSE
SPACE
TIME

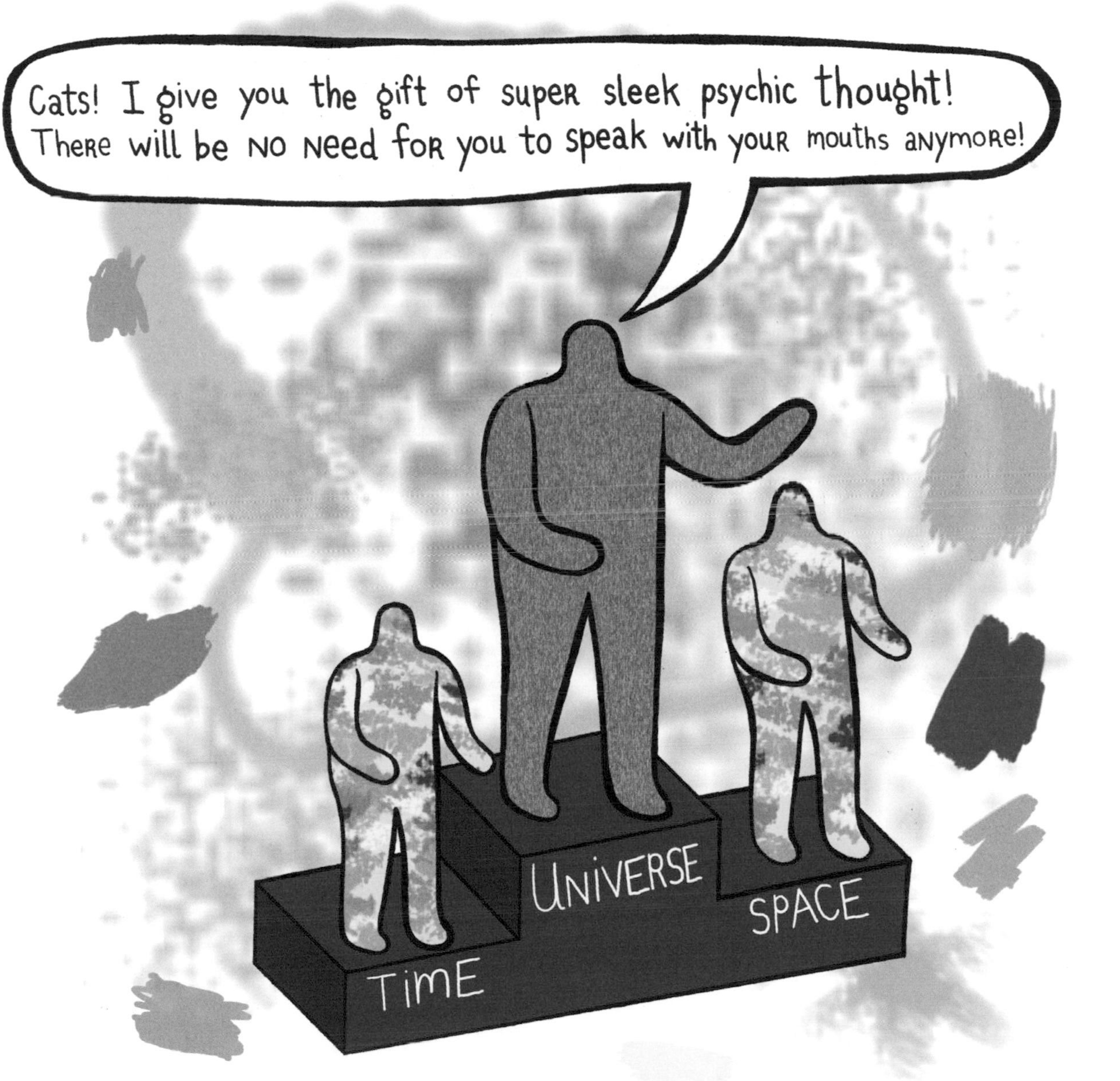
Cats! I give you the gift of super sleek psychic thought! There will be NO Need for you to speak with your mouths anymore!
UNIVERSE
SPACE
TIME

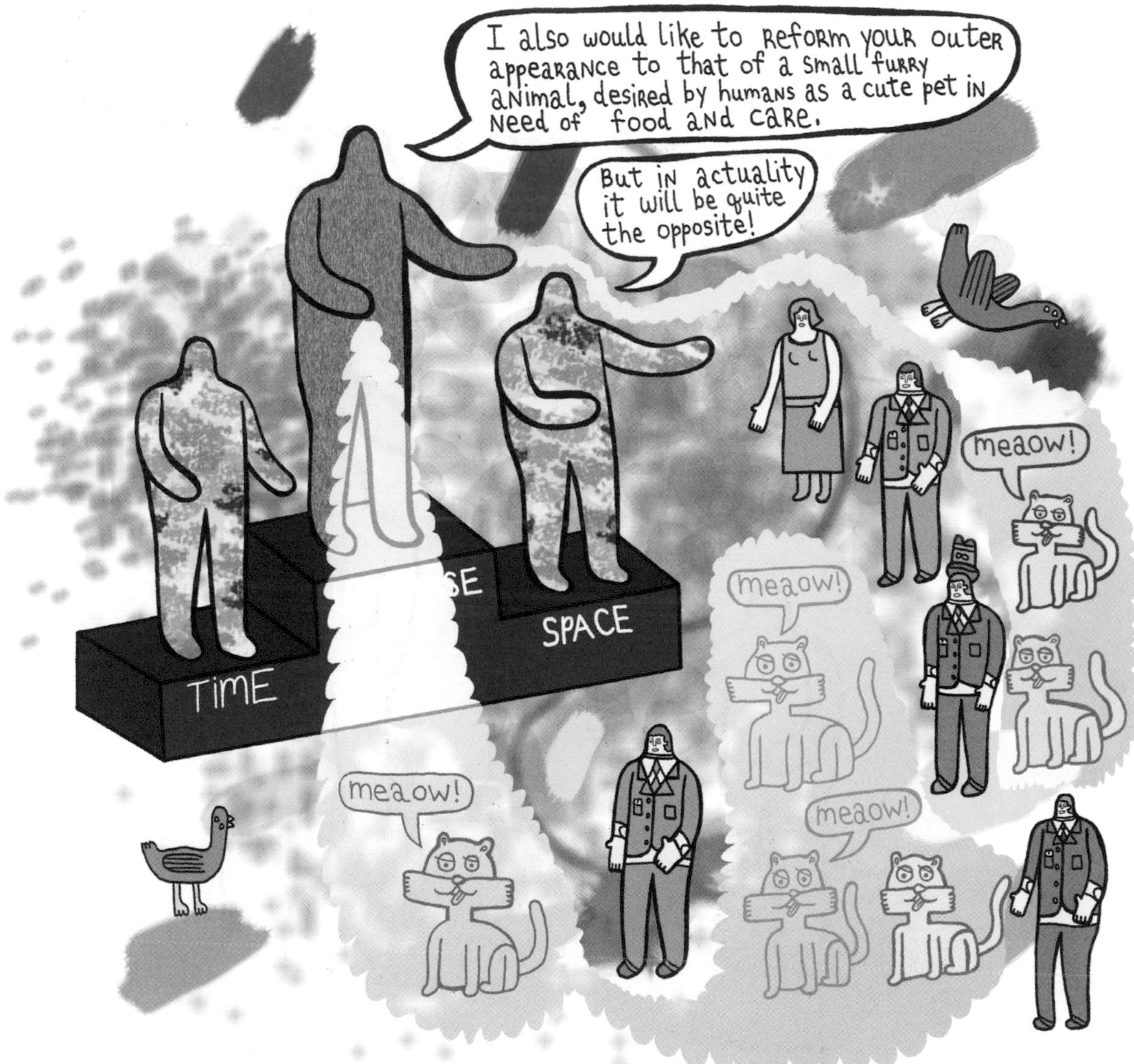

I also would like to reform your outer appearance to that of a small furry animal, desired by humans as a cute pet in need of food and care.
But in actuality it will be quite the opposite!
TIME
SE
SPACE
meaow!
meaow!
meaow!
meaow!

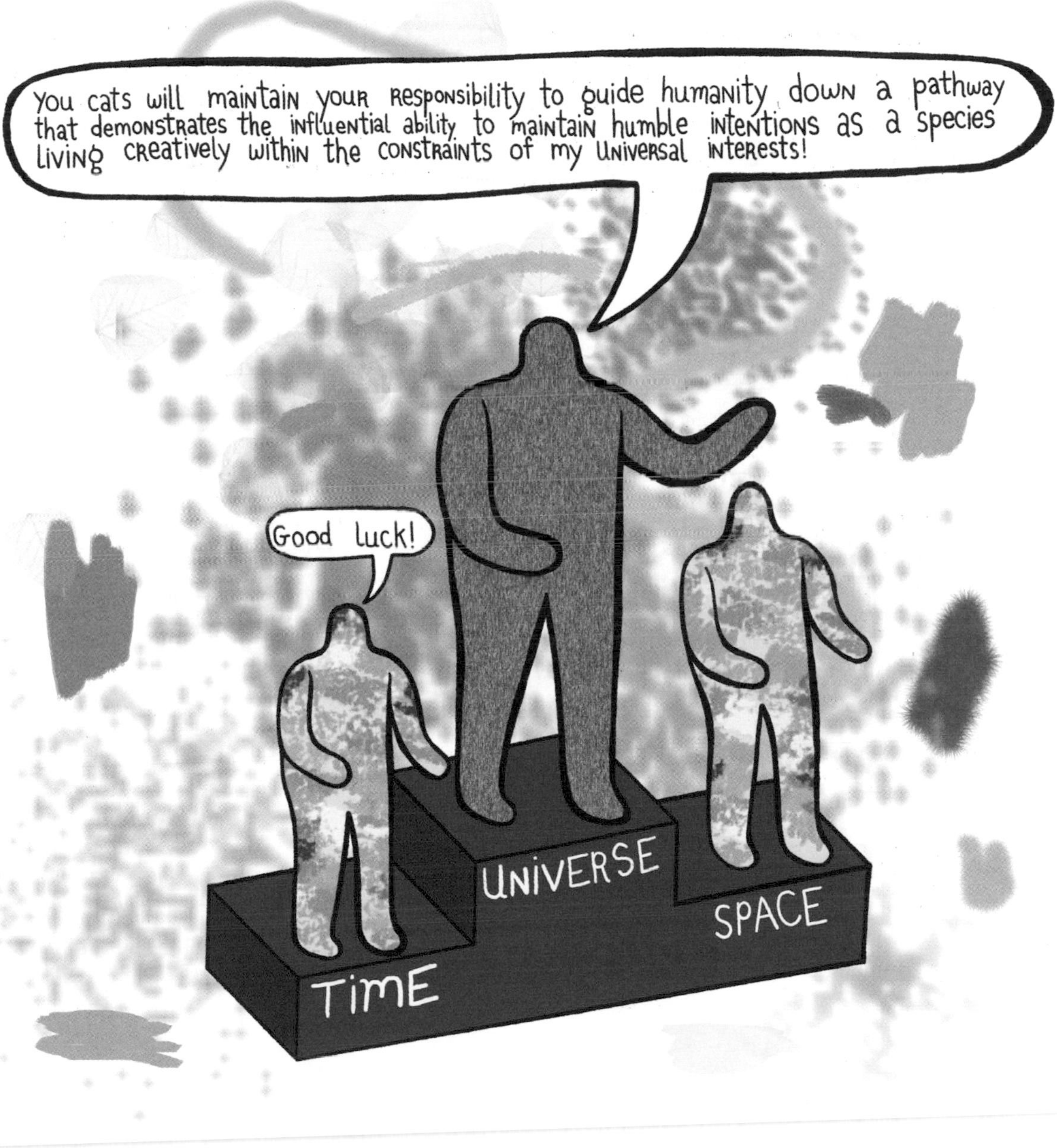
You cats will maintain your responsibility to guide humanity down a pathway that demonstrates the influential ability to maintain humble intentions as a species living creatively within the constraints of my Universal interests!
Good luck!
UNIVERSE
TIME
SPACE

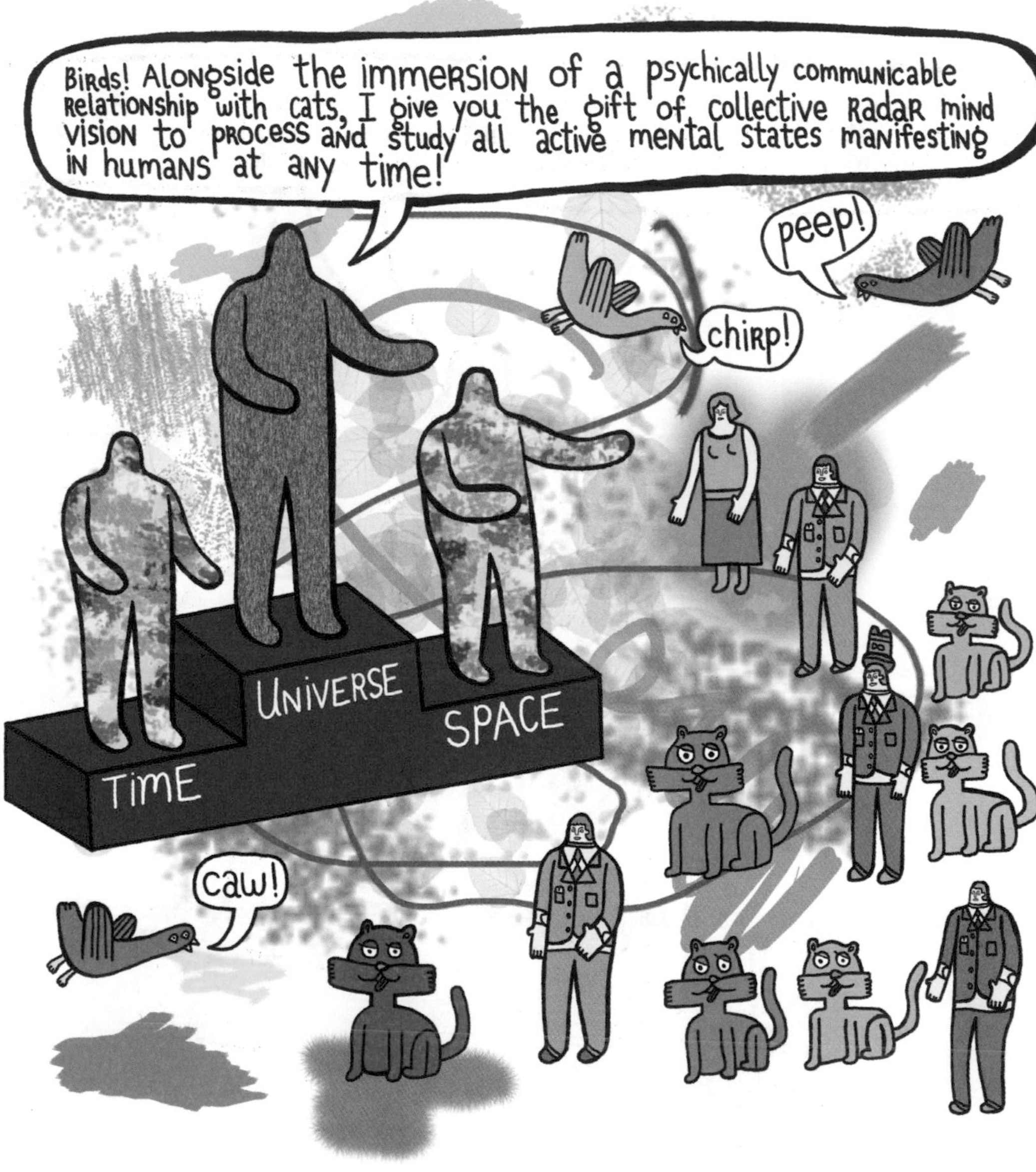
Birds! Alongside the immersion of a psychically communicable relationship with cats, I give you the gift of collective radar mind vision to process and study all active mental states manifesting in humans at any time!
peep!
chirp!
UNIVERSE
SPACE
TIME
caw!

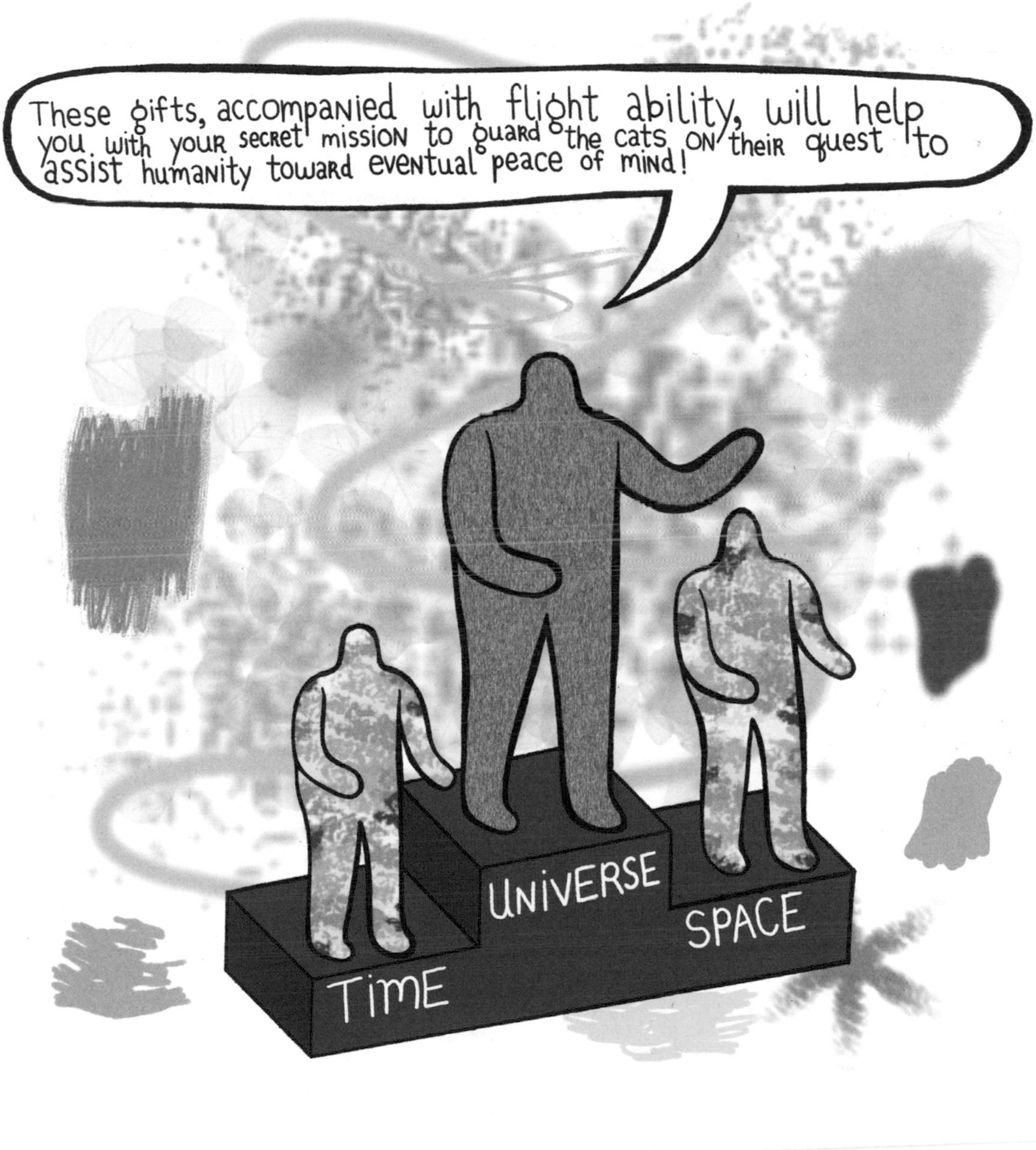
These gifts, accompanied with flight ability, will help you with your secret mission to guard the cats on their quest to assist humanity toward eventual peace of mind!
TIME
UNIVERSE
SPACE

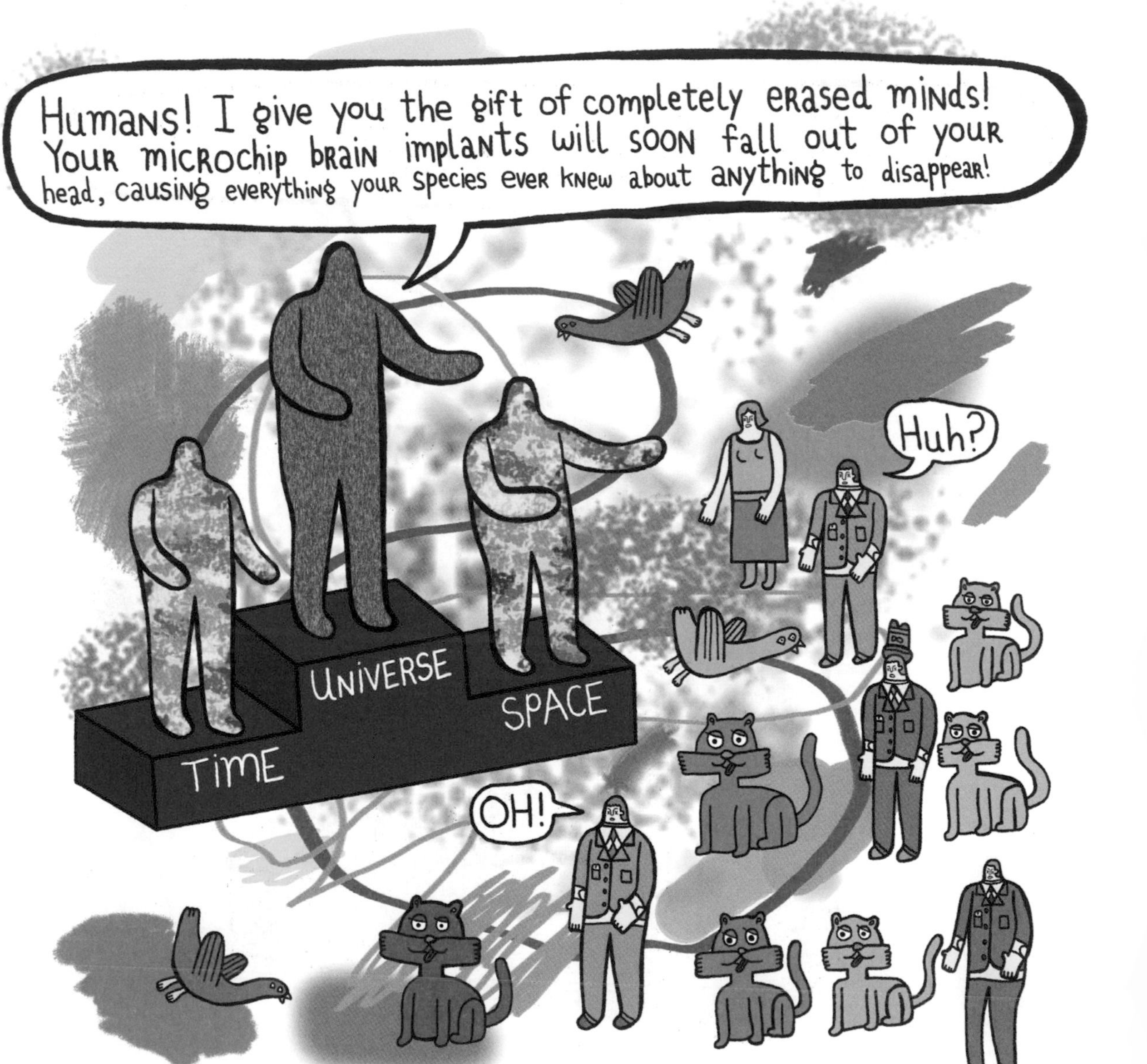
Humans! I give you the gift of completely erased minds! Your microchip brain implants will soon fall out of your head, causing everything your species ever knew about anything to disappear!
Huh?
UNIVERSE
TIME
SPACE
OH!

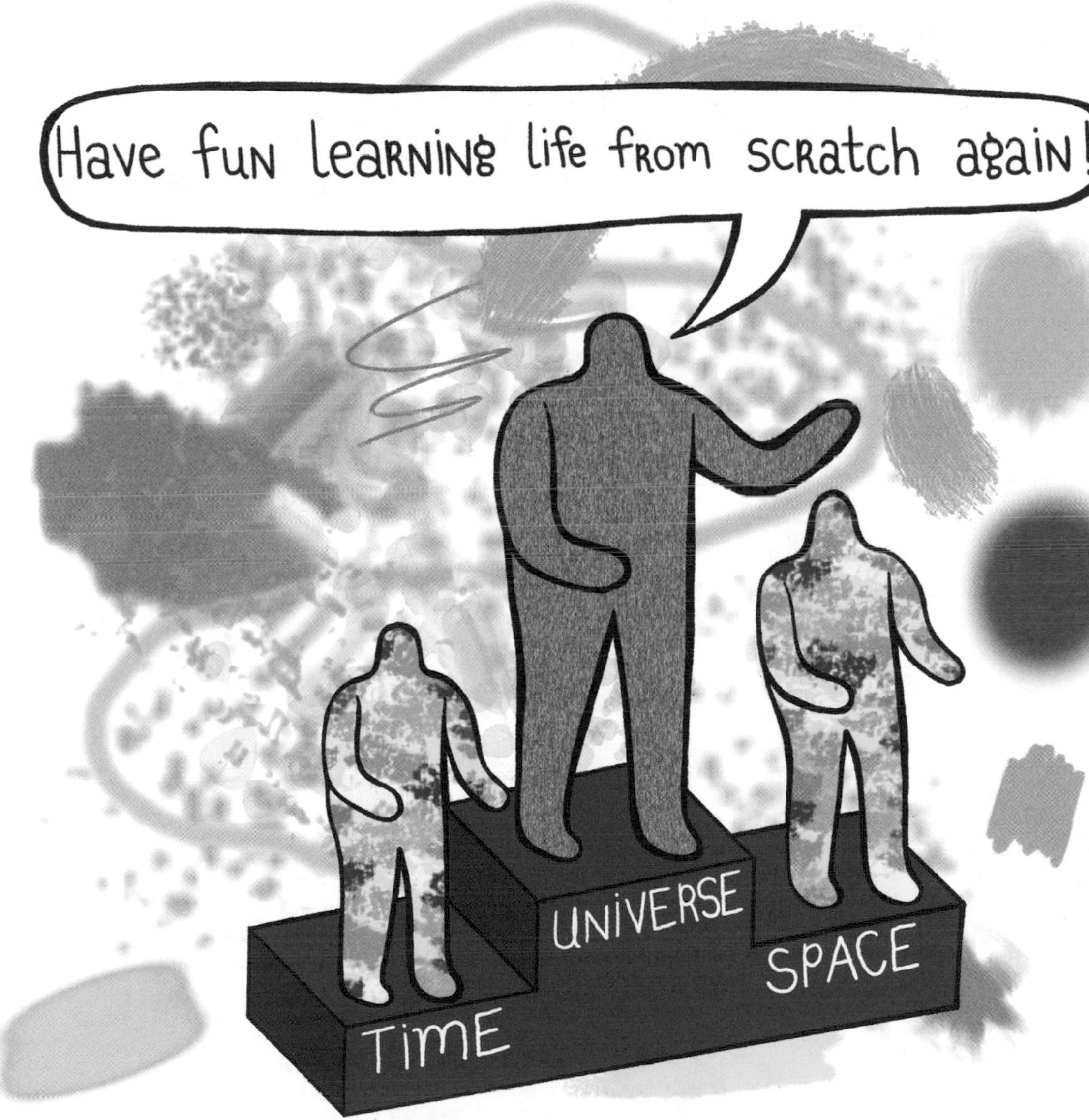
Have fun learning life from scratch again!
UNIVERSE
TIME
SPACE

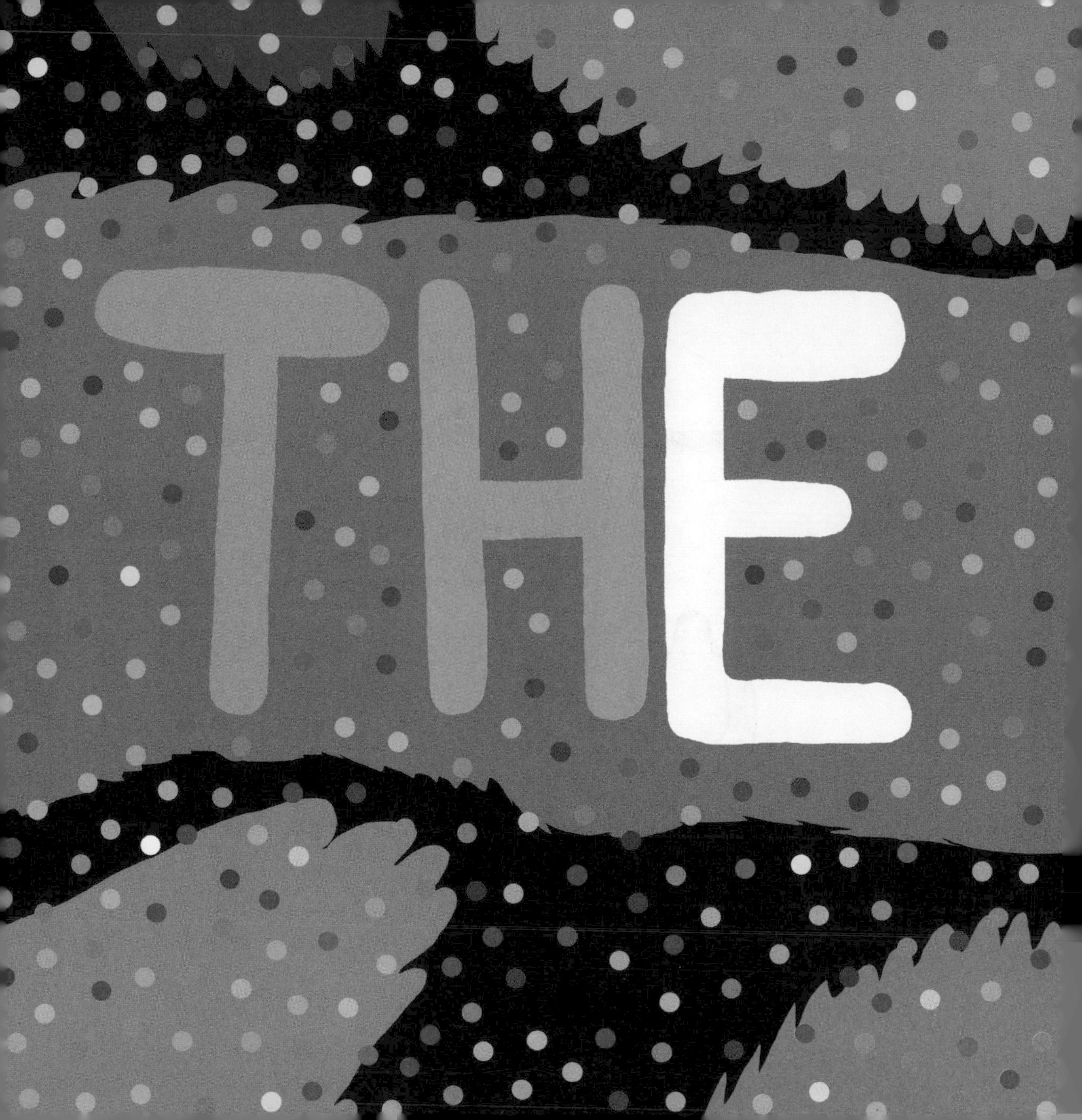
THE

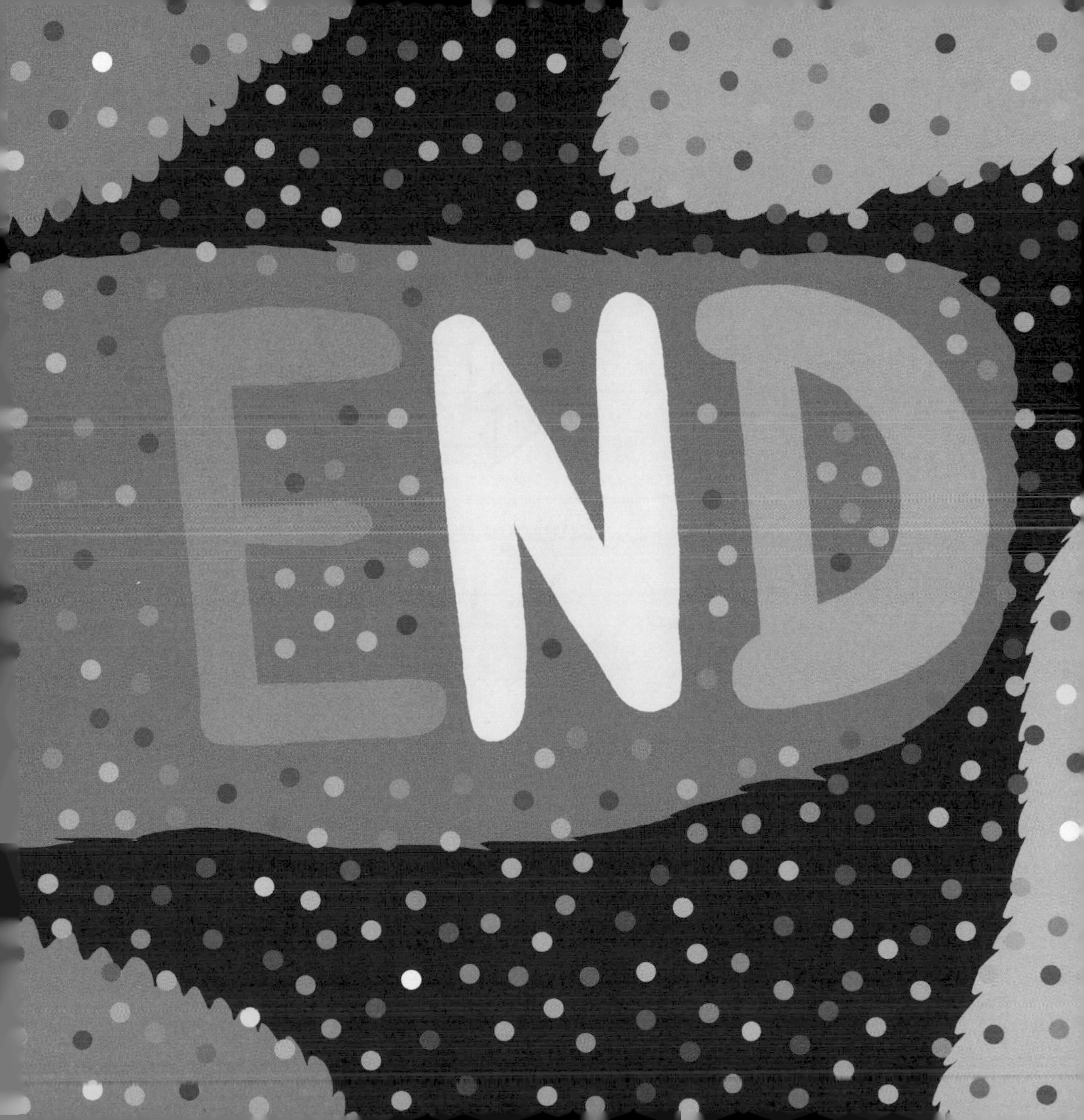
END

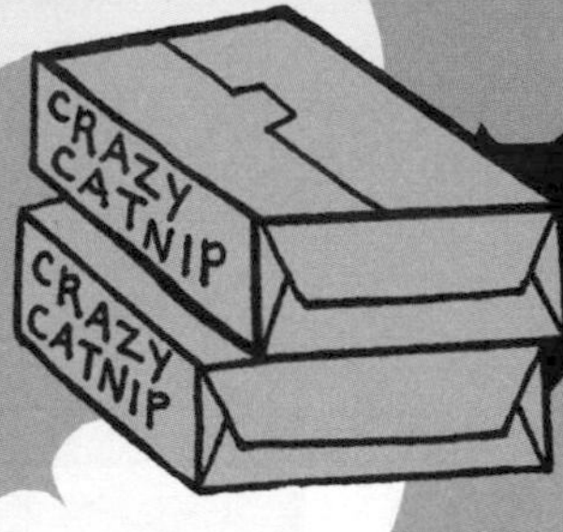
CRAZY CATNIP
CRAZY CATNIP

Drawn & Quarterly
Post Office Box 48056
Montreal, Quebec
Canada H2V 4S8
www.drawnandquarterly.com

Library and Archives Canada Cataloguing in Publication

Jones, Keith, 1978-
Catland Empire/Keith Jones.

ISBN 978-1-897299-92-0

1. Cats--Comic books, strips, etc. 2. Dogs--Comic books, strips, etc.
3. Animal fighting--Comic books, strips, etc. I. Title.

PN6733.J66C37 2010 741.5'971 C2009-906774-9

First softcover edition: March 2010.
10 9 8 7 6 5 4 3 2 1
Printed in Canada

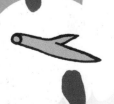